John Ray
William Ray

D0870838

Sams **Teach Yourself**

Xcode° 4

in **24**
Hours

800 East 96th Street, Indianapolis, Indiana, 46240 USA

Sams Teach Yourself Xcode® 4 in 24 Hours

ISBN-13: 978-0-672-33587-7
ISBN-10: 0-672-33587-5

The Library of Congress Cataloging-in-Publication data is on file.

Printed in the United States of America

First Printing June 2012

Trademarks

All terms mentioned in this book that are known to be trademarks or service marks have been appropriately capitalized. Sams Publishing cannot attest to the accuracy of this information. Use of a term in this book should not be regarded as affecting the validity of any trademark or service mark.

Warning and Disclaimer

Every effort has been made to make this book as complete and as accurate as possible, but no warranty or fitness is implied. The information provided is on an "as is" basis. The author and the publisher shall have neither liability nor responsibility to any person or entity with respect to any loss or damages arising from the information contained in this book.

Bulk Sales

Sams Publishing offers excellent discounts on this book when ordered in quantity for bulk purchases or special sales. For more information, please contact

U.S. Corporate and Government Sales
1-800-382-3419
corpsales@pearsontechgroup.com

For sales outside of the U.S., please contact

International Sales
international@pearsoned.com

Editor-in-Chief
Greg Wiegand

Acquisitions Editor
Laura Norman

Development Editor
Keith Cline

Managing Editor
Kristy Hart

Project Editor
Andy Beaster

Copy Editor
Keith Cline

Indexer
Tim Wright

Proofreader
Chrissy White

Technical Editor
Greg Kettell

Publishing Coordinator
Cindy Teeters

Book Designer
Gary Adair

Compositor
Nonie Ratcliff

Contents at a Glance

Table of Contents

x

Sams Teach Yourself Xcode 4 in 24 Hours

About the Authors

John Ray is currently serving as a Senior Business Analyst and Development Team Manager for the Ohio State University Office of Research. He has written numerous books for Macmillan/Sams/Que, including *Using TCP/IP: Special Edition, Teach Yourself Dreamweaver MX in 21 Days, Mac OS X Unleashed*, and *Teach Yourself iOS 5 Development in 24 Hours*. As a Macintosh user since 1984, he strives to ensure that each project presents the Macintosh with the equality and depth it deserves. Even technical titles such as *Using TCP/IP* contain extensive information about the Macintosh and its applications and have garnered numerous positive reviews for their straightforward approach and accessibility to beginner and intermediate audiences.

Will Ray is an assistant professor of pediatrics in the Battelle Center for Mathematical Medicine at Nationwide Children's Hospital. Trained as a biophysicist in computational biology and scientific visualization, Dr. Ray's group is working to bring cutting-edge computational technology to end users, through simplified user interfaces. He has been developing training materials and teaching users and programmers to live at the intersection of Macintosh and UNIX technologies since 1989.

You can visit their Xcode book website at http://teachyourselfxcode.com or follow their book-related tweets on Twitter at #XcodeIn24.

Dedication

Since Will and I couldn't agree on dedicating this to his parents or mine, we hereby dedicate this book to the game #Starhawk. Come play the authors and discuss Xcode in the regularly appearing "Old-N-Slow" server.

Acknowledgments

Thank you to the group at Sams Publishing—Laura Norman, Keith Cline, Greg Kettell—for working through the table of content changes, schedule conflicts, and on-the-fly revisions. You've made this book a reality and deciphered many 2 a.m. sentences that were barely more than random keyboard mashing.

Thanks to everyone around us—family, friends, distant relations, strangers, and pets—for providing food, ibuprofen, and paying the bills.

We Want to Hear from You!

As the reader of this book, *you* are our most important critic and commentator. We value your opinion and want to know what we're doing right, what we could do better, what areas you'd like to see us publish in, and any other words of wisdom you're willing to pass our way.

You can e-mail or write me directly to let me know what you did or didn't like about this book—as well as what we can do to make our books stronger.

Please note that I cannot help you with technical problems related to the topic of this book, and that due to the high volume of mail I receive, I might not be able to reply to every message.

When you write, please be sure to include this book's title and author as well as your name and phone number or e-mail address. I will carefully review your comments and share them with the author and editors who worked on the book.

E-mail: consumer@samspublishing.com

Mail: Greg Wiegand
Editor-in-Chief
Sams Publishing
800 East 96th Street
Indianapolis, IN 46240 USA

Reader Services

Visit our website and register this book at informit.com/register for convenient access to any updates, downloads, and errata that might be available for this book.

Introduction

So you've decided to write applications for OS X or iOS. You sit down at your Macintosh, start up Xcode, and... what? Create a project? Create a file? Make a storyboard? Build a Core Data model? What?

For an operating system that prides itself on being accessible to many, Xcode can appear as an insurmountable obstacle to an unprepared developer. With an iTunes-like interface, and more panels, palettes, menus, and buttons than you can count, even a simple Hello World application can seem daunting. Apple, while diligent in providing documentation, provides very few resources for developers who understand programming fundamentals but not their OS X/iOS implementation. That's where this book comes in.

Xcode offers a range of integrated tools for everything from data modeling to performance analysis and optimization. *Teach Yourself Xcode in 24 Hours* takes 24 of the most important aspects of Xcode development and condenses them down into easily understandable chunks. To help convey some of the core concepts, you work with real projects for both iOS and OS X that demonstrate important features such as shared libraries/frameworks, storyboards, Core Data models, and even hands-on debugger practice.

Xcode 4 represents an entirely redesigned version of Apple's development suite. Despite reaching version 4.4 (in beta) during this writing, it has only been in developer's hands for slightly more than a year. Unfortunately, this means it is a still a bit rough around the edges. We point out the issues where we encounter them, but don't be shy about filing bug reports with Apple if features don't quite work as anticipated. With the help of the OS X/iOS community, Xcode is being improved and enhanced rapidly. Each new release brings more consistency and reliability to the product.

Our goal for this book is to open Xcode development to programmers who may have previously eyed the platform with trepidation. A learning curve applies to becoming an Xcode developer, but once you begin to understand how Apple intends the tools to be used, you'll find that OS X and iOS development can be fast and, most important, fun.

Who Should Use This Book?

This book targets individuals who have used programming tools but who are new to the Xcode development platform. Although no previous development experience is required to complete the book, an understanding of programming fundamentals is helpful. To be clear, even though we provide code samples and an introduction to Objective-C, we do not have the space in 24 hours to teach the concepts of loops, arrays, and other foundation topics.

In addition, to be successful, we recommend that you spend time reading the Apple developer documentation and researching the topics presented in this book. A vast amount of information about OS X/iOS development is available, and it is constantly changing. Apple's integrated online documentation system makes it possible to stay up-to-date on your development knowledge and learn the details of available technologies from the comfort of your desktop Mac or iPad.

The material in this book specifically targets Xcode 4.3 and later. If you are running an earlier version, you definitely want to upgrade before moving too far along. In addition, many lessons are accompanied by project files that include sample code. While opening a project and clicking Run can be fun, we prefer that you follow along, when possible, and build the application yourself.

Be sure to download the project files from the book's website at http://teachyourselfxcode.com. If you have issues with any projects, view the posts on this site to see whether a solution has been posted.

In addition to the support website, you can follow along on Twitter. Search for #XcodeIn24 on Twitter to receive official updates and tweets from other readers. Use the hashtag #XcodeIn24 in your tweets to join the conversation. To send me messages via Twitter, begin each tweet with @johnemeryray.

Due to the complexity of the topics discussed, some figures in this book are very detailed and are intended only to provide a high-level view of concepts. Those figures are representational and not intended to be read in detail. If you prefer to view these figures on your computer, you can download them at informit.com/title/9780672335877.

HOUR 1

Xcode 4

What You'll Learn in This Hour:

▶ How to download and install Xcode

▶ Differences from Xcode 3

▶ The Xcode interface basics

▶ Benefits of being a paid developer

▶ What to expect during the first few hours of this book

Do you love using your Mac or iOS device? If so, you can thank Xcode. Xcode is the starting point for nearly all the applications you know and love on your favorite operating system. It contains the tools for writing code, developing interfaces, testing performance, and even submitting your creations to the Mac or iOS App Store for distribution.

This hour walks you through the evolution of Xcode, including the difference between Xcode 4 and Xcode 3, and the addition of iOS development tools to what was traditionally a desktop application development environment. You also learn the benefits of joining a paid developer program, how to install Xcode, and begin to find your way around its user interface. The hour concludes with the steps you need to take if you want to test code directly on your own iDevice rather than in a simulator.

Welcome to Xcode

There are many different reasons to learn Xcode. Perhaps you want to develop iOS applications for the iPhone, iPad, and whatever other devices Apple has up its sleeves. Perhaps you want to take the desktop route and focus on creating applications that run on your Mac. Maybe you just want to write some quick utilities in AppleScript. Regardless of what you're looking to do, Xcode is the place to do it.

Xcode Evolves

Xcode 4 is the start of a new development environment from Apple. For the first time since the inception of Mac OS X, Apple has dramatically changed the development experience. Xcode, when introduced with Mac OS X, was an adaptation of the NeXTSTEP/OpenStep development tools. These tools were widely heralded as easy to use and innovative for their object-oriented approach.

Although features have been added over the past decade, the general development workflow went untouched. In Xcode 4, Apple is attempting to simplify and modernize the developer toolset. This isn't to say that if you've used earlier versions of Xcode you won't be able to catch on quickly, but Xcode 4 feels and acts like a new product.

> To learn more about the transition from NeXTSTEP to Mac OS X, and see a side-by-side comparison of the development process, check out this video presentation from SecondConf in 2010: http://cdn.secondconf.com/2010/videos/SecondConf-GeneBacklin-17425.mp4.

Some of the biggest changes between Xcode 3 and Xcode 4 include the following:

▶ A single-window unified development environment

▶ Instant-access editors and viewers for code files, interfaces, data models, and more

▶ Detailed code analysis and error detection

▶ Integrated interface builder

▶ Updated compiler and debugger

▶ Storyboard interface development for iOS applications

▶ Workspaces for combining multiple related projects

▶ Save-as-you go editing

▶ Integrated source control options, including local Git support

Figure 1.1 shows what an iOS project looks like Xcode 3.2, compared to Xcode 4.2 in Figure 1.2.

As you read through each hour's lesson, you'll see that although the tools are new, the development fundamentals you use in Xcode are the same as they have always been. If you have never used Xcode before, I think you're going to like what you see.

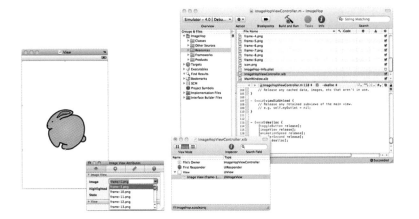

FIGURE 1.1
A simple iOS
project in
Xcode 3.2.

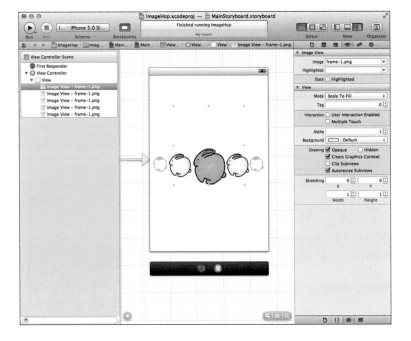

FIGURE 1.2
The same iOS
project in Xcode
4.2.

iOS Versus Mac OS X Development

Xcode, although originally built for desktop application development, is now the
primary method of deploying applications on the iOS mobile platform. While the
skills necessary for writing applications on both iOS and Mac OS X are similar, the
workflow differs significantly. The goal here is to present Xcode in a way that takes
into account all the Apple platforms.

Let's take a few minutes to review some of the main differences between Mac OS X and iOS development.

Frameworks

The Mac OS X frameworks are adapted and improved versions of what was available in NeXTSTEP and OpenStep. They have been defined and refined over more than a decade. iOS, in contrast, is a new OS, based on Mac OS X. Although it includes many of the same frameworks, they are largely "light" versions that do not offer the same depth of features as their desktop counterpart.

Core Image, for example, provides advanced image-processing capabilities in Mac OS X. In iOS 5, the Core Image was introduced, but without support for many of the advanced features of its desktop brethren. The lack of a one-to-one mapping between the two platforms is a frustration to developers, but with each iteration of iOS and Mac OS X, the two operating systems grow closer and closer together.

Deployment

As you already know, iOS applications are deployed on an iPhone/iPad, and Mac OS X applications are deployed on a Mac. Although this might seem obvious, the implications for developers might not be. First, iOS applications must be run and debugged in a simulator, as shown in Figure 1.3 (unless separate development hardware is available). Mac applications are developed and debugged directly on your development machine—no simulator required.

Second, iOS applications, even those that you write for yourself on your own iOS hardware, are tied to a time-limited development certificate. Without a paid developer license, iOS developers are limited to using the simulator only. Mac developers have no such restrictions. You can write a Mac application in Xcode that runs on any computer at any time.

Interface Development

After Xcode 4 shipped, Apple added an iOS specific feature called storyboarding. This presents one of biggest advances in iOS GUI development and also one of the biggest differences between iOS and Mac OS X projects. On the Mac, application interfaces are created independently of one another. Even though clicking a button in one window might lead to another window opening, no such relationship is represented when designing the interface.

iOS storyboards take a more holistic approach to the UI design. Each screen (window) within an application can be defined, and the transitions and relationships between them defined visually. Using iOS storyboarding, it is possible to create a working application UI with almost no code written.

FIGURE 1.3
iOS applications run in a simulator; Mac applications run directly on your Mac.

Application Access

Another big distinction between iOS and Macintosh applications is the level of access that you, the developer, have to low-level file system and operating system internals. On the Mac, developers can do almost anything they want—because they are free to distribute an app however they please. Software submitted to the Mac App Store does have to meet a strict set of requirements, but it is a choice, not a compulsion.

The opposite is true for iOS. To publicly distribute an app for iOS means that your creation must be a well-behaved citizen of iOS and follow very strict guidelines for resource usage. Some of these restrictions are forced based on resource limits (threads, memory, storage), whereas others require you, the developer, to pay attention to Apple coding guidelines. Using Xcode, for example, you can easily create an application that accesses information across the iOS file system and that runs indefinitely in the background. You can create it, but Apple is not going to approve it.

Now that you have an idea of what to expect from Xcode, and the differences between iOS and Mac OS X development, it's time to begin preparing your development environment. Your next step is to determine whether joining a developer program is worth your time (and money).

The Apple Developer Programs

There are two types of developers: paid and unpaid. For free, you can download the latest stable Xcode release from the Mac App Store and begin writing applications that run either on your Mac or in the iOS simulator. You even have access to the full Xcode documentation and sample projects. You cannot, however, run applications directly on iOS hardware or submit apps (iOS or Mac) to the App Store.

For hobbyists or individuals wanting to gain experience with iOS development, paid developer membership offers few advantages. Those who are committed to the deployment of a product on either iOS or Mac OS X, however, are best served by a paid membership.

Paid memberships offers early access to iOS and Mac OS X operating system releases, as well as to beta releases of Xcode. In fact, developers had access to Xcode 4 beta for the better part of a year before it was finally released in 2011. In addition, being part of a paid developer program grants you access to discussion forums, beta documentation, *Worldwide Developers Conference* (WWDC) materials, and in some cases, direct support from Apple.

 By the Way

> ### Test Before the Rest
> Testing products on new pre-release versions of an OS and its development tools is an important part of a serious developer's process. With each new release of iOS and Mac OS X, developers scramble to update applications, fix bugs, and implement new features. Those who take advantage of the pre-release program, however, can get their creations on the market day and date with Apple's latest and greatest.

The cost of iOS and Mac OS X developer program memberships is currently $99/year each for an individual or a company. Corporate iOS developers seeking to deploy iOS applications in house can pay $299/year for a special enterprise-level program.

For a summary of all the current membership levels, visit http://developer.apple.com/programs/which-program/.

Big or small, free or paid, your venture into Xcode development begins on the Apple website by registering as an Apple developer.

Registering as a Developer

To start, visit the Apple Developer Registration portal (http://developer.apple.com/programs/register/) shown in Figure 1.4. If you have an existing Apple ID from using iTunes, iCloud, or other Apple services, you can to use it for your developer account. If not, or if you want a new ID to use solely for development, you have the option of creating a new Apple ID during the registration process.

FIGURE 1.4
Visit an Apple developer center to begin the enrollment process.

Click the Get Started link in the upper right. When the registration starts, decide whether to create an Apple ID or jump-start registration by choosing to Use an Existing Apple ID, as shown in Figure 1.5. After making your choice, click Continue.

The registration process walks you through the process of creating a new Apple ID (if needed) and collects information about your development interests and experience, as shown in Figure 1.6.

If you choose to create a new ID, Apple verifies your email address by sending you a clickable link to activate your account.

Joining a Paid Developer Program (Optional)

After you have a registered and activated Apple ID, you can decide to join a paid program or to continue and use the free developer resources. If you choose to join a paid program, point your browser to the Developer Program list (http://developer. apple.com/programs/which-program/), pick the link to the program you want, and then and click the Enroll link on the subsequent page. After reading the introductory text, click Continue to begin the enrollment process.

FIGURE 1.5
You use an
Apple ID to
access all the
developer
resources.

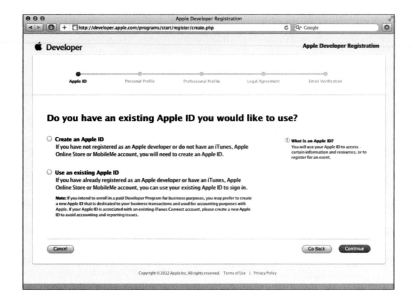

FIGURE 1.5
You use an
Apple ID to
access all the
developer
resources.

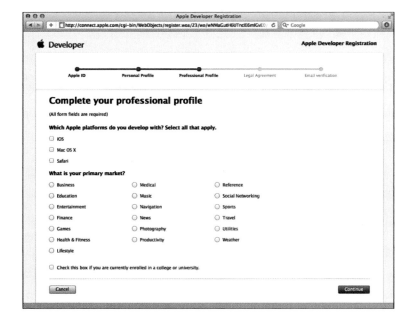

FIGURE 1.6
Provide Apple
with information
about your
development
experience.

When prompted, choose I'm Registered as a Developer with Apple and Would Like to Enroll in a Paid Apple Developer Program, and then click Continue.

The registration tool then guides you through applying for the paid programs, including choosing between the individual and company options, as shown in Figure 1.7.

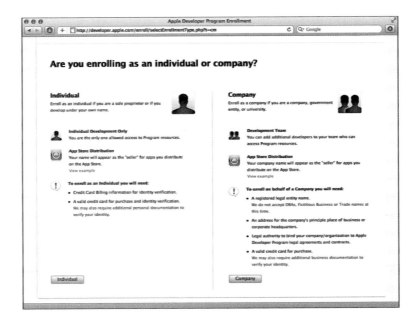

FIGURE 1.7
Choose whether to enroll as a company or an individual.

Unlike the free developer membership, the paid developer program does not take effect immediately. When the iOS developer program started, it took months for new developers to be approved into the program. Today, it might take hours—be patient.

Installing the Xcode Developer Tools

Downloading the Xcode developer suite is as easy as point and click. Open the App Store from your Dock, search for Xcode, and download it for free, as shown in Figure 1.8. Sit back while your Mac downloads the large (~3GB) installer. If you prefer not to use the App Store, or have difficulty with the download, you can also download the software by going to http://developer.apple.com/, choosing the developer program you enrolled in (iOS or Mac), and then logging in to access a direct-download installer for Xcode.

FIGURE 1.8
Download Xcode
from the Mac
App Store.

By the
Way

If you have the free developer membership and log in to the Dev Center, you see just a single installer for Xcode. If you've become a paid program member, you might see additional links for different versions of Xcode, iOS, Mac OS X, and other pre-release software. I recommend, when first starting out, to use the stable release version of the tools.

When the download completes, you have either an installer (if you downloaded from the Mac App Store) or a disk image (if you downloaded from the developer site). Open the disk image, if necessary, and run the installer. You do not have to change any of the defaults during the installation process, so just read and agree to the software license and click Continue to proceed through the steps.

Like most applications, Xcode 4.3+ is installed in your Applications folder. Additional tools are installed within the application bundle itself at the path `/Applications/Xcode.app/Contents/Developer`. Inside the Developer folder are dozens of files and folders containing developer frameworks, source code files, and additional developer applications. Most of your time will be spent in Xcode (see Figure 1.9), but you'll have quick access to the additional developer tools through the Xcode, Open Developer Tool menu.

Xcode

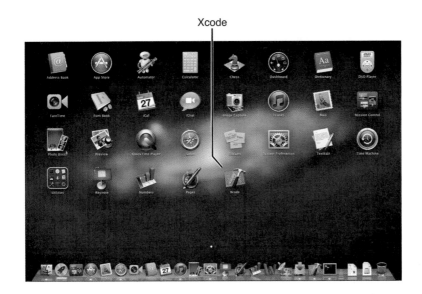

FIGURE 1.9
Start Xcode
directly from
Launchpad.

At the time of this writing, versions of Xcode installed from Apple's developer portal (as opposed to the Mac App Store) use the path "/Developer/Applications" at the root level of your hard drive. In other words, if you don't see Xcode installed in your main Applications folder, check your drive for a "Developer" folder—if you see it, you'll find Xcode within *that* Applications folder.

Did You Know?

The Nickel Tour

If you're like me, it's pretty much impossible to install a piece of software and not immediately start it. To get an idea of what you're going to encounter in Xcode, let's take a few minutes to walk through the basics of the Xcode interface.

Starting Up

Launching Xcode displays a welcome screen (unless you've disabled it) that provides quick access to online resources and common project functions—connecting to source control repositories, opening projects, and creating new projects. This window, shown in Figure 1.10, is a convenient way to access your most frequently used projects without having to delve into any local folders you've created.

Creating Projects

Creating a new project (either through the welcome screen or the File menu) displays a project template selection dialog, as shown in Figure 1.11. This might seem like a bold statement to make, but you won't be creating any applications without using a template (even if it is an empty application template). The Xcode application templates set up properly configured projects for a variety of different development scenarios.

FIGURE 1.10
Use the welcome screen to access your projects, create new projects, or view online resources.

FIGURE 1.11
Navigate the templates for iOS and Mac OS X applications.

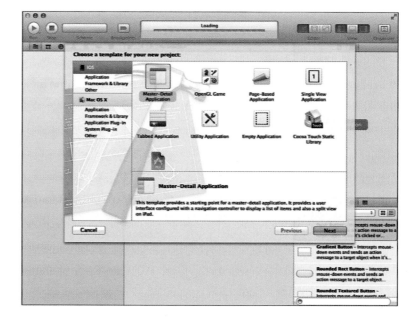

On the left side of the project creation screen, you choose the operating system (currently iOS and Mac OS X), and then select from a number of template categories for that OS, and finally select an individual template from within the category. For example, to create a screen saver for Mac OS X, you choose Mac OS X, System Plug-In, and Screen Saver, as shown in Figure 1.12.

Operating System   Template

Category

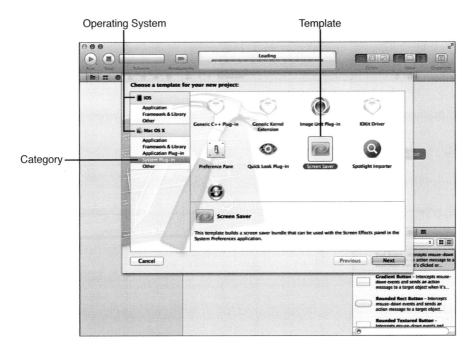

FIGURE 1.12
Get a quick start on almost any type of project.

After selecting a template, you are guided, wizard style, through a series of dialogs to configure any additional attributes for your project. Xcode then presents your workspace, ready for coding.

Navigating the Xcode Workspace

The Xcode 4 workspace looks like a more cluttered version of iTunes; all the development tools are contained within a single window. If you're used to Xcode 3.x, this will come as a bit of a shock. You have much less flexibility in how you arrange your tools. However, the consistency in the interface makes it easy to switch between different editing modes and jump between interface, code, and back without losing your focus.

The Xcode IDE consists of five different functional areas, as shown in Figure 1.13.

▶ **Toolbar**: Displays project status and provides easy access to common functions

▶ **Navigator**: Manages files, groups, and other information related to your project or collection of projects

▶ **Editor**: Edits or displays the currently selected project resource, such as a code file, interface file, or plist (property list)

▶ **Utility**: Provides quick access to object inspectors, help, and object/code palettes

▶ **Debug**: Visible during application debugging, the debug area provides console feedback and debugger output

FIGURE 1.13
The Xcode interface is divided into five areas.

We delve into each of these areas in depth in subsequent hours, so don't worry—this isn't the last time you'll hear about them. Xcode can be an overwhelming application for someone who is just starting development or who is moving from another *interface development environment* (IDE). The toolset is immense, and it is not difficult to get lost clicking between the hundreds of configuration options available. The goal of this book is to provide an understanding of Xcode's major functions and to give you the background you need to start coding productively. The first half of this book examines the Xcode tools. The second half reviews specific examples of how you can use the tools.

Before I wrap up this first hour's lesson, I want like to provide a bit of instruction for those readers who are anxious to begin iOS projects: how to prepare your iDevice for running your own code.

Preparing Your iOS Device (Optional)

If you're planning to use Xcode for creating iOS applications (and have joined a paid iOS developer program), you'll likely want to run your creations on your actual device. Although I had been programming for most of my life, seeing my first iOS app run on my iPhone was an absolute thrill.

> **Watch Out!**
>
> **Pay to Play**
>
> You absolutely must have a paid iOS developer program to run your Xcode projects on an iDevice. If you try to complete these steps without paying, don't expect it to work—but you can still use the iOS simulator.

Like it or not, Apple's current approach to iOS development is to make absolutely certain that the development process is controlled—and that groups cannot just distribute software to anyone they want. The result is a rather confusing process that ties together information about you, any development team members, and your application into a *provisioning profile*.

A development provisioning profile identifies the developer who may install an application, an ID for the application being developed, and the *unique device identifiers* for each device that will run the application. This is *only* for the development process. When you are ready to distribute an application via the App Store or to a group of testers (or friends) via ad hoc means, you need to create a separate *distribution* profile.

Installing a Development Profile

Apple has dramatically streamlined the process of creating a provisioning profile in Xcode. To install the development provisioning profile, first make sure that your device is connected to your computer, and then launch Xcode and follow these steps:

1. When Xcode launches, dismiss any welcome windows that appear.

2. Choose Window, Organizer from the menu. You should see your iDevice listed in the leftmost column of the Organizer under the Devices section, as shown in Figure 1.14.

FIGURE 1.14
Identify your
device in the
Organizer.

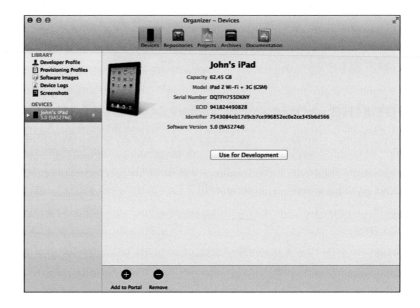

3. Click the device icon to select it, and then click the Use for Development button.

4. Enter the Apple ID login associated with your paid developer membership when prompted.

5. In the background, Xcode is adding a unique identity to the iOS developer portal that identifies you and is used to digitally sign any applications you generate. It also registers your device with Apple so that it can run the software you create (and beta releases of iOS). If this is the first time you have been through the process, you are prompted as to whether a development certificate should be generated, as shown in Figure 1.15. Click Submit Request to continue.

6. Xcode communicates with Apple to create a development profile that is named Team Provisioning Profile and a unique App ID. This ID identifies a shared portion of the iOS device keychain that your application will have access to. Xcode then transparently uploads the profile to your device.

7. To view the details of the profile (and verify it has been installed), expand the disclosure arrow beside your device name in the Organizer, and then click the Provisioning Profiles line, shown in Figure 1.16.

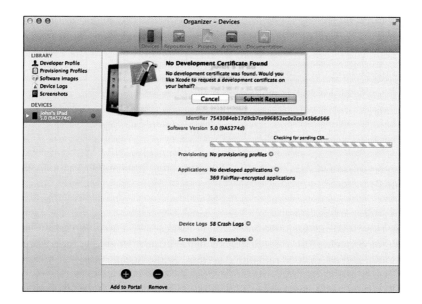

FIGURE 1.15
Create a development certificate.

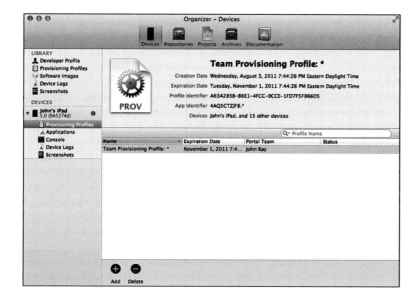

FIGURE 1.16
Verify that the device is installed.

That's it! Your iDevice is ready to go, and any projects you create can be installed and executed on your hardware. You learn more about device provisioning in Hour 22, "Managing and Provisioning iOS Devices," but you probably did not want to wait that long to run your first app.

Summary

In this hour, you learned about Xcode 4 and its relationship to Xcode 3, including the primary differences between the two IDEs. You also learned several of the ways in which development differs between iOS and Mac OS X projects.

You should now be in a position to choose between the paid and unpaid developer programs. Mac developers can develop and deploy software without paying a cent. iOS developers, however, are required to be in a paid program to test software on iDevices. Both types of developers must pay to submit applications to their corresponding App Stores.

Next, you walked through the basics of the Xcode interface. Although the interface is divided into a few general areas, the use of these areas is consistent regardless of the task you are completing. You'll quickly get a sense of where the tools you need are located based on the five functional sections of the application.

Finally, iOS developers in a paid program were taken through the steps of preparing their devices to run their project code. Because Xcode provides an iOS simulator, this is not strictly necessary, but there is something satisfying about seeing your creation running on your very own iPhone or iPad.

Q&A

Q. *If I have older projects created in Xcode 3.2, will they work in Xcode 4?*

A. Yes, Xcode 4 will open your old projects, but they will not be upgraded to take advantage of all the new features of Xcode 4.

Q. *Can I join just one paid developer program to get access to betas?*

A. Yes and no. Joining the iOS program gets you access to the Xcode betas and iOS software releases, but not beta releases of Mac OS X. Similarly, the Mac developer program includes Xcode releases and Mac OS X betas, but not iOS releases.

Q. *Are there any other good reasons to join a paid program?*

A. Keep in mind that beta releases are under NDA (nondisclosure agreement), meaning that you cannot discuss them publicly. Being in a paid developer program not only lets you try out features before they are publicly available, but the Apple forums present the *only* legal opportunity for discussing bugs, development practices, and exchanging ideas prior to the software's public release.

Workshop

Quiz

1. iOS and Mac OS X development are identical except for screen size. True or false?

2. A single paid developer program covers both Mac OS X and iOS. True or false?

3. Can you publish a Mac OS X app without a paid developer membership?

Answers

1. False. iOS development provides a subset of the features of Mac OS X and includes additional touch-related features not currently found in Mac OS X.

2. False. Both Mac OS X and iOS development have individual paid memberships starting at $99.

3. Yes. Although you cannot publish the app to the Mac App Store, you can still write, compile, and distribute an application on your own. The same, however, cannot be said for iOS apps.

Activities

1. Download and install the Xcode developer tools using the Mac App Store.

2. Open Xcode and use the welcome screen to create a new project. Using the new project's workspace, click through the various functional areas of Xcode. Quit Xcode and throw away the project folder when finished.

3. If you have joined a paid iOS developer program, follow the steps in the "Preparing Your iOS Device" section to provision your iDevice for development.

HOUR 2

Just Enough Objective-C and Cocoa

What You'll Learn in This Hour:

▶ What Objective-C is

▶ The Objective-C terminology

▶ How to create classes, categories, and protocols

▶ Basic programming concepts

▶ The purpose of Cocoa and Cocoa Touch

This hour provides a glimpse of what it means to *code* for OS X and iOS. Both OS X and iOS share a common development environment and, with them, a common development language: Objective-C.

Objective-C provides the syntax and structure for creating applications on Apple platforms. For many, learning Objective-C can be daunting, but with patience, it may quickly become the favorite choice for many development projects. This hour takes you through the steps you need to know to be comfortable with Objective-C and also gives you a short introduction to Cocoa and Cocoa Touch—the frameworks that make Objective-C useful.

Object-Oriented Programming and Objective-C

To better understand the scope of this hour, take a few minutes to search for Objective-C or object-oriented programming in your favorite online bookstore. You will find quite a few books—lengthy books—on these topics. In this book, roughly 20 pages cover what other books teach in hundreds of pages. Although it is not possible to fully cover

Objective-C and object-oriented development in this single hour, we can make sure that you understand enough to develop fairly complex apps.

To provide you with the information you need to be successful in OS X and iOS development, this hour concentrates on fundamentals—the core concepts that are used in examples in this book and sample projects you'll find in Apple's documentation. The approach in this hour is to introduce you to a programming topic in general terms. Before beginning, let's look a bit closer at Objective-C and object-oriented programming.

What Is Object-Oriented Programming?

Most people have an idea of what programming is and have even written a simple program. Everything from setting your TiVo to record a show to configuring a cooking cycle for your microwave is a type of programming. You use data (such as times) and instructions (like *record*) to tell your devices to complete a specific task. This certainly is a long way from developing an application, but in a way the biggest difference is in the amount of data you can provide and manipulate and the number of different instructions available to you.

Imperative Development

There are two primary development paradigms. First, *imperative programming* (a subset of which is called *procedural programming*) implements a sequence of commands that should be performed. The application follows the sequence and carries out activities as directed. Although there might be branches in the sequence or movement back and forth between some of the steps, the flow is from a starting condition to an ending condition, with all the logic to make things *work* sitting in the middle.

The problem with imperative programming is that it lends itself to growing, without structure, into an amorphous blob. Applications gain features when developers tack on bits of code here and there. Often, instructions that implement a piece of functionality are repeated over and over wherever something needs to take place. Procedural programming refers to an imperative programming structure that attempts to avoid repetition by creating functions (or procedures) that can be reused. This works to some extent, but long-term still frequently results in code bloat. The benefit of this approach, however, is that it is quite easy to pick up and learn: You create a series of instructions, the computer follows them.

The Object-Oriented Approach

The other development approach, and what we use in this book, is *object-oriented programming* (OOP). OOP uses the same types of instructions as imperative development, but structures them in a way that makes your applications easy to maintain and promotes code reuse whenever possible. In OOP, you create objects that hold the data that describes something together with the instructions to manipulate that data. Perhaps an example is in order.

Consider a program that enables you to track reminders. With each reminder, you want to store information about the event that will take place—a name, a time to sound an alarm, a location, and any additional miscellaneous notes that you might want to store. In addition, you need to be able to reschedule a reminder's alarm time or completely cancel an alarm.

In the imperative approach, you have to write the steps necessary to track all the reminders, write all the data in the reminders, check every reminder to see whether an alarm should sound, and so on. It is certainly possible, but just trying to wrap your mind around everything that the application needs to do could cause some serious headaches. An object-oriented approach brings some sanity to the situation.

In an object-oriented model, you could implement a reminder as a single object. The reminder object would know how to store the properties such as the name, location, and so on. It would implement just enough functionality to sound its own alarm and reschedule or cancel its alarm. Writing the code, in fact, would be very similar to writing an imperative program that only has to manage a single reminder. By encapsulating this functionality into an object, however, we can then create multiple copies of the object within an application and have them each fully capable of handling separate reminders. No fuss and no messy code.

Another important facet of OOP is inheritance. Suppose you want to create a special type of reminder for birthdays that includes a list of birthday presents that a person has requested. Instead of tacking this onto the reminder object, you could create an entirely new *birthday reminder* that inherits all the features and properties of a reminder and then adds in the list of presents and anything else specific to birthdays.

What Is Objective-C?

A few years ago, I would have answered this question with "one of the strangest-looking languages I've ever seen." Today, I love it (and so will you). Objective-C was created in the 1980s, and is an extension of the C language. It adds many additional features to C and, most important, an OOP structure. Objective-C is primarily used for developing OS X and iOS applications and has attracted a devoted group of followers who appreciate its capabilities and syntax.

Objective-C statements are easier to read than other programming languages and often can be deciphered just by looking at them. For example, consider the following line that compares whether the contents of a variable called myName is equal to John:

```
[myName isEqualToString:@"John"]
```

It does not take a very large mental leap to see what is going on in the code snippet. In traditional C, this might be written as follows:

```
strcmp(myName,"John")
```

The C statement is a bit shorter, but does little to convey what the code is actually doing. Because Objective-C is implemented as a layer on top of C, it is still fully compatible with code that is written entirely in C. In fact, Apple has left a bit of cruft in their SDK that relies on C-language syntax. You'll encounter this infrequently, and it is not difficult to code with when it occurs, but it does take away from the elegance of Objective-C just a little.

By the Way

> Objective-C is case sensitive. If a program is failing, make sure you aren't mixing case somewhere in the code.

The Terminology of Objective-C Development

OOP and Objective-C bring a whole range of terminology that you need to get accustomed to seeing in this book (and in Apple's documentation). The more familiar you are with these terms, the easier it is to look for solutions to problems and interact with other developers. Let's establish some basic vocabulary now:

- ▶ **Class:** The code, usually consisting of a header/interface file and implementation file, which defines an object and what it can do.

- ▶ **Subclass:** A class that builds upon another class, adding additional features. Almost everything you use in your development will be a subclass of something else, inheriting all the properties and capabilities of its parent class.

- ▶ **Superclass/parent class:** The class that another class inherits from.

- ▶ **Singleton:** A class that is instantiated only once during the lifetime of a program. For example, a class to read your device's orientation is implemented as a singleton because only one sensor returns tilt information.

- ▶ **Object/instance:** A class that has been invoked and is active in your code. Classes are the code that makes an object work, whereas an object is the actual class *in action*. This is also known as an *instance* of a class.

► **Instantiation**: The process of creating an active object from a class.

► **Instance method**: A basic piece of program functionality implemented in a class. For the `reminder` class, for instance, this might be something like `setAlarm` to set the alarm for a given reminder.

► **Category**: Provide a means of extending a class without modifying the class code itself.

► **Class method**: Similar to an instance method, but applicable to all the objects created from a class. The `reminder` class, for example, might implement a method called `countReminders` that provides a count of all the `reminder` objects that have been created. If you are familiar with other OO languages, you might recognize this as a *static method*.

► **Message**: When you want to use a method in an object, you send the object a message (the name of the method). This process is also referred to as *calling the method*.

► **Instance variable**: A storage place for a piece of information specific to a class. The name of a reminder, for example, might be stored in an instance variable. All variables in Objective-C have a specific *type* that describes the contents of what they will be holding. Instance variables are rarely accessed directly and, instead, should be used via properties.

► **Variable**: A storage location for a piece of information. Unlike instance variables, a "normal" variable is only accessible in the method where it is defined.

► **Parameter**: A piece of information that is provided to a method when it is messaged. If you were to send a `reminder` object the `setAlarm` method, you would presumably need to include the time to set. The time, in this case, would be a parameter used with the `setAlarm` method.

► **Property**: An abstraction of an instance variable that has been configured using special directives to provide easy access to your code.

► **Protocol**: Protocols declare methods that can be implemented by a class— usually to provide functionality needed for an object. A class that implements a protocol is said to *conform* to that protocol. This is similar to a Java interface.

► **self**: A way to refer to an object within its own methods. When an instance method or property is used in an application, it must be used with a specific object. If you're writing code within a class and you want it to access one of its own methods or properties, you use `self` to refer to the object.

> You might be wondering, if almost everything in Objective-C development is a sub-class of something else, is there some sort of base class that *starts* this tree of inheritance? The answer is yes. The NSObject class is the parent to all classes in Apple's implementation of Objective-C.

It is important to know that when you develop for iOS and OS X, you're going to be taking advantage of hundreds of classes that Apple has already written for you. Everything from creating onscreen buttons to manipulating dates and writing files is covered by prebuilt classes. You'll occasionally want to customize some of the functionality in those classes, but you'll start out with a toolkit already overflowing with functionality.

You will spend the majority of your time in Xcode adding Objective-C methods in class files that Xcode creates for you when you start a project, as shown in Figure 2.1, or that you add after the fact.

FIGURE 2.1
You'll create and modify classes within your Xcode projects.

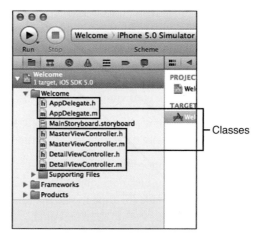

Right now, we need to get a handle on what these classes actually look like and what to expect when you begin coding in them.

Header/Interface Files

Creating a class creates two different files: an interface (or header) file (.h) and an implementation file (.m). The interface file is used to define a list of all the methods and properties that your class will be using. This is useful for other parts of your program, and the Xcode Interface Builder editor itself (which you learn about in Hour 8, "Creating User Interfaces") to determine how to access information and features in your class.

The implementation file is where you go to write the code that makes everything defined in the header file work. Let's review the structure of the very short, and entirely contrived, interface file in Listing 2.1.

LISTING 2.1   A Sample Interface File

```
 1: #import <UIKit/UIKit.h>
 2:
 3: @interface myClass : myParent <myProtocol> {
 4:    NSString *myString;
 5:    IBOutlet UILabel *myLabel;
 6: }
 7:
 8: +(NSString)myClassMethod:(NSString)aString;
 9:
10: -(NSDate)myInstanceMethod:(NSString)aString anotherParameter:(NSURL)aURL;
11:
12: @property (strong, nonatomic) NSString *myString;
13:
14: @end
```

The #import Directive

```
 1: #import <UIKit/UIKit.h>
```

First, in line 1, the interface file uses the #import directive to include any other interface files that our application needs to access. The string <UIKit/UIKit.h> designates the specific file (in this case, UIKit, which gives an iOS application access to a vast majority of the iOS user interface classes).

Wait a Sec, What's a Directive?

Directives are commands that are added to your files that help Xcode and its associated tools build your application. They do not implement the logic that makes your app work, but they are necessary for providing information on how your applications are structured so that Xcode knows how to deal with them.

The @interface Directive and Instance Variables

Line 3 uses the @interface directive to begin a set of lines (enclosed in {} braces) to describe all the instance variables that your class will be providing:

```
 3: @interface myClass : myParent <myProtocol> {
 4:    NSString *myString;
 5:    IBOutlet UILabel *myLabel;
 6: }
```

In this example, a variable that contains an object of type NSString named myString is declared, along with an object of type UILabel that will be referenced by the variable myLabel. An additional keyword IBOutlet is added to the front of the UILabel declaration to indicate that this is an object that will be defined in Interface Builder. You learn more about IBOutlet in Hour 3, "Understanding the MVC Design Pattern."

End Correctly

All instance variables, method declaration lines, and property declarations must end with a semicolon (;).

Notice that line 3 includes a few additional items after the @interface directive: myClass : myParent <myProtocol>. The first of these is the name that we're giving the class that we're working on. Here, we have decided the class will be called myClass. The class name is then followed by a colon (:) and a list of the classes that this class is inheriting from (that is, the *parent* classes). Finally, the parent classes are followed by a list of *protocols* enclosed within angle brackets, <>.

The implementation and interface files for a class usually share the name of the class. Here, the interface file would be named myClass.h, and the implementation file myClass.m.

Protocol... What's a Protocol?

Protocols are a feature of Objective-C that sound complicated but really aren't. Sometimes you will come across features that require you to write methods to support their use—such as providing a list of items to be displayed in a table. The methods that you need to write are grouped together under a common name; this is known as a *protocol*.

Some protocol methods are required, others are optional. It just depends on the features you need. A class that implements a protocol is said to *conform* to that protocol. You learn a little about protocols later this hour.

Defining Methods

Lines 8 and 10 declare two methods that need to be implemented in the class:

```
 8: +(NSString)myClassMethod:(NSString)aString;
 9:
10: -(NSDate)myInstanceMethod:(NSString)aString anotherParameter:(NSURL)aURL;
```

Method declarations (called *prototypes*) follow a simple structure. They begin with a + or -. The + denotes a class method, and - indicates an instance method. Next, the type of information the method returns is provided in parentheses, followed by the name of the method itself. If the method takes a parameter, the name is followed by a colon, the type of information the method is expecting, and the variable name that the method uses to refer to that information. If multiple parameters are needed, a short descriptive label is added, followed by another colon, data type, and variable name. This pattern can repeat for as many parameters as needed.

In the example file, line 8 defines a class method named `myClassMethod` that returns an `NSString` object and accepts an `NSString` object as a parameter. The input parameter is made available in a variable called `aString`.

Line 10 defines an instance method named `myInstanceMethod` that returns an `NSDate` object, also takes an `NSString` as a parameter, and includes a second parameter of the type `NSURL` that will be available to the method via the variable `aURL`.

> **By the Way**
>
> You learn more about an `NSString`, `NSDate`, and `NSURL` a bit later this hour, but as you might guess, these are objects for storing and manipulating strings, dates, and URLs, respectively.

> **Did You Know?**
>
> You will often see methods that accept or return objects of the type `id`. This is a special type in Objective-C that can reference any kind of object and proves useful if you do not know exactly what you'll be passing to a method or if you want to be able to return different types of objects from a single method.
>
> Another common return type for methods is `void`. When you see `void` used, it means that the method returns nothing.

The @property Directive

The final functional piece of the interface file is the addition of `@property` directives, demonstrated in line 12:

```
12: @property (strong, nonatomic) NSString *myString;
```

The `@property` directive is used in conjunction with another command `@synthesize` in the implementation file to simplify how you interact with the instance variables that you have defined in your interface. In essence, defining a property provides a layer of abstraction on top of an instance variable. Instead of interacting with a variable directly (and potentially in ways you shouldn't), you use a property.

In the traditional way to interact with the contents of your instance variables, you have to use (and *write*) methods called *getters* and *setters* (or accessors and mutators, if you want to sound a bit more exotic). These methods, as their names suggest, are created to get and set values in your instance variable objects. For example, an NSString object, like what we reference with the myString instance variable in line 12, represents text we are storing in our class. If we create an instance of myClass called myClassObject, how would we access the myString instance variable? Without using @property and @synthesize or manually writing a getter or setter, we couldn't!

What these two important directives do is write the getter and setter for us and give us a really nice way of using them. The getter is simply the name of the property, and the setter is the property name with the prefix set. For example, to set myString, you could use the following:

```
[myClassObject setMyString:@"Hello World"];
```

And to retrieve value from the myString, you use this:

```
theStringInMyObject=[myClassObject myString];
```

Not too tough, but it is not as easy as it could be. Using @property and synthesize also allows us to read and write instance variable values just by typing the name of the object that contains the property, followed by a period, and the name of the property. This is called *dot notation*:

```
myClassObject.myString=@"Hello World";
theStringInMyObject=myClassObject.mystring;
```

We make use of this feature nearly everywhere that we need easy access to instance variables. After we have given this treatment to an instance variable, we almost always refer to the property rather than the variable itself. That leads us to two final points that can lead to a ton of confusion.

First, because properties and instance variables are so closely related, Objective-C makes it possible to implicitly declare an instance variable *just* by declaring the property. In other words, line 12

```
12: @property (strong, nonatomic) NSString *myString;
```

is all that is actually needed to declare the instance variable myString and its associated property; line 4 is entirely optional. You'll encounter this often in Apple's project templates—a property declaration with no corresponding instance variable declaration.

The second *extremely* important point is that in this discussion we have talked about properties and instance variables as if they have the same name. In many cases, that is because they do, but this is not a rule. In fact, some developers use the convention of declaring properties with different names from the instance variables—often with the instance variable prefixed with an underscore (_). This is performed by the @synthesize directive in the implementation file, which you learn about shortly.

Property Attributes

Notice that the property directive includes attributes (here strong and nonatomic). These directives affect the getter/setter behavior for the property. These are the attributes you'll encounter most often:

readwrite (the default)   Both a getter and setter are created for the property.

readonly   Only a getter method is needed for the property; you may not assign values.

strong   Creates a *strong* reference to the object referred to by the property. This ensures that the object will not be released until the property is set to nil. See "Memory Management and ARC," later this hour, for more information.

weak   Creates a *weak* reference to the object. This helps avoid issues with objects that are retained because of circular references.

copy   Uses a copy of the object when an assignment is made.

atomic (the default)   Ensures that the accessors are thread-safe. Any access to the object is locked and you are guaranteed clean access to the full object.

nonatomic   Much faster than atomic accessors, nonatomic getters/setters cannot guarantee consistency of the data when multiple threads access a property simultaneously. Not an issue you are worried about in your project? Use this for much faster property access.

If you are not sure what to use, strong and atomic are the safest bet. If you are not worried about multithread access, strong and nonatomic are fine.

Ending the Interface File

To end the interface file, add @end on its own line, as shown on line 14 of the example file:

```
14: @end
```

That's it for the interface. Although that might seem like quite a bit to digest, it covers almost everything you'll see in an interface/header file. Now let's look at the file where the actual work gets done: the implementation file.

Implementation Files

After you have defined your instance variables, properties, and methods in your interface file, you need to do the work of writing code to implement the logic of your application. The implementation file (.m) holds all the "stuff" that makes your class work. Let's take a look at Listing 2.2, a sample skeleton file myClass.m that corresponds to the interface file we have been reviewing.

LISTING 2.2   A Sample Implementation File

```
 1: #import "myClass.h"
 2:
 3: @implementation myClass
 4:
 5: @synthesize myLabel;
 6:
 7: +(NSString)myClassMethod:(NSString)aString {
 8:    // Implement the Class Method Here!
 9: }
10:
11: -(NSString)myInstanceMethod:(NSString)aString anotherParameter:(NSURL)aURL {
12:    // Implement the Instance Method Here!
13: }
14:
15: @end
```

The #import Directive

The #import directive kicks things off in line 1 by importing the interface file associated with the class:

```
1: #import "myClass.h"
```

When you create your projects and classes in Xcode, the interface file is automatically added to the code for you. If any additional interface files need to be imported, you should add them to the top of your interface file rather than here.

The @implementation Directive

The implementation directive, shown in line 3, tells Xcode what class the file is going to be implementing. In this case, the file should contain the code to implement myClass:

```
3: @implementation myClass
```

The @synthesize Directive

In line 5, we use the @synthesize directive to, behind the scenes, generate the code for the getters and setters of an instance variable:

```
5: @synthesize myLabel;
```

Used along with the @property directive, this ensures that we have a straightforward way to access and modify the contents of our instance variables as described earlier.

You'll also remember that we mentioned earlier that property names do not necessarily have to match an instance variable's name. Although this is not something that you'll often want to do yourself, it is something you will encounter in Apple templates and, perhaps, code examples you find online. The syntax for declaring that a property be set up with a different name from an instance variable is as follows:

```
@synthesize <myPropertyName>=<myInstanceVariableName>
```

You'll see this used in Apple's templates to name the instance variable when a property is used to implicitly define the variable. You'll also often see the specified instance variable name prefixed with an underscore (_) character. This is just one additional visual cue to differentiate between referring to a property versus an instance variable.

If My Properties and Instance Variables Share a Name, How Do I Know Which I'm Using in My Class Methods?

I'm glad you asked. The default Interface Builder editor code-writing behavior has been to name properties the same as their instance variable (a behavior that might change by the time you read this). So, how can you tell is which?

If you're writing code that instantiates an object and you want to retrieve a property that object contains, you write *<objectname>.<propertyname>* to access it.

That's fine. But what if you want to access the property from inside the class where it is defined? Simple: You do exactly the same thing, but use self to refer to the object, as in self.*<propertyname>*. If you were to use just the property name by itself, Xcode has no idea if you mean the property or the instance variable, so it assumes the instance variable.

Implementing Methods

To provide an area to write your code, the implementation file must restate the method definitions, but instead of ending them with a semicolon (;), a set of curly

braces, {}, is added at the end, as shown in lines 7–9 and 11–13. All the magic of
your programming takes place between these braces:

```
 7: +(NSString)myClassMethod:(NSString)aString {
 8:    // Implement the Class Method Here!
 9: }
10:
11: -(NSString)myInstanceMethod:(NSString)aString anotherParameter:(NSURL)aURL {
12:    // Implement the Instance Method Here!
13: }
```

> You can add a text comment on any line within your class files by prefixing the line
> with the // characters. If you want to create a comment that spans multiple lines,
> you can begin the comment with the characters /* and end with */.

Ending the Interface File

To end the implementation file, add @end on its own line just like the interface file,
as shown on line 15 of the example:

```
15: @end
```

Structure for Free

Even though we've just spent quite a bit of time going through the structure of the
interface and implementation files, you rarely (if ever) need to type it all out by
hand. Whenever you add a new class to your Xcode project, the structure of the file
is set up for you; the @interface and @implementation directives and overall file
structure are in place before you write a single line of code. What's more, you can
do much of the work of declaring properties, instances variables, and methods visually. Of course, you still need to know how to write code manually, but Xcode 4 goes
a long way toward making sure you don't have to sweat the details.

> The class structure seems simple enough, but where will the coding take place?
> When you create a new project, you see quite a few different files staring back at
> you. For OS X applications, your application processing starts with a method
> applicationDidFinishLaunching in the AppDelegate class. iOS apps begin
> processing with application:didFinishLaunchingWithOptions, also in the
> AppDelegate class. From there, the application execution typically branches out in
> additional classes, such as a view controller. You learn more about view con-
> trollers and the design pattern used by Xcode applications in Hour 6, "Using the
> Xcode Code Editor."

Categories and Protocols

In addition to writing classes, you can define functionality through Objective-C's categories and protocols. A category enables you to add methods to a class without subclassing or override a class's existing methods. This means that you could, for example, add new methods to Cocoa's built-in classes, like NSString.

A protocol does not implement functionality, but defines what another class *may* or *must* implement to comply with the protocol. In other words, you can define a protocol that enables other classes to interface with your code, which is often done with objects like the iOS UITable, which expects certain methods to exist in your code so as to provide it with data. For Java developers, this is similar to the idea of an *interface*.

Defining a Category

To define a category, you just decide what class your category is going to add methods to and what your category is going to be named (presumably based on the features it provides), and then you create a new interface file using this format:

```
@interface ClassNameToUpdate (CategoryName)
      // Declarations for new (or overridden) methods go here
@end
```

The implementation file follows:

```
@implementation ClassNameToUpdate (CategoryName)
        // Implementations of new methods go here
@end
```

The naming conventions for category files are the class name you want to update plus (+) the name of the category (for example, ClassNameToUpdate+CategoryName.h and ClassNameToUpdate+CategoryName.m).

After you have created your category, you can import the interface file into your other classes and code away. Your application will behave as if the original class now includes the methods you wrote.

No Instance Variables for You!

Note that you can override methods with a category, but you cannot add new instance variables.

Watch Out!

Creating a Protocol

Creating a new protocol is easier than creating a class or a category because you're just defining functionality to be implemented elsewhere. To define a new protocol, create a new interface file with what you want to name your protocol. The contents of the file should follow this format:

```
@protocol ANewProtocol <NSObject>
        @optional
                // Declarations for optional methods
        @required
                // Declarations for required methods
@end
```

The `<NSObject>` denotes the base protocol that this protocol will be based on (similar to inheriting from a class). Methods that must be implemented to conform to the protocol are found under the `@required` directive, and optional ones are under the `@optional` directive.

> Methods defined without `@optional` or `@required` preceding them are assumed to be required.

Objective-C Programming Basics

We've explored the notion of classes, categories, protocols, methods, and instance variables, but not how to go about making a program *do* something. So, this section reviews several key programming tasks that you use to implement your methods:

- ▶ Declaring variables
- ▶ Allocating and initializing objects
- ▶ Using an object's instance methods
- ▶ Making decisions with expressions
- ▶ Branching and looping

Declaring Variables

Earlier we documented what instance variables in your interface file will look like, but we did not really get into the process of *how* you declare (or define) them (or use them). Instance variables are also only a small subset of the variables you use in your projects. Instance variables store information that is available across all the methods in your class, but they're not really appropriate for small temporary storage tasks, such as formatting a line of text to output to a user. Most commonly, you declare several variables at the start of your methods, using them for various calculations, and then get rid of them when you have finished with them.

Whatever the purpose, you declare your variables using this syntax:

```
<Type> <Variable Name>;
```

The type is either a primitive data type or the name of a class that you want to instantiate and use.

Primitive Data Types

Primitive data types are defined in the C language and are used to hold very basic values. Common types you'll encounter include the following:

- **int**: Integers (whole numbers such as 1, 0, and –99)

- **float**: Floating-point numbers (numbers with decimal points in them)

- **double**: Highly precise floating-point numbers that can handle a large number of digits

For example, to declare an integer variable that will hold a user's age, you might enter the following:

```
int userAge;
```

After a primitive data type is declared, the variable can be used for assignments and mathematical operations. The following code, for example, declares two variables, userAge and userAgeInDays, and then assigns a value to one and calculates the other:

```
int userAge;
int userAgeInDays;
userAge=30;
userAgeInDays=userAge*365;
```

Pretty easy, don't you think? Primitive data types, however, make up only a very small number of the types of variables that you use. Most variables you declare are used to store objects.

Object Data Types and Pointers

Just about everything within your applications is an object. Text strings, for example, are instances of the class NSString. Buttons that you display on the screen are objects of the class UIButton (iOS) or NSButton (OS X). Apple has literally provided hundreds of different classes that you can use to store and manipulate data.

Unfortunately for us, for a computer to work with an object, it cannot just store it like a primitive data type. Objects have associated instance variables and methods, making them far more complex. To declare a variable as an object of a specific class, we must declare the variable as a *pointer* to an object. A pointer references the place in memory where the object is stored, rather than a value. To declare a variable as a pointer, prefix the name of the variable with an asterisk. For example, to declare a variable of type NSString with the intention of holding a user's name, we might type this:

```
NSString *userName;
```

Once declared, you can use the variable without the asterisk. It is only used in the declaration to identify the variable as a pointer to the object.

When a variable is a pointer to an object, it is said to reference or point to the object. This is in contrast to a variable of a primitive data type, which is said to store the data. Pointers, although largely concealed in basic Cocoa development, are an important topic to understand. For a quick introduction, watch this video: http://www.youtube.com/watch?v=7-EppTJK7WQ.

Even after a variable has been declared as a pointer to an object, it still is not ready to be used. Xcode, at this point, only knows what object you intend the variable to reference. Before the object actually exists, you must manually prepare the memory it will use and perform any initial setup required. This is handled via the processes of allocation and initialization, which we review next.

Allocating and Initializing Objects

Before an object can be used, memory must be allocated and the contents of the object initialized. This is handled by sending an alloc message to the class that you're going to be using, followed by an init message to what is returned by alloc. The syntax you use is this:

```
[[<class name> alloc] init];
```

For example, to declare and create a new instance of UILabel class (used for showing onscreen text labels in iOS), you could use the following code:

```
UILabel *myLabel;
myLabel=[[UILabel alloc] init];
```

Once allocated and initialized, the object is ready to use.

We haven't covered the method messaging syntax in Objective-C, but we do so shortly. For now, it's just important to know the pattern for creating objects.

Convenience Methods

When we initialized the UILabel instance, we *did* create a *usable* object, but it does not yet have any of the additional information that makes it *useful*. Properties such as what the label should say or where it should be shown on the screen have yet to be set. We would need to use several of the object's other methods to really make use of the object.

These configuration steps are sometimes a necessary evil, but Apple classes often provide a special initialization method called a *convenience method*. These methods can be invoked to set up an object with a basic set of properties so that it can be used almost immediately.

For example, the NSURL class, which is used to work with web addresses, defines a convenience method called initWithString.

To declare and initialize an NSURL object that points to the website http://www.teachyourselfxcode.com, we might type the following:

```
NSURL *xcodeURL;
xcodeURL=[[NSURL alloc] initWithString:@"http://www.teachyourselfxcode.com/"];
```

Without any additional work, we allocated and initialized a URL with an actual web address in a single line of code.

> **Did You Know?**
>
> In this example, we actually created another object, too: an NSString. By typing the @ symbol followed by characters in quotes, you allocate and initialize a string. This feature exists because strings are so commonly used that having to allocate and initialize them each time you need one would make development quite cumbersome.

Using Methods and Messaging

You've already seen the methods used to allocate and initialize objects, but this is only a tiny picture of the methods you'll use in your applications. Let's start by reviewing the syntax of methods and messaging.

Messaging Syntax

To send an object a message, give the name of the variable that is referencing the object followed by the name of the method—all within square brackets. If you're using a class method, just provide the name of the class rather than a variable name:

```
[<object variable or class name> <method name>];
```

Things start to look a little more complicated when the method has parameters. A single parameter method call looks like this:

```
[<object variable> <method name>:<parameter value>];
```

Multiple parameters look even more bizarre:

```
[<object variable> <method name>:<parameter value>
➥additionalParameter:<parameter value>];
```

An actual example of using a multiple parameter method looks like this:

```
[userName compare:@"John" options:NSCaseInsensitive];
```

Here an object `userName` (presumably an `NSString`) uses the `compare:options` method to compare itself to the string `"John"` in a non-case-sensitive manner. The result of this particular method is a Boolean value (`true` or `false`), which could be used as part of an expression to make a decision in your application. (We review expressions and decision making next.)

Did You Know?

> A useful predefined value in Objective-C is `nil`. The `nil` value indicates a lack of any value at all. You use `nil` in some methods that call for a parameter that you do not have available. A method that receives `nil` in place of an object can actually pass messages to `nil` without creating an error—`nil` simply returns another `nil` as the result.

Nested Messaging

Something that you'll see when looking at Objective-C code is that the result of a method is sometimes used directly as a parameter within another method. In some cases, if the result of a method is an object, a developer sends a message directly to that result.

In both of these cases, using the results directly avoids the need to create a variable to hold the results. Want an example that puts all of this together? We've got one for you.

Assume you have two `NSString` variables, `userFirstName` and `userLastName`, that you want to capitalize and concatenate, storing the results in another `NSString` called `finalString`. To keep this simple, we assume a space is already concatenated onto the `userFirstName` variable.

The `NSString` instance method `capitalizedString` returns a capitalized string, and `stringByAppendingString` takes a second string as a parameter and concatenates it onto the string invoking the message. Putting this together (disregarding the variable declarations), the code looks like this:

```
tempCapitalizedFirstName=[userFirstName capitalizedString];
tempCapitalizedSecondName=[userLastName capitalizedString];
finalString=[tempCapitalizedFirstName
     stringByAppendingString:tempCapitalizedSecondName];
```

Instead of using these temporary variables, however, you could just substitute the method calls into a single combined line:

```
finalString=[[userFirstName capitalizedString]
→stringByAppendingString:[userLastName capitalizedString]];
```

This can be a powerful way to structure your code, but it can also lead to long and rather confusing statements. Do what makes you comfortable—both approaches are equally valid and have the same outcome.

> A confession. I have a difficult time referring to using a method as sending a "message to an object." Although this is the preferred terminology for OOP, all we're really doing is executing an object's method by providing the name of the object and the name of the method.

Blocks

Although most of your coding will be within methods, Objective-C also supports the notion of *blocks*. Sometimes referred to as a *handler block* in the Xcode documentation, these are chunks of code that can be passed as a value when calling a method. They provide instructions that the method should run when reacting to a certain event.

For example, imagine a `personInformation` object with a method called `setDisplayName` that defines a format for showing a person's name. Instead of just showing the name, however, `setDisplayName` might use a block to let you define, programmatically, how the name should be shown:

```
[personInformation setDisplayName:^(NSString firstName, NSString lastName)
               {
                  // Implement code here to modify the first name and last name
                  // and display it however you want.
               }];
```

Interesting, isn't it? You might be used to using anonymous functions in other languages. It is the same concept, but with a rather (in my opinion) unusual syntax. If you want to learn more about these unique creatures, read Apple's "A Short Practical Guide to Blocks" in the Xcode documentation.

Expressions and Decision Making

For an application to react to user input and process information, it must be capable of making decisions. Every decision in an app boils down to a yes or no result based on evaluating a set of tests. These can be as simple as comparing two values, to something as complex as checking the results of a complicated mathematical calculation. The combination of tests used to make a decision is called an *expression*.

Using Expressions

If you recall your high school algebra, you'll be right at home with expressions. An expression can combine arithmetic, comparison, and logical operations.

A simple numeric comparison checking to see whether a variable userAge is greater than 30 could be written as follows:

```
userAge>30
```

When working with objects, we need to use properties within the object and values returned from methods to create expressions. To check to see whether a string stored in an object userName is equal to "John", we could use this:

```
[userName compare:@"John"]
```

Expressions are not limited to the evaluation of a single condition. We could easily combine the previous two expressions to find a user who is over 30 and named John:

```
userAge>30 && [userName compare:@"John"]
```

Common Expression Syntax

()	Groups expressions together, forcing evaluation of the innermost group first
==	Tests to see whether two values are equal (for example, userAge==30)
!=	Tests to see whether two values are not equal (for example, userAge!=30)
&&	Implements a logical AND condition (for example, userAge>30 && userAge<40)
||	Implements a logical OR condition (for example, userAge>30 || userAge<10)
!	Negates the result of an expression, returning the opposite of the original result (for example, !(userAge==30) is the same as userAge!=30)

For a complete list of C expression syntax, refer to http://en.wikipedia.org/wiki/Operators_in_C_and_C%2B%2B.

As mentioned repeatedly, you're going to be spending lots of time working with complex objects and using the methods within the objects. You cannot make direct comparisons between objects as you can with simple primitive data types. To successfully create expressions for the myriad objects you'll be using, you must review each object's methods and properties.

Making Decisions with `if-then-else` and `switch` Statements

Typically, depending on the outcome of the evaluated expression, different code statements are executed. The most common way of defining these different execution paths is with an if-then-else statement:

```
if (<expression>) {
   // do this, the expression is true.
} else {
   // the expression isn't true, do this instead!
}
```

For example, consider the comparison we used earlier to check a userName NSString variable to see whether its contents were set to a specific name. If we want to react to that comparison, we might write the following:

```
If ([userName compare:@"John"]) {
   userMessage=@"I like your name";
} else {
   userMessage=@"Your name isn't John, but I still like it!";
}
```

Another approach to implementing different code paths when there are potentially many different outcomes to an expression is to use a switch statement. A switch statement checks a variable for a value, and then executes different blocks of code depending on the value that is found:

```
switch (<numeric value>) {
   case <numeric option 1>:
      // The value matches this option
      break;
   case <numeric option 2>:
      // The value matches this option
      break;
   default:
      // None of the options match the number.
}
```

Applying this to a situation where we might want to check a user's age (stored in userAge) for some key milestones and then set an appropriate userMessage string if they are found, the result might look like this:

```
switch (userAge) {
   case 18:
      userMessage=@"Congratulations, you're an adult!";
```

```
      break;
    case 21:
      userMessage=@"Congratulations, you can drink champagne!";
      break;
    case 50:
      userMessage=@"You're half a century old!";
      break;
    default:
      userMessage=@"Sorry, there's nothing special about your age.";
}
```

Repetition with Loops

Sometimes you'll have a situation where you need to repeat several instructions over and over in your code. Instead of typing the lines repeatedly, you can loop over them. A loop defines the start and end of several lines of code. As long as the loop is running, the program executes the lines from top to bottom, and then restarts again from the top. The loops you use are of two types: count-based and condition-based.

In a count-based loop, the statements are repeated a certain number of times. In a condition-based loop, an expression determines whether a loop should occur.

The count-based loop you use is called a for loop and has this syntax:

```
for (<initialization>;<test condition>;<count update>) {
  // Do this, over and over!
}
```

The three *unknowns* in the for statement syntax are a statement to initialize a counter to track the number of times the loop has executed, a condition to check to see whether the loop should continue, and finally, an increment for the counter. An example of a loop that uses the integer variable count to loop 50 times could be written as follows:

```
int count;
for (count=0;count<50;count=count+1) {
  // Do this, 50 times!
}
```

The for loop starts by setting the count variable to 0. The loop then starts and continues as long as the condition of count<50 remains true. When the loop hits the bottom curly brace (}) and starts over, the increment operation is carried out and count is increased by 1.

In C and C-like languages, like Objective-C, integers are usually incremented by using ++ at the end of the variable name. In other words, rather than using count=count+1, most often you'll encounter count++, which does the same thing. Decrementing works the same way, but with --.

In a condition-based loop, the loop continues while an expression remains true. There are two variables of this loop type that you'll encounter, while and do-while:

```
while (<expression>) {
  // Do this, over and over, while the expression is true!
}
```

and

```
do {
  // Do this, over and over, while the expression is true!
} while (<expression>);
```

The only difference between these two loops is when the expression is evaluated. In a standard while loop, the check is done at the beginning of the loop. In the do-while loop, however, the expression is evaluated at the end of every loop. In practice, this difference ensures that in a do-while loop the code block is executed at least once; a while loop might not execute the block at all.

For example, suppose you are asking users to input their names and you want to keep prompting them until they type John. You might format a do-while loop like this:

```
do {
  // Get the user's input in this part of the loop
} while (![userName compare:@"John"]);
```

The assumption is that the name is stored in a string object called userName. Because you would not have requested the user's input when the loop first starts, you would use a do-while loop to put the test condition at the end. Also, the value returned by the string compare method has to been negated with the ! operator because you want to continue looping as long as the comparison of the userName to "John" *isn't* true.

Loops are a very useful part of programming and, along with the decision statements, form the basis for structuring the code within your object methods. They allow code to branch and extend beyond a linear flow.

Although an all-encompassing picture of programming is beyond the scope of this book, this should give you some sense of what to expect in the rest of the book. Let's now close our Objective-C intro with a topic that causes quite a bit of confusion for many developers: memory management.

Memory Management and Automatic Reference Counting

No matter how much memory we have in our Macs or iDevices, applications will always want more. As a developer, it is important to use memory judiciously so that our applications have access to the resources we want, when we want them. Proper memory management is the difference between applications that run smoothly and applications that crash or grow to use a humungous amount of memory over time.

The Old Way: Retaining and Releasing Objects

Each time you allocate memory for an object, you're using up memory on your Mac or iDevice. If you allocate too many objects, you run out of memory, and your application crashes or is forced to quit. To avoid a memory problem, keep objects around long enough to use them only, and then get rid of them.

If you have read some Objective-C books, or even browsed online source code, chances are you have encountered the `retain` and `release` messages (probably many, many times). These messages, when passed to an object, indicate that the object is needed or that it is no longer being used (`release`).

Behind the scenes, the system maintains a `retain` count to determine when it can get rid of an object. For example, when an object is first allocated, the `retain` count is incremented. Any use of the `retain` message on the object also increases the count.

The `release` message, in contrast, decrements the count. As long as the retain count remains above 0, the object is not removed from memory. When the count reaches 0, the object is considered unused and is removed.

What this looked like in code was that scattered throughout an application you needed to `release` any object you allocated. Think about that on a large scale: applications with hundreds or thousands of objects, manually needing to be retained or released. If you missed one, memory leaks and application crashes occurred. If you released an object too soon, more application crashes.

Consider the earlier example of allocating an instance of NSURL:

```
NSURL *xcodeURL;
xcodeURL=[[NSURL alloc] initWithString:@"http://www.teachyourselfxcode/"];
```

Suppose that after you allocate and initialize the URL you use it to load a web page. After the page loads, and you're done with the object, you need to manually to tell Xcode that you no longer have a need for it by writing the following:

```
[xcodeURL release];
```

In Xcode 4, all of that changes. Manually releasing and retaining objects is a thing of the past, thanks to ARC.

The New Way: ARC

In Xcode 4, Apple implemented a new compiler called LLVM, along with a feature known as *Automatic Reference Counting* (ARC). ARC uses a powerful code analyzer to look at how your objects are allocated and used and then automatically retains and releases them as needed. When nothing is referencing an object, ARC ensures it is automatically removed from memory. No more retain or release messages to be sent, no more phantom crashes and memory leaks; you simply code and it works.

All new projects that you build in Xcode 4 will take advantage of ARC as long as you click the Use Automatic Reference Counting check box when creating your project. ARC is so good at what it does it will not *let* you write applications that include release, retain, dealloc, or autorelease. So, how does this translate into your development process? Just as you would hope: You write the code you need, initialize and use objects when you want, and when they are no longer referenced by anything else, the memory they occupied is automatically freed. It's as simple as that.

In certain instances, ARC cannot clean up after an object. Consider an object A that references an object B. B, in turn, references C, which references D, which references B again. This is a case of a cyclical reference. The object A can be completely done using object B, but because there is a circular reference between B, C, and D, those three objects cannot be released.

To get around this, you could use what are called *weak references* (remember the weak attribute for properties?). This isn't something you're likely to encounter often, but you can learn more about it in the "Programming with ARC" reference in the Apple library.

By the Way

Of course, it is hyperbole to say that with ARC crashes won't happen. There are still plenty of places for even the most experienced developer to make mistakes. Keep in mind that a typical Objective-C book spends multiple chapters on these topics, so the goal here is just to give you a starting point that makes the template code and sample projects seem a bit less foreign to the beginner.

To complete this hour's lesson, let's take a quick look at Cocoa—the collection of frameworks that will make your apps behave like proper OS X or iOS software.

What Is Cocoa?

You've learned about the Objective-C language, the basic syntax, and what it looks like. Objective-C forms the functional skeleton of your applications. It helps you structure your applications and make logical decisions during the life cycle of your application, and it enables you to control how and when events will take place. What Objective-C does not provide, however, is a way to access the core features that make your Mac and iDevice compelling devices to use.

Consider the following Hello World application:

```
int main(int argc, char *argv[]) {
    printf("Hello World");
}
```

This code is typical of a beginner Hello World application written in C. It compiles and executes on your Mac and iDevice, but because these platforms rely on Cocoa for creating interfaces and handling user input and output, this version of Hello World is close to meaningless. Cocoa is the collection of software frameworks that is used to build applications and the runtime that those applications are executed within. Cocoa includes hundreds of classes for managing everything from buttons and URLs to manipulating photos and performing facial recognition.

Returning to the Hello World example, if we had defined a text label object named `outputLabel` within a project, we could set it to read `Hello World` using Objective-C and the appropriate class property like this:

```
[self.outputLabel.text=@"Hello World"];
```

Seems simple enough, as long as we know that the `UILabel` object has a text property, right?

The Apple Xcode documentation (see Hour 7, "Working with the Xcode 4 Documentation," for more information) includes a complete reference for every class available to OS X and iOS. Plenty of sample applications are available through the documentation system, and many tutorial guides, as well. If you think there should be a feature available to you through Cocoa, just search the help. Chances are, you will find it!

One of the most compelling advantages to programming using Cocoa versus platforms is that the Cocoa frameworks are amazingly mature. Cocoa was borne out of the NeXTSTEP platform—the environment that was used by NeXT computers in the mid-1980s. In the early 1990s, NeXTSTEP evolved into the cross-platform OpenStep. Finally, in 1996, Apple purchased NeXT Computer, and over the next decade the

NeXTSTEP/OpenStep framework became the de facto standard for Macintosh development and was renamed Cocoa. You'll notice that there are still signs of Cocoa's origins in class names that begin with NS.

Cocoa Versus Cocoa Touch

Cocoa is the development framework used for most native OS X applications. iOS, although based on many of the foundational technologies of OS X, is not quite the same. Cocoa Touch is heavily customized for a touch interface and working within the constraints of a handheld system. Desktop application components that would traditionally require extensive screen real estate have been replaced by simpler multiple-view components, mouse clicks with "touch up" and "touch down" events.

Cocoa (Mac) applications make use of two important frameworks: AppKit, which defines how applications present their user interface, process events, and start and stop; and Foundation, which provides object management and common data types and operating system interactivity. Cocoa Touch (iOS) applications, like Cocoa, rely on the Foundation framework, but replace AppKit with UIKit.

Other frameworks, such as Core Graphics and Core Animation, are implemented in similar ways across both platforms—although iOS implementations are often just a subset of the features in the OS X framework.

> **By the Way**
>
> Just because AppKit and UIKit have different names does not mean they're entirely dissimilar. As you work with Cocoa and Cocoa Touch, you'll notice that frequently objects in UIKit have AppKit counterparts: UIButton/NSButton, UITextField/NSTextField, and so on.

I strongly recommend reading Apple's "Cocoa Fundamentals" guide for a full introduction to this important piece of the OS X/iOS development puzzle: https://developer.apple.com/library/mac/documentation/Cocoa/Conceptual/CocoaFundamentals/CocoaFundamentals.pdf.

Data Type Classes

The primitive Cocoa data types made available through the Foundation classes represent one of the important parts that is shared between iOS/OS X development. This hour wraps up with a review of some of these objects because I suspect you'll encounter them often in your code explorations.

Strings (`NSString`/`NSMutableString`)

Strings are collections of characters—numbers, letters, and symbols. We use strings to collect user input and to create and format user output frequently throughout this book.

As with many of the data type objects you use, there are two string classes: `NSString` and `NSMutableString`. The difference, as the name describes, is that one of the classes can be used to create strings that can be changed (mutable). An `NSString` instance remains static once it is initialized, whereas an `NSMutableString` can be changed (lengthened, shortened, replaced, and so on).

Strings are used so frequently in Cocoa Touch applications that you can create and initialize an `NSString` using the notation `@"<my string value>"`. For example, if you needed to set the `text` property of an object called `myLabel` to a new string that reads `Hello World!`, you could use the following:

```
myLabel.text=@"Hello World!"
```

Strings can also be initialized with the values of other variables, such as integers, floating-point numbers, and so on.

Arrays (`NSArray`/`NSMutableArray`)

A useful category of data type is a collection. Collections enable your applications to store multiple pieces of information in a single object. An `NSArray` is an example of a collection data type that can hold multiple objects, accessed by a numeric index.

You might, for instance, create an array that contains all the user feedback strings you want to display in an application:

```
myMessages = [[NSArray alloc] initWithObjects: @"Good Job!",@"Bad job!",nil]
```

A `nil` value is always used to end the list of objects when initializing an array. To access the strings, you use the index value. This is the number that represents its position in the list, starting with 0. To return the `Bad job!` message, we use the `objectAtIndex` method:

```
[myMessages objectAtIndex: 1]
```

As with strings, a mutable `NSMutableArray` class creates an array that can be changed after it has been created.

Dictionaries (`NSDictionary`/`NSMutableDictionary`)

Like arrays, dictionaries are another collection data type, but with an important difference. Whereas the objects in an array are accessed by a numeric index, dictionaries store information as object/key pairs. The key is an arbitrary string, whereas the object can be anything you want, such as a string. If the previous array were to be created as an NSDictionary instead, it might look like this:

```
myMessages = [[NSDictionary alloc] initwithObjectsAndKeys:@"Good
        Job!",@"positive",@"Bad
        Job!",@"negative",nil];
```

Now, instead of accessing the strings by a numeric index, they can be accessed by the keys "positive" and "negative" with the objectForKey method, as follows:

```
[myMessages objectForKey:@"negative"]
```

Dictionaries are useful because they let you store and access data in abstract ways rather than in a strict numeric order. Once again, the mutable form of the dictionaries, NSMutableDictionary, can be modified after it has been created.

Numbers (NSNumber/NSDecimalNumber)

We can store strings and collections of objects, but what about numbers? Working with numbers is a bit different. In general, if you need to work with an integer, you use the C data type int, and for floating-point numbers, float. You do not need to worry about classes and methods and object-oriented programming at all.

So, what about the classes that refer to numbers? The purpose of the NSNumber class is to take a numeric C data type and store it as an NSNumber object. The following line creates a number object with the value 100:

```
myNumberObject = [[NSNumber alloc] numberWithInt: 100]
```

You can then work with the number as an object—adding it to arrays, dictionaries, and so on. NSDecimalNumber, a subclass of NSNumber, can be used to perform decimal arithmetic on very large numbers, but will be needed only in special cases.

Dates (NSDate)

If you have ever tried to work with a date manually (interpreting a date string in a program, or even just doing date arithmetic by hand), you know it can be a great cause of headaches. How many days were there in September? Was this a leap year? And so on. The NSDate class provides a convenient way to work with dates as an object.

For example, assume you have a user-provided date (userDate) and want to use it for a calculation, but only if it is earlier than the current date, in which case, you want to use *that* date. Typically, this would be a bunch of nasty comparisons and assignments. With `NSDate`, you create a date object with the current date in it (provided automatically by the `init` method):

```
myDate=[[NSDate alloc] init]
```

And then grab the earlier of the two dates using the `earlierDate` method:

```
[myDate earlierDate: userDate]
```

Obviously, you can perform many other operations, but you can avoid much of the ugliness of data and time manipulation using `NSDate` objects.

URLs (NSURL)

URLs are certainly a different type of data from what we're accustomed to thinking about, but on an Internet-connected device like the iPhone and iPad, you'll find that the ability to manipulate URLs comes in handy. The `NSURL` class enables you to manage URLs with ease. For example, suppose you have the URL http://www.floraphotographs.com/index.html and want to get just the machine name out of the string. You could create an `NSURL` object:

```
MyURL=[[NSURL alloc] initWithString:
      @"http://www.floraphotographs.com/index.html"]
```

Then use the `host` method to automatically parse the URL and grab the text www.floraphotographs.com:

```
[MyURL host]
```

This will come in handy as you start to create Internet-enabled applications. Of course, many more data type objects are available, and as mentioned earlier, Apple provides a ton of documentation to help you find exactly what you'll need for your own projects.

Summary

In this hour's lesson, you learned about object-oriented development and the Objective-C language. Objective-C will form the structure of your applications and give you tools to collect and react to user input and other changes. After reading this hour's lesson, you should understand how to make classes, instantiate objects, call methods, create protocols and categories, and use decision and looping statements to create code that implements more complex logic than a simple top-to-bottom workflow. You should understand memory management and how it works under the ARC system.

To finish up the hour, you explored a tiny fraction of what Cocoa provides to iOS and OS X developers. Much more functionality is implemented in the Cocoa frameworks than can be covered in an entire 24 hours book, but with Apple's documentation tools, you'll be able to find the features you need easily.

Q&A

Q. *I'm trying to do XYZ in my iOS project and it doesn't work. Why does it work just fine in my OS X project?*

A. The frameworks available and features in those frameworks are not identical between OS X and iOS. Core Image for OS X, for example, includes methods and default filters that are not available on iOS, despite the framework itself being available.

Q. *Should I use primitive C data types or Objective-C data types?*

A. This is usually determined by the methods you're using and the context of the development. There is no reason to instantiate an object to store an integer if all you want to do is some simple math, for example.

Q. *Why aren't Cocoa and Cocoa Touch the same?*

A. I suspect that over time they will merge. For many people the biggest hurdle is coding UIKit on one platform versus AppKit on the other. To that end, you might want to look into the Chameleon Project (http://chameleonproject.org/) which offers a clean implementation of UIKit on OS X.

Workshop

Quiz

1. An interface file defines the user interface for an application. True or false?

2. I want to manage my object memory myself. Why should I use ARC?

3. Cocoa Touch and Cocoa are names for exactly the same thing. True or false?

Answers

1. False. Interface (.h) files describe how code will interface with your class. It contains instance variables, properties, and method declarations.

2. ARC is built around the idea that Objective-C is very structured and predictable. By being able to analyze your code at compile time, ARC and LLVM are able to optimize memory management in a way that mere mortals would have a difficult time replicating.

3. False. Although similar in features, Cocoa Touch was developed for handheld touchable devices, not mouse/touchpad-driven desktop applications.

Activities

1. Start Xcode and create a new application project using the OS X or iOS templates. Review the contents of the classes in the project Xcode Classes folder. With the information you have read in this hour, you should now be able to read and navigate the structure of these files.

2. Review the Apple Objective-C documentation found at https://developer.apple. com/library/mac/documentation/cocoa/conceptual/objectivec/ObjC.pdf.

HOUR 3

Understanding the MVC Design Pattern

What You'll Learn in This Hour:

▶ What a design pattern is
▶ The goal of the model-view-controller design pattern
▶ How Xcode implements MVC
▶ What an MVC application project looks like

If you have programmed within other environments before, chances are you have gotten used to doing things in a certain way. Xcode and Mac OS X/iOS development is flexible, but you will find that using a development approach known as *model-view-controller* (MVC) will make your projects flow smoothly and make them easier to update in the future.

This hour explores the MVC approach and discusses why it can be a benefit to your development as well as how you can implement it within the Xcode toolset. You learn the forms a data model may take and how views are created and connected to controllers. This is a relatively short hour and an easy read, but the concepts introduced will be used in almost everything you do.

Development, Design Patterns, and MVC

When you start programming, you'll quickly come to the conclusion that more than one "correct" way exists to do just about everything. Part of the joy of programming is that it is a creative process in which you can be as clever as your imagination allows. This does not mean, however, that adding structure to the development process is a bad idea. Having a defined and documented structure means that other developers can work with your code, projects large and small are easy to navigate, and you can reuse your best work in multiple applications.

The approach that you will use for many applications in Xcode is a design pattern known as model-view-controller; it will help you create clean, efficient applications.

What Is a Design Pattern?

A design pattern, in software engineering, is a reusable approach to that can be used to solve a common problem. That sounds innocuous enough, right? But what does it mean? It means developers frequently encounter problems while coding, and over the years, effective approaches have been identified to mitigate these problems.

Dozens of design patterns are in use, many of which you will end up using in your applications, even if you are unaware of it. For example, object-oriented development usually includes a chain-of-responsibility pattern. In this design pattern, lower-level objects that are asked to perform processing of an item (data, an event, and so on) can identify which portions they can process, then pass the rest to a higher-level object, and so on. You see this exact same behavior in Xcode when dealing with responses to events, and you will likely include similar functionality in your own classes and subclasses.

> If you have been through software engineering classes, chances are you have been taught many design patterns as "this is how you should be programming." That's fine, but do not assume that no other approaches also work. Programming is about problem solving, and design patterns develop and evolve as languages and computer capabilities evolve.

So, what is the problem that the MVC design pattern is going to solve? To understand that, we need to have dinner.

Making Spaghetti

When creating an application that interacts with a user, you must take into account several things. First, the user interface. You must present something that the user interacts with: buttons, fields, and so on. Second, handling and reacting to the user input. Finally, the application must store the information necessary to correctly react to the user (often in the form of a database).

One approach to incorporating all these pieces is to combine them into a single class. The code that displays the interface is mixed with the code that implements the logic and the code that handles data. This can be a straightforward development methodology, but it limits the developer in several ways:

▶ When code is mixed together, it is difficult for multiple developers to work together because no clear division exists between any of the functional units.

▶ The interface, application logic, and data are unlikely to be reusable in other applications because the combination of the three is too specific to the current project to be useful elsewhere.

▶ The application is difficult to extend. Adding features requires working around existing code. The developer must modify the existing code to include new features, even if they are unrelated.

▶ As user interfaces or data storage changes, *all* the code must be updated, making it difficult to scale the application to new technologies.

In short, mixing code, logic, and data leads to a mess. This is known as *spaghetti code* and is the exact opposite of what you want for your applications. MVC presents a solution to this problem.

Structured Application Design with MVC

MVC defines a clean separation between the critical components of our apps. As implied by the name, MVC defines three parts of an application:

▶ **Model**: A model provides the underlying data and methods that provide information to the rest of the application. The model does not define how the application will look or how it will act.

▶ **View**: One or more views make up the user interface. A view consists of the different onscreen widgets (buttons, fields, switches, and so forth) that a user can interact with.

▶ **Controller**: A controller is typically paired with a view. The controller is responsible for receiving the user's input and acting accordingly. Controllers may access and update a view using information from the model and update the model using the results of user interactions in the view. In short, it bridges the MVC components.

The logical isolation created between the functional parts of an application, illustrated in Figure 3.1, means the code becomes more easily maintainable, reusable, and extendable—the exact opposite of spaghetti code.

Unfortunately, MVC comes as an afterthought in many application development environments. A question that I am often asked when suggesting MVC design is, "How do I do that?" This question does not indicate a misunderstanding of what MVC is or how it works, but a lack of a clear means of implementing it.

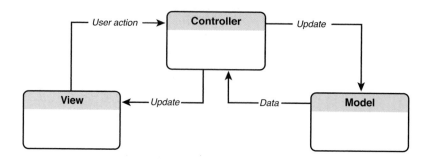

In Xcode, MVC design is natural. (You could even say *forced* in most iOS applications.) As you create new projects and start coding, you are guided into using MVC design patterns automatically. It actually becomes more difficult to program poorly than it does to build a well-structured app.

How Xcode Implements MVC

Before you start creating projects and designing your user interfaces, it is important to get a sense for how Xcode implements MVC. This will help ensure that you are working with the tools, rather than against them.

Because the MVC design pattern consists of three parts, let's look at each one, and then see how they are (or can be) implemented in an Xcode project.

Models

Xcode provides a number of different ways to implement a data model. The simplest approach is to create a class that accesses and stores information through a series of setters and getters. You might also use a plist file (property list) to store a series of key/value pairs.

For applications that have more complex data needs, Core Data can be used. Core Data provides a persistent data store that can be used to store information in a way similar to a relational database. You learn more about Core Data in Hour 17, "Attaching Big Data: Using Core Data in Your Applications."

By the Way

Incidentally, Core Data provides a very clean abstraction of the SQLite database engine. By using Core Data in your application, you gain the speed and power of SQLite, without needing to worry about writing SQL.

What's more, Core Data models are created in a way that makes swapping out their implementation relatively straightforward, thus giving you the flexibility to change your application's data model without requiring drastic changes to your controller.

Views

Views, although possible to create programmatically, are often designed visually with the Interface Builder Editor. Views can consist of many different interface elements: buttons, switches, check boxes, and so on (as shown in Figure 3.2). When loaded at runtime, views create any number of objects that can implement a basic level of interactivity on their own (such as a text field opening a keyboard when touched). Even so, a view is entirely independent of any application logic. This clear separation is one of the core principles of the MVC approach.

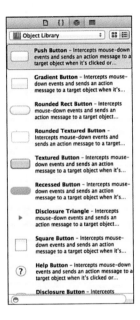

FIGURE 3.2
The Interface Builder Editor gives you access to a wealth of UI components.

For the objects in a view to interact with application logic, they require a connection point to be defined. These connections come in two varieties: outlets and actions. An *outlet* defines a path between the code and the view that can be used to read and write values. An *action* defines a method in your application that can be triggered via an event within a view, such as a touch or swipe.

So, how do outlets and actions actually get created? Xcode certainly cannot "guess" where in your code you want to create a connection; instead, you must define the outlets and actions that in the corresponding controller. Don't worry, you learn how to do this starting Hour 9, "Connecting a GUI to Code."

Controllers

As you learned, a controller is the "glue" that coordinates the action between a model and a view. You'll usually be working with a subclass of UIViewController on iOS projects, and *possibly* NSViewControllers in Mac OS X. I say "possibly" because using a subclass of the NSViewController class provides only a few benefits to you over a generic subclass of NSObject. In iOS, however, subclassing UIViewController is necessary because of the support for handling device orientation.

Whatever your class type, it will handle the interactions with your interface and establish the connection points for outlets and actions. To accomplish this, two special directives, IBAction and IBOutlet, are added to your project's code. IBAction and IBOutlet are markers that the Interface Builder Editor recognizes; they serve no other purpose within Objective-C. You add these directives to the interface files of your view controller either manually or by using the Interface Builder Editor's connections to generate the code automatically, as shown in Figure 3.3 (Hour 9).

FIGURE 3.3
The Interface Builder Editor helps define connections to your code.

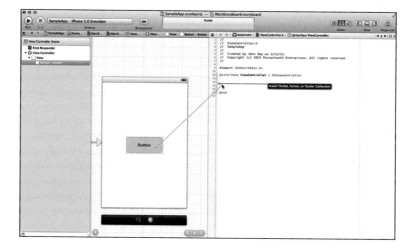

Let's review what this code will ultimately look like through a brief introduction to IBOutlet and IBAction.

Did You Know?

Controllers hold the logic that glues your app together, but they do not have to be the *only* place where you implement your functionality. You can develop as many supporting classes as you need to create your application. In some cases, you will not need any; in others, you might have dozens. The controller just ties it all together.

IBOutlet

An IBOutlet is added to your controller's interface (.h) file to enable your code to talk to objects within views. For example, consider an iOS text label (UILabel) that you have added to a view. If you want to create an instance variable and property for the label under the name myLabel within your view controller, you could explicitly declare both, or you might use the @property directive alone to implicitly declare the instance variable and add a corresponding property:

```
@property (strong, nonatomic) UILabel *myLabel;
```

This gives your application a place to store the reference to the text label and a property to access it with, but it still does not provide a way to connect it to the label in the interface. To do this, you include the IBOutlet keyword as part of the property declaration:

```
@property (strong, nonatomic) IBOutlet UILabel *myLabel;
```

Once IBOutlet is added, the Interface Builder Editor enables you to visually connect the view's label object to the myLabel variable and property. Your code can then use the property to fully interact with the onscreen label object—changing the label's text, calling its methods, and so on.

IBAction

An IBAction is used to "advertise" a method in your code that should be called when a certain event takes place. For instance, if a button is pushed, or a field updated, you will probably want your application to take action and react appropriately. When you have written a method that implements your event-driven logic, you can declare it with IBAction in the controller class interface file (.h), which subsequently exposes it to the Interface Builder Editor.

For instance, a method doCalculation might be declared like this:

```
-(IBAction)doCalculation:(id)sender;
```

The declaration includes a sender parameter with the type of id. This is a generic type that you can use when you do not know (or need to know) the type of object you will be working with. By using id, you can write code that does not tie itself to a specific class, making it easier to adapt to different situations.

When creating a method that will be used as an action (like the doCalculation example), you can identify and interact with the object that invoked the action through the sender variable.

There's Room for All Styles!

You will sometimes write apps that have no separate data model. You will write apps that create and present their interface through code in the controller. That's okay.

Xcode and Apple embrace the MVC design pattern, but that does not mean it fits in all cases, or that every program requires the overhead of setting up a separate data model from the controller, and so on. The examples in this book take a few different approaches. Why were things done this way? To provide a demonstration of the techniques in the allotted space. Is it the only way to do it? Not at all.

If you are just starting out, do what works, and refine your style over time. If you are a seasoned developer with a proven process, keep using it. The Xcode tools and structure are here to help you, not to limit you.

An MVC Walkthrough

To finish this hour, open the Library sample iOS application that is included in the code downloads for the book (within the Hour 3 folder). This is a simple piece of software that reads a database of books and displays them in a list, including the publication year and author, as shown in Figure 3.4.

The Data Model

Open the Library project file and click the Library.xcdatamodeld file in the Project Navigator (the column on the left side of the Xcode window).

The Core Data Editor appears, as shown in Figure 3.5. Two entities (think database tables) are represented in the project. The first, Books, describes a book by its title and a publication year. The second, Authors, describes an author with their first name, last name, and an email address. The two entities are related to one another in that a book can have one author, while an author can have written many books. Xcode (and the operating system) hide the actual implementation of this model behind the scenes.

FIGURE 3.4
The Library application accesses a database of books and presents them through several different views.

One-to-many relationship

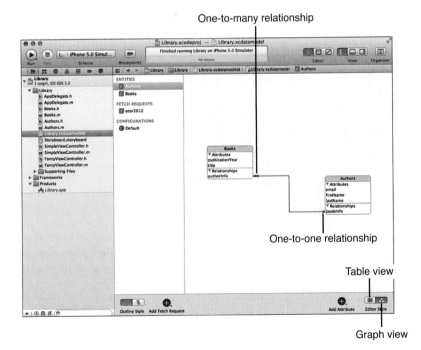

One-to-one relationship

Table view

Graph view

FIGURE 3.5
The Core Data Editor provides a visual means of viewing and designing your data model.

In code, these entities are accessed via Core Data framework methods and two NSManagedObject subclasses—essentially, the data is made available through the classes Books and Authors, which are automatically created for us (and visible in the Project Navigator).

The Views

To display information, the Library application includes two views: one a simple text field that lists information, another that displays the information in a table. A third view (the initial view seen by the user) presents an option of showing the simple text list, or the pretty table.

Click the Storyboard.storyboard file in the Project Navigator to open the Interface Builder Editor and display the design, as shown in Figure 3.6.

FIGURE 3.6
In the Interface Builder Editor, you design the Library interfaces and add the basic navigation logic.

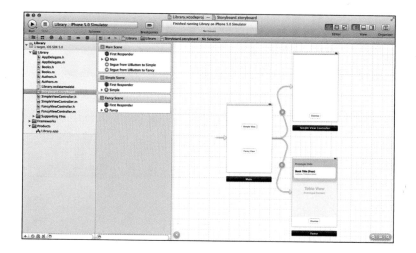

The interface design becomes obvious in the Interface Builder Editor. The initial screen connects to the two information displays—one named Simple and another named Fancy—using connections created entirely in the Interface Builder Editor.

The Simple view contains a scrolling text field that the controller will insert data into, and the Fancy view uses a table that also ties to a controller to be populated with information. Buttons on both the Fancy and Simple views are created to return the user to the initial screen.

Did You Know?

The transitions between the initial view and the Simple and Fancy views are created using a feature in Xcode called *storyboards*. The functionality is defined in the storyboard rather than coded in a method. As a result, the initial view requires *no* code at all, and no corresponding view controller.

Unfortunately, storyboards are currently iOS-only.

The Controllers

The simple and fancy views in the storyboard UI design have corresponding view controllers that tie their interface to the information contained in the data model. Look to the Project Navigator again. Notice that the project contains two classes, `SimpleViewController` and `FancyViewController`, as shown in Figure 3.7.

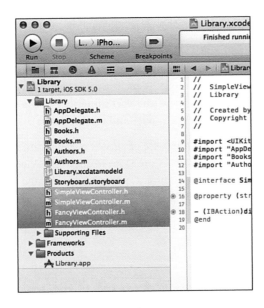

FIGURE 3.7
Each view is supported by an underlying controller.

The `SimpleViewController` includes an outlet for connecting the scrolling text field and an action for handling the user's touch of the Dismiss button. It also provides the logic to read data from data model and populate the text field.

Similarly, the `FancyViewController` include the logic for reading the data and populating a table view—but it does so by being a delegate of the table view rather than through an outlet. It does, however, include the same action to handle the Dismiss button.

> **By the Way**
>
> Feel free to open up the SimpleViewController.h and FancyViewController.h files to view the outlets, actions, and delegate protocol declarations. The project is for poking around, so have at it.

> If you run the application on your system, it, by default, will not have any information stored in it. Each time it is run, however, a single book title (STY Xcode 4 Development in 24 Hours) is stored. This happens at application launch in the AppDelegate.m implementation file.

Summary

In this hour, you learned how to the model-view-controller design pattern prevents spaghetti code before it starts. The MVC approach separates an application into three primary components: the model (which provides access to any underlying data needed for processing), the view (the user's interface to the application), and the controller (the glue that ties the model and view together).

Xcode implements MVC through the use of classes representing the data model—often provided by the iOS/Mac OS X Core Data frameworks. Views are created visually through the Interface Builder Editor. Controllers are created as subclasses of UIViewController (iOS) and NSViewController (Mac OS X) and tied to views via outlets and actions.

Q&A

Q. *I have code that I wrote that draws its own UI from scratch. Do I have to use MVC to port it to the Mac or iOS?*

A. No. As mentioned earlier, Xcode is flexible. You can create a window/view from scratch and draw directly within it. Keep in mind, however, that Mac and iDevice users expect native interfaces.

Q. *Is designing Mac/iOS interfaces the same?*

A. No. You use very similar tools, but, for one thing, Mac applications use windows and menus, whereas iOS applications have a single "window" that presents one or more views. In addition, iOS applications have a different set of UI elements that work well with touch rather than with mouse/trackpad events.

Q. *I'm thinking of writing an application, but I do not seem to need a data model. What am I doing wrong?*

A. Nothing. Use MVC where it makes sense. If your application does not require a data source, that's fine.

Workshop

Quiz

1. Spaghetti code is an example of a design pattern. True or false?

2. The Interface Builder Editor connects to a controller how?

3. Core Data requires knowledge of SQL to use. True or false?

Answers

1. False. A design pattern provides a solution to a commonly occurring problem. Spaghetti code is one of the problems that MVC seeks to solve.

2. The Interface Builder Editor connects to outlets (IBOutlet) and actions (IBAction) that are added to the interface file (.h) of the controller class.

3. False. The underlying storage mechanism is abstracted in Core Data. It might use SQLite behind the scenes, but it is not something you need to worry about.

Activities

1. Read the "Cocoa Design Patterns" section within the *Cocoa Fundamentals Guide* (https://developer.apple.com/library/mac/documentation/Cocoa/Conceptual/C ocoaFundamentals/CocoaFundamentals.pdf). This presents a full background of the design patterns used in Cocoa, with a focus on MVC.

2. Open the sample application and view the data design. Use the sample code in the AppDelegate.m implementation file to add additional books and authors, or additional books for a single author. Consider how you might go about presenting this data in an iOS application versus an Mac OS X application.

HOUR 4

Using Xcode Templates to Create Projects

In the past few hours, you have learned how to install Xcode, what Objective-C looks like, and how the *model-view-controller* (MVC) development methodology can lead to well-structured projects. Starting with this hour, it is time to work directly with Xcode.

In this hour, you learn about the Xcode project templates and how to create and test an application using the templates. One of the best things about the Xcode templates is that they provide a starting point for a variety of different applications. Before deciding to reinvent the wheel, take a look at the available Xcode templates and consider using one of them as your starting point; it might save you hours of coding.

Available Project Types

In Hour 1, "Xcode 4," you learned that project templates in Xcode are divided between iOS and OS X applications. This division is more than superficial. Creating an iOS project sets up the compiler, target platforms, interface, and controllers for an iDevice deployment. Similarly, a OS X project contains project resources that are just as specific to the Mac. In other words, don't plan on creating a new project with the idea it will be "truly" cross-platform.

iOS and OS X: Where the Paths Cross

You can create common classes to be shared between OS X and iOS, but your implementation is constrained to the intersection of Cocoa and Cocoa Touch. Opportunities for code reuse are improving, but don't plan on a large overlap between iOS and Mac projects.

Let's begin by exploring many of the different types of projects templates in Xcode. Apple changes these somewhat frequently, so do not be surprised if the names don't quite match up. The basic functionality, however, seems to be consistent between Xcode releases.

iOS Project Templates

We start with the iOS project rather than Mac project templates because, frankly, they are more interesting. They provide starting points across a wide variety of different application interface styles. The Mac templates, in contrast, are more basic and require you, the developer, to determine what the final product will look like.

The iOS templates are divided into three categories: Application, Framework & Library, and Other. Within each category are a number of templates, as follows:

- ▶ **Application**

    Master-Detail Application

    OpenGL Game

    Page-Based Application

    Tabbed Application

    Single View Application

    Utility Application

    Empty Application

- ▶ **Framework & Library**

    Cocoa Touch Static Library

- ▶ **Other**

    Empty

In this hour, we walk through each category and each template type within. As you'll see, chances are your time will be spent with Application projects more than anything else.

> Selecting iOS or OS X in the project creation screen shows *all* available templates for that platform. Choosing the individual categories under the platform filters the choices appropriately.

Master-Detail Application

The first template, called the Master-Detail template (and previously known as the Split View template), creates an iPad or iPhone application that displays hierarchical information and enables users to drill down to more detailed items, ultimately displaying a screen containing a detailed description of what they have selected.

An app that catalogs flowers, for example, might let the user pick a geographic region, and then display a screen listing species in that area, and then finally show details on the chosen species. Figure 4.1 shows an example of the Master-Detail application template in use.

FIGURE 4.1
Use the Master-Detail template to show structured information.

A unique feature of this template is that you can use it to build universal applications for iPhones and iPads, even though the interface differs strikingly between these devices.

OpenGL Game

iOS (like OS X and many other operating systems) uses OpenGL for creating interactive 3D scenes. To get a quick start on creating your own OpenGL masterpiece, you can use the OpenGL Game template. The default template implements an OpenGL ES drawing context with a few 3D objects, and a timer that can be used to check for updates and apply them to the scene. Figure 4.2 shows the OpenGL template and its default scene of floating blocks.

By the Way

Although the template is referred to as a Game template, nothing stops you from using for any 3D application you want to implement. The basic pieces are all in place; that is, you can use the drawing context and a timer in any type of application. You just need to provide code to process user input and control the OpenGL scene accordingly.

Page-Based Application

The Page-Based Application template emulates a book (similar to iBooks), with a familiar 3D page-turning effect, as shown in Figure 4.3. Although available for both iPhone and iPad (and universal) deployment, the effect and user experience is far superior on the iPad.

Although this template might seem like a no-brainer for creating interactive iOS books, you should choose it only if you need to build a digital book that offers more interactivity than possible with iBooks Author. Yes, the Page-Based Application template looks like a book, but it has all the features of a typical iOS app at its disposal. If you need that, great. If not, you might find it harder to maintain your content and that your development takes longer than if you just use the Apple digital iBooks content-creation tool.

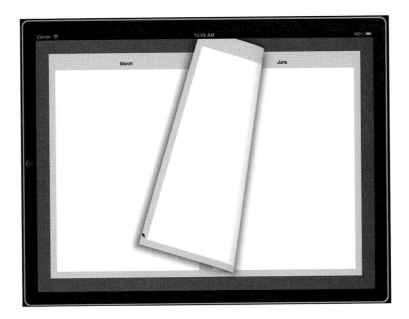

FIGURE 4.3
Use the page-based template to create interactive linear content.

Single View Application

The Single View Application template is the most "generic" of the iOS templates and your likely starting point for applications for which you want to develop your own interface. As its name suggests, this template provides a single empty view when the application starts.

Tabbed Application

Applications that provide different functions (for example, a conversion app that has conversions for measurements distance, volume, and temperature) can provide different "areas" within a single piece of software by adopting the tabbed application template. In this template, a tab bar (a bar with icons on it) displays at the bottom of the iOS device screen, as shown in Figure 4.4.

Using the tabs, a user can navigate between different views within the application, giving you (and them) plenty of space to work in.

> Tabbed applications are more common on the iPhone than on the iPad because of the smaller amount of screen real estate available. If you're creating a universal application that uses a tabbed interface on the iPhone, you might want to consider a different UI for iPad users.

Did You Know?

Utility Application

Utility applications are simple applications with a primary content view and a secondary view (often reserved for configuration). The iPhone version of the Utility
Application template provides a single blank view with an information button (i)
that triggers a flipping effect on the screen to transition to the secondary view.
When finished with the secondary view, the user can touch a Done button to return
to the primary, as shown in Figure 4.5. iPad users do not get the flipping effect and
instead access the secondary view via a button and a popover displayed on the
primary view.

You should use this template for applications that provide their functionality within
a single view but that might also require some setup. Timers, clocks, weather
widgets—simple content-consumption apps—are prime examples of applications
that fit this template structure.

Empty Application

The Empty Application template is a properly configured iOS template with
absolutely no UI in place, nor any code to support a UI. If you want to build an app
from the ground up, this is the proper starting place.

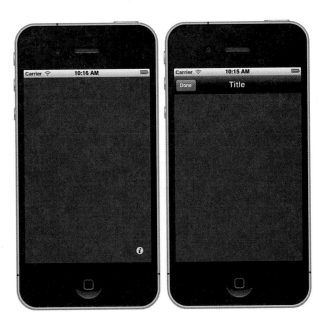

FIGURE 4.5
Quickly transition to and from a primary and secondary view with a utility application.

Cocoa Touch Static Library

In the Framework & Library category of templates, you find the Cocoa Touch Static Library. Using this template, you can build your own code library for use in other projects or distribution to other developers.

Creating a library is different from creating and sharing a class. A class is the raw code that implements functionality. A library is compiled code that implements functionality. If you develop a new handwriting-recognition engine that you want to share with other developers (without giving them access to your code), you do this by using the Cocoa Touch Static Library template.

Empty

The final iOS template (located in the Other category) is named Empty and does nothing except create an empty project structure that you can fill with code. The empty template does not include any code or files beyond the project folder. You'll not likely ever want to use this, but it is there if you do.

OS X Project Templates

OS X projects are divided into five different categories: Application, Framework & Library, Application Plug-In, System Plug-In, and Other. Unlike for iOS, you can develop software that integrates much deeper into OS X, so you'll find a greater breadth of project templates here, but they are less fully developed than the iOS application templates.

▶ **Application**

Cocoa Application

Cocoa-AppleScript Application

Command Line Tool

▶ **Framework & Library**

Cocoa Framework

Cocoa Library

Bundle

XPC Service

C/C++ Library

STL C++ Library

▶ **Application Plug-In**

Automator Action

Address Book Action Plug-In

Installer Plug-In

Quartz Composer Plug-In

▶ **System Plug-In**

Generic Kernel Extension

Image Unit Plug-In

IOKit Driver

Preference Pane

Quick Look Plug-In

Screen Saver

Spotlight Importer

Sync Schema

▶ **Other**

Empty

External Build System

If you are learning to program and want to write some simple C/C++/Objective-C code without dealing with complexities of Cocoa, pay close attention to the Command Line Tool template. This gives you what you need to start programming with minimal overhead.

Cocoa Application

The Cocoa Application template delivers a bare-bones window-based application that can cover two scenarios: applications that present their functionality in a window (a calendar, for example), and applications where the user works within a document window, as shown in Figure 4.6.

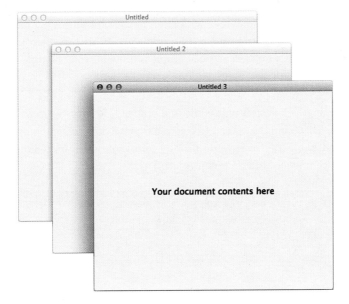

FIGURE 4.6
Quickly set up a skeleton app that functions from a single window or many document windows.

The template does not handle the process of creating files or providing any features beyond displaying one or more windows; it just sets up the basic methods and UI for your app. Consider this the equivalent of the Single View iOS application template.

Cocoa-AppleScript Application

If you're an experienced AppleScript application developer, you can develop full Mac applications using AppleScript rather than Objective-C. You still use the Cocoa classes, but you do not need to learn a whole new language. Aside from the language, this template is identical to the Cocoa Application template.

> To get started with AppleScript Xcode development, visit
> http://www.macosxautomation.com/applescript/develop/index.html for
> more information. Hour 13, "Xcode-Supported Languages," includes more
> information about using other languages in Xcode.

Command Line Tool

Developers coming from a UNIX background may be used to creating a `main()`
function and coding from there. In addition, if you're in the progress of learning
basic development skills, chances are you are not worried about building user interfaces or using the MVC design. In these cases, the Command Line Tool template
may be exactly what is needed.

This template enables you to choose a base language, and then sets up a `main()`
function and lets you code from there. Your application runs via the command line
and produces output in text. Sometimes simple is all you need or want.

Cocoa Framework

The Cocoa Framework project type is the first of the OS X Framework & Library project templates. This template is used to create a *framework*, a collection of independent but shared resources. Frameworks usually consist of one or more libraries and
can include multimedia, interface objects, and more.

> To learn more about frameworks and the role they serve in OS X, be sure to read
> the document "Framework Programming Guide" in the Apple Xcode documenta-
> tion. Hour 7, "Working with the Xcode Documentation," discusses the documenta-
> tion system.

Cocoa Library

Use the Cocoa Library framework to create a distributable binary library that provides a common set of functions to other applications. Libraries can be used as
standalone tools or combined with other related libraries and resources to form a
framework.

Bundle

Bundles are similar to frameworks (and libraries) in that they encapsulate functionality and resources. Rather than provide those features to arbitrary applications,
however, they are written to extend existing applications. You can build OS X soft-

ware to accept bundles to extend and enhance features. To create a bundle, you can start with this template, but you also need information about the bundle architecture required by the software you want to extend. In other words, you need developer documentation for the software you're enhancing *before* you start building a bundle.

XPC Services

XPC services are used by OS X applications to implement interprocess communications. They act as small, standalone helpers that enable two or more independent (but related) processes to communicate safely. With this go-between established, applications can be safely extended or broken into smaller components that only expose system resources to the parts of the app that need it. A browser, for example, might communicate with its plug-ins via an XPC service, removing the ability for a plug-in to directly affect the browser in a negative way.

Use the XPC Service template to set up a project for building a new service for your application.

C/C++ Library

The C/C++ Library is the same as a Cocoa Library, but it is developed for use with C/C++.

STL C++ Library

The STL C++ Library uses the C++ Standard Template Library (a variation of the C++ Standard Library). Learn more about STL C++ at http://en.wikipedia.org/wiki/Standard_Template_Library.

Automator Action

The Automator Action template starts off the Application Plug-In template category. This template is used to create a new action for use with the Automator OS X automation/scripting system. The template includes the required Automator input/output method and an empty UI that displays within the Automator workflow.

Address Book Action Plug-In

Address Book Actions extend the OS X Address Book application by providing custom functions that you can apply to entries. The plug-in template creates a sample action that uses the OS X speech synthesizer to speak information about a selected contact.

Installer Plug-In

Applications that use the OS X installer can customize the GUI of the system installer by writing installer plug-ins. This template does not provide any functionality, but it does include method stubs and an empty interface for designing your own installer plug-in.

Quartz Composer Plug-In

Quartz is a graphical rendering environment that enables developers to layer processing modules (creating what is called a *composition*) to visualize data, without having to write code. Quartz plug-ins are custom processing modules that you can add to a composition. This template provides no example, but it implements all the method stubs that you'll need to complete.

Generic Kernel Extension

Need to extend the core system-level functionality of OS X? Use this template to create a dynamically loadable extension for the Darwin kernel. Few development efforts require creating kernel extensions, so it is unlikely that you'll use this often.

Image Unit Plug-In

Core Image is a framework for OS X (and also iOS 5+) that enables advanced image manipulation through the application of nondestructive filters called an *image unit*. This template enables you to create your own Core Image filters that can be loaded and applied in other applications. (It contains a sample filter implementation by default.)

IOKit Driver

Use the IOKit Driver template to get a start on developing drivers for communicating with external hardware. Like kernel extensions, this is highly specialized and rarely needed by most developers.

Preference Pane

To create a program that presents itself through the OS X System Preferences application, use the Preference Pane template. Preference panes are typically just used for configuration and control of another service. Unlike iOS preferences, however, they are complete applications themselves. The default template provides an empty slate and UI for development.

Quick Look Plug-In

Quick Look makes it possible for a user to quickly preview the contents of a file from within the Finder, Mail, and other enabled applications. You can extend Quick Look capabilities beyond the built-in file types by creating a Quick Look plug-in. This template includes empty method stubs for building your own plug-in to preview files of your choosing.

Screen Saver

Don't like the built-in OS X screen savers? Build your own with the Screen Saver template. Unfortunately, the template does not provide sample code beyond method stubs, so you'll be starting from scratch in your implementation.

Spotlight Importer

You can extend Spotlight, much as you can Quick Look, to handle new types of content. By creating a Spotlight Importer, you can enable the OS X system to intelligently index files that normally would be ignored or not provide useful information. The Spotlight Importer template sets up the methods you need to do so.

Empty

Like the iOS Empty template, the OS X template contains absolutely nothing. This is your starting point for a project where you want to determine all the details (not Xcode).

External Build System

This template, like the Empty template, is a starting point for just about anything. The only difference is that the External Build System template is configured for a command-line build system (such as make). Many of us started development by creating C applications that built with Makefiles. This is where we go to relive the old days.

The Project-Creation Process

Creating a project in Xcode follows a wizard/assistant-like process that walks you through a set of screens to configure how the template is applied. With all the different template types and options that can be used with each template, your projects can inherit hundreds of possible starting points.

Obviously, we cannot cover all of these in a meaningful way, but we walk through the creation of an iOS project and discuss the most common template options you'll encounter. Why an iOS project? Because the iOS templates include almost all the same configuration options of Mac templates, *plus* a few that are unique to iOS.

By the Way

> When you create a new project in Xcode, all the source files contain a copyright message at the top with your name, date, and company. Xcode grabs this information from the My Card identified in Address Book. If you haven't properly set this card, the text in your files will be wrong.
>
> Be sure to start Address Book and choose Card, Go to My Card to see your current contact data. Choose Card, Make This My Card while browsing a contact to choose a new card as your personal card.

Choosing the Template

To begin creating a new project, use either the Create New Xcode Project button in the Xcode welcome window, or choose File, New, New Project after starting Xcode. Figure 4.7 shows the template selection screen.

FIGURE 4.7
Choose your platform, category, and then a project template.

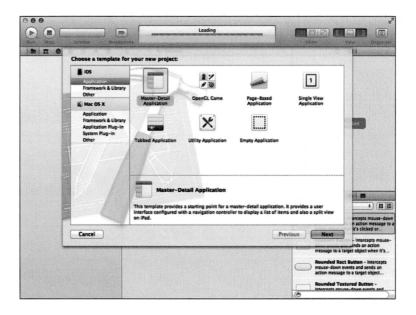

Use the column on the left to choose your deployment OS, the category, and finally the individual template that you want to use. Click the Next button in the lower-right corner of the template screen when happy with your selection.

Configuring the Template

After choosing the template, you are prompted for a product name, identifier, and a variety of other values, as shown in Figure 4.8. Let's start by working through the basic naming conventions, and then look at the other possible options you might encounter.

Product Naming

The product name is the name of your application, and the company identifier is the domain name, in reverse order, of the organization or individual producing the app (Apple's convention, not mine). Together, these two values make up something called the *bundle identifier*, which uniquely identifies your application among all other apps.

For example, assume I am creating an app called Welcome. This becomes the product name. I own the domain teachyourselfxcode.com, so I enter com.teachyourselfxcode as the company identifier. The final bundle identifier for the application becomes com.teachyourselfxcode.Welcome. If you do not own a domain name, you can just use the default identifier for your initial development.

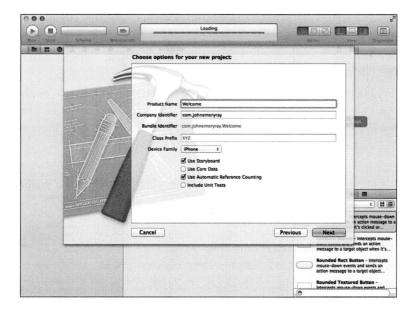

FIGURE 4.8
Choose the options to customize your template.

The *class prefix* is an arbitrary string that is appended onto the start of the filenames in an Xcode application template. Apple has traditionally automatically assigned the product name as the prefix, but changed this in recent versions of Xcode. Leave this blank or provide any value you want.

Additional Attributes

After setting the naming conventions to be used by your application and classes, you still have several possible settings to choose from. Many of these cannot be reset after the fact, so make sure you pick what you need:

- ▶ **App Store Category:** This sets the primary category that your application will be offered under in the Mac App Store if you choose to publish it there. (OS X only)

- ▶ **Create Document-Based Application:** Includes code in the template for basic handling of document windows and document creation. You must still write the load/save code yourself, but the method stubs are all in place if you check this check box. (OS X only)

- ▶ **Document Extension:** In document-based applications, you use this to define the file extension that your application's documents will be saved with. (OS X only)

- ▶ **Device Family:** Unlike when creating a OS X application, iOS apps must target a specific device. Use the device family attribute to create projects for iPhone or iPad. You can also create universal projects that include resources for both devices. (iOS only)

- ▶ **Include Unit Tests:** Unit tests are short coded tests that, when run, verify that your code is working the way it should be. You learn more about unit tests in Hour 18, "Test Early, Test Often." Until you're ready to use them, leave this box unchecked. (OS X and iOS)

- ▶ **Include Spotlight Importer:** When this check box is checked, your project includes the method stubs for a Spotlight Importer for your application's documents. Remember, there is also an Importer project template, so you can always build one later. (OS X only)

- ▶ **Use Automatic Reference Counting:** Switches the project to use ARC (automatic reference counting). Apple prefers that new projects include automatic reference counting, instead of relying on garbage collection (OS X) or manual reference counting (OS X/iOS). (OS X and iOS)

- ▶ **Use Core Data:** When this box is checked, this option includes a Core Data data model and the framework for accessing it. Core Data is a built-in relational database engine that applications can use if they have complex data requirements.

▶ **Use Storyboard**: Like ARC, it is probably best to check this option in your iOS apps. Storyboard is a new method for designing and storing interfaces and interface transitions and is considered the future of iOS interface development. You learn to use the storyboarding tools in Hour 8, "Creating User Interfaces." (iOS only)

When satisfied with your settings, click Next.

Saving the Template

Xcode prompts for a save location for the project, as shown in Figure 4.9. Navigate to an appropriate location on your drive and then click Create. Xcode makes a folder with the name of the project and places all the associated template files within that folder.

FIGURE 4.9
Choose your save location.

Notice the availability of a Source Control check box when choosing where to save your project. This helps you track versions of files in your project, see changes between versions, and restore earlier files if needed. You learn more about source control in Hour 12, "Using Source Control."

You've Got a Project

Okay, so you've got a project... now what? The answer to that question is provided over the next few hours. For now, though, let's take a look at what you should see after creating a project.

Project Files

First, after walking through the template configuration and choosing a save location, you arrive in the main Xcode workspace. On the left side of the Xcode interface, you see the project Navigator and all the files associated with your project, as shown in Figure 4.10.

FIGURE 4.10
Xcode displays
your project
files and
resources in
the Navigator.

One thing you want to be aware of is that the representation of the project in Xcode is not a mirror of what was been created in your file system. The folders (called *groups*) are logical divisions of content. They are used for organization within the project and do not influence the project's actual folder structure.

If you browse to the location on your disk where the project is stored, you see a top-level project folder that contains a file with the extension .xcodeproj, as shown in Figure 4.11. This is the file you need to open to return to your project workspace after exiting Xcode.

You'll also notice another folder (also named after the project) within your main project folder. This contains all the class and supporting files for the project. Additional folders might also be visible for supporting localization (en.lproj for English projects, for example) and for resources you manually add to the project.

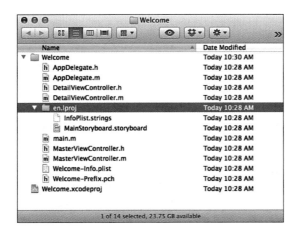

FIGURE 4.11
Don't expect to see the same folder structure shown in Xcode in your actual project directory.

Project Configuration

To review your project configuration, click the top-level icon in the project Navigator in Xcode. To the right of the Navigator, make sure the application icon under Targets is selected, and then click the Summary tab. Doing so displays a summary of how the project is configured, as shown in Figure 4.12.

FIGURE 4.12
Review your project summary.

The project configuration contains information that describes how your project will work and look. Settings such as deployment target (operating system version), icons, and even (on OS X) which capabilities the application is going to have.

Building the Template

Even if you haven't written any code, the templates Apple provides will compile and (unless completely empty) run. To run and view the output of an application, click the Run button in the upper-right corner. OS X applications will run, just as you expect. iOS applications will run in a simulator, as shown in Figure 4.13.

FIGURE 4.13
Click Run to build and run an application.

Stop

Build and Run

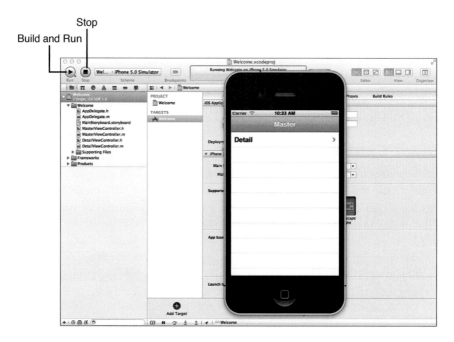

To stop an application that is executing, click the Xcode Stop button. You learn more about building applications and the simulator in Hour 11, "Building an Application," but this should give you enough information to get started exploring live examples of the Xcode templates.

Customizing the Xcode Templates

The Xcode templates are actually project files that you can open and edit to customize with your own code and resources. To do this, you must first make a copy of the project template you want to change. OS X projects are located in /Applications/Xcode.app/Contents/Developer/Library/Xcode/Templates/Project Templates/Mac. You can find iOS templates at /Applications/Xcode.app/Contents/Developer/Platforms/iPhoneOS.platform/Developer/Library/Xcode/Templates/Project Templates.

After changing the template, do not copy the updated template back overtop the factory-installed templates. Instead, create the folder structure Developer/Xcode/ Templates/*Category* within the Library folder in your home directory. The *Category* can be anything you want to help categorize your templates (Applications, Games, or so on). Place the updated project templates inside these folders, and Xcode will immediately recognize them.

Summary

Developers often approach a problem with the mindset of "I'm going to build this from scratch." This, however, is rarely needed when working with Xcode. In this hour, you learned about the project-creation process, which templates are available, and how you can configure them for both iOS and OS X platforms. Although you are most likely interested in creating applications, Xcode provides starting points for libraries and frameworks, command-line utilities, image filters, and even screen savers.

After a project is created, we reviewed "what happens next": A project workspace opens, and the project files are stored on your hard drive. You can now review your project configuration and even build and run the project to get a sense for what the template has provided. Obviously, you want to expand the project beyond just creating a template, so keep on reading.

Q&A

Q. *The templates I'm seeing don't exactly match what you've listed here. Why not?*

A. Apple continually tweaks and updates the templates included with Xcode. The functionality usually remains very similar, but don't be surprised to see template names change over time.

Q. *Are templates my only starting point?*

A. Absolutely not. Dozens of sample projects are provided in the Xcode documentation (see Hour 7) that you can use for experimentation or adapt to your own use. I encourage you to use these samples as a means of exploring Xcode and Objective-C.

Q. *What options do you recommend selecting when creating new projects?*

A. For beginning developers, I recommend making sure that ARC is enabled, Storyboarding (for iOS) is selected, a single (iPad/iPhone) device is chosen, and that Document-Based Application, Unit Tests, and Source Control are disabled. This results in a project that uses the latest technologies and does not include any extra cruft that will just get in the way.

Workshop

Quiz

1. What type of template provides a means of browsing hierarchically arranged information on iOS?

2. The OS X and iOS projects have a great deal in common. True or false?

3. You cannot build and run a project immediately after creating it from a template. True or false?

Answers

1. The Master-Detail template creates unique interfaces on both iPhone and iPad devices that enable a user to drill down through information to ever-increasing details.

2. True and false. Although the skills and many libraries needed to develop for OS X and iOS are very similar (true), the user interaction in an application dictates very different starting points and application resources (false).

3. False. The templates, in most cases, will create a perfectly valid project that will build and execute. It may not do much, but it does give you a quick way to start experimenting with functionality without performing any additional setup.

Activities

1. Walk through the creation of one or two projects (for OS X and iOS) using the application templates. Review the Xcode workspace that is created and compare it to the project folders saved on your disk.

2. Create and run an iOS application using one of the available templates. Notice that the application runs within the iOS simulator. Although this is covered in a later hour, test the simulator and get a feel for how it compares to a real iOS device.

HOUR 5

Managing Projects and Resources

What You'll Learn in This Hour:

▶ How to find your way around a project
▶ The file templates available in Xcode
▶ Ways to add new files and resources
▶ Where to add frameworks and libraries
▶ How to manage target properties

In the preceding hour, you learned how to create projects in Xcode using the built-in project templates. That's a good start, but without the ability to add new classes and resources to your creation, you limit what you could potentially create.

This hour explores how you can add new files, resources, and frameworks to your project. You also learn how to manage the files that make up your project, how to create groups, and even how to configure some of the basic target properties that define how the applications your project creates appear and function. When you have finished, you can create projects with 1 or 100 classes; it's up to you.

Getting Your Bearings

After you have created or opened a project in Xcode, the interface displays an iTunes-like window that you use for everything from writing code to designing your application interfaces. We briefly discussed the important parts of the interface (shown in Figure 5.1) in the first hour, but let's review them now as a refresher.

FIGURE 5.1
Xcode's single
window is
divided into five
functional
areas.

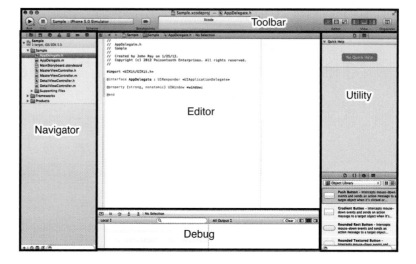

▶ **Toolbar**: Displays project status and provides easy access to common functions

▶ **Navigator**: Manages files, groups, and other information related to your project or collection of projects

▶ **Editor**: Edits or displays the currently selected project resource, such as a code file, interface file, or *property list* (plist)

▶ **Utility**: Provides quick access to object inspectors, help, and object/code palettes

▶ **Debug**: Visible during application debugging, the debug area provides console feedback and debugger output

By default, the Utility area is hidden. You can toggle its visibility using the third button in the View area of the toolbar. Likewise, you can hide and show the Navigator using the first view button. The middle button reveals a fifth area, the Debug area. The debugger is displayed below the editor automatically when needed. In this hour, we focus on the Navigator (and a bit on the Editor). The next hour is devoted to using the Editor in depth.

By the Way

If you ever find that your display seems completely different from what you expect, use the View menu on the Xcode menu bar to show the toolbar, Navigator, or any other pieces that have gone missing. Of course, you can use this in reverse as well—hiding pieces of the interface that are getting in your way.

Navigating a Project

The Navigator can operate in many different modes, from navigating your project files to reviewing search results and error messages. You change modes by using the icons immediately above the Navigator area. The folder icon shows the project Navigator and is the where you will spend most of your time.

The project Navigator displays a top-level icon representing (and named after) your project; this is the project group. You can use the disclosure arrow in front of the project group to open and show the files and groups that make up your application. Let's take a look at the project Navigator for a project named Sample created using the Mac OS X Cocoa Application template (others will be very similar.) Figure 5.2 shows the project Navigator for Sample.

FIGURE 5.2
Your project is defined by the contents of the project Navigator.

Within the project group are three subgroups that you will find useful:

▶ **Project Code:** Named after the project, this folder contains the code for the class files and resources that you add to your project. As you learn in the next hour, classes group together application features that complement one another. Most of your development will be within a file located here. If you dig a bit further, you'll find a Supporting Files group within the project code folder. This contains files that, although necessary for your application to work correctly, are rarely edited by hand.

▶ **Frameworks:** Frameworks are the core code and resource libraries that give your application a certain level of functionality. By default, Xcode includes the basic frameworks for you, but if you want to add special features, you might need an additional framework. We walk through the process of adding frameworks in a few minutes.

▶ **Products**: Anything produced by Xcode is included here (typically, the executable application).

As mentioned in the preceding hour, the folder divisions shown in the project Navigator are logical groupings; they do not directly correspond to a folder structure on your hard drive. In a few minutes, you learn how to create new groups to help organize your projects in a way that makes sense to you.

If Xcode cannot find a file that it expects to be part of a project, that file is highlighted in red in the Xcode interface. This might happen if you accidentally use the Finder to delete a file from the project folder. It also occurs when Xcode knows that an application file will be created by a project but the application has not been generated yet. In this case, you can safely ignore the red .app file within the Products group.

Finding Your Way with Filtering

A project with two or three files is easy to work with visually, but large projects can have dozens of classes and resources and become unwieldy. To help manage the cruft, you can use the Navigator filter.

At the bottom of the Navigator area is a small toolbar, shown in Figure 5.3, that you can use to filter or adjust what is currently being displayed. In the project Navigator, for example, you can enter text in the Search field to only display project resources (groups or files) that match. You can also use the icons to the right of the field to limit the results to recent files or files that have not been saved (the clock and pen/paper icons, respectively). The box-shaped icon is used with source control, discussed in Hour 12, "Using Source Control."

FIGURE 5.3
Filter files in the Xcode project Navigator.

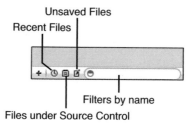

The filtering options are contextual; they change based on what is currently being displayed in the Navigator. Be sure to take advantage of Xcode's extensive tooltips to explore the interface as you encounter new areas and features.

Managing Project Files

Even though the Apple Xcode templates give you a great starting point for your development, eventually you will need to add additional code files to supplement the base project. This portion of the lesson describes how to add and remove files from your project.

Adding Template-Based Files

Much as Xcode can create projects with a base amount of functionality, it an also add new class files (or other useful files) to your project that already have method stubs or other features built in.

Using the File Template Wizard

To add a new template-based file to a project, follow these steps:

1. Highlight the group you want to add the file to (usually the project code group).

2. Choose File, New or click the + button located at the bottom-left corner of the Navigator.

   In an interface similar to the project templates, Xcode prompts you, as shown in Figure 5.4, for the category and type of file that you want to add to the project.

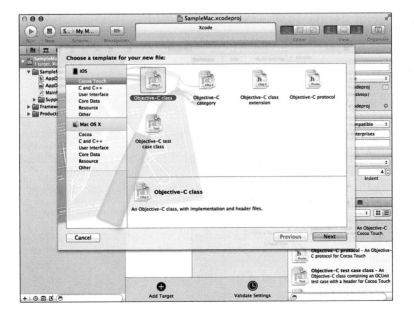

FIGURE 5.4
Choose the type of file to add.

To learn how to add arbitrary resources to a project (such as images), skip ahead to the "Adding External Resources" section.

Unlike project templates, file templates are more focused and contain a few method stubs to help you get started with your implementation. Let's review a few of the templates that are available under the Cocoa Touch/Cocoa categories for iOS and Mac OS X, respectively. Like projects, these are subject to change at Apple's whim:

▶ **Objective-C class**: Adds a new generic class implementation and interface file to the project. You can choose the name for the class and what it should be a subclass of—NSObject being the topmost level object that you can subclass.

▶ **Objective-C category**: Creates a new category in your project. Categories, as you learned in Hour 2, "Just Enough Objective-C and Cocoa," extend the functionality of a class and all its subclasses. Using this template, you can name the category and choose which class it extends.

▶ **Objective-C protocol**: A protocol file defines a set of methods that a class must implement to "conform" to a protocol. In other words, this is a means of providing forced consistency between classes. Again, refer to Hour 2 for more details. This template adds a single empty protocol file to your project.

▶ **Objective-C test case class**: Adds a class to your project that is used to implement unit tests. The class template contains a sample method, but you need to add the SenTestingKit framework to your project before you can compile it. Learn more about how to add a framework in the "Managing Frameworks and Libraries" section, later this hour.

▶ **Objective-C extension**: Similar to a category, extensions anonymously extend the features of a class. Use this template to create a new extension by providing a name and the class to be extended.

I See More Templates. What Are They?

These templates listed here are the ones you will likely use for the vast majority of your development, but others are available under the other categories:

C and C++   Within the C and C++ category, for example, are simple C/C++ and header file templates. If you choose one of these, you end up with a largely empty file added to your project.

User Interface   In the User Interface category, choose from a variety of UI documents that can use used to add new interface features to your application. The iOS templates, while similar to the Mac OS X options, are superseded by the storyboard file and shouldn't be used in new applications. It is also useful to note that any of the interface templates can be built from scratch in seconds within the Interface Builder editor (Hour 8, "Creating User Interfaces").

Core Data The Core Data templates are added to projects that want to use Mac OS X/iOS's internal relational database system.

Resources In the Resources category, choose from a variety of generic file types that can be added as file resources in your project. Plists, rich text files, and so on are contained here.

Other Finally, the Other category contains templates for empty (yes, completely empty) files, shell scripts, and assembly language files. It is unlikely that you will need these templates often.

3. After picking your template, click Next.

   You are then prompted for the name of the class, category, or protocol that you are creating. If you choose to make a subclass of a UIViewController (iOS only), you also have the option to add a corresponding NIB interface file and target it for the iPad, as shown in Figure 5.5.

4. Assuming you are using storyboarding, you do not want (or need) either of these options. Click Next to continue.

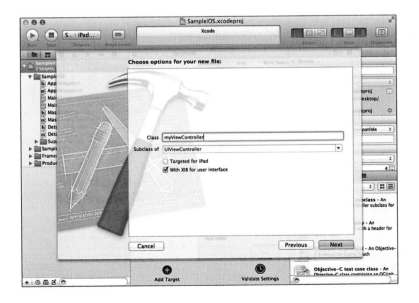

FIGURE 5.5
Set the options for the code template that you are creating.

5. Choose where the new files will be stored.

Typically, this is inside the main project code directory (as shown in Figure 5.6). In some instances, however, you might want to add the files to one of the localization directories within the project or into an arbitrary directory. Remember that this is an actual directory, not an Xcode group.

6. To set the Xcode group, use the Group pop-up menu near the bottom of the dialog box. You should also make sure that the appropriate targets are checked.

The targets are the products that are produced by building the application. For example, you might have an iOS project with individual targets for the iPad and iPhone. You do not necessarily want a new interface file for the iPhone to be included with the iPad target, or vice versa.

FIGURE 5.6
Choose where
to create
the file.

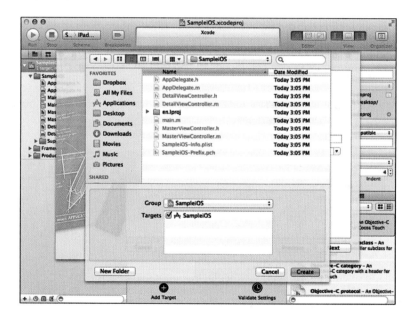

7. When satisfied with your choices, click Create.

Notice that the new files are immediately visible within the project Navigator, as shown in Figure 5.7.

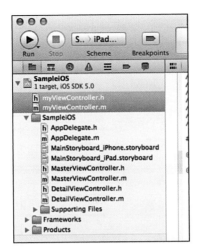

FIGURE 5.7
The files are added to the project Navigator.

> **By the Way**
>
> If your new files do not show up in the groups that you expect, you can move them after the fact. Just click and drag the file icons within the project Navigator to move them to and from any group.

Using the File Template Library

Not satisfied with one perfectly acceptable way of adding files to your project? Neither was Apple. If you prefer to have an always-visible collection of file templates at your disposal, you can use the File Template Library to add your files. To make this tool visible within the Utility area of Xcode, choose View, Utilities, Show File Template Library (Control+Option+Command+1). The File Template Library appears in the lower right of the Utility area, as shown in Figure 5.8.

> **By the Way**
>
> To increase (or decrease) the size of the File Template Library (or any other panel), just click and drag up and down on the top border of the panel.
>
> You can also switch the File Template Library between icon and list (the default) view using the buttons in the upper-right corner. The icon view fits more onto the screen but does not provide a description of the template.

To add a file from the library to your project, scroll through the library to find the file you want (you can filter the list with the field at the bottom of the pane), and then click and drag the icon in the library to the project Navigator. When you release your mouse button, you are prompted to name the file (or class), choose a save location, and pick the targets that will use the file, as shown in Figure 5.9.

FIGURE 5.8
The File
Template Library
is visible in the
Utility area.

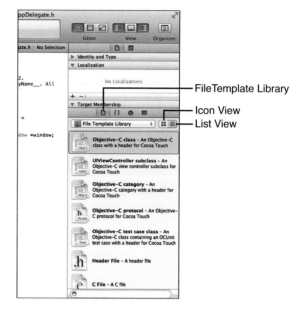

FIGURE 5.9
Complete the
details to add
file to your
project.

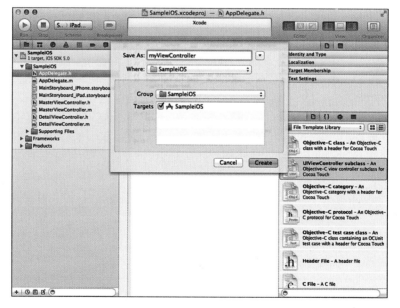

Notice that the file library does not (currently) present the full multistep wizard for configuring the template. Unfortunately, this means that you might end up with files you do not want. For example, the UIViewController template for iOS automatically adds a NIB file for an iOS interface—even if your project is using a storyboard.

> If you target a project group when dragging your template, the files are automatically added to the group. As always, you can drag and rearrange the files later.

Adding General Files

Many applications require sound or image files that you integrate into your development. Obviously, Xcode cannot help you "create" these files with a template, so you must add them by hand. To do this, just click and drag the file from its location in the Finder into the project code group in Xcode. You are prompted to copy the files. If you are not sharing files between multiple projects, make sure the Copy check box is selected so that Xcode can put the files where they need to go within your project directory and that the appropriate targets that will use the files are selected, as shown in Figure 5.10.

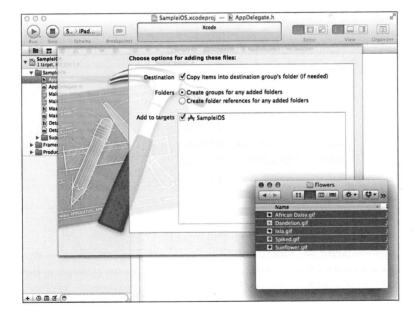

FIGURE 5.10
Copy the files to the project.

When you add new files in this method, notice that you have the option of creating folder references or groups for the files. If you choose to create a folder reference, the project creates a link to the folder on your drive (the folder itself is not copied). If you create a group, Xcode automatically creates a new logical group that contains the files.

By the Way

> You can add any type of file using this method, including your own code files. Just keep in mind that adding the template-based files buys you a head start in coding with method stubs and properly formatted class files.

Renaming Files

To rename a file within the project Navigator, click to select the file in the Navigator and then press Return or move your mouse back and forth over the name. The name changes to an editable field, as shown in Figure 5.11. Enter your changes, and then click off of the file to save them.

FIGURE 5.11
Change the name of any project file.

Be aware that changing a filename in the navigator *will* change the filename on your hard disk. If the file is referenced from any other files or lines of code, you also need to update them. To change the name of a class or other object and have it automatically propagated throughout your project, look at the refactoring features discussed in the next hour's lesson.

Removing Files

If you have added something to Xcode that you decide you do not want, you can delete it easily. To remove a file or resource from your project, just select it within the project Navigator and then press the Delete key. Xcode gives you the option to delete any references to the file from the project and move the file to the trash or just to delete the references (see Figure 5.12).

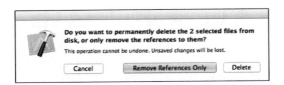

FIGURE 5.12
Delete the files
(or just their
references).

If you choose to delete references, the file itself remains but is no longer visible in the project.

Locating Your Files in the Finder

When working in Xcode, it is sometimes helpful to be able to quickly jump to a file in the finder—perhaps to open it in another application, get some information about it, or in the case of an Xcode "product," find where your compiled application has been saved.

To jump to any file that you can see in the project Navigator, right-click it, and then choose Show in Finder, as shown in Figure 5.13.

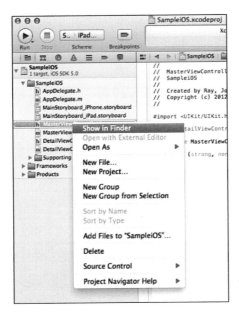

FIGURE 5.13
Show your files
in the Finder.

Remember that if you want to delete or rename a file, you should do so directly in Xcode; otherwise, the Xcode project Navigator gets out of sync with the files that are actually stored on your disk.

Managing Frameworks and Libraries

Frameworks are bundles of files (libraries, headers, and other resources) that you can use to add functionality to your projects. Projects that you create from templates already include the base frameworks that you need, but you'll likely want to add more as you use new Cocoa or Cocoa Touch features.

Adding Frameworks and Libraries to a Project

To add a framework (or library), follow these steps:

1. Select the top-level project group in the project Navigator, and then the application icon in the Targets section that appears in the column to the right of the Navigator.

2. Make sure the Summary tab is highlighted at the top of the Editor area.

3. Scroll down the summary until you find the section called Linked Frameworks and Libraries. Click the + button below the list.

   A list of all available frameworks and libraries appropriate to your project appears, as shown in Figure 5.14.

FIGURE 5.14
Choose a framework or library to add.

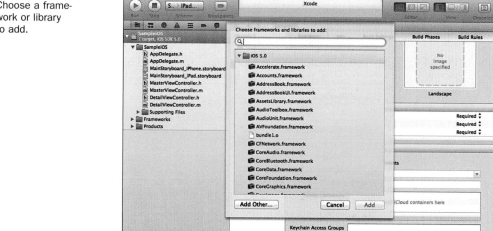

Select the item you want, and then click Add.

The framework now appears in both the Summary area and within the project Navigator. You must drag it to the Frameworks group in your project. This is not necessary for the project to work, but it keeps things neat and orderly (and that's a good thing).

If you know the location of your framework/library and/or it isn't in the list, you can click Add Other to browse your drive and choose from another location.

Finding the Framework Headers

To successfully use a framework (or library), you need to include its header (interface file) within the class code that needs to access the framework's methods. For a library, you must know exactly where the headers are located—but for a framework, the headers are included directly in the framework itself. You can expand any framework to examine its header files, as shown in Figure 5.15.

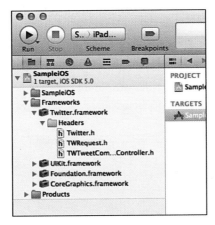

FIGURE 5.15
Explore the headers included in a framework.

A top-level header file—named after the framework itself—includes all the other header files in the framework, and it is what you want to include in your code using this naming convention:

```
#import <Framework/Framework.h>
```

For example, if you need to include the UIKit framework for iOS manually (it is included automatically, by the way), you use the following:

```
#import <UIKit/UIKit.h>
```

Removing Frameworks and Libraries

Removing a framework is just like removing any other file from your project. Just select the icon in the project manager and press the Delete key on your keyboard. Be sure to only delete the reference, not the actual files. Even if you do not need a framework today, that doesn't mean you won't want to include it somewhere tomorrow.

Managing Groups

You have already learned one way to add groups to the project navigator by dragging an existing Finder folder into the Navigator, but you can also add them directly without leaving Xcode.

Adding Groups

There are two different ways to create a group: either by grouping a set of existing files or by creating a new empty group. To add a new empty group, right-click in the project Navigator and choose New Group. A group, labeled New Group is then added to the project. You can rename it as described in the "Renaming Files" section, earlier in this hour.

If you are adding a group to collect a set of existing files, you can do it all at one time by selecting the files in the Navigator and right-clicking and choosing New Group from Selection, as shown in Figure 5.16.

FIGURE 5.16
Collect existing files into a new group.

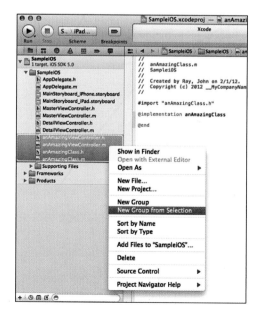

On Mac OS X, you can select noncontiguous ranges of files by holding Command and clicking the filename. You cannot, however, make a new group out of files that are already contained within different groups—you need to drag the files to a common level first.

If you're a more menu-centric user, you can access these functions by choosing File, New.

After creating your groups, add your files to them by clicking and dragging. Because this is just a logical view of the files, you can even arrange the individual files in the order you want—they are not forced into any particular sequence.

Removing Groups

If you create too many groups and decide you do not want them, just select a group and press the Delete button. If you choose a group with files, you are prompted with the standard Xcode file-deletion confirmation. If you choose to delete an empty group, it disappears silently.

Managing Target Properties

To finish this hour's lesson, let's focus on something a bit different: the properties that describe a target. A target is the application that your project produces. I sometimes refer to these as project properties, but because technically a project can have multiple targets, that is not quite the reality. I bring this up now because you access these through the project Navigator.

In this book and most simple development, a project almost always has a single target, so equating a project and a target is not unusual.

Basic Properties

By default, your target is going to contain lots of settings for building an application—and you're not going to need to change them. We talk about build settings more throughout the book, but there are several settings that affect how your project is built that you *will* need to access early on.

For iOS applications, this includes icons, launch images, supported device orientations, and so on. Mac OS X applications have similar settings, including a list of the attributes your software needs to run. So, where is this stored and edited? The answer is the target plist file.

This file, found in a project's Supporting Files folder, is created automatically when you start a new project or add a new target, and is prefixed with the project/target name and ends in Info.plist. Although you can edit the values directly in the plist file, Xcode provides an easier approach, as follows:

Within the project Navigator, click the top-level project icon (a blue document icon). After selecting this, you can pick the target to focus on (usually just one) from the column beside the Navigator. Once you have chosen this, the Editor area refreshes to display several tabs across the top, as shown in Figure 5.17.

FIGURE 5.17
Set your target
properties.

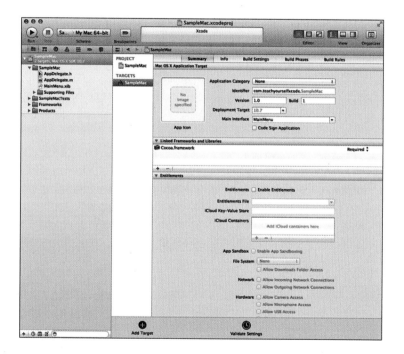

In the first, Summary, you can set many of the target plist options visually. The second, Info, provides direct access to the plist file contents without any digging around to file the plist file itself. We get to the others later; they contain settings that you probably will not need to modify for most day-to-day development.

Some of the properties you'll encounter are as follows:

▶ **Version/Build:** The version number of your application

▶ **Deployment Target:** The OS version you are building for

▶ **Devices**: Which devices will run the software (iOS only)

▶ **Identifier**: The unique identifier for your application (added when the project is created)

▶ **Main interface**: The file that contains your primary application interface

▶ **Supported Device Orientations**: Which iDevice orientations your app will support running in (iOS only)

▶ **App Icon(s)**: The icons to associate with your application

▶ **Launch images**: The images to show while launching your app (iOS only)

▶ **Entitlements**: Access rights that your application can ask for during execution (access to iCloud, network services, and so on)

Setting an Application Icon

Although we cannot go through every target property that exists (the Apple documentation system you learn about in Hour 7, "Working with the Xcode Documentation," more than suffices for giving you every esoteric detail), we cover the one example that every application needs: an icon.

For iOS devices, there are currently four different sizes of icons that you might need:

iPhone – Non-Retina display – 57x57 pixels

iPhone – Retina display – 114x114 pixels

iPad – Non-Retina display – 72x72 pixels

iPad – Retina display – 144x144 pixels

For Mac OS X, you should start with an icon sized at 1024x1024 pixels, although you can also include smaller sizes in your project.

To set an icon, create a PNG file of the appropriate dimensions. iOS icons should not have rounded corners or any visual effects. (iOS automatically adds the glossy look for you.) Just drag the icon file from the Finder into the appropriate image well, as shown in Figure 5.18. "Regular" display icons are named as Icon.png, and Retina display icons are named Icon@2x.png.

FIGURE 5.18
Add an icon to
your application.

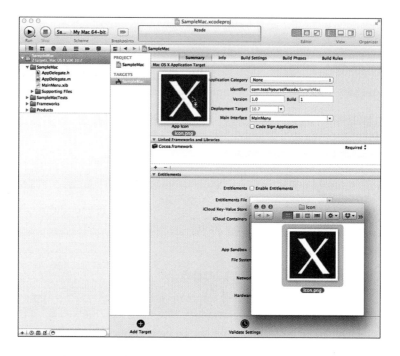

The @2x naming convention is used in iOS to support the Retina display. In fact, if an application is running on a device with a Retina display and is asked to display an image, it automatically substitutes (if available) an image resource with the same name and the suffix @2x. This enables developers to support Retina displays without changing any code in their applications. I suspect that when Retina displays are added to the Mac line, the same conventions will apply.

Again, this is just meant to provide you with a starting point for configuring some of the attributes that define how your project targets will look and function. Dozens of additional options do not even display in the simple summary interface, so explore when you have a chance.

Summary

In this hour, you learned how to add new files to your project and how the file templates can give you a better starting point in your coding than simply adding a new file. You also learned how to manage files and resources in your projects, and how to create new groups to logically arrange your code in a way that makes sense.

Although these things might seem like simple steps, they are critical to working effectively on a project. Getting files in and out of Xcode is not as simple as working in the project folder in the Finder, so knowing how to manage your project and get to the resources you need is a useful skill as we move forward.

Q&A

Q. *The file templates I'm seeing don't exactly match what you've listed here. Why not?*

A. Like project templates, the file templates may change over time. I suspect Apple will change the iOS interface templates given the advent of Storyboard, for example.

Q. *What happens to the source files if I delete a reference to them?*

A. Not a thing. The reference is just a link to the files. If you delete a reference accidentally, you can find the original file within the project directory and drag it back into the project Navigator.

Q. *What other options, besides icon settings, are available for targets?*

A. This depends on the OS you are deploying on, and is a moving target (no pun intended). If you are interested in which attributes of a target can be controlled by their plist, you want to search the Apple documentation for a full reference.

Workshop

Quiz

1. What file template is used to define a set of methods that other classes (should they choose to adopt it) must implement?

2. Deleting a file reference deletes the file. True or false?

3. The maximum size for a Mac OS X icon is 512x512 pixels. True or false?

Answers

1. The protocol template. Protocols define a standard collection of methods. To conform to a protocol, a class must implement those methods.

2. False. Deleting a file reference does not change the file on the disk.

3. False. The maximum Mac OS X icon size is 1024x1024. I suspect that this will increase to 2048x2048 when Retina displays become common across the Mac lineup.

Activities

1. Walk through the creation of a project and use it to test the activities described in this hour. Add and remove a class, add a new external resource, add and remove a group, and add a new framework.

2. Create an application using one of the available templates. Use the target properties to set an icon, and then view the icon in the iOS simulator (iOS apps) or the Finder (Mac OS X).

HOUR 6

Using the Xcode Source Editor

What You'll Learn in This Hour:

▶ Xcode Source Editor basics

▶ How to use autoformatting features

▶ The use of pragma marks to identify different pieces of code

▶ Ways to find and correct errors before your app even runs

▶ How to refactor existing code

Over the past few hours, you have learned how to create projects, add files, add frameworks, and do much of the work necessary to successfully build you own application projects. What we have not touched on, however, is the Xcode Source Editor itself, which you use to edit, unsurprisingly, source code. You've got your project and files; now how about editing them?

This hour walks through the different Source Editor features—from automatic code completion to code refactoring. You learn how the Source Editor can help you write clean, well-formatted code and even identify problems before you even try to run your application. Even if you have played around with editing files already, you're still likely to find a few undiscovered tricks in this hour.

Understanding Editor Basics

Let's be serious: If you're learning how to program in Xcode, you know how to edit a text file. I am not going to bore you with details on how to move your cursor or copy and paste. The Xcode Source Editor works just like any text editor, with several additions that may make your life easier. To follow along with this hour's lesson, create a new project called **HelloXcode** using the Mac OS X Cocoa Application template and the configuration shown in Figure 6.1. We'll edit this so that it displays a simple message (Hello Xcode) in the application's window. Nothing earth shattering, but you'll find it handy to keep this open so that you can test the tools as you read.

FIGURE 6.1
Create a new Mac OS X Cocoa application.

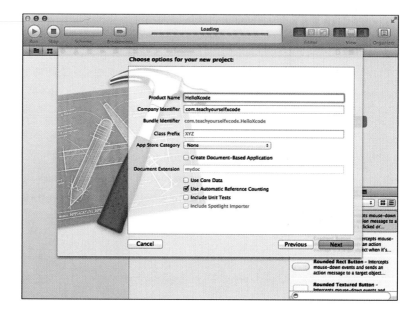

To edit code in Xcode, use the Project Navigator to find the file you want to work on, and then click the filename. The editable contents of the file are shown in the Editor area of the Xcode interface. For our sample application, click the AppDelegate.m file, as shown in Figure 6.2.

Code Completion

Using the Source Editor, start entering the following text to implement the applicationDidFinishLaunching method. Start a new line immediately following the existing comment "Insert code here to initialize your application." Update the method as shown in Listing 6.1.

LISTING 6.1   A Short Sample Mac OS X Application

```
1: - (void)applicationDidFinishLaunching:(NSNotification *)aNotification
2: {
3:      // Insert code here to initialize your application
4:      NSTextField *myMessage;
5:      NSTextField *myUnusedMessage;
6:      myMessage=[[NSTextField alloc] init];
```

LISTING 6.1 Continued

```
 7:        myMessage.font=[NSFont systemFontOfSize:72.0];
 8:        myMessage.stringValue=@"Hello Xcode";
 9:        myMessage.textColor=[NSColor blueColor];
10:        myMessage.editable=NO;
11:        [self.window setContentView:myMessage];
12: }
```

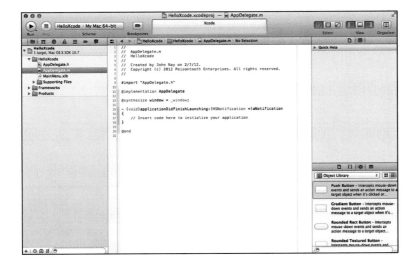

FIGURE 6.2
Choose a file to edit.

As you enter the code, notice that when you are typing a method or class name that Xcode recognizes, a pop-up dialog appears near your cursor, as shown in Figure 6.3. Here, the systemFontOfSize method is being typed, and Xcode is presenting potential options for autocompletion as I type.

To choose an autocompletion value, use the arrow keys to highlight the value you want to use, and then press Return to insert it into your code. You can also press Escape to make the pop-up disappear.

If you are completing a method name, chances are that you need to provide parameters as well. (In the case of systemFontOfSize, it is a floating-point value that describes the size of the text.) You can again use the arrow keys to move between the parameter fields and enter the values you want, or you can just press Tab to skip from parameter to parameter.

FIGURE 6.3
Xcode autocompletes recognized methods, classes, and symbols.

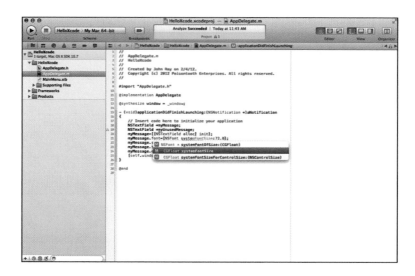

By the Way

If you have already finished typing (or autocompleted) a line in your code and discover that it is not what you want, you can click anywhere within the line and then choose Editor, Show Completions (Control+Spacebar) or press Escape. Doing so displays the autocomplete pop-up dialog with all the potential matches wherever your cursor is located—as if the rest of the line does not exist.

You can adjust the code completion options in the Xcode preferences within the Text Editing section.

Auto-Indentation

Clean code is easier to read and easier to maintain, and Xcode works behind the scenes to keep your code nicely formatted through auto-indention. As you program, Xcode automatically indents lines so that they fall either directly under the previous line or as appropriate to the structure of the statements you are writing.

Code within conditional blocks and loops, for example, are indented farther than surrounding code to visually show that they are a cohesive block. This has no effect on execution, but it can make reading through a source code file *much* easier than if each line's code starts at the first character.

You can control the logic for the Xcode auto-indentation system using the Text Editing panel of the application preferences (Xcode, Preferences) and the Indentation button within that, as shown in Figure 6.4.

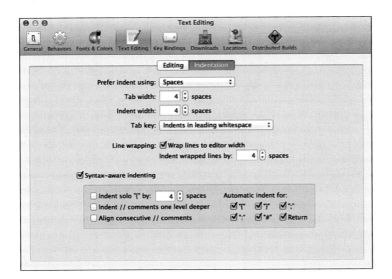

FIGURE 6.4
Configure the
Xcode indenta-
tion logic.

A nice feature of Xcode is that indentation isn't just applied while you're typing and then lost. Although you can certainly move your code around and make it into a mess, you can always apply the indentation rules again, as follows:

1. Within the sample project, add tabs and spaces in front of some of the lines in applicationDidFinishLaunching.

2. Delete the indentation from some of the lines, as well.

3. After you have made the method sufficiently ugly in appearance, select the lines of code.

4. Choose Editor, Structure, Re-Indent (Control+I).

Xcode reformats the code, and all is well again, as shown in Figure 6.5.

> **By the Way**
>
> You can access the Structure menu by right-clicking directly in the Xcode Source Editor. This can be a useful menu to access while editing, so the faster you can get to it, the better.

FIGURE 6.5
Before and after
applying the
indentation
logic.

Balancing Delimiters

Indentation may be "just for looks," but delimiters are not. Properly balanced delimiters are the difference between code that works the way you want and code that seems to have a mind of its own. When coding in Objective-C, you work with three primary types of block delimiters:

()   Parentheses for function calls

[]   Square brackets for Objective-C messaging

{}   Curly brackets for logical programming blocks

Each time you type one of these delimiters, you need another matching one added to your code. If you happen to miss one or put one in the wrong place, chances are your code won't run. Worse yet, it might run and not do what you expect.

To help you keep track of where your delimiters are (or aren't) balanced, Xcode automatically highlights the first delimiter when you type the second (or move the cursor to the immediate right of the second delimiter).

For example, return to the sample method that you wrote earlier (applicationDidFinishLaunching), position your text entry cursor immediately before the right curly bracket, }, at the end of the method. Next, press the right arrow to move the text cursor to the right of the curly bracket. As you do this, notice that the left curly bracket, {, at the start of the method is briefly highlighted. This same behavior occurs with parentheses and square brackets, too.

To select all of the code that is contained within a set of delimiters, right-click within the code, and then choose Structure, Balance Delimiter (also available from the Editor menu), as shown in Figure 6.6.

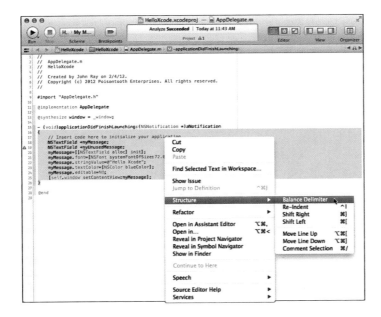

FIGURE 6.6
Select the code between two delimiters.

When you are entering your code, Xcode automatically inserts matching curly and square brackets when you type the first bracket. In other words, if you type {, Xcode automatically adds a corresponding } for you. You can disable this behavior in the Xcode Text Editing preferences (Xcode, Preferences, Text Editing, Editing).

By the Way

Code Folding

Working in conjunction with your code delimiters and the logical blocks/methods you define in your code, Xcode's code-folding features let you focus on editing a specific piece of code and hide the rest. To the immediate right of your Editor is the gutter, which typically holds line numbers (enabled in Xcode's Text Editing preferences) and error/warning icons. The very right side of the gutter is the *code-folding ribbon*. By clicking in the ribbon, you can *fold* (collapse) your methods and functions and comment blocks.

For example, view the code in the `applicationDidFinishLaunching` method. Click immediately to the left of the method in the code-folding ribbon. The code collapses and is replaced with an ellipsis (...), as shown in Figure 6.7. You can expand the code again by double-clicking the ellipsis or by using the disclosure arrow that appears in the ribbon.

FIGURE 6.7
Collapse your code to improve your focus.

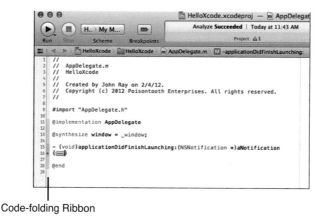

Code-folding Ribbon

By the Way

To help identify what blocks of your code can be collapsed, Xcode lightly shades the code folding ribbon. Blocks within blocks are successively darker in color. Hovering your mouse over a shaded portion of the code-folding ribbon highlights the relevant block within Xcode.

You can quickly collapse all comment blocks (text between /* and */) and function/methods using the Editor, Code Folding menu.

The Other Bits

As with any application, some settings and options (although useful to some) do not warrant a full discussion. The Xcode Source Editor has a number of other features that might come in handy but that do not necessarily pertain to the editing process itself.

What follows are a few configuration tweaks and editing functions that you might want to use in your projects.

Line Numbers

To enable or disable the display of line numbers beside your code, use the Line Numbers check box accessed within the Text Editing section of Xcode preferences.

Line numbers are a great help when debugging code or describing your code to other developers.

Edit All in Scope

If you've ever written a function or method only to smack yourself in the head and say, "I should have named that variable something else," you will love the Edit All in Scope feature. To simultaneously change all the instances of a variable name within a method, select the variable name, and then choose Editor, Edit All in Scope (Control+Command+E). Each instance of the variable highlights, and all update as you edit one, as shown in Figure 6.8.

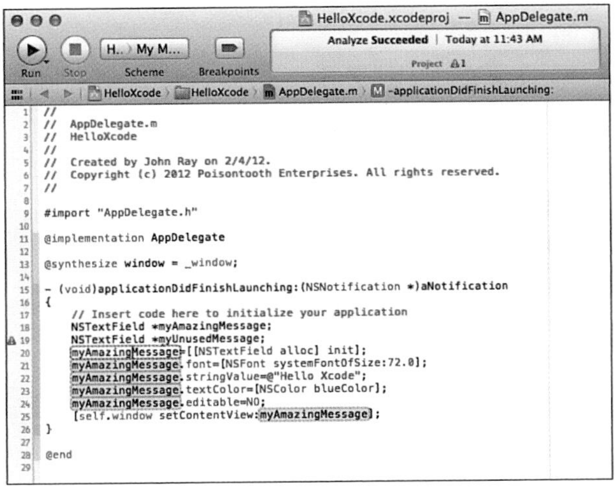

FIGURE 6.8
Quickly change symbol names using Edit All in Scope.

Shift, Move, or Comment

The Structure contextual menu (also accessible from the Editor menu) contains commands for shifting (indenting/outdenting) your code left or right, moving it up or down, or commenting it out. Use these functions to quickly act on a selection of lines, rather than changing each one individually.

Hide/Show Invisibles

There's more to your code than you can see. To get a glimpse at how the code is formatted (tabs/spaces/return characters) or check for any gremlins that may have crept into your code from pasting from other applications, use the Editor, Show Invisibles command. This displays all normally invisible characters directly within your code listing. To hide the characters, choose Editor, Hide Invisibles.

Syntax Coloring

Normally, Xcode colors your code based on the type of file you are editing. You can override the chosen syntax-highlighting scheme by choosing Editor, Syntax Coloring from the menu. You can also change the syntax colors entirely using the Xcode Fonts & Colors preferences, shown in Figure 6.9.

FIGURE 6.9
Change the syntax color rules to suit your sensibilities.

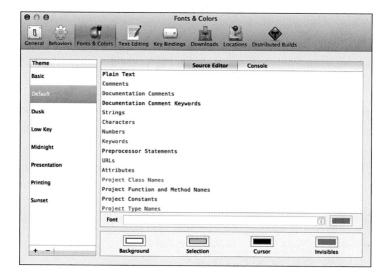

Navigating Within and Between Files

Now that you know the basic code-editing features provided by Xcode, we can turn our attention to some of the features that simplify working with multiple files. Except in the most rudimentary development, your projects will consist of multiple source files with multiple methods spread between them. Becoming efficient and jumping between these files is a skill that becomes increasingly valuable as your applications increase in scale.

This section examines some of the tools you can use when working with multiple files (or very large individual files).

Tabbed Editing

Tabbed editing is just like tabbed browsing in your favorite web browser. Using tabbed editing, you can have many files open simultaneously and switch between them by clicking tabs at the top of the Editor area.

To create a new tab, choose File, New, New Tab (Command+T). A new tab appears with the contents of the file you are currently editing. You can switch the contents of the tab to whatever you want by clicking a file in the Project Navigator. You can repeat this process to create as many tabs as you want, with whatever file contents to want, as shown in Figure 6.10.

Tabs   Close Tabs

FIGURE 6.10
Keep multiple editors open simultaneously with tabs.

To close a tab, click the X that is displayed on the left side of the tab when hovering over it with your mouse. As with all files in Xcode, the files you edit in tabs are automatically saved when you close them; you do not have to explicitly use the Save command.

The Jump Bar

When editing a file, you might have noticed that above the Editor area is a visual path to the file you are editing and several buttons. This is collectively known as the *jump bar*. Clicking any portion of the path reveals a pop-up menu for quickly jumping to other files in same location, as shown in Figure 6.11. The last segment (on the right) of the jump bar is special: You can click it to view and jump between the symbols (methods, properties, and so on) within the file you are currently editing.

Related Files   File Path   Symbols

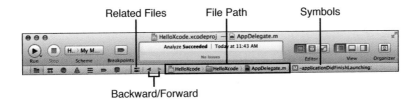

Backward/Forward

FIGURE 6.11
Quickly navigate your project hierarchy.

To the left of the path are forward and back arrows. The arrows move back and forth between files that you have been editing—just like pages you visit in a web browser. Finally, to the left of the arrows is the Related Files button.

Use the Related Files button to show a pop-up menu of categorized files such as recently opened or unsaved. This menu even displays files that are just referenced (even if just included or imported) in the file currently open in the Source Editor. Figure 6.12 shows the contents of the menu when editing the application delegate file for an empty iOS application.

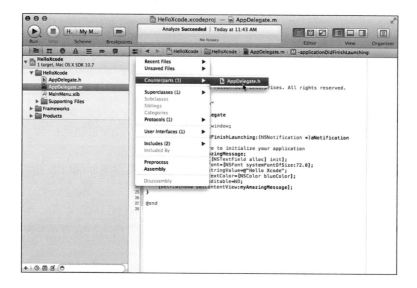

The Symbol Navigator

The easiest way to find a method or property within a source code file is to use the Symbol Navigator, opened by clicking the icon to the immediate right of the Project Navigator. This view, shown in Figure 6.13, enables you to expand your project classes to show all the methods, properties, and variables that are defined. Choosing an item from the list jumps to and highlights the relevant line in your source code.

Symbol Navigator

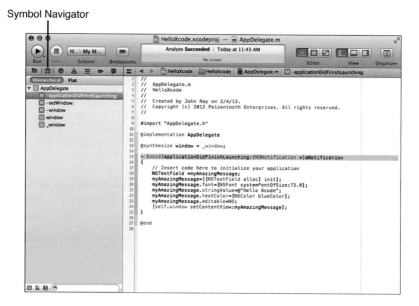

For example, with the HelloXcode project open, switch to the Symbol Navigator and expand the AppDelegate item. This is the only object used in this application. Next, find and select `applicationDidFinishLaunching` from the list that is displayed. Xcode jumps to the finds and select the line where the method begins.

The Search Navigator

Searching for text anywhere in your project is trivial using the Search Navigator. To access this search feature, click the magnifying glass icon in the icon bar above the Navigator. A Search field displays at the top of the Navigator area, into which you can enter whatever you want to find. As you type, a drop-down menu appears, as shown in Figure 6.14, that shows potential options for refining your search. Choose one of the options or press Return to perform a non-case-sensitive search of the text you enter.

Search Navigator

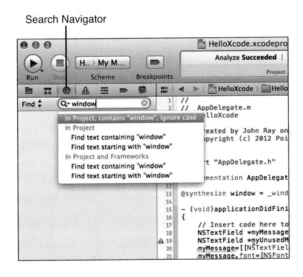

FIGURE 6.14
Use the Search Navigator to find text in your project.

The search results display below the Search field, along with a snippet of the file containing the text you were looking for, as shown in Figure 6.15. Clicking a search result opens the corresponding file in the Source Editor and jumps to the line containing your search string.

To make things even more interesting, you can use the Filter field at the bottom of the Search Navigator to filter your search results by a secondary term. You can also click the Find label at the top of the Search Navigator to switch to a Replace mode, enabling you to perform projectwide find and replace.

FIGURE 6.15
Search results
are displayed
along with the
context of the
match.

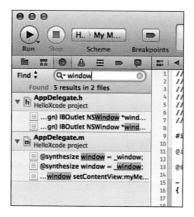

If you're looking for a string within a file you are actively editing, choose Edit, Find, Find (Command+F) to open a more traditional Find field at the top of the Source Editor. This gives you quick access to find (or find/replace) within a given file, rather than across the entire project.

Pragma Marks

Sometimes navigating code by symbols or with a search is not very efficient. To help denote important pieces of code in plain English, you can insert a #pragma mark directive. Pragma marks do not add any features to your application; instead, they create logical sections within your code. These sections are then are displayed, with the rest of the code symbols, when you click the last item in the visual path above the Editor area.

There are two common types of pragma marks:

```
#pragma mark -
```

and

```
#pragma mark <label name>
```

The first inserts a horizontal line in the symbol menu; the second inserts an arbitrary label name. You can use both together to add a section heading to your code. For example, to add a section called Methods for starting and stopping the application followed by a horizontal line, you can enter the following:

```
#pragma mark Methods for starting and stopping the application
#pragma mark -
```

After the pragma mark has been added to your code and saved, the symbol menu updates accordingly, as shown in Figure 6.16. Choosing a pragma mark from the Symbol menu jumps to that portion of the code.

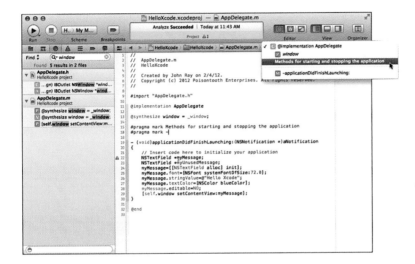

FIGURE 6.16
Use pragma marks to add logical delimiters to your code.

Using the Assistant Editor

As you work with Xcode projects, you will quickly realize that most program functionality comes from editing one of two related files: an implementation file (.m extension) and an interface file (.h extension). You'll also learn that when you make changes to one of these two files, you'll often need to make changes to the other. You will see a similar pattern emerge when you start editing GUIs in Xcode.

Xcode simplifies this back-and-forth editing with the Assistant Editor mode. The Assistant Editor (or just called Assistant in Apple documentation) automatically looks at the file you have opened for editing and opens, right beside it (or under it, if you prefer), the related file that you also need to work on, as shown in Figure 6.17.

To switch between Standard and Assistant Editor modes, you use the first and second buttons, respectively, in the Editor section of the Xcode toolbar.

In the upper-right corner of the Assistant Editor's jump bar, notice a + icon and an X icon. The + icon adds *another* Assistant Editor to your screen; the X icon closes the current Assistant Editor.

By the Way

FIGURE 6.17
Xcode opens
the file related
to what you are
working on.

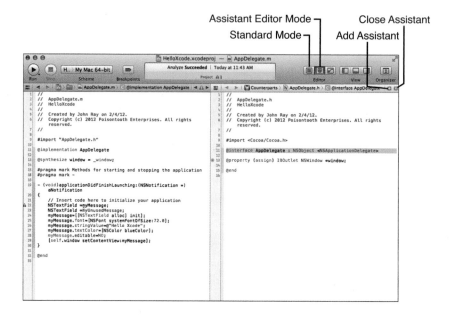

Choosing the Assistant File

When you are using the Assistant Editor, it sometimes chooses a file that it thinks
you want to edit but that really is not what you had in mind. To view all the
Assistant's recommended options, click the Assistant Editor icon (a little suit and
bowtie) displayed in the jump bar located at the top of the Assistant Editor view.
This displays a menu of all the related files that the Assistant Editor has identified,
sorted by type, as shown in Figure 6.18.

Changing the Assistant Editor Layout

As you can see, the Assistant Editor occupies more than a little bit of screen space. If
you are coding on a MacBook Air (which I love), you'll find that you need to hide
the Navigator/Utility areas to make the full Assistant Editor work.

To change how the Assistant Editor displays in the Xcode interface, choose View,
Assistant Editor, as shown in Figure 6.19. From there, you can choose how the
Assistant Editor is added to the display and what will happen if multiple Assistant
Editors are in use.

To set up shortcuts for when the Assistant Editor (or tabs) are used, open the
Xcode general preferences (Xcode, Preferences, General). You have several
options to fine-tune how you invoke the special editing modes of Xcode.

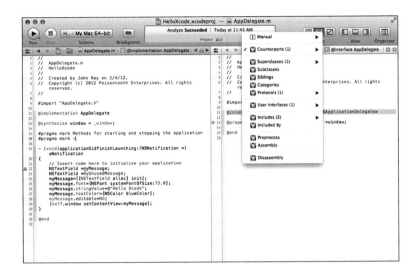

FIGURE 6.18
Choose a different file to edit.

FIGURE 6.19
Configure how the Assistant Editors will appear in the display.

Correcting Errors and Warnings in the Issue Navigator

As you write your code, Xcode is sitting in the background judging you, but do not take it personally—it only wants to help. Xcode analyzes your code and detects issues that might be (or are) problems and displays warnings and errors before you ever click the Run button.

Error Types

You can receive three general types of feedback from Xcode when it analyzes your application: errors, warnings, and logic problems. Warnings are potential problems that might cause your application to misbehave; a yellow caution sign warns you of these. Errors, however, are complete showstoppers. You cannot run your application if you have an error. The symbol for an error, appropriately enough, is a red stop sign.

Logic problems, found by the Xcode analyze process, are shown as a blue badge. All of these bugs, across all your files, are consolidated in the Issue Navigator. The Issue Navigator displays automatically if problems are found during a build or analyze process. You can also open it directly by clicking the exclamation point icon (on the toolbar above the Navigator area).

For example, the method `applicationDidFinishLaunching` that you wrote earlier contains an unused variable (`myUnusedMessage`). This is highlighted with a yellow exclamation point in the Issue Navigator (Unused Entity Issue), as shown in Figure 6.20.

Issue Navigator

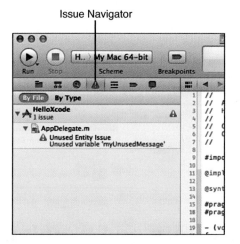

FIGURE 6.20
Use the Issue Navigator to browse all your project's potential problems.

Logic problems must be detected by choosing Product, Analyze from the menu bar. Warnings and errors are shown immediately as you code.

Jumping to an Error

To jump to an error in your code, just click it in the Issue Navigator. The corresponding code is opened, and the error message is visible directly after the line that caused the problem. To remove the warning from the sample method, just delete the line `NSTextField *myUnusedMessage;` to empty the Issue Navigator.

If you are in the middle of editing a file that contains errors, you'll see the errors immediately displayed onscreen—so no need to jump back and forth to the Issue Navigator. You can also quickly cycle through your errors using the forward and backward arrows found at the rightmost side of the window, directly above the Editor area. These controls are visible only if errors are present, however.

Fixing Errors to Find Others

With the warning message still visible in the `applicationDidFinishLaunching` method (add the code line back in, if you need to), try adding a line of complete garbage into the code. Pay attention to what happens when you click off of the line.

What you will see is that the new code is flagged as an error (red stop sign), but the original warning has disappeared. This brings up an important point: Sometimes not all errors or warnings are detected and displayed in the Issue Navigator or in a source file. You might find, after fixing a line or two, that new and previously undetected errors appear. Conversely, you'll also occasionally see false errors that disappear when you correct others.

To control which issues are visible (hiding warnings, for example), choose Editor, Issues from the menu bar.

Refactoring Code

Earlier in this hour, you learned how to use Edit All in Scope to change the name of a variable within a method. But what happens if you need to make a more massive change, such as changing the name of a class? Making changes like this is called *refactoring* and can involve a ridiculous amount of work given the amount of code that needs to be touched, filenames that need to change, and so on. If you find yourself in this situation, however, Xcode offers refactoring features to help get you out of a jam.

To access the refactoring tools, choose Edit, Refactor from the menu bar or right-click in your code to use the Refactor contextual menu item.

Renaming

To rename a symbol across your entire project, including any files named after that symbol, follow these steps:

1. Select the symbol in your project.

2. Choose Edit, Refactor, Rename from the menu bar.

You are prompted for the new name, and whether to rename any associated files, as shown in Figure 6.21.

FIGURE 6.21
Rename a symbol (variable, class, method, etc. across your project).

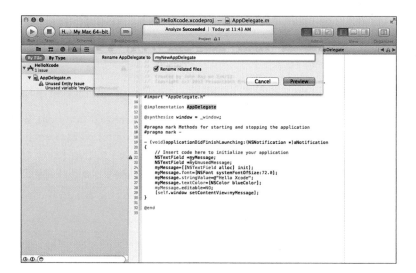

3. After you have made your naming choice, click Preview to show the files that will be changed and the differences between the original and new versions, as shown in Figure 6.22.

From this window, you can choose which files to change (check or uncheck the boxes in front of their names) and even edit the code directly in the comparison views.

4. Click Save to make the changes across the entire project.

The remaining refactoring options work in a similar way, but with different effects.

Extracting

If you find that you have written code for a method but that code would be better suited in its own method or function that is called by the current method, you can use the Extract function. Simply select the code you want to move out of the current method, and then choose Edit, Refactor, Extract.

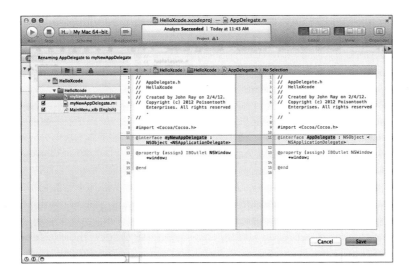

FIGURE 6.22
Confirm the changes that will be made.

You are prompted for the new function or method name, then presented with a preview of the change. Xcode automatically analyzes the code to determine what parameters are necessary for the new method, and even includes the method/function call in your original method.

Watch
Out!

Double-Check Xcode's Work!

Be sure to double-check the methods that Xcode creates when using the Extract feature. I have had mixed results with its ability to correctly parse the method parameters.

Creating Superclasses

Sometimes, when writing a class, you might discover that it would have made more sense for the class you're building to be a subclass of a larger superclass. To quickly create a superclass, select the class name, and then choose Edit, Refactor, Create Superclass, and, again, follow the onscreen prompts to name and save the new class file.

Moving Up/Down

After creating a superclass (or if you already have one), it might make sense to move some of the variables or methods from your current class into the superclass. Conversely, you might have a superclass symbol that make more sense being contained in one of its subclasses. Use the Edit, Refactor, Move Up/Down functions to move a variable/method into a class's superclass or a superclass's variable/method into a subclass.

Encapsulating

When you use the Edit, Refactor, Encapsulate action on an instance variable, it creates explicit getters and setters for that variable. In most cases, however, the `@property`/`@synthesize` combination should be enough to handle setting up your accessors.

> If you need a refresher on instance variables, classes, setters, getters, and so on, refer back to Hour 2, "Just Enough Objective-C and Cocoa." These are important concepts to understand, so be sure you have got a good grip on the basics before moving on.

Using Code Snippets

When you are writing code, you will often find yourself typing statements that are *very* similar to one another: `catch-try` blocks, `if-then` statements, `switch` statements, and so on. Instead of having to remember the syntax of each of these common code sequences, you can make use of the built-in Xcode Code Snippet Library.

You can access the Code Snippet Library from the Xcode Source Editor by choosing View, Utilities, Show Code Snippet Library, or by pressing Control+Option+Command+2. The library appears in the Utility area and is represented by the {} icon, as shown in Figure 6.23.

Viewing Snippets

To view what a snippet contains, click its entry in the library. A popover window appears displaying the contents of the snippet, as shown in Figure 6.24.

Notice that certain parts of the snippet are highlighted in gray. These represent portions of the code that you need to provide. When a snippet is inserted into your code, you can use the Tab key to jump between these areas. Click the Done button when viewing the snippet code to hide the popover.

Code Snippet Library

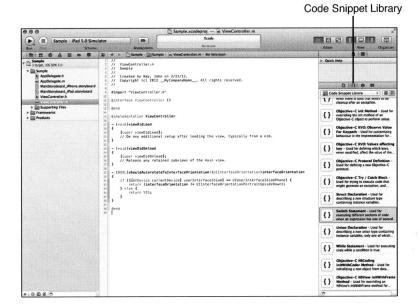

FIGURE 6.23
The Code Snippet Library contains snippets of useful code.

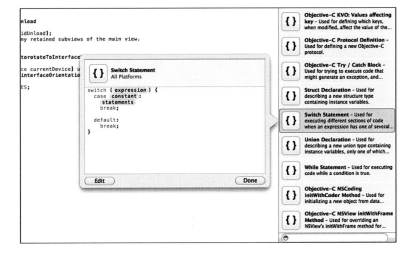

FIGURE 6.24
View the contents of a snippet.

Inserting Snippets

To insert a code snippet into your class files, just drag and drop from the Code Snippet Library into your code. Wherever your cursor points, the snippet is inserted, exactly as if you had typed the code yourself.

Adding Snippets

Not only can you use the existing snippets to help code, but when you write useful code sequences of your own, you can add them to the Code Snippet Library as user-defined snippets. To do this, follow these steps:

1. Select the code in the Source Editor that you want to turn into a snippet.

2. Make sure the Code Snippet Library is visible (Control+Option+Command+2).

3. Click and drag from the selected text to the Code Snippet Library, as shown in Figure 6.25.

FIGURE 6.25
Drag the code to the Code Snippet Library.

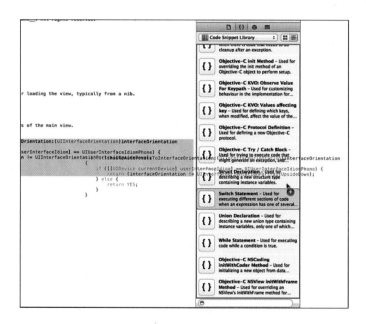

The text is added to the library under the title My Code Snippet, as shown in Figure 6.26.

FIGURE 6.26
The new snippet is visible in the library.

Because the default name is not very descriptive, you will probably want to edit it to reflect its purpose.

Editing Snippets

To edit a snippet you have defined, follow these steps:

1. Click it in the library so that the popover appears displaying its code.

2. Click the Edit button in the lower-left corner. Figure 6.27 shows a snippet in edit mode.

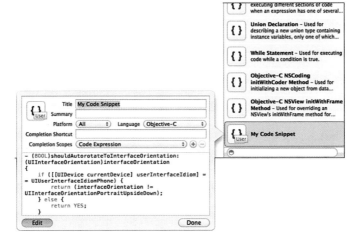

FIGURE 6.27
Edit the snippet and the information stored about the snippet.

3. Use the fields in the Source Editor to set a title and summary for the snippet and define the platform and development language the snippet applies to.

4. Enter a shortcut that can be typed to automatically insert the snippet and the different areas (scopes) within a typical source file where the completion shortcut should be active.

5. Click Done to save the snippet.

To remove a snippet from the library, just click once to select it in the Code Snippet Library and then press the Delete key on your keyboard.

By the Way

Summary

In this hour, you learned how to use the Xcode Source Editor for more than just typing text. We looked at special features like automatic code completion, auto-indentation, and code folding. You also learned how the Assistant Editor mode makes working on multiple related files a pain-free process.

In addition to the Source Editor itself, you explored the tools for identifying and correcting errors in your code, for searching and replacing text across your entire project, and for refactoring existing code. Although it is technically true that you can develop an application using any text editor you want, using Xcode gets you best-of-breed tools that are specific to the language and methodology of the Apple development platform.

Q&A

Q. *I really hate editing files in a huge window. Can I break out into just a single window per file?*

A. Yes. Just double-click the file in the Navigator to open a new window with all features disabled except the Source Editor. You can turn this into a single-click in the Xcode preferences if you prefer.

Q. *I'm confused. What is a symbol?*

A. Think of a symbol as anything you've named within your code. Typically, this means variables/properties—but it can also be method names, class names, and so on.

Q. *Xcode keeps autocompleting methods that I don't want. What do I do?*

A. Unless you press Tab or the arrow keys, Xcode will not autocomplete at all. You can either just keep typing and enter the full name yourself, or you can disable autocompletion in the Text Editing area of the Xcode preferences.

Workshop

Quiz

1. I use a MacBook for my development. How will I ever get the Assistant Editor to fit on my screen?

2. Besides the Assistant Editor, you can only have a single file open at once. True or false?

3. It is impossible to easily rename a class after creating it. True or false?

Answers

1. Learn to use the View buttons on the Xcode toolbar. If you disable the Project Navigator and Utility area, you'll find that the Assistant Editor fits quite nicely on your screen.

2. False. Using the tabbed editing feature, you can open as many files simultaneously as you want, using the tabs below the Xcode toolbar to switch between them.

3. False. The Rename refactoring tool simplifies the process of changing a class name after the fact.

Activities

1. Using the sample project you created this hour, walk through the different features of the Source Editor and Assistant Editor. Try your hand at Edit All in Scope and refactoring.

2. Create errors your HelloXcode application by duplicating lines or methods in the AppDelegate class files. Add a few lines with arbitrary text for good measure. Note where and when Xcode detects the errors. Does it find all the erroneous lines at once, or does it present one error, which, when fixed, shows another, and so on? Get used to this behavior; it is rare you'll write perfect code, and knowing how Xcode presents errors and warnings is a big help when things do not work right.

HOUR 7

Working with the Xcode 4 Documentation

What You'll Learn in This Hour:

▶ The different parts of the Xcode documentation system
▶ How to configure automatic documentation updates
▶ Ways to search and browse the developer documentation
▶ How the Research Assistant can help you as you code
▶ How to access sample projects referenced in the Apple documentation

A discussion that I frequently have with prospective developers is what they need to know to be successful. Is the sign of a good developer someone who can recite all the classes available in a language? Is it someone who can tell you the order of parameters in all the methods in a given *application programming interface* (API)? No. A good developer might be able to do those things, but in practice, memorization is much less valuable than applied logic skills.

Good developers can easily move between different programming languages because they understand the logic of development. All they need is a proper reference and an understanding of a language's syntax, and the platform becomes meaningless. Xcode provides nearly all the documentation and examples you need to learn Objective-C and Cocoa—all accessible within its interface. This hour introduces you to the documentation tools and how you can use them to master Mac OS X and iOS development.

Overview of Documentation Resources

Apple makes their developer documentation available in a variety of different formats and through several different mechanisms. Which you use depends on what you are trying to do and what resources you have at your disposal.

Web-Based Documentation

If you want to learn about Xcode on the go, the web-based version of the documentation might be the most useful. You can access either the Mac or iOS documentation from the developer resources URL at http://developer.apple.com/resources/.

If you view the online documentation on your iPad, it is even formatted for the device like a native app (see Figure 7.1). This makes using the iPad as your documentation consumption device particularly appealing if you can set one up near your development station.

FIGURE 7.1
Browsing the Apple documentation on the iPad enables special tablet formatting.

By the Way

> If you want to read without an Internet connection, most of the developer documents include a PDF link in the upper-right corner (or upper-left corner on mobile devices). Use this link in mobile Safari to download the document, and then open it in iBooks for an always-available copy of whatever you're interested in.

Xcode Help Viewer

The Xcode Help viewer, shown in Figure 7.2, provides a convenient browser-like interface to the documentation, but with features that go above and beyond Safari. (We take an in-depth look at its use in a few minutes.)

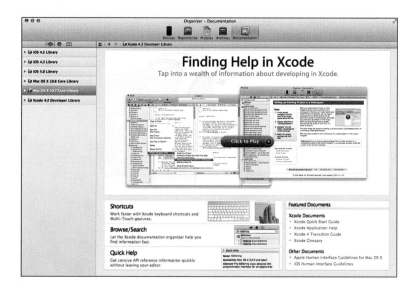

FIGURE 7.2
The Xcode Help viewer provides all available documentation within a convenient interface.

To access the Xcode Help, you can either open the Xcode Organizer (the last tab on the right within the Organizer window), or choose Help, Xcode Help from the menu bar.

> Notice the several help resources under the Xcode Help menu. These are just shortcuts to different documents within the Xcode Help system. If you want to access help, it doesn't really matter which you choose; you can navigate all of the Help system after the viewer opens.

Did You Know?

Quick Help

The final form of developer documentation comes in the form of Xcode's Quick Help system. Quick Help is not meant to replace the primary Help system but acts as a quick reference while coding. Shown in Figure 7.3, you can invoke Quick Help at any time in the coding process; it provides links to the full documentation if needed.

FIGURE 7.3
Quick Help
brings help
directly to the
coding
process—
no need to
lift a finger.

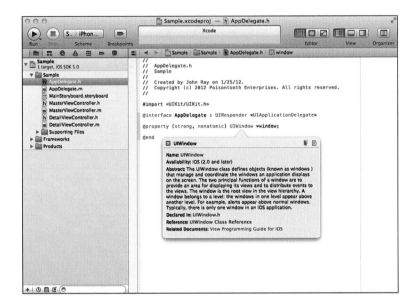

Configuring the Xcode Documentation Downloads

As you might have noticed, operating systems do not remain static. Roughly once a year, Apple issues major releases to iOS and Mac OS X, with more than a few interim releases in-between. As the operating system changes, so does the documentation you need to effectively develop for it. To keep things up-to-date, Xcode provides a documentation system that updates as needed by downloading docset files that include all the documentation for a given operating system release.

To configure your Xcode documentation downloads, choose Xcode, Preferences from the menu, and then click the Downloads icon on the Preferences toolbar. In the Documentation pane, shown in Figure 7.4, click the Check For and Install Updates Automatically check box. As long as this is selected, Xcode periodically connects to Apple servers and automatically updates your local documentation. Also notice that additional documentation sets may be listed for different versions of the operating system. If you intend to target earlier OS releases, keeping a copy of the appropriate documentation on hand can prove helpful.

Click the Install button beside any of the listed items to download and automatically include it in any future updates.

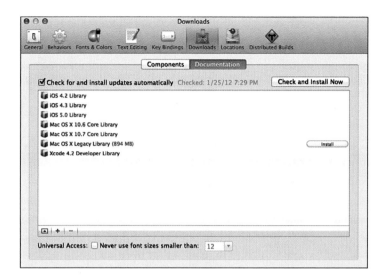

FIGURE 7.4
Choose the documentation sets to download and keep updated.

Each documentation set can take up several hundred megabytes of space. If this is an issue, you might want to keep only the most recent sets installed on your computer.

Did You Know?

In the lower-right corner of the documentation list are + and – buttons. By clicking the + button, you can enter a URL for a third-party docset file that you want to add to Xcode. For example, the third-party iOS PDF library FastPdfKit (http://www.fastpdfkit.com/), provides their developer documentation in the form of a docset. If you use a third-party tool in your projects, check to see whether a docset is provided and add it to Xcode for integrated help.

Understanding the Documentation Resources

It would be easy to point you to the developer documentation resources and say "have at it." But, as a beginning Xcode developer, your first impression might not be a positive one. The Apple developer documentation is full of information in many different forms. If your first experience with the library is stumbling across a document that is so terse and outdated that it dissuades you from ever using documentation again, we've done you a great disservice.

Before diving into the documentation viewer, let's quickly review the types of documents found in a docset and what to expect from them. Note that these are listed here in alphabetic order (as Apple does), which most certainly will bear little semblance to their usefulness to a developer.

> Not all docsets have all the following document types. This does not necessarily mean that similar sorts of information are not available in other places. For example, the iOS *How-To* documents, which are not included for Mac OS X, are very similar to the *Guide* document type.

Articles

Articles are short, focused content on a very specific topic. For example, the article "Using Phusion Passenger as a Ruby on Rails Server" describes how to install a Ruby on Rails server—hardly a topic for a Mac OS X reference guide, but still useful enough that Apple chose to include it. Articles may be stories about technology, applications of technology, or individual developers who have used Mac OS X or iOS in interesting ways.

These are more useful for casual reading than fir learning how to program, so do not expect to spend much time browsing articles and finding answers to your questions.

> ### This Just In: Outdated Information!
> Articles are one of the areas of the developer documentation that Apple does not update as frequently as they should. The article on Phusion Passenger, in fact, was written to target the Leopard operating system, but is included in the core Lion docset. Although the information contained in the article might still be accurate, you may want to look for online resources to supplement what is described in an article.

Coding How-Tos

Currently unique to the iOS docsets, the *coding how-tos*, shown in Figure 7.5, provide access to answers to common coding questions, such as "How do I display data from a website?" Each question is linked to a short code sample of how to solve a particular problem.

In general, the coding how-tos are most useful for tracking down a topic and finding more information than they are for answering practical questions. Although it is unlikely that the exact question you want answered will be covered in a how-to, chances are you can find references to class documentation that points you in the right direction.

FIGURE 7.5
Coding how-tos present informa-tion as a series of questions and answers.

Getting Started

Getting Started documents are short descriptions of a broad topic area, such as "Audio and View," that contain links to prerequisite information and links to coding guides for implementing a particular technology. These are good documents to find all the resources and gain the background you need to implement features such as cryptography, iCloud, and so on with your projects.

If you are looking for a class reference or coding examples, Getting Started documents are a bit too high level. You'll want to look through the Guides or Reference documents to get to the nitty-gritty.

Guides

Guides are similar to Getting Started documents, but they contain more targeted links to technical information and less introductory content. A view controller guide, for example, provides technical information on how view controllers work and links to sample code and class references. Browse the docset guides when you know exactly what topic you need information on but are not sure of the class names associated with it.

Reference

Reference documents are the lifeblood of the developer. These are the class and framework references that provide method names, input and output parameters, code samples, and a full technical description of how, when, where, and why a particularly piece of code is needed, as shown in Figure 7.6. References also document when particular pieces of code have been deprecated or when they should not be used in conjunction with other features.

FIGURE 7.6
References provide the details needed to code successfully.

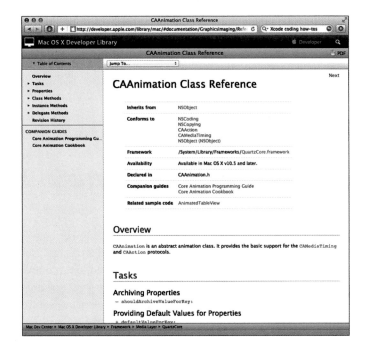

Reference documents contain many cross-reference links to other documents that you'll find helpful. When method parameters call for constants that are defined elsewhere, for example, you see a link to the list of constants. As you browse reference documents, it is not uncommon to find that you have jumped between several difference references while looking up the information you need.

By the Way

If you view the developer documentation in a browser, returning to an earlier document is just a matter of clicking the Back button. As you learn shortly, the Xcode Help view works in much the same way, making it easy to cope with all the interlinked documents you traverse in your research.

Release Notes

Release notes describe the changes and new features added to the OS release described by a docset. These documents are a must-read if you've implemented a technology in an earlier version of your software and are intending to update the application for a new version of the Apple OS. With iOS especially, it is not unusual for applications that access advanced features to require updates to work correctly when the operating system updates. The release note documentation presents these changes clearly and provides links to the reference documents where detailed information can be found.

Sample Code

When browsing any one of the types of documents available in the developer documentation, you might encounter links to *sample code*. These aren't just links to text documents full of Objective-C; they're links to actual project files that you can open and explore in Xcode. The sample code included with Xcode covers a vast array of topics and presents examples of some of the most useful coding scenarios that you are likely to encounter.

When you happen upon a sample code link, clicking it opens a description of the sample project, as shown in Figure 7.7.

FIGURE 7.7
Sample code is available for a wide range of topics and is presented as a ready-to-go Xcode project.

To use the sample when accessing docs directly from Xcode, click the Open Project button and, when prompted, provide a save location for the project files. Xcode opens the project within the IDE, and you can run or edit it immediately.

> If you are using a web browser to access sample code (shown in Figure 7.7), you will see a Download Sample Code button, and the project will be downloaded to your Downloads folder. You must locate and open the project file manually.

Technical Notes

Technical notes are short help documents that describe how to troubleshoot or implement a given technology in a very specific situation. "Troubleshooting Push Notifications," for example, is an available technical note for iOS and Mac OS X developers that helps identify why notifications may not be working as expected.

Although technical notes are helpful, their day-to-day benefit is limited. They are useful only in very specific circumstances—and have little information that applies to general development.

Technical Q&As

A *technical Q&A* is similar to a technical note but is presented as a single question and answer. Again, the question (and corresponding answer) is applicable in only a very specific circumstance, and (I say this cynically) never one that applies to me.

It's likely that the only time you'll end up reading a technical note or Q&A is when it is returned as the result of a document search. Browsing these two document categories can lead to some interesting discoveries, but is not very useful for learning development.

Xcode Tasks

I'm not sure why this resource type exists on its own, but it does. *Xcode tasks* are essentially Getting Started guides for tasks related to Xcode but that do not necessarily take place within the application. The current Xcode tasks available in the iOS and Mac OS X docsets are related to provisioning your iDevices and managing/preparing applications for submission to the App Store. Not much to see here, folks.

Video

Rarely included in Apple's documentation are *how-to videos*. When you encounter a video, take an opportunity to watch it. I find Apple's video tutorials useful, easy to watch, and quick to deliver information. Unfortunately, they are few and far between. If you are seeking more video content, I recommend that you visit the online developer portals and watch the *Worldwide Developers Conference* (WWDC) session videos. These are highly technical and provide a solid introduction to many important development topics.

Using the Xcode Help Viewer

The Xcode Help viewer, as mentioned earlier, works much like Safari for browsing documentation, but includes several additional features to make navigating the available information much easier.

To open the Xcode documentation, choose Help, Xcode Help from the menu bar. The Help system launches, as shown in Figure 7.8.

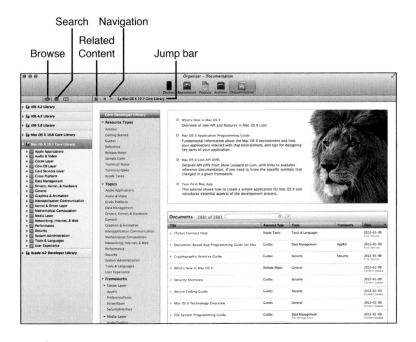

FIGURE 7.8
Browse or search the available help documents.

Browsing the Library

If you do not know exactly what you're looking for, sometimes the best option is to just browse. Click the eye icon to browse all the available documentation. Browsing starts at the top of each docset, with the docsets listed in the left column—called the Navigator. Expanding a docset lists the topics and individual documents within, enabling you to select and view a file or to drill down further to lower-level topics. When a document or topic area is clicked, the corresponding content is shown on the right side of the window—just like when you choose a file and open its editor in Xcode.

> If you aren't sure what document you want, you can click a topic area, or even the top-level docset to view a different organization of information. The top-level view of a topic or docset includes a description of what you will find in that area, along with an organization of the docset documents by resource type, topic, and framework.

When you have arrived at a document that interests you, you can read and navigate within the document using the blue links. You can also move forward and backward between documents using the arrow buttons located above the content—just as with a web browser.

Just to the left of the arrows is a button showing two short dashed lines. This is a drop-down menu that provides easy access to related content. Unfortunately, that is not quite what it sounds like. The related content (which you might validly assume a cross-reference to other classes) is actually just "attachments" referenced in the document. If sample code or a PDF of the document is available, you can access it by clicking it in the related content menu.

> To quickly move between documents in a topic area, or even sections within an individual document, use the jump bar, which shows the path to the document you are actively viewing and is located directly above the content area.

Adding Bookmarks

The Help view is much like a browser in that you can add bookmarks for later reading. To create a bookmark, right-click either an item in the Navigator or click the content itself, and then choose Add Bookmark for Current Page from the contextual menu. You can access all your documentation bookmarks by clicking the book icon at the top of the Navigator, as shown in Figure 7.9.

Bookmarks

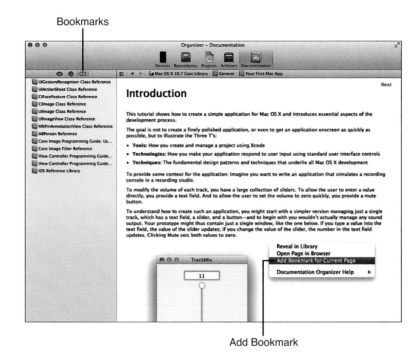

FIGURE 7.9
Bookmark com-
monly used help
documents.

Add Bookmark

To delete a bookmark, make sure it is selected in the Navigator, and then press the Delete button on your keyboard. You receive no confirmation that it's going to be removed, so make sure you are deleting the reference you want, not a bookmark to some esoteric class that took two hours to find.

Searching the Library

Browsing is great for exploring, but not that useful for finding references on exact topics—like class method names or individual properties. To search the Xcode documentation, click the magnifying glass, and then type into the Search field. You can enter class, method, or property names, or just type in a concept that you're interested in. As you type, Xcode begins returning results below the Search field, as shown in Figure 7.10.

Search results resources are divided into groups, including Reference (API documentation), System Guides/Tool Guides (explanatory/tutorial text), and Sample Code (example Xcode projects).

Search

FIGURE 7.10
Search to find
specific topics
quickly.

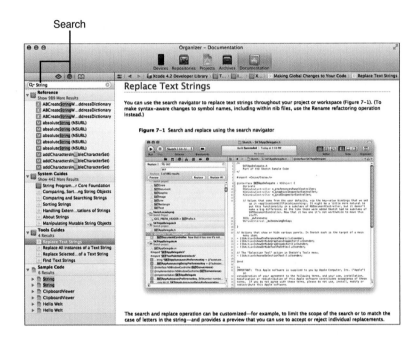

You can fine-tune your search criteria by clicking the magnifying glass located within the Search field. This displays a pop-up menu with selections for limiting your search to specific document sets and reviewing recently completed searches.

Using the Quick Help Assistant

One of the fastest and easiest ways to get help while coding is through the Xcode Quick Help assistant. Instead of searching help for a particular topic, Quick Help integrates directly with the code editor and can be used to directly reference a topic as you program.

Accessing Quick Help

Open the assistant by holding down Option and clicking a symbol in Xcode (for example, a class name or method name) or choose Help, Quick Help. A small window opens with basic information about the symbol and links to other documentation resources.

For example, consider the following line that allocates and initializes a string with the contents of an integer variable:

```
myString=[[NSString alloc] initWithFormat:@"%d",myValue];
```

In this sample, there is a class (NSString) and two methods (alloc and initWithFormat). To get information about the initWithFormat: method, hold down Option, and then click initWithFormat:. The Quick Help popover appears, as shown in Figure 7.11.

FIGURE 7.11
Open the Quick Help assistant directly within your code stream.

Interpreting Quick Help Results

Quick Help displays context-sensitive information related to your code in up to eight different sections. What you see depends on the type of symbol you have selected. A class property, for example, does not have a return type, but a class method does:

▶ **Abstract**: A description of the feature that the class, method, or other symbol provides

▶ **Availability**: The versions of the operating system where the feature is available

- ▶ **Declaration**: The structure of a method or definition of a data type

- ▶ **Parameters**: The required or option information that can be provided to a method

- ▶ **Return Value**: What information will be returned by a method when it completes

- ▶ **Declared In**: The file that defines the selected symbol

- ▶ **Reference**: The official reference documentation for the system

- ▶ **Related API**: Other methods within the same class as your selected method

- ▶ **Related Documents**: Additional documentation that references the selected symbol

- ▶ **Sample Code**: Sample code files that include examples of class/method/ property use

To open the full Xcode documentation for the symbol, click the book icon in the upper-right corner. You can also click any of the hyperlinks in Quick Help results to jump to a specific piece of documentation or code.

Activating the Quick Help Inspector

Quick Help is fast, but it can be even faster, and possibly answer your questions before you even have them. By turning on the Quick Help Inspector, you can display help information all the time. Xcode actually displays context-aware help for whatever you're typing, as you type it.

To display the Quick Help Inspector, activate the Utility area of the Xcode window using the third (rightmost) View button. Next, click the show Quick Help Inspector icon (wavy lines in a dark square), located in the Utility area, as shown in Figure 7.12. Quick Help automatically displays a reference for whatever code your text-entry cursor is located in.

Although Quick Help and the Quick Help Inspector do not offer the depth of information contained in the main Xcode documentation, they do give you the primary details needed to correctly implement the code you're working on. As you can see, memorizing documentation is not a requirement in Xcode. (Save your brain cells for something more important—like your anniversary date.)

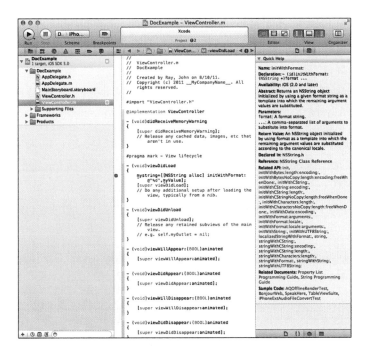

FIGURE 7.12
View Quick Help wherever you are, for whatever you're coding.

Summary

Documentation can make or break a developer. You can visualize a breakthrough algorithm in your mind, but without the means of turning the idea into code, it might never see the light of day. Thankfully, Apple provides a wide range of developer documentation resources that you can access from your browser, iPad, or directly within the Xcode development suite.

In this hour's lesson, you explored the documentation resources available, what they are used for, and which offer the greatest benefit for typical development. You learned how to configure Xcode's docset download facility, and how to browse, search, and bookmark resources—even access sample projects—all within the Xcode help viewer.

For on-the-fly help, we discussed how to invoke the Xcode Quick Help feature and display always-on information with the Quick Help Inspector. In short, if you need help coding in Xcode, you should now know where to find it.

Q&A

Q. *Can I access the developer documentation through any browser, or only in Safari?*

A. You can access the documentation in any browser you want. Only browsers that identify themselves as Mobile Safari on the iPad see the iPad-specific view, however.

Q. *Can I access earlier iOS/Mac OS documentation releases through my browser?*

A. No. Only the latest release is available through your web browser. You can access earlier versions by downloading the appropriate docsets in Xcode.

Q. *I'm searching for a document, but I keep returning results for versions of iOS/Mac OS X that I do not want. What do I do?*

A. Click the magnifying glass within the help viewer Search field and choose Show Find Options. A small configuration area that appears below the field enables you to choose which docsets are searched.

Workshop

Quiz

1. iOS and Mac OS X documentation is combined in a single docset. True or false?

2. Do the Guide documents contain detailed information about implementing a particular technology?

3. The Quick Help system is only available when coding for iOS. True or false?

Answers

1. False. Each iOS release and Mac OS X release has its own docset.

2. No. Guides provide links to technical documents, but rarely contain technical/implementation details themselves.

3. False. The Quick Help and Quick Help Inspector work across all project types to bring you instant information with no searching.

Activities

1. Configure your Xcode docset downloads so that the latest version of the iOS and Mac OS X documentation is downloaded as well as the previous release.

2. Open an Xcode project and activate the Quick Help Inspector. Try writing a line or two of code (feel free to use the example from this hour's lesson) and watch what happens. Use the links within the Quick Help to open and access detailed documentation in the Xcode help viewer.

HOUR 8

Creating User Interfaces

What You'll Learn in This Hour:

▶ What the Interface Builder editor does and what makes it special

▶ The differences between XIB and storyboard files

▶ How to create user interfaces using the Object Library

▶ The use of Auto Layout features in OS X

▶ How to instantiate any object in an Interface Builder document

Over the past few hours, you've become familiar with the core Xcode functions, including project management and coding features. Although these are certainly important skills for becoming a successful developer, there's nothing quite like building your application interface and seeing it come alive on the screen.

In this hour, we introduce the Interface Builder editor. Interface Builder provides a visual approach to application interface design, but behind the scenes, it does much, much more. As you read through this hour, keep in mind that Interface Builder is *integral* to the OS X/iOS application development workflow. You're going to be seeing a lot more of it through the rest of the book.

What Is Interface Builder?

Let's get it out of the way up front: Yes, the Interface Builder editor (or IB for short) does help you create interfaces for your applications, but it isn't a just a drawing tool for GUIs; it helps you symbolically build application functionality without writing code. This translates to fewer bugs, less development time, and easier-to-maintain projects.

Originally a standalone application, it is now integrated into Xcode 4. In this hour, we focus on navigating through Interface Builder's components. We also spend time with it over the next 2 hours—getting to know how it ties back to your code files and its iOS-specific features.

The Interface Builder Approach

Using Xcode and the Cocoa toolset, you can program OS X and iOS interfaces by hand—instantiating interface objects, defining where they appear on the screen, setting attributes for the objects, and, finally, making them visible. Over the years, there have been many different approaches to graphical interface builders. One of the most common implementations is to enable the user to "draw" an interface, but behind the scenes create the code that generates that interface. Any tweaks require the code to be edited by hand—hardly an acceptable situation.

Another tactic is to maintain the interface definition symbolically but to attach the code that implements functionality directly to interface elements. This, unfortunately, means that if you want to change your interface, or swap functionality from one UI element to another, you have to move the code as well.

Interface Builder works differently. Rather than autogenerating interface code or tying source listings directly to interface elements, IB builds live objects that connect to your application code through simple links called *connections*. Want to change how a feature of your app is triggered? Just change the connection. As you learn a bit later, changing how your application works with the objects you create in Interface Builder is, quite literally, a matter of connecting or reconnecting the dots as you see fit.

Beyond the UI

Something that isn't immediately obvious to many developers is that Interface Builder isn't just for interfaces. In fact, you can use it to instantiate any object that you want, even your custom classes. When your interface file is loaded, OS X and iOS create instances of any objects described in the file (or scene).

As long as you provide a connection to your object (which you learn about in the next hour), you can create these instances exactly as if you had allocated and initialized them in code. Why is this valuable? Because it saves time and simplifies development. Need an instance of a controller to manage your interface? Add a controller object. The more complex your applications become, the more you'll appreciate the code you *don't* have to write.

Interface Builder XIB Versus Storyboard

One of the most confusing aspects of writing about the Interface Builder editor is that it works a bit differently between OS X and iOS applications.

In an OS X application, your work in Interface Builder results in an XML file called an XIB or (for legacy reasons) NIB file, containing a hierarchy of objects. Your application delegate loads the XIB file and becomes what is called the *File's Owner* for the objects in the XIB file. Other classes can load additional XIB files to further build the application interface, becoming the File's Owner for whatever objects they load. This parent-children relationship is clearly denoted in Interface Builder and makes it easy for interface objects to connect to the classes that instantiated them.

Unlike OS X applications that lend themselves to being built up from multiple components (multiple windows, palettes, etc.), iOS applications focus on a single, full-screen interface. That interface may certainly go through transitions from one appearance to another, but the application only presents a single "face" at a time.

Storyboards provide a way of defining multiple *scenes* within a single file: a storyboard file. When an application starts, it loads a default storyboard file and scene. The objects within that scene are instantiated, just like a XIB file. Using code or point-and-click connections (which you learn about in Hour 10, "Creating iOS Application Workflows with Storyboards"), you can transition to other scenes and so on.

Unlike a XIB, a storyboard does not have a File's Owner object that it can reference. Instead, each scene must define a view controller class (that is, a class that will manage the objects in the scene). You can certainly add view controllers to your OS X XIB files and develop in a manner similar to iOS, but Apple forces a more structured approach with the storyboard approach.

Where It All Begins

By default, OS X application projects are set to load their initial interface from MainMenu.xib. iOS projects load the storyboard from MainStoryboard.storyboard or from MainStoryboard_iPad.storyboard and MainStoryboard_iPhone.storyboard for universal projects.

You can change this behavior by selecting the top-level project group in the Project Navigator, selecting your application target, then using the Main Interface or Main Storyboard fields in the Summary area to choose a new file, as shown in Figure 8.1.

FIGURE 8.1
Set the interface file loaded when the application starts.

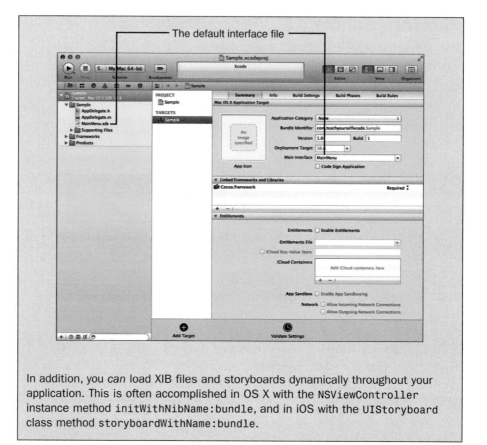

In addition, you *can* load XIB files and storyboards dynamically throughout your application. This is often accomplished in OS X with the `NSViewController` instance method `initWithNibName:bundle`, and in iOS with the `UIStoryboard` class method `storyboardWithName:bundle`.

Watch Out!

Storyboards Are the Way to Go

iOS applications can still be built using XIB files if you uncheck Use Storyboard when creating a new project. I suspect Apple will eventually drop support for XIB files in iOS, so I recommend avoiding new non-storyboard projects.

The Anatomy of an Interface Builder File

What do XIB files and storyboard files look like in IB? Let's start with a XIB file. Open the Hour 8 Projects folder and double-click the file MainMenu.xib to open Interface Builder and display a sample XIB file. The contents of the file are shown in the IB editor, as shown in Figure 8.2.

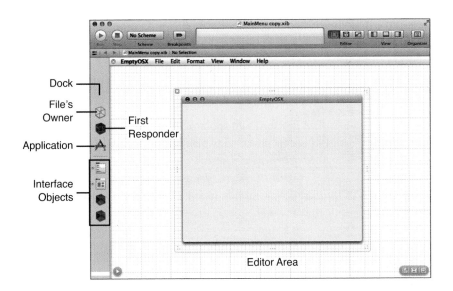

FIGURE 8.2
An XIB file's
objects are
represented
by icons.

The objects represented within the interface are visible in the dock (the column along the left side of the Editor area). The icons are divided into a top portion (called the placeholder objects), and a bottom portion (called the interface objects). To make this a big clearer, click and drag the right side of the dock to show the Document Outline (or choose Editor, Show Document Outline). The Document Outline is a *much* easier to understand view of the objects in the XIB (or storyboard) file. From here on, that's the view we show (see Figure 8.3).

Placeholder Objects

In this sample XIB file, three placeholder icons are visible: File's Owner, First Responder, and Application. These are special icons used to represent unique objects in our application and these will be present in all XIB files that you work with.

▶ **File's Owner:** The File's Owner icon denotes the object that loads the XIB file in your running application. This is the object that effectively instantiates all the other objects described in the XIB file. For example, you may have an interface defined in myInterface.xib, which is loaded by an object you've written called myInterfaceController. In this case, the File's Owner would represent the myInterfaceController object. You learn more about the relationship between interfaces and code in Hour 9, "Connecting a GUI to Code."

▶ **First Responder:** The First Responder icon denotes the object currently in control and interacting with the user. A text field that the user is typing into, for example, is the First Responder until the user moves to another field or control.

▶ **Application:** The Application icon denotes the shared Application object (NSApplication, a global singleton) within your XIB. This object provides the main event loop and manages windows and menus for your application.

FIGURE 8.3
The Document
Outline view
within the
Interface Builder
editor.

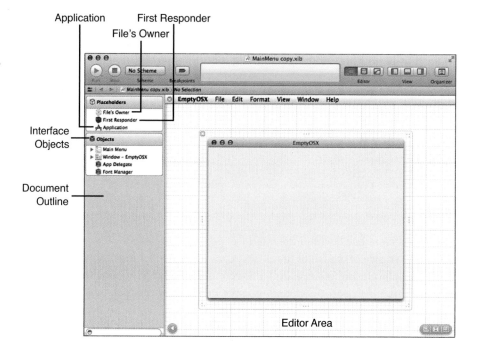

Interface Objects

Below the placeholder objects are the interface objects. By default, a Main Menu object, which defines the contents of the menu bar, and a single Window object are included in the OS X Cocoa application template.

> For the OS X application template, you'll also see two non-UI objects included with the interface objects. The Font Manager object handles application fonts, and the App Delegate object represents the application delegate class within your project.

Many objects are hierarchical in nature. This means that as you add objects to your interface, they will be contained *within* other objects—views within windows, buttons within views, and so on. You can use the disclosure arrow located to the left of any object to expand it in the Document Outline, as shown in Figure 8.4.

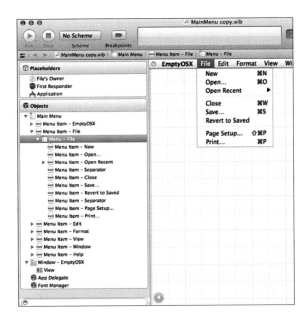

FIGURE 8.4
Expand objects
to view the
other objects it
contains.

By the Way

At their most basic level, all interface objects are subclasses of NSView (OS X) or UIView (iOS). A view is a rectangular region that can contain content and respond to user events. All the controls (buttons, fields, and so on) that you'll add to a view are, in fact, subclasses of a view. This isn't necessarily something you need to be worried about, except that you'll be encountering documentation that refers to buttons and other interface elements referred to as *subviews* and the views that contain them as *superviews*.

Just keep in the back of your mind that pretty much everything you see on the screen can be considered a "view" and the terminology will seem a little less alien.

Working with the Object Icons

The Document Outline (and Interface Builder dock) show icons for objects in your application, but what good are they? Aside from presenting a nice list, do the icons provide any functionality?

Absolutely. The icons give you a visual means of referring to the objects they represent. You interact with the icons by dragging to and from them to create the connections that drive your application's features.

Consider an onscreen control, such as a button, that needs to be able to trigger an action in your code. By dragging from the button to the File's Owner icon, you can create a connection from the GUI element you've drawn to a method you've written in the object that loaded the XIB file.

We go through two hands-on examples in the next hour so that you can get a feel for how this works on both OS X and iOS projects.

The Storyboard Differences

Now that you've seen what a XIB file looks like, return to your Projects folder for this hour and open the file MainStoryboard.storyboard. This is the default storyboard file for the iOS Single View Application type. When loaded, the Interface Builder editor is a bit different, as shown in Figure 8.5, than it was with the XIB file.

FIGURE 8.5
Storyboard files appear a bit differently in Interface Builder.

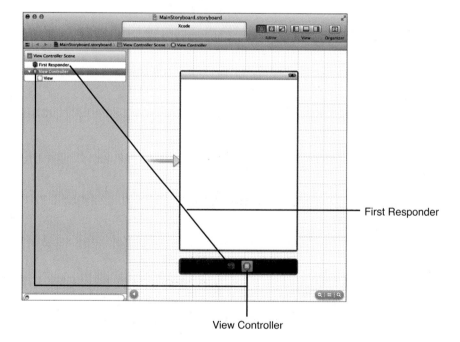

First Responder

View Controller

First, the icon dock isn't available in storyboard files. This makes sense because the storyboard can grow to have many different scenes (more on this in Hour 10), and trying to interpret what was what would get seriously confusing. Second, there are only two placeholder icons, and they are displayed both in the Document Outline and in a bar underneath the iOS application view.

By default, any storyboard scene contains two objects:

▶ **First Responder:** A placeholder, just like the First Responder in OS X XIB files.

▶ **View Controller:** Represents the object that is responsible for handling your interface events. In a vanilla iOS application, this is just the ViewController class.

Unlike OS X XIB files where the objects that make up the interface sat outside of the noninterface objects, here the interface objects sit *inside* the View Controller object. Expand the View Controller object by clicking the disclosure arrow in front of its name. You will see a third object appear: View (visible in Figure 8.5). This is the view that will be controlled by the View Controller object. You build your interfaces within a view, as demonstrated by a completed storyboard in Figure 8.6.

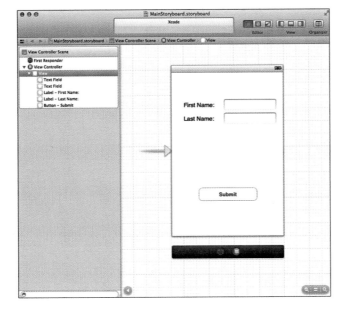

FIGURE 8.6
You build your interfaces in the view controller's view.

Guided Structure

You should be seeing at this point that iOS development guides your application structure in a much more rigid manner than OS X development. In an OS X application, your interface can be handled by the class that loaded it, or by entirely separate classes that you instantiate in your XIB file. (We discuss adding arbitrary objects representing any class later this hour.) You can add as many windows as you want and, basically, create a complete mess if that's your thing.

In iOS applications, it is certainly possible to create a mess, but the storyboard files are structured so that you *must* have a `ViewController` class that manages a view. You build your interface starting from the view, and if additional displays are necessary (read "multiple scenes"), they too will have a view controller and a view.

Creating User Interfaces

You've seen the default state of a OS X application interface and an iOS interface, but how do we go from that to an application interface that works? Figure 8.7 shows a simple functional application UI that you work with in the next hour.

FIGURE 8.7
From nothing, to something.

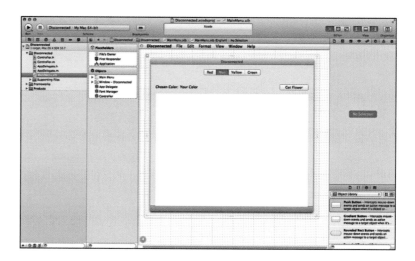

In this section, we explore how interfaces are created with the Interface Builder editor. In other words, it's time for the fun stuff.

If you haven't already, open the MainMenu.xib file or MainStoryboard.storyboard file included in this hour's Projects folder. Use the Document Outline to open select and display a window (or an iOS view) in the editor.

The Object Library

Everything that you add to a view, from buttons and images to web content, comes from the Object Library. You can view the library by choosing View, Utilities, Show Object Library from the menu bar (Control+Option+Command+3). If it isn't already visible, the Utility area of the Xcode interface opens, and Object Library is displayed in the lower-right. Make sure that the Objects item is selected in the pop-up menu at the top of the library so that all available options are visible.

Watch
Out!

Libraries, Libraries, Everywhere!

Xcode has more than one library. The Object Library contains the UI elements you'll be adding in Interface Builder, but there are also File Template, Code Snippet, and Media libraries that you can activate by clicking the icons immediately above the library area.

If you find yourself staring at a library that doesn't seem to show what you're expecting, click the cube icon above the library, or reselect the object library from the menu to make sure you're in the right place.

When you click and hover over an element in the library, a popover is displayed with a description of how the object can be used in the interface, as shown in Figure 8.8. This provides a convenient way of exploring your UI options without having to open the Xcode documentation.

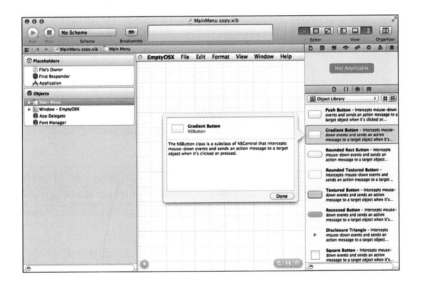

FIGURE 8.8
Learn about the objects you can add to your XIB or storyboard file.

Did You
Know?

Using view buttons at the top of the library, you can switch between list and icon views of the available objects. You can also focus in on specific UI elements using the pop-up menu above the library listing. If you know the name of an object but can't locate it in the list, use the Filter field at the bottom of the library to quickly find it, or the pop-up menu at the top of the list to limit what is shown to specific subset of objects.

Adding and Removing UI Objects

To add an object to a view, click and drag from the library to the view. For example, find the label object in the Object Library and drag it into the center of the OS X window's views or into the iOS storyboard scene's view. The label should appear in your UI and read Label. Double-click the label and type **Hello World**. The text will update, as shown in Figure 8.9, just as you would expect.

FIGURE 8.9
Add objects by dragging them into your OS X or iOS views.

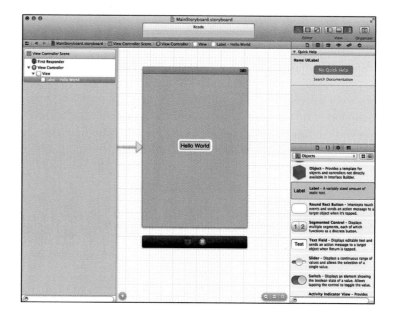

With that simple action, you've written a Hello World application. Try dragging other objects from the Object Library into the view (buttons, text fields, and so on). With few exceptions, the objects should appear and behave just the way you expect.

To remove an object from the view, click to select it, and then press the Delete key. If you find it difficult to target an object directly in the user interface, select it from the Document Outline instead.

By the Way

In storyboard files, the +/- magnifying glasses in the lower right of the Editor area will zoom in and out on your interface for fine-tuning a scene. This proves useful when creating storyboards with multiple scenes. Unfortunately, you cannot edit a scene when zoomed out, so Apple provides the = button to quickly jump back and forth between a 100% view and your last chosen zoom setting.

OS X XIB files get an entirely different menu in the lower-right corner for arranging and managing the UI spacing and sizing. More on that later.

Not all objects are UI objects. Some objects (controllers for other objects, for instance) have no onscreen representation. These objects are dragged from the Object Library directly into the Document Outline area, where they are added to a scene (storyboard) or object list (XIB).

Working with the IB Layout Tools

Instead of relying on your visual acuity to position objects in a view, Apple has included some useful tools for fine-tuning your layout. If you've ever used a drawing program like OmniGraffle or Adobe Illustrator, you'll find many of these familiar.

Guides

As you drag objects in a view, you'll notice guides appearing to help with the layout. These blue dotted lines are displayed to align objects along the margins of the view, to the centers of other objects in the view, and to the baseline of the fonts used in the labels and object titles, as shown in Figure 8.10.

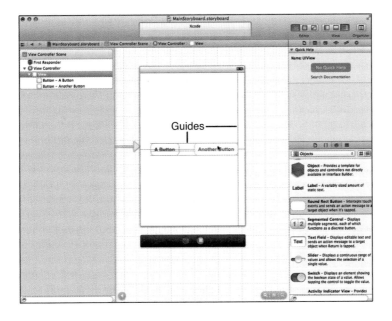

FIGURE 8.10
Use the guides to help position your objects.

As an added bonus, guides automatically appear to indicate the approximate spacing requirements of Apple interface guidelines. If you're not sure why it is showing you a particular margin guide, it is likely that your object is in a position that Interface Builder considers "appropriate" for something of that type and size.

You can manually add your own guides by selecting a view and choosing Editor, Add Horizontal Guide or by choosing Editor, Add Vertical Guide.

Selection Handles

In addition to the layout guides, most objects include selection handles to stretch an object either horizontally, vertically, or both. Using the small boxes that appear alongside an object when it is selected, just click and drag to change its size, as demonstrated in Figure 8.11.

FIGURE 8.11
Use the handles to resize your objects.

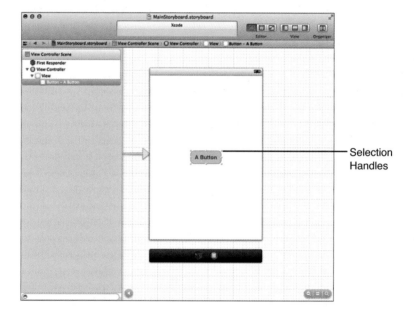

Selection Handles

Some objects constrain how you can resize them; this preserves a level of consistency within the application interfaces.

OS X windows work a bit differently. To resize windows, use the gray border that Xcode adds around their onscreen display in the Interface Builder editor. Also, be aware that clicking the X in the upper-left corner of the window border closes it, but the Window object is still part of the XIB file. Double-clicking it in the document outline opens it again.

Alignment

To quickly align several objects within a view, select them by clicking and dragging a selection rectangle around them or by holding down the Shift key, and then choose Editor, Align and an appropriate alignment type from the menu.

For example, try dragging several buttons into your view, placing them in a variety of different positions. To align them based on their horizontal center (a line that runs vertically through each button's center), select the buttons, and then choose Editor, Align, Horizontal Centers. Figure 8.12 shows the before and after results.

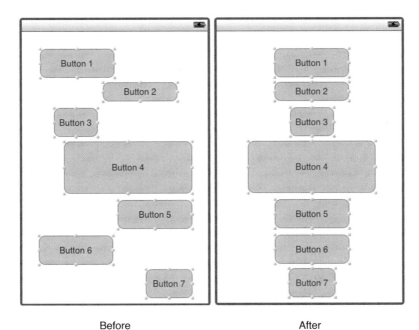

Before   After

FIGURE 8.12
Use the Align menu to quickly align a group of items to an edge or center.

OS X developers can get even faster access to alignment features using the Align pop-up menu in the lower-right corner of the editor.

To fine-tune an object's position within a view, select it, and then use the arrow keys to position it left, right, up, or down, 1 pixel at a time.

The Size Inspector

Another tool that you may want to use for controlling your layout is the Size Inspector. Interface Builder has a number of "inspectors" for examining the attributes of an object. As the name implies, the Size Inspector provides information about sizes, but also position and alignment. To open the Size Inspector, first select the object (or objects) that you want to work with, and then click the ruler icon at the top of the Utility area in Xcode. Alternatively, choose View, Utilities, Show Size Inspector or press Option+Command+5. Figure 8.13 shows the OS X version of the inspector.

FIGURE 8.13
The Size Inspector enables you to adjust the size and position of one or more objects.

Size Inspector

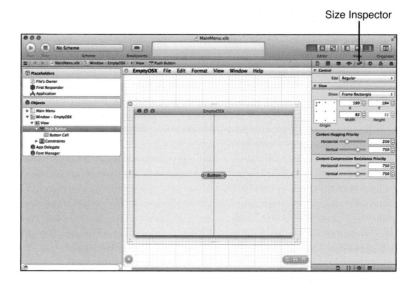

At the top of the inspector is a Control section, which enables you to choose between different sizes of a given UI control. Next, in the View section, you can change the size and position of the object by changing the coordinates in the Height/Width and X/Y fields. You can also view the coordinates of a specific portion of an object by clicking one of the black dots in the size and grid to indicate where the reading should come from.

By the Way

Within the Size and Position settings, notice a drop-down menu where you can choose between Frame Rectangle and Layout Rectangle. These two settings are usually very similar, but there is a slight difference. The frame values represent the exact area an object occupies onscreen, whereas the layout values take into account spacing around the object.

By the Way

When an object is selected, press the Option button to quickly get a read on the distances (in view coordinates, starting at 0,0 in the upper left) between the edges of an object and the view it is within.

Auto Layout and Content Hugging and Compression

By default, OS X applications now enable a feature called Auto Layout. This makes it possible for application controls to dynamically adjust their sizing as their views change size (most often from a user resizing a window). We look at the Auto Layout features in a few minutes.

If you prefer to disable Auto Layout in your application and instead use the autosizing features available in iOS applications, open the File Inspector for the XIB file (Option+Command+1) and uncheck the Use Auto Layout check box, as shown in Figure 8.14.

File Inspector ———

Disable Auto Layout ———

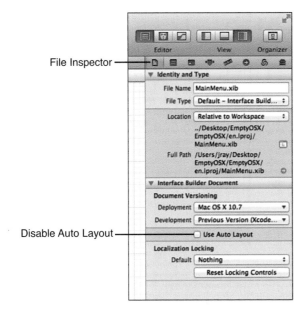

FIGURE 8.14
Disable Auto Layout to use the same autosizing features as iOS.

Autosizing

The autosizing settings of the Size Inspector determine how controls resize/reposition themselves when a window (OS X) changes sizes or a device (iOS) changes orientation.

This deceptively simple "square in a square" interface provides everything you need to tell Interface Builder where to anchor your controls and in which directions (horizontally or vertically) they can stretch.

To understand how this works, imagine that the inner square represents one of your interface elements and the outer square is the view that contains the element. The lines between the inner and outer square are the anchors. When clicked, they toggle between solid and dashed lines. Solid lines are anchors that are set. This means that those distances will be maintained when the interface changes size.

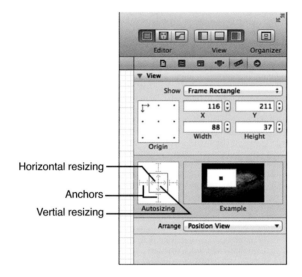

Horizontal resizing —
Anchors —
Vertial resizing —

Within the inner square are two double-headed arrows, representing horizontal and vertical resizing. Clicking these arrows toggles between solid and dashed lines. Solid arrows indicate that the item is allowed to resize horizontally, vertically, or both.

For example, to create a button that stays in the center of the screen and grows/shrinks proportionally when the view changes sizes, follow these steps using the MainStoryboard.storyboard file:

1. Add a button to the center of the view.

2. Open the Size Inspector (Option+Command+5).

3. Remove any existing anchors around the edges of the center box.

4. Click the horizontal arrowed line in the center of the box to enable horizontal resizing, as shown in Figure 8.16.

If you need a more "visual" means of understanding the autosizing controls, just look to the right of the two squares. The rectangle to the right shows an animated preview of what will happen to your control (represented as a red rectangle) when the view changes size around it. The easiest way to understand the relationship between anchors, resizing, and view size/orientation is to configure the anchors/resize arrows and then watch the preview to see the effect.

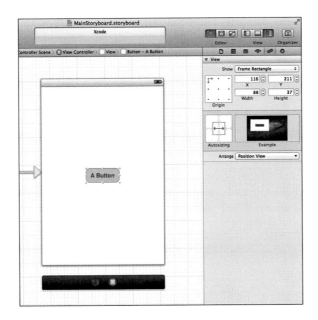

FIGURE 8.16
Create a button that floats in the center of the screen and resizes horizontally when the view changes size.

The Auto Layout System

While the guides, Size Inspector, and other tools are helpful for laying out interfaces—even interfaces that can adapt to view changes—OS X applications can take advantage of a new powerful tool for managing layouts: the Auto Layout system. Auto layouts are OS X only and are enabled by default on new projects. Review the previous section, "Auto Layout and Content Hugging and Compression," for more information on enabling or disabling auto layouts.

Understanding Constraints

Auto Layout works by building a series of constraints for your onscreen objects. The constraints define distances between objects and how flexible these relationships are. For example, try adding a button to the window in MainMenu.xib; make sure it is located toward the top-left side of the view. Notice that parallel to the button in the object hierarchy a new Constraints entry shows up, as shown in Figure 8.17.

Within the Constraints object are two constraints: horizontal space and vertical space constraint. The horizontal constraint states that the left side of the button will be a certain number of points from the left edge of the view. The vertical constraint is the distance from the top of the view to the top of the button. What constraints are added depend on where the object is in relation to its containing view.

FIGURE 8.17
The Constraints
object repre-
sents the
positioning
relationships
within a view.

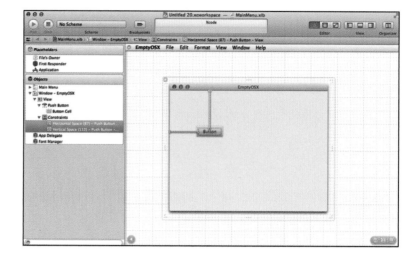

Constraints, however, are more than just entries that tie an object to the view it is within. They can be flexible, ensuring that an object maintains *at least* or *at most* a certain distance from another object, or even that two objects, when resized, maintain the same distance between one another.

Constraints that set a specific size or distance between objects are called *pinning*. The flexibility (or inflexibility of a constraint) is managed by configuring a *relationship*.

Alignment of objects is also listed as a constraint, but is managed using the alignment tools you've already seen.

Setting Constraints and Relationships

Let's look at an example of two buttons that are located a set distance (150 points) from either side of a window that will grow farther apart or closer together when the window is resized but *won't* allow themselves to be any closer than 75 points apart.

To do this, begin by adding your buttons:

1. If you already have a push button added to a window in the MainWindow.xib file, you're in good shape. If not, add one now. Position the button along the left side of the window.

2. Repeat this for a second button, positioning it along the right side of the window. Use the guides to align the baseline of each button's label.

Xcode should automatically create constraints for the first button that tie it to the top of the left side and top of the view (or center of the view, if centered vertically). The second button will be tied to the baseline of the first button and the right side of the view, as shown in Figure 8.18.

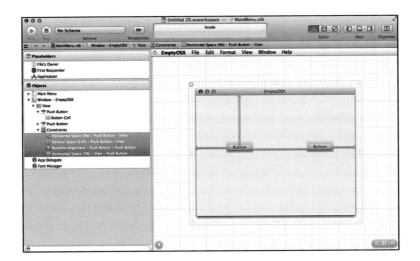

FIGURE 8.18
Four constraints should exist for the two buttons.

Now, adjust the two buttons so that they are located 150 points from the sides of the view:

1. Select the Horizontal Space constraint for the first button within the Constraints object in Document Outline.

2. Open the Attributes Inspector (Option+Command+4). Here you can define the constraint relationship.

   Because we want the button to be exactly 150 points from the side of the view, the Constant field is set to 150, and the Relation pop-up is set to Equal, as shown in Figure 8.19. The other settings are left at their defaults.

3. Repeat this set for the other button's horizontal constraint. They will now be located exactly 150 points from the edges of the view.

FIGURE 8.19
Set constraints
to tie your
objects to
the view.

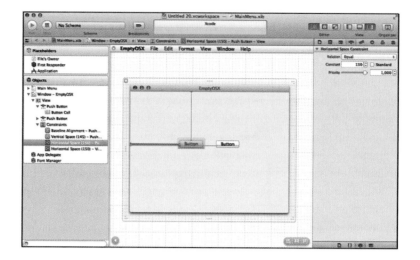

FIGURE 8.19
Set constraints
to tie your
objects to
the view.

The final thing you must do is tell the interface that no matter how it is resized, the
buttons should never be closer together than 75 points. This involves creating and
configuring a new relationship:

1. Select both buttons. (Click to select one and then hold Shift and click to select
   the other.)

2. Use the middle icon of the layout button at the bottom of the editor (or the
   Editor, Pin menu) to choose Horizontal Spacing. This creates a constraint that
   manages the spacing between the two buttons.

3. Select this constraint and then open the Attributes Inspector
   (Option+Command+4). This time set the relation to Greater Than or Equal,
   meaning the horizontal spacing will always be equal to or larger than the
   provided value.

4. Set the constant to 75, meaning the buttons will be at least 75 points apart at
   all times, as shown in Figure 8.20.

You can now test your constraints by resizing the window in the Interface Builder
editor. Notice that the buttons go apart as expected, but limit the window from
shrinking to a size that would violate the 75-point horizontal-spacing constraint.

**Did You
Know?**

When defining the constraint relationships in the Attributes Inspector, you may
have noticed a Priority slider and a Standard check box. The Priority slider determines how "strong" the constraint relationship is. There may, for example, be
instances when multiple constraints must be evaluated against one another.

The priority setting determines the importance of any given constraint. A value of 1000 is a constraint that is required. If you move the Constraint slider, Xcode shows a description of what to expect at a given constraint priority.

The Standard check box lets Xcode use its internal database of spacing to set the recommended space between two objects. This, in many cases, is preferred because it ensures a consistent interface.

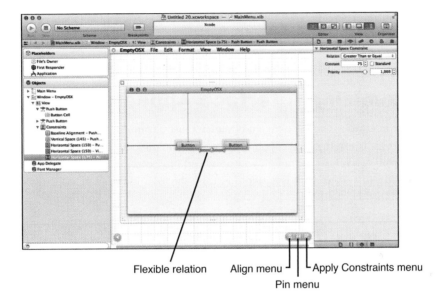

Flexible relation   Align menu   Apply Constraints menu

                        Pin menu

FIGURE 8.20
Create a flexible constraint.

Content Hugging and Content Compression Resistance

Earlier in the hour, you learned that the Content Hugging and Compression Resistance settings in the Size Inspector (refer to Figure 8.14) are related to Auto Layout. So, where do these tie in?

When inspecting an object that is within an Auto Layout XIB, these settings control how closely the sides of an object "hug" the content in the object and how much the content can be compressed or clipped. A button, for example, can expand horizontally (so horizontal hugging is a low priority) but shouldn't grow vertically (making vertical hugging a very high priority). Similarly, the content (the button label) should not be compressed or clipped at all, so the content compression resistance settings for both horizontal and vertical compression should be very high priority.

You will not often need to adjust these settings beyond their defaults, which Interface Builder adds for you.

> ## Wait... There's More
>
> There is far more to the Auto Layout system than can be described in an hour. Be sure to explore the Pin menu to see the different types of constraints that you can put in place. Width/height constraints enforce a given width or height on an object. Equal width/height constraints ensure multiple objects maintain an equal width or height. The leading/trailing space pinnings tie the left side of an object to the left side of its parent view (leading), or the right side of an object to the right side of its parent view (trailing).
>
> Review Apple's documentation, starting with "Cocoa Auto Layout Guide," for more information.

Customizing Interface Appearance

How your interface appears to the end user isn't just a combination of control sizes and positions. For many kinds of objects, there are literally dozens of different attributes that you can adjust. Although you could certainly configure things such as colors and fonts in your code, it is easier to just use the tools included in the Interface Builder editor.

Using the Attributes Inspector

The most common place you'll tweak the way your interface objects appear is through the Attributes Inspector, available by clicking the slider icon at the top of the Utility area. You can also choose View, Utilities, Show Attributes Inspector (Option+Command+4) if the Utility area isn't currently visible. Let's run through a quick example to see how this works.

Open the MainStoryboard.storyboard file and add a label to your view. Select the label and then open the Attributes Inspector, shown in Figure 8.21.

The top portion of the Attributes Inspector contains attributes for the specific object. In the case of the text object, this includes settings such as font, size, color, and alignment—everything you'd expect to find for editing text. Try changing a few of the settings and see what happens to the label. You should be able to easily set its size, color, and font.

In the lower portion of the inspector are additional inherited attributes. Remember that onscreen elements are a subclass of a view? This means that many of the standard view attributes are also available for the object and for your tinkering enjoyment (and, for OS X, NSControl attributes). In many cases, you'll want to leave these alone, but settings such as background and transparency can come in handy.

Attributes Inspector

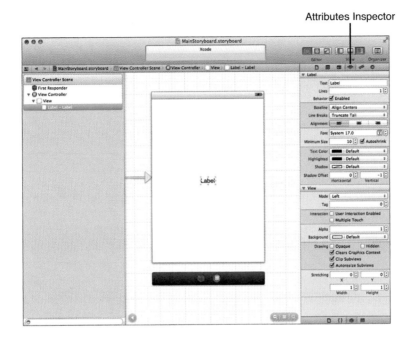

FIGURE 8.21
To change how an object looks and behaves, select it, and then open the Attributes Inspector.

OS X UI objects behave a bit differently from most iOS objects. When you are working with iOS objects in the Document Outline, they are represented as just a single configurable object. A button is a button, end of story. OS X objects, however, are very often a hierarchy of objects, each with its own attributes to be configured. A table view, for example, expands to show objects for each column. You might use the top-level table view object to choose whether column headings are visible, but then drill down to a column to choose whether clicking its heading results in the table contents sorting.

By the Way

The attributes you change in Interface Builder are simply properties of the object's class. To help identify what an attribute does, use the documentation tool in Xcode to look up the object's class and review the descriptions of its properties. Don't spend your time trying to memorize these—there's no point in filling your head with this minutia.

Did You Know?

Simulating the Interface

At any point in time during the construction of your interface, you can test the layout without having to build the full project. To test the interface, choose Editor, Simulate Document. After a few seconds, the interface appears in the Cocoa

Simulator. You can resize windows, click controls, and generally give your interface design a workout.

Less Than Meets the Eye

When you use the Simulate Document command, only the interface code is being run. Nothing that you may have written in the code editor is included. Therefore, you can simulate interfaces even before you've written a single line of supporting code or if your code has errors. However, it also means that if your code modifies the display in any way, you won't see those changes onscreen.

Unfortunately, you lose the ability to simulate the interface with iOS storyboards. If you're developing an iOS application, you *must* run the application code if you want to see an interface. You learn more about the iOS simulation tool and its role in testing in Hour 11, "Building and Executing Applications." That said, one of the biggest reasons to test an iOS interface is to see how it performs under rotation events. You *can* do this in the storyboard by selecting the View Controller object and opening the Attributes Inspector (Option+Command+4). Use the Orientation setting under Simulated Metrics to force a scene to be visible in Landscape mode, as shown in Figure 8.22. This *does* take into account all settings made within the Size Inspector and re-lays out the display as needed.

FIGURE 8.22
Simulate Landscape iOS views without leaving the Interface Builder editor.

Set Interface Orientation

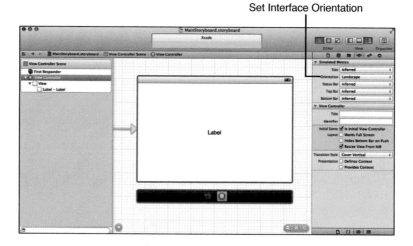

When you simulate an OS X Cocoa application interface, it starts the Cocoa Simulator. This is nothing more than a XIB simulator and has nothing in common with the iOS simulator that you'll learn about in Hour 11. The iOS simulator runs your full iOS apps without an iOS device present.

Setting Object Identities

As we finish this introduction to Interface Builder, we would be remiss if we didn't introduce one more feature: the Identity Inspector. As you drag objects into the interface, you're creating instances of classes that already exist (buttons, labels, and so on). Often, however, you'll build custom classes that also need to be referenced in Interface Builder. In these cases, you need to help Interface Builder out by identifying the subclass it should use.

For example, suppose we create a subclass of the standard button class that we name ourFancyButtonClass. We might drag a button into Interface Builder to represent our fancy button, but when the XIB or storyboard file loads, it just creates the same old UIButton.

To fix the problem, we select the button we've added to the view, open the Identity Inspector by choosing Tools, Identity Inspector (Option+Command+3), and then use the drop-down menu/field to enter the class that we really want instantiated at runtime (see Figure 8.23).

Identity Inspector

Custom Label   Custom Class

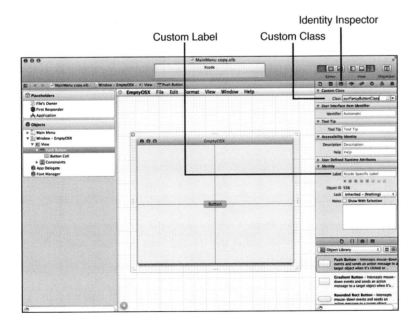

FIGURE 8.23
If you're using a custom class, you need to manually set the identity of your objects in Interface Builder.

> You'll use this often to set the class that implements an iOS scene's view controller. You use the Document Outline to select the View Controller object in the scene, then within the Identity Inspector, set the custom class to the name of the class in your project that implements your view controller behavior.

By the Way

Use the Identity Inspector's Label field to set a custom label that will be used in the display of the object in the Document Outline. For complex interfaces, this can help you tell dozens of similarly named objects from one another.

Adding Custom Objects to Interface Builder

To add an instance of an entirely custom/arbitrary object, search the Object Library for the Object item, as shown in Figure 8.24. You can drag this into your storyboard or XIB file Document Outline to instantiate any object you want.

FIGURE 8.24
The Object item can represent any class instance you want.

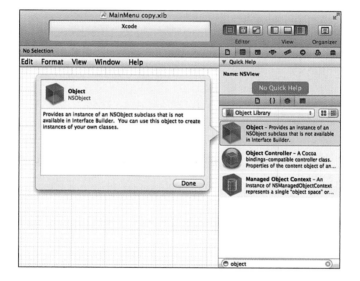

Once this is visible in the Document Outline, open the Identity Inspector (Option+Command+3), type or choose the class in your application that this object should be an instance of, exactly as you saw in Figure 8.23.

When adding objects for your custom classes to the Document Outline, be sure to choose the objects that *best* represent your class. The generic "object" shown in Figure 8.24 can represent *anything*, but provides the fewest features to the rest of the objects in Interface Builder. A View Controller object, for example, would be a better representation of a custom subclass of NSViewController (OS X) or UIViewController (iOS) and would be your best choice for representing a custom view controller.

Inspectors Here, There, and Everywhere!

Several other inspectors that relate to the objects you use in Interface Builder have not been discussed this hour. The Connections Inspector helps connect interfaces to code and is the focus of the next hour. The Bindings Inspector enables you to connect OS X (not iOS) interfaces directly to data and is the topic of Hour 17, "Attaching Big Data: Using Core Data in Your Applications."

Unfortunately, the View Effects Inspector, which enables you to apply visual effects to a view, is beyond the scope of this book. You can learn more about the View Effects Inspector in the Xcode document "Interface Builder User Guide" in the section "Attaching Graphical Effects in Mac OS X."

Summary

This hour covered Interface Builder and the tools it provides for building rich graphical interfaces for your applications. You learned how to navigate the IB editor window and access the interface objects from the Object Library. Using the various inspector tools within Interface Builder, you reviewed how to customize the look and feel of the onscreen controls and their layout.

There are some significant differences to how XIB and storyboard documents look in Interface Builder, but the basic process for editing and managing the documents is the same. Hour 9 shows how these interfaces, be they iOS or OS X, are connected back to code; and Hour 10 focuses on what makes storyboards truly unique and powerful.

Q&A

Q. *Why do I keep seeing things referred to as NIB files?*

A. The origins of Interface Builder trace back to the NeXT Computer, which made use of NIB files. These files, in fact, still bore the same name when Mac OS X was released. In recent years, however, Apple has renamed the files to have the XIB extension—unfortunately, habits (and documentation) rarely change, so they are still commonly called NIB files.

Q. *Some of the objects in the Interface Builder Library cannot be added to my view. What gives?*

A. Not all of the library objects are interface objects. Some represent objects that provide functionality to your application. These are added directly to the object list in the Document Outline.

Q. *I'm using control XYZ on OS X but don't see it on iOS.*

A. Although there are many similarities between OS X and iOS development, many differences also exist. The UI controls, while performing similar functions across both platforms, are often implemented by very different objects. Search for generic terms instead of using specific class names.

Workshop

Quiz

1. Simulating an interface from IB also compiles the project's code in Xcode. True or false?

2. What is a constraint relationship?

3. It is impossible to represent custom classes in Interface Builder. Yes or no?

Answers

1. False. Simulating the interface does not use the project code at all. As a result, the interface will not perform any coded logic that may be assigned.

2. A constraint relationship defines how an interface element relates to another element, such as a distance that should be maintained between them.

3. No. Using the Identity Inspector, you can set the class that should be instantiated for any object represented in Interface Builder.

Activities

1. Practice using the interface layout tools on the MainMenu.xib file or MainStoryboard.storyboard file. Add each available interface object to your view, and then review the Attributes Inspector for that object. If an attribute doesn't make sense, remember that you can review documentation for the class to identify the role of each of its properties.

2. Read the Xcode "Interface Builder User Guide." This document can be helpful to get a sense for where various features and settings are tucked within the myriad of interface builder menus and inspectors.

HOUR 9

Connecting a GUI to Code

What You'll Learn in This Hour:

▶ The code that supports outlets, properties, and actions
▶ How to use the Connections Inspector
▶ The process for making outlet and action connections
▶ How Xcode can generate connection code for you

After the preceding hour's lesson, you know how to make an interface. But how do you make it do something? As mentioned previously, connecting an interface to code is just a matter of "connecting the dots." In this hour, you learn how to do just that: take an *graphical user interface* (GUI) and connect it to the code that makes it into a functional application. You also learn how to automatically create the outlets and actions in your code that make these connections possible.

Outlet, Actions, and Properties: A Review

Although covered in previous hours, let's quickly review the purpose of outlets and actions, how they relate to properties, and the additional code that you must write when creating an outlet or an action.

Outlets and Properties

An outlet connects a property to an interface object. For example, if you had created a field in the Interface Builder editor intending that it would be used to collect a user's name, you might want to create an outlet for it in your controller's interface file (.h) called userName. Using this outlet and the corresponding property, you could then access or change the contents of the field:

```
@property (strong, nonatomic) IBOutlet UITextField *userName;
```

A property also requires a corresponding @synthesize line be added to the start of your implementation file to create the property's accessors. (This can also define the name of the instance variable that the property references.)

For example, to synthesize accessors for the userName property and set its instance variable name to _userName, I could add this line to my controller's implementation file (.m) file:

```
@synthesize userName=_userName;
```

Finally, in your controller's cleanup method, you also need to add code that removes the property's reference to your object, freeing it to be removed from memory:

```
[self setUserName:nil];
```

As you can see, not much code is involved, but interfaces can be complex, and the number of outlets (and corresponding properties) you need in your code will likely be much more than you see in the simple examples in this book. These things add up quickly, so the more code you can have Xcode write for you, the better (more on that in a minute).

Advanced development projects can take advantage of IBOutletCollections rather than IBOutlets. These are simply an NSArray that enables us to reference all of a particular type of object simultaneously. For a tutorial on how this can be used with iOS switches, visit http://useyourloaf.com/blog/2011/3/28/interface-builder-outlet-collections.html.

Actions

An action is a method within your code that is called when an event takes place. Certain objects, such as buttons and switches, can trigger actions when a user interacts with them through an event (such as clicking or, in iOS, touching) When you define actions in your code, Interface Builder can make them available to the onscreen objects.

To define an action, doCalculation, that is triggered from my UI, I could add this to my controller's interface file (.h):

```
-(IBAction)doCalculation:(id)sender;
```

Obviously, for the action, there must be a real method implementation in the controller's implementation (.m) file. But presumably that is why you want to be a developer: to write code that actually *does* something.

Let Xcode Do It for You

Now that outlets and actions and properties synthesize, and all this interrelated "stuff" are fresh in your mind, let's get to the point.

We all want to concentrate on writing code that does interesting things. Managing properties, outlets, synthesize statements, and keeping track of the syntax of it all is busy-work, and Xcode will do it for us. Using the Interface Builder editor's Connections Inspector and the Xcode Assistant Editor, you can create your outlets, properties, instance variables, cleanup calls, and method stubs—with only a drag and a drop.

This hour contains two tutorials. In the first, you connect to outlets and actions that are already defined to your controller class's interface (.h) file. In the second, you use the Interface Builder Editor to write the outlet and action code automatically. The best way to see how both of these processes work is to walk through the steps of making the connections with an actual application, so that's exactly what we do next.

Making Connections to Outlets and Actions

For the first tutorial, we use the OS X project named Disconnected contained within the Hour 9 OS X Projects folder. Open the folder and double-click the Disconnected.xcodeproj file to open the project in Xcode, as shown in Figure 9.1.

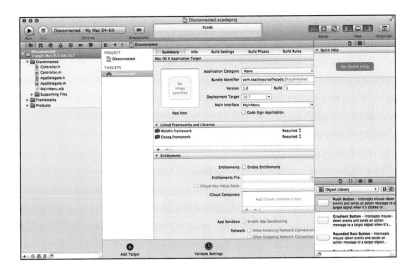

FIGURE 9.1
To begin, open the project in Xcode.

After the project is loaded, expand the project code group (Disconnected) and click the MainMenu.xib file. This contains the window and view that this application displays as its interface. Xcode refreshes and displays the objects in the Interface Builder Editor, as shown in Figure 9.2.

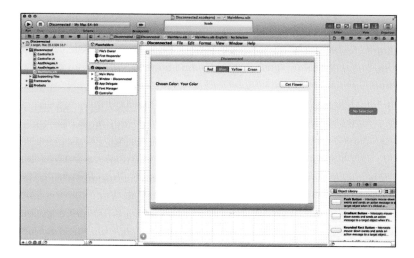

Implementation Overview

The interface contains four interactive elements: a button bar (called a segmented control), a push button, an output label (a text field), and a web view (an integrated web browser component). Together, these controls interface with application code to enable a user to pick a flower color, click the Get Flower button, and then display the chosen color in the static text field along with a matching flower photo fetched from the website http://www.floraphotographs.com. Figure 9.3 shows the final result.

Right now, the application does nothing. The interface is not connected to any application code, so it is hardly more than a pretty picture. To make it work, we must create connections to outlets and actions that have been defined using IBOutlet and IBAction in the application controller's interface file (Controller.h).

Identifying the Outlets and Actions

For the Disconnected app to function, we need to create connections to the predefined outlets and actions. Let's step through each of the outlets and actions as I've named them in the code:

▶ **colorChoice**: An outlet created for the segmented control in order to access the color the user has selected

- **chosenColor**: An outlet for the label that will be updated by getFlower to show the name of the chosen color

- **flowerView**: An outlet for the web view that will be updated by getFlower to show the image

- **getFlower**: An action that retrieves a flower from the Web, displays it, and updates a static text field label with the chosen color

FIGURE 9.3
The finished application enables a user to choose a color and have a flower image returned that matches that color.

Now that we know what object is connecting to what outlet, it's time to go ahead and make some connections. Make sure that the Interface Builder Editor is open and that you can see as much of the application interface on your screen as possible.

Creating Connections to Outlets

To create a connection from an interface item to an outlet, Control-drag from the controller object's icon in the Document Outline to either the visual representation of the object in the view or in the Document Outline. Try this with the segmented control:

1. Pressing Control, click and drag from the object named Controller in the Document Outline.

2. Drag to the onscreen image of the segmented control.

A line will appear as you drag, enabling you to easily point to the object that you want to use for the connection, as shown in Figure 9.4.

FIGURE 9.4
Control-drag
from the con-
troller object to
the segmented
control.

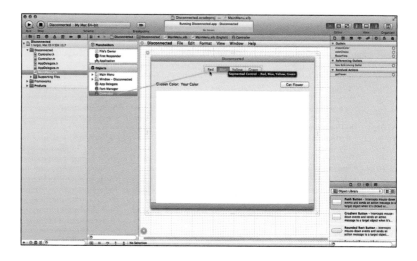

3. Release the mouse button after pointing to the segmented control.

   The available connections are shown in a pop-up menu (see Figure 9.5).

4. Pick colorChoice to make your connection.

FIGURE 9.5
Choose from
the outlets
available for the
targeted object.

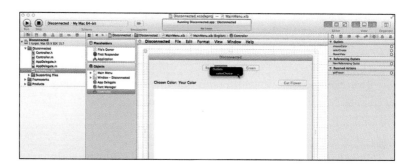

Interface Builder knows what type of object is allowed to connect to a given outlet, so it displays only the outlets appropriate for the connection you are trying to make.

Repeat this process for the static text field with the text **Your Color**, connecting it to the chosenColor outlet, and the web view, connecting to flowerView.

Connecting to Actions

Connecting to actions is a bit different. An object's events trigger actions (methods) in your code. So, the connection direction reverses; you connect from the object invoking an event to the view controller of its scene.

Although it is possible to Control-drag and create a connection in the same manner you did with outlets, this is not recommended for iOS apps. Many objects have more than a single possible event associated with them (putting your find down on a button versus picking it up, for example). In OS X development, objects typically connect to an action via a single selector (a named method), so the process is more straightforward.

To create your connection, select the object that will be connecting to the action and open the Connections Inspector by clicking the arrow icon at the top of the Xcode Utility area. You can also show the inspector by choosing View, Utilities, Show Connections Inspector (or by pressing Option+Command+6).

The Connections Inspector, shown in Figure 9.6, shows a list of the events that the object, or, in the case of an NSButton, a selector under Sent Actions. Beside the event (or selector) is an open circle. To connect to an action in your code, click and drag from one of these circles to the controller object in the Document Outline.

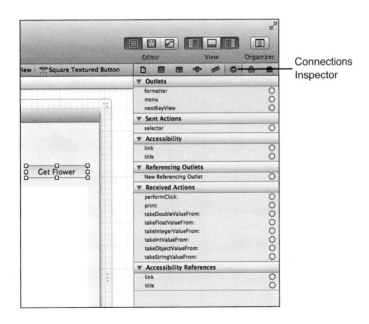

Connections Inspector

FIGURE 9.6
Use the Connections Inspector to view existing connections and to make new ones.

For example, to connect the Get Flower button to the `getFlower` method, follow these steps:

1. Select the button.

2. Open the Connections Inspector (Option+Command+6).

3. Drag from the circle beside the Sent Action selector to the Controller object, as demonstrated in Figure 9.7.

FIGURE 9.7
Drag from the selector or event to the controller.

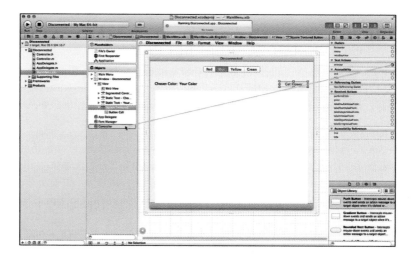

4. When prompted, choose the `getFlower` action, shown in Figure 9.8.

FIGURE 9.8
Choose the action you want the interface element to invoke.

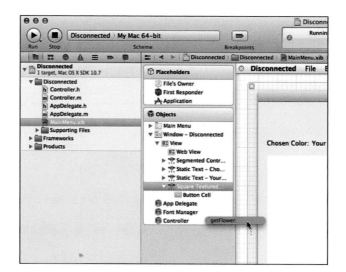

Repeat this same process for the segmented control, connecting its selector to the same getFlower action. This adds functionality so that when users update their color selection, a new flower is grabbed without users having to click the Get Flower button.

After a connection has been made, the inspector updates to show the event and the action that it calls, as shown in Figure 9.9. If you click other already-connected objects, you'll notice that the Connections Inspector shows their connections to outlets and actions (under the Referencing Outlets section).

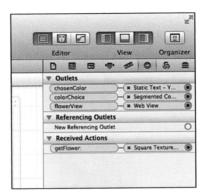

FIGURE 9.9
The Connections Inspector updates to show the actions and outlets that an object references (here, the controller).

Well done! You have just linked an interface to the code that supports it. Click Run on the Xcode toolbar to build and run the application.

Prebuilt Actions

Although most of your connections in Interface Builder will be between objects and outlets and actions you have defined in your code, certain objects implement built-in actions that do not require you to write a single line of code. These are listed in the Connections Inspector as received actions.

The web view, for example, implements actions, including goForward and goBack. Using these actions, you could add basic navigation functionality to a web view by dragging from a button's event or selector directly to the web view object (rather than dragging to the controller itself). As described previously, you are prompted for the action to connect to, but this time, it isn't an action you have had to code yourself.

The Accessibility sections within the Connections Inspector are used for creating applications accessible to those with special needs. Unfortunately, developing for accessibility is beyond the scope of this book, but you'll find plenty of information available by searching for "accessibility" in the Xcode documentation.

Did You Know?

Editing Connections with the Quick Inspector

One of the errors that I commonly make when connecting my interfaces is creating
a connection that I didn't intend. A bit of overzealous dragging, and suddenly your
interface is wired up incorrectly and won't work. To review the connections that are
in place, you select an object and use the Connections Inspector discussed previously, or you can open the Quick Inspector by right-clicking any object in the
Interface Builder editor or Document Outline. This opens a floating window that
contains all the outlets and actions either referenced or received by the object, as
shown in Figure 9.10.

FIGURE 9.10
Right-click to
quickly inspect
any object
connections.

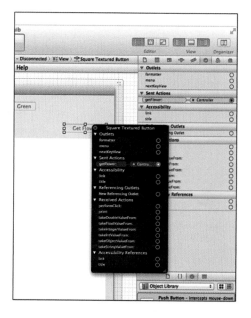

Besides viewing the connections that are in place, you can remove a connection by
clicking the X next to a connected object (see Figure 9.10). You can even create new
connections using the same "click and drag from the circle to an object" approach
that you performed with the Connections Inspector. Click the X in the upper-left corner of the window to close the Quick Inspector.

By the Way

Clicking an object, such as a button, shows you all the connections related to that
object, but it does *not* show you everything you have connected in the Interface
Builder editor. Because almost all the connections you create will go to and from a
view's controller, choosing it and then opening the inspector (or the Quick
Inspector) will give you a more complete picture of what connections you have
made.

Writing Connection Code with Interface Builder

You have now created connections from user interface objects to the corresponding outlets and actions that have already been defined in code. But how did those outlet and action definitions get written? You could certainly have coded them by hand, as described earlier this hour. But why do that when Xcode will do all the setup for you?

Although it is impossible for Xcode to write your application, it will create the instance variables and properties for your app's interface objects, as well as "stubs" of the methods your interface will trigger. All you need to do is drag and drop the Interface Builder objects into your source code files. Using this feature is completely optional, but it does help save time and avoid syntax errors. To demonstrate this process, we re-create the exact same application, but this time for the iPhone or iPad. We start with a defined interface, but no outlets, actions, or connections. After a bit of clicking and dragging, we have a full app.

Open the Hour 9 projects folder, choose either the iPad or iPhone project folders, and then drill down to the Disconnected project within. Double-click the Disconnected.xcodeproj file to open the project in Xcode. Again, expand the project code group (Disconnected), but this time, click the MainStoryboard.storyboard file. Interface Builder updates and shows the scene for the application, as shown in Figure 9.11.

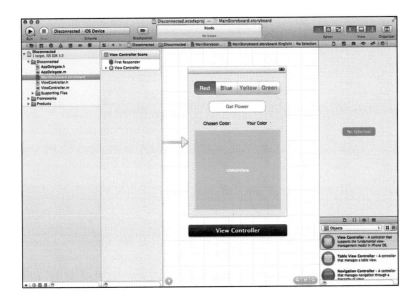

FIGURE 9.11
The scene for the iOS version of the application is displayed.

Implementation Overview

As with the previous tutorial, you are working with an interface that consists of a segmented button bar, a push button, text label, and a web view. This time, however, instead of just connecting to predefined outlets and actions, you actually create the outlets and actions from scratch. The project you have just opened is based on the Single View iOS application template and has had no code added to the classes; only a basic interface has been created in the storyboard.

Identifying the Outlets and Actions

In this exercise, we create outlets and actions that are identical to the ones that we used for connections earlier. To recap, we have three outlets:

- **colorChoice**: The segmented control
- **chosenColor**: The label
- **flowerView**: The web view

And we have a single action:

- **getFlower**: Triggered by the button Get Flower and by touching the segmented control

I recommend creating a list of your XIB/storyboard objects and their corresponding properties and actions during the planning phase of your development. This will keep you on track and help make sure that you wire your interfaces correctly as you work through your implementation.

Creating Outlets

To create our outlets, we need to be able to drag from the Interface Builder editor to the area of the code where we want to add an outlet or an action. In other words, we need to be able to see the ViewController.h file at the same time we see the view that we are connecting. This is where the Assistant Editor feature of Xcode comes in very handy.

With the MainStoryboard.storyboard visible in the Interface Builder editor, click the Assistant Editor button (the middle button in the Editor section of the toolbar). The ViewController.h file automatically opens to the right of the interface because Xcode knows that is the file that you need to work with while editing the view.

How Does Xcode Know Which File Goes with the UI?

Xcode knows the class `ViewController` is the view controller class responsible for controlling the view. This relationship is established by selecting the View Controller object in the Document Outline and then using the Interface Builder Identity Inspector to choose which class implements the controller.

If you're on a MacBook, you're likely to find your workspace a bit cramped. To conserve space, use the leftmost and rightmost "view" buttons on the toolbar to disable the Navigation and Utility areas of the Xcode window. You can also use the disclosure arrow in the lower-left corner of Interface Builder editor itself to toggle the Document Outline off.

Start by connecting the segmented control we created for choosing a color. Recall that we want this to be represented by an instance variable and corresponding property called `colorChoice`. When this is in place, we repeat the process for the remaining outlets:

1. Control-drag from the segmented control or its icon in the Document Outline. Drag all the way into the source editor for ViewController.h, releasing the mouse button when your cursor is just under the `@interface` line. As you drag, you see a visual indication of what Xcode is planning to insert when you release the button, as shown in Figure 9.12.

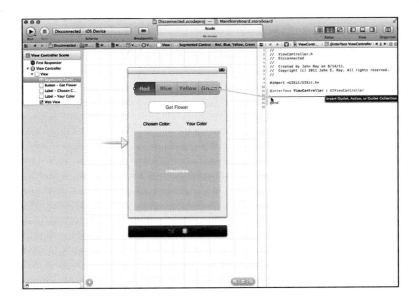

FIGURE 9.12
Xcode indicates where it will insert code.

2. When you release the mouse button, you are prompted to define an outlet. Be sure that the Connection menu is set to Outlet, storage is Strong, and the type is set to `UISegmentedControl`, because that's what the object is. Finally, specify the name you want to use for the instance variable and property (`colorChoice`), and then click Connect, as shown in Figure 9.13.

FIGURE 9.13
Define your
outlet.

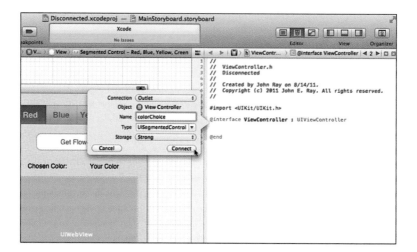

3. When you click Connect, Xcode automatically inserts the proper `@property` directive with `IBOutlet`, `@synthesize` directive (in ViewController.m), and cleanup code (also in ViewController.m). What's more, it has made the connection between the outlet you just defined, and the code itself. If you want to verify this, just check the Connections Inspector or right-click the field to open the Quick Inspector, as you learned earlier this hour.

Repeat the process for the text label, dragging from it to just below the `@property` line that was inserted. This time choose `UILabel` as the type and `chosenColor` as the name of the outlet. And now do this one more time for the web view: Drag from it to below the last `@property` line. Use `UIWebView` as the type and `flowerView` as the name of the outlet.

You've just made all the outlets, properties, and connections for the user interface. Now let's see how to go about creating and connecting the action.

Creating Actions

Adding the action and making the connection between the button (Get Flower) and the action follows the exact same pattern as the outlets you just added. The only difference is that actions are usually defined after properties in an interface file, so you just drag to a slightly different location:

So, to add the action and make the connection between the button and the action, follow these steps:

1. Control-drag from the button in the view to the area of the interface file (ViewController.h) just below the three @property directives that you added. Again, as you drag, you see Xcode provide visual feedback about where it is going to insert code. Release the mouse button when you've targeted the line where you want the action code to be inserted.

2. As with the outlets, you are prompted to configure the connection, as demonstrated in Figure 9.14. This time, be sure to choose Action as the connection type; otherwise, Xcode tries to insert another outlet.

3. Set the name to getFlower (the method name chosen earlier).

4. Be sure that the Event pop-up menu is set to Touch Up Inside to configure the event that will trigger the action.

5. Leave the rest of the fields set to their defaults and click Connect.

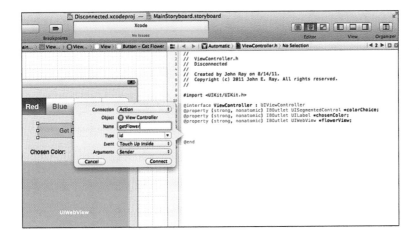

FIGURE 9.14
Create the action.

That's it. You have just set up your action. You still need to implement the logic, but the Get Flower button will now trigger the getFlower method. You'll even find a stub for this method in the ViewController.m file.

As a final step in finishing up the UI connections, use the technique you practiced in the first tutorial to connect the Value Changed or Touch Up Inside event for the segmented control to the getFlower action you've created. Because the action is already defined, you need to drag from the Connections Inspector to the View Controller object; don't redefine the method in your code. Making this connection is optional, but it does enable touches in the segmented control to retrieve a new flower image.

Implementing the getFlower Logic

To make this a fully functional application, you need to implement the getFlower method in ViewController.m. Open this file in the source editor, and edit the stub method to match the code in Listing 9.1.

LISTING 9.1   A Possible getFlower Implementation

```
-(IBAction)getFlower:(id)sender {
        NSString *outputHTML;
        NSString *color;
        NSString *colorVal;
        int colorNum;
        colorNum=colorChoice.selectedSegmentIndex;
        switch (colorNum) {
                case 0:
                        color=@"Red";
                        colorVal=@"red";
                        break;
                case 1:
                        color=@"Blue";
                        colorVal=@"blue";
                        break;
                case 2:
                        color=@"Yellow";
                        colorVal=@"yellow";
                        break;
                case 3:
                        color=@"Green";
                        colorVal=@"green";
                        break;
        }
        chosenColor.text=[[NSString alloc] initWithFormat:@"%@",color];
        outputHTML=[[NSString alloc] initWithFormat:@"<body style='margin:
         0px; padding: 0px'><img height='1200'
         src='http://www.floraphotographs.com/showrandom.php?color=%@'></body>"
         ,colorVal];
        [flowerView loadHTMLString:outputHTML baseURL:nil];
}
```

**Watch
Out!**

Type Without Line Breaks

To get the code to fit on the page, the outputHTML initialization and assignment
line was broken across several lines in this listing. When entering this code, you
must type it as a single line.

Run the application and test the interface. It should work exactly as planned, as
shown in Figure 9.15.

FIGURE 9.15
The working
Disconnected
iPhone app.

Summary

This was a very hands-on hour that walked you through the process of connecting
objects to outlets and actions. First, you practiced using predefined outlets and
actions. You learned how to use the Connections Inspector to target specific events
for an object, and how to use it to see the existing connections that are already in
place. You also practiced using the Xcode tools to create outlets and actions from
scratch. Using the Assistant Editor, you built new outlets and properties and wired
them to your interface without having to type a single line of code.

You will use these processes in nearly every project that you create, so being comfortable with them is a key piece of being a successful Xcode developer. Keep practicing,
and you'll find that making connections from Interface Builder quickly becomes second nature.

Q&A

Q. *I keep seeing references to segues in the Connections Inspector. What are they?*

A. Segues are used in iOS to transition from one scene to another. Revisit Hour 8, "Creating User Interfaces," for more information.

Q. *Is there a way to make all of my connections from one place?*

A. Absolutely. The Connections Inspector can be your one-stop-shop for all your outlet and action connections. Instead of dragging from objects in the UI design to your interface (.h) file, you can use the Connections Inspector's New Referencing Outlet connection as the starting point for dragging into the interface file, thereby creating a new outlet or action.

Q. *How do I know what objects support what events and actions?*

A. Read the documentation. Over time, you'll start to recognize that similar controls support similar actions and events. The only way to learn what the options are, however, is to experiment with using the controls and read the documentation for their classes.

Workshop

Quiz

1. The Assistant Editor is not useful when you are creating outlets and actions. True or false?

2. Are the events supported by controls shared between iOS and OS X?

3. A single UI object can trigger actions. True or false?

Answers

1. False. The Assistant Editor enables you to insert outlets and actions by dragging from your interface into the corresponding controller code file.

2. No. Use the Connections Inspector to see what events (actions) your controls support. iOS tends to have many more possible events per UI control than OS X.

3. False. You can create connections to an action from any number of UI objects.

Activities

1. Complete the tutorials provided within this hour's lesson, and then review the connections using the Connections Inspector. Try to remove a connection. What happens, if anything, to the underlying code? Next, try to delete the underlying code for an outlet. Does it also delete the UI connection?

2. Create a new project (OS X or iOS) and begin exploring the different UI objects that are available. Add each to a storyboard/XIB file, and then use the Connections Inspector to see what types of events (actions) they can receive or act on. Feel free to use the provided apps as a starting point for this exploration.

HOUR 10

Creating iOS Application Workflows with Storyboards

What You'll Learn in This Hour:

▶ How to create multiple scenes in the storyboard

▶ The use of segues to transition between scenes

▶ Ways to share data between scenes

▶ How to build applications with navigation and tab bar controllers

In the preceding hour, you learned how to connect an iOS application UI to code. This took place within a single scene, which is good for simple apps, but limiting for serious development. In this hour, we break through the single-scene limit and introduce the ability to create applications with multiple scenes—in other words, multiple view controllers and multiple views.

You learn how to create new scenes and the new view controller classes needed to back them up. You also explore how to visually define your transitions between scenes and trigger them automatically, or programmatically. Because it is easier to understand these concepts by using them, this hour ends with some hands-on practice for multiscene development.

The Power of Storyboards

Over the past few hours, you have learned how the Interface Builder editor can create interfaces and connect them to code. What you haven't seen, however, is how iOS applications can use storyboarding to develop their entire workflow.

Many iOS apps lend themselves to a single-view approach—which is all you have seen so far in the storyboard examples. It is rare to download an app that doesn't have configuration screens, help screens, or other displays of information that go beyond the initial view that is loaded at runtime.

To use features like these in your apps, you must create multiple scenes in your storyboard file. Recall that a scene is defined by the presence of a view controller and a view. Imagine how much functionality you could introduce with unlimited scenes (views and view controllers). With the iOS project storyboard, that's exactly what you can do.

Not only that, but you can literally "draw" the connections between different scenes. Want to display an information screen if the user touches a Help button? Just drag from your button to a new scene. It "just works." Figure 10.1 shows a multiscene application design with segues.

FIGURE 10.1
A multiscene application design.

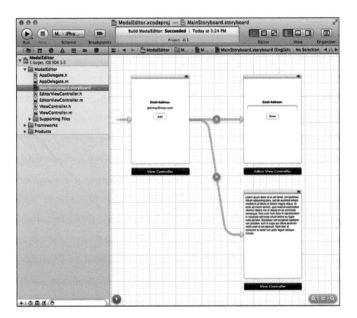

Storyboard Terminology

Before we head into the specifics of multiscene development, you should learn a few terms. Several of these terms you have learned previously but might not have really had to think about the until now include

- ▶ **View controller:** A class that manages the user's interactions with their iDevice interface.

- ▶ **View:** The visual layout that a user sees onscreen.

▶ **Scene:** A unique combination of view controller and view. Imagine you're building an image-editing application. You may choose to develop scenes for selecting files to edit, another scene for implementing the editor, another for applying filters, and so on.

▶ **Segue:** A segue is a transition between scenes, often with a visual transition effect applied. There are multiple different types of segues available depending on the type of view controller you're using.

▶ **Modal Views:** A modal view is one that is displayed over top of an original view when user interactions are required. A segue to a modal view is segue you'll make most often.

▶ **Relationship:** A "segue" of sorts for certain types of view controllers, such as the tab bar controller. Relationships are created between buttons on a master "tab bar" that display independent scenes when touched.

▶ **Storyboard:** The file that contains the scene, segue, and relationship definitions for your project.

You need to create new class files to support the requirement for multiple view controllers. If you need a quick refresher on adding new files to Xcode, see Hour 5, "Managing Files in Xcode." Other than that, the only prerequisite is the ability to Control-drag—something you should be very good at after Hour 9, "Connecting a GUI to Code."

The storyboard concepts in this hour require a bit of supporting code, so skimming is not recommended.

A Different Perspective

You have just read about the different pieces that you need to know to create a multiscene application, but this doesn't necessarily help you conceptualize what Apple's "storyboarding" concept is trying to achieve.

Think of it this way: A storyboard provides an area where you can sketch out, visually, your application's visual design and workflow. Each scene is a different screen that your user will encounter. Each segue is a transition between scenes. If you're the type of person who thinks visually, you'll find that with a little practice, you can go from a paper sketch of an application's operation and design to a working prototype in the Xcode storyboard very, very quickly.

The Anatomy of a Multiscene Project

To create an application with multiple scenes and segues, you must first know how to add new view controller and view pairings to your project. For each of these, you also need supporting class files where you can code up the logic for your additional scenes. To give you a better idea of how this works, let's use a typical iOS Single View Application template as a starting point. Feel free to follow along with an empty iOS project if you want—but we build a simple (but complete) example of a multiscene application at the end of the hour.

The Single View Application template has a single view controller and a single view—in other words, a single scene. This doesn't mean, however, that we're stuck with that configuration. You can expand a single-view application to support as many scenes as you want; the template just provides a convenient starting point.

Adding Additional Scenes to a Storyboard

To add a new scene to a storyboard, follow these steps:

1. Open the project's storyboard file (often MainStoryboard.storyboard) in the Interface Builder editor.

2. Make sure the Object Library (Control+Option+Command+3) is visible and type **view controller** in the Search field to show the view controller objects that are available, as shown in Figure 10.2.

FIGURE 10.2
Find the view controller objects in the Object Library.

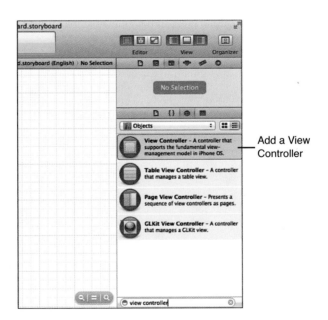

3. Drag the View Controller object into an empty portion of the Editor area.

The view controller adds itself, with a corresponding view, to your storyboard, and just like that, you'll have a new scene, as shown in Figure 10.3.

You can drag the new view around in the storyboard editor to position it somewhere convenient.

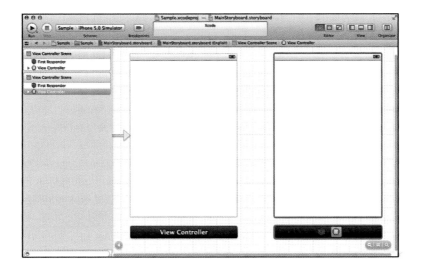

FIGURE 10.3
Adding a new view controller/view creates a new scene.

> If you find it difficult to grab and drag the new view around in the editor, use the object bar beneath it. It provides a convenient handle for moving the object around.

By the Way

Naming Scenes

After adding a new scene to a project, you'll notice there's a bit of a problem brewing in the Document Outline (Editor, Show Document Outline). By default, each scene is named based on its view controller class. By default, Single View Application templates include a view controller class called `ViewController`, so the Document Outline shows the default scene as View Controller Scene. Once we add a new scene, it doesn't have a view controller class assigned yet, so it also appears as View Controller Scene. Add another, and the scene also appears as View Controller Scene...and so on.

To deal with the ambiguity, you have two options: First, you can add and assign view controller classes to the new scenes; the scenes adopt the name of the class. This is necessary anyway, but sometimes its nicer to have a plain English name for a scene that can be anything we want without it reflecting the underlying code (John's Awesome Image Editor Scene makes a horrible name for a view controller class).

This brings us to the second approach: applying your own name to the scene. To label a scene using any arbitrary string you want, select its view controller in the Document Outline, and then open the Identity Inspector and expand the Identity section, as shown in Figure 10.4. Use the Label field to enter a name for the scene. Xcode automatically tacks *Scene* onto the end, so there's no need to add that.

FIGURE 10.4
Label the view controller to help differentiate between scenes.

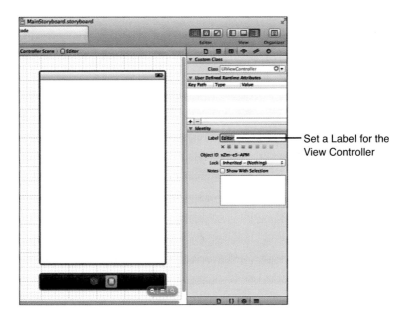

Set a Label for the View Controller

Adding Supporting View Controller Subclasses

After establishing the new scenes in your storyboard, you need to couple them to actual code. In the iOS Single View Application template, the initial view's view controller is already configured to be an instance of the ViewController class—implemented by editing the ViewController.h and ViewController.m files. You need to create similar files to support any new scenes that are added.

> If you're just adding a scene that displays static content (such as a Help or About page), you do not need to add a custom subclass. You can use the default class assigned to the scene, UIViewController, but you won't be able to add any interactivity.

To add a new subclass of `UIViewController` to your project, make sure that the Project Navigator is visible (Command+1), and then click the + icon at the bottom-left corner of the window. When prompted, choose the iOS Cocoa Touch template category, click the Objective-C class icon, and then click Next.

You are asked to name your class. Name it something that differentiates it from other view controllers in your project. **EditorViewController** is better than **ViewControllerTwo**, for example. Choose a subclass of `UIViewController`, as shown in Figure 10.5. If you're creating the controller for use in an iPad project, check the Targeted for iPad check box, and then click Next.

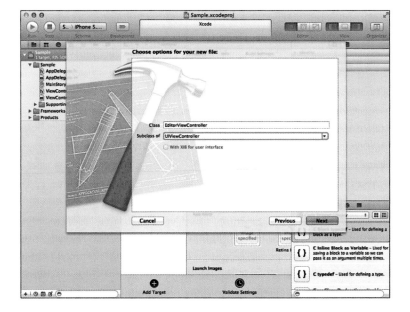

FIGURE 10.5
Choose the `UIViewController` subclass.

Finally, you're prompted for where to save your new class. Use the group pop-up menu at the bottom of the dialog to choose your main project code group, and then click Create. Your new class is added to the project and ready for coding—but it still isn't connected to the scene you defined.

To associate a scene's view controller with the `UIViewController` subclass, shift your attention back to the Interface Builder editor. Within the Document Outline, select the view controller line for the new scene, and then open the Identity Inspector (Option+Command+3). In the Custom Class section, use the drop-down menu to select the name of the class you just created (such as `EditorViewController`), as shown in Figure 10.6.

FIGURE 10.6
Associate the
view controller
with the new
class.

After the view controller is assigned to a class, you can develop in the new scene exactly in the same way you developed the initial scene—but the code will go in your new view controller's class. This takes us most of the way to creating a multi-scene application, but the two scenes are still completely independent. If you develop for the new scene, it's essentially like developing a new application; there is no way for the scenes to exchange data and no way to transition between them.

Sharing Properties and Methods

As you add multiple view controllers (and any other classes) to your project, there's a good chance they need to display and exchange information. For your classes to "know about each other" programmatically, they need to import one another's interface files. For example, if MyEditorClass needs to access properties and methods in MyGraphicsClass, MyEditorClass.h includes #import "MyGraphicsClass.h" at its start.

Simple enough, right? Unfortunately, it isn't always that easy. If both classes need access to one another, and both try to import the interface file from the other class, you'll most likely end up with an error because the import lines have just created a reference loop. One class references the other, which references the other, which references the other, and so on.

To deal with this situation, you must change your code around a bit and make use of the @class directive. @class enables an interface file to reference another class without creating a loop. Using the hypothetical `MyGraphicsClass` and `MyEditorClass` as examples of classes that both need to reference one another, the references could be added like this:

1. In MyEditorClass.h, add `#import "MyGraphicsClass.h"`. One half of the two references can be implemented with just an `#import`; nothing special needs to happen.

2. In MyGraphicsClass.h, add `@class MyEditorClass;` after the existing `#import` lines.

3. In MyGraphicsClass.m, add the `#import "MyEditorClass.h"` line after the existing `#import` lines.

The first `#import` is performed normally, but to get around the circular reference, the second class's `#import` moves to the implementation file, and a `@class` directive is added to the second class's interface file. This may seem convoluted, but it works.

After you have created your new scenes, assigned the view controller classes, and added the appropriate references between classes, you're ready to create segues—the mechanism that enables you to transition from scene to scene.

Creating a Segue

Creating a segue between scenes uses the same Control-drag mechanism that you saw in Hour 9 for making connections between an object and an outlet. For example, consider a two-scene storyboard where you want to add a button to the initial scene that, when clicked, transitions to the Second Scene. To create this segue, you Control-drag from the button to the second scene's view controller (targeting either the visual representation of the scene itself or the view controller line in the Document Outline), as shown in Figure 10.7.

When you release your mouse button, a Storyboard Segues box appears, as shown in Figure 10.8. Here you can choose the style of segue that you're creating—most likely Modal. A total of five potential options may appear:

▶ **Modal:** Transition to another scene for the purposes of completing a task. When finished, we dismiss the scene, and it transitions back to the original view. This is the primary segue we will be using.

▶ **Push:** Create a chain of scenes where the user can move forward or back. This is used with navigation view controllers.

▶ **Replace (iPad only):** Replace the current scene with another. This is used in some specialized iPad view controllers. This is used with a popular iPad view controller called the "split-view controller."

▶ **Popover (iPad only):** Displays the scene in a pop-up "window" over top of the current view.

▶ **Custom:** Used for programming a custom transition between scenes.

FIGURE 10.7
Control-drag from the object to the new scene's view controller.

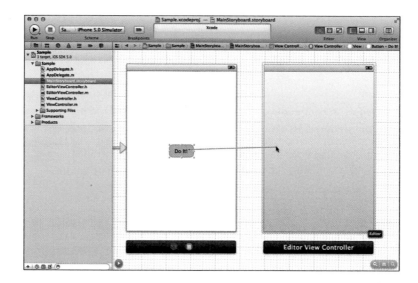

FIGURE 10.8
Choose the segue style to create.

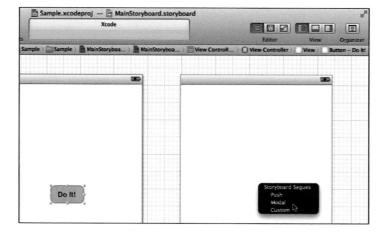

For most projects, you'll want to choose a modal transition—which is what we use here. The other segues are used in very specific conditions, some of which we cover later this hour.

You can create a segue that is not attached to any particular UI element by Control-dragging from one scene's view controller to another. This creates a segue that you can trigger, in your code, from a gesture or other event.

Configuring a Segue

Once the segue is added to your project, you see a line added to the Editor area that visually ties your two scenes together. You can rearrange the individual scenes within the editor to create a layout that maps how the application will flow. This layout is solely for your benefit; it doesn't change how the application will operate.

Notice, as well, a representation of it in your Document Outline. The scene that initiates a segue shows a new line in the outline: Segue from <origin> to <destination>. Selecting the segue line gives you the opportunity to configure its style, transition type, identifier, and presentation (iPad only), as shown in Figure 10.9.

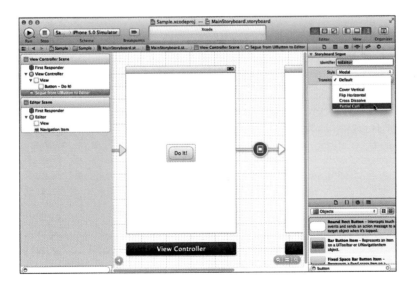

FIGURE 10.9
Configure each segue you add.

The identifier is an arbitrary string that you can use to trigger a segue manually or to identify which segue is underway programmatically (if you have multiple segues configured). Even if you do not plan to use multiple segues, it is a good idea to name this something meaningful (toEditor, toGameView, and so on).

The transition type is a visual animation that is played as iOS moves from one scene to another. You have four possible options:

▶ **Cover vertical:** The new scene slides up over the old scene.

▶ **Flip horizontal:** The view flips around horizontally, revealing the new scene on the "back."

▶ **Cross dissolve:** The old scene fades out while the new scene fades in.

▶ **Partial curl:** The old scene "curls up" like a piece of paper, revealing the new scene underneath.

On the iPad, you can also set a presentation attribute. This determines how the new modal view is displayed on the screen. The iPad has more screen real estate than an iPhone, so it can do things a little differently. You can choose from four possible presentation styles:

▶ **Form sheet:** Sizes the scene smaller than the screen (regardless of orientation), showing the original scene behind it. This, for all intents and purposes, is the iPad equivalent of a "window."

▶ **Page sheet:** Sizes the scene so that it is presented in the portrait format.

▶ **Full screen:** Sizes the view so that covers the full screen.

▶ **Current context:** Uses the same style display as the scene that is displaying it.

> **Match Your Styles with Suitable Transitions**
>
> Not all styles are compatible with all transitions. A page curl, for example, cannot take place on a form sheet that does not completely fill the screen. Attempting to use an incompatible combination will result in a crash. So, if you have chosen a bad pair, you'll find out pretty quickly (or you could review the documentation for the transition/style you plan to use).

After setting the identifier, style, transition, and presentation for a segue, you're ready to use it. Without the developer writing any code, an application that has followed these steps can now present two fully interactive views and transition between them. What it cannot do, however, is interact with them programmatically. In addition, once you transition from one view to another, you cannot transition back. For that, you need some code. Let's take a look at how you can create and trigger modal segues programmatically, and, perhaps most important, dismiss a modal segue when you have finished using it.

Controlling Modal Segues Manually

Although it is easy to create segues with a single Control-drag, you need to interact with them manually in several situations. If you create a modal segue between view controllers that you want to trigger manually, for example, you need to know how to initiate it in code. When a user is done with the task in another scene, he also needs a mechanism to dismiss the modal scene and transition back to the original scene. Let's handle these scenarios now.

Starting the Segue

First, to transition to an scene using a segue that you have defined in your storyboard but don't want to be triggered automatically, you use the UIViewController instance method performSegueWithIdentifier:sender. For example, within your initial view controller, you can initiate a segue with the identifier toMyGame using the following line:

```
[self performSegueWithIdentifier:@"toMyGame" sender:self];
```

That's it! As soon as the line is executed, the segue starts and the transition occurs. The sender parameter should be set to the object that initiated the segue (it doesn't matter what that object is)—it is made available as a property during the segue if your code needs to determine what object started the process.

Dismissing a Modal Scene

When you execute a modal segue (either automatically or manually), there's one teensy problem: There is no way back to your original scene. After users have finished interacting with your view, you'll probably want to provide them with a means of getting back to where they started. At present, there is no facility in modal segues to allow for this, so you must turn to code. The UIViewController method dismissViewControllerAnimated:completion can be used in either the view controller that displayed the modal scene or the modal scene's view controller to transition back to the original scene:

```
[self dismissViewControllerAnimated:YES completion:nil];
```

The completion block is an optional block of code that is executed when the transition has completed. After you have dismissed a scene presented modally, control is returned to the original scene, and users can interact with it as they normally would.

Passing Data Between Scenes

You know how to create and display scenes, but one very critical piece of the puzzle is missing: the ability to share information between the different scenes in an application. Right now, they act as entirely independent applications—which is perfectly fine if that is your intention, but chances are, you want an integrated user experience. Let's make that happen.

The most straightforward way for any class to exchange information with any other is through properties and methods that it exposes in its interface file. The only trouble with this is that we need to be able to get an instance of one scene's view controller from another, and, at present, when using a segue we create visually, these are not entirely obvious.

The prepareForSegue:sender Method

One way to get references to the view controllers in a segue is by implementing the prepareForSegue:sender method. This method is automatically called on the initiating view controller when a segue is about to take place away from it. It returns an instance of UIStoryboardSegue and the object that initiated the segue. The UIStoryboard object contains the properties sourceViewController and destinationViewController, representing the view controller starting the segue (the source) and the view controller about to be displayed (the destination).

Listing 10.1 shows a simple implementation of this approach. In this example, the code transitions from an initial view controller (an instance of ViewController) to a new view controller, which is an instance of a hypothetical EditorViewController class.

LISTING 10.1   Use prepareForSegue:sender to Grab the View Controllers

```
- (void)prepareForSegue:(UIStoryboardSegue *)segue sender:(id)sender {

    ViewController *startingViewController;
    EditorViewController *destinationViewController;

    startingViewController=(ViewController *)segue.sourceViewController;
    destinationViewController=
            (EditorViewController *)segue.destinationViewController;

}
```

First, the method declares two variables to reference the source and destination controllers. Then they are assigned to typecast versions of the source and destination properties returned by the UIStoryboardSegue object.

Once there is a reference to the destination view controller, however, you can set and access properties on it—even changing the presentation and transition styles before it is displayed. If it is assigned to an instance variable/property, it can be accessed anywhere within the source view controller.

What if you want the destination view controller to send information back to the source? In this case, only the source can communicate with the destination because that's where the prepareForSegue:sender method is implemented. One option is to create a property on the destination controller that stores a reference to the source controller. Another approach is to use built-in properties of UIViewController that make working with modally presented scenes *easy easy easy*.

It's Not Just for Getting the Controllers

The prepareForSegue:sender isn't just for getting the view controllers involved in a segue. It can also be used to make decisions during a segue. Because a scene can define multiple different segues, you may need to know which segue is happening and react accordingly. To do this, use the UIStoryboardSegue property identifier to get the identifier string you set for the segue:

```
if ([segue.identifier isEqualToString:@"myAwesomeSegue"]) {
    // Do something unique for this segue
}
```

The Easy Way

The prepareForSegue:sender gives us a generic way to work with any segue that is taking place in an application, but it doesn't always represent the easiest way to get a handle on the view controllers involved. For modal segues, the UIViewController class gives us properties that make it easy to reference the source and destination view controllers: presentingViewController and presentedViewController.

In other words, you can reference the original (source) view controller within a view controller that has just been displayed by accessing self.presentingViewController. Similarly, you can get a reference to the destination view controller from the original controller with self.presentedViewController. It's as easy as that. For example, assume that the original view controller is an instance of the class ViewController and that the destination view controller is an instance of EditorViewController.

From the EditorViewController, you can access properties in the original view controller with the following syntax:

```
((ViewController *)self.presentingViewController).<property>
```

And within the original view controller, you can manipulate properties in the destination view controller with this:

```
((EditorViewController *)self.presentedViewController).<property>
```

The parentheses with the class name is necessary to typecast the `presentingViewController`/`presentedViewController` properties to the right object types. Without this notation, Xcode would not know what types of view controllers these were, and we wouldn't be able to access their properties.

Making Advanced Segues

Segues can do more than just link two scenes together: They can work with specialized iOS view controllers to add advanced functionality to applications. In this section, we review how segues work with two common types of iOS controllers: navigation controllers and tab bar controllers.

Storyboarding Navigation Controllers

The navigation controller (`UINavigationController`) class presents a series of scenes that represent hierarchical information. In other words, one scene presents a high-level view of a topic, a second scene drills down further, a third scene even further, and so on. For example, the iPhone version of the Contacts application presents a list of contact groups. Touching a group opens a list of contacts within that group. Touching an individual contact displays details on that person, as shown in Figure 10.10. At any point in time, a user can back out of a level of detail and return to the previous level—or jump all the way to the starting point, called the root.

Managing this transition between scenes is the navigation controller. It creates a "stack" of view controllers. The root view controller is at the bottom. As a user navigates deeper into the scenes, each successive view controller is pushed on the stack, with the current scene's view controller at the very top. To return to a previous level, the navigation controller pops the topmost controller off the stack and returns to the one below it.

The terminology of *push* and *pop* is used to describe navigation controllers throughout the iOS documentation. You'll even be showing new scenes under a navigation controller by using the push segue.

FIGURE 10.10
Navigation
controllers are
prevalent
in iOS.

Navigation Bars, Items, and Bar Button Items

In addition to managing the stack of view controllers, the navigation controller manages a navigation bar (UINavigationBar). A navigation bar is populated from an instance of a navigation item (UINavigationItem) that is added to each scene that falls under the navigation controller.

By default, the navigation item for a scene contains a title for that scene and a Back button. The Back button is added as a bar button item (UIBarButtonItem) within the navigation item. You can even drag additional bar button items into the navigation item to add your own custom buttons to the navigation bar that is displayed for that scene.

I fully expect that if you have made it through that description, you're getting a bit worried about having to manually handle all of those different objects (and that's why doing this in code is not trivial). Don't fear. Interface Builder makes it painless, and after you see how each scene is constructed, you'll have no problem working with all these objects in your apps.

Using Navigation Controllers with Storyboards

Adding a navigation controller to a storyboard is very similar to adding a view controller. It looks a bit different, but the process is the same. Let's assume you're starting with a Single View Application template. Now, just follow these steps:

1. Establish the code files for one or more view controller subclasses to handle the user's interactions within a given navigation controller scene. This is the same as any other scene.

2. Open the application storyboard file in the Interface Builder editor.

3. If you want your entire application to fall under the navigation controller, select the view controller in the default view and delete it. (Remove the corresponding ViewController.m and .h files, as well.) This removes the default scene.

4. Drag an instance of the Navigation Controller object from the Object Library into the Document Outline or the Editor area. This adds what appears to be two scenes to your project, as shown in Figure 10.11.

FIGURE 10.11
Add a navigation controller to your project.

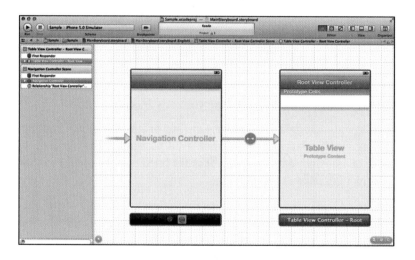

The scene labeled Navigation Controller Scene represents the navigation controller. It is just a placeholder for the object that is going to control all the scenes that fall underneath it. Although you won't want to change much about the controller, you can use the Attributes Inspector to customize its appearance slightly (choosing a color scheme/tint, for example, if you want).

The navigation controller is connected via a *relationship* to a table view controller scene called Root View Controller. This is the scene where you begin your editing. Although Apple initially gives you a table view controller (UITableViewController) as your Root View Controller scene, you can replace it with anything you want, including a simple view controller (UIViewController). Whatever scene you present will have the navigation bar at the top, and you'll be able to use a push segue to transition to another scene.

Setting the Navigation Bar Item Attributes

To change the title in the navigation bar, just double-click and start editing, or select the navigation item in the scene and open the Attributes Inspector (Option+Command+4), as shown in Figure 10.12.

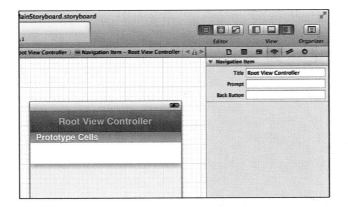

FIGURE 10.12
Customize the Navigation Item for the scene.

You can change three attributes:

▶ **Title:** The title string that is shown at the top of the view

▶ **Prompt:** A line of text that provides instruction to the user (if needed) and is shown above the title

▶ **Back button:** The text that appears in the Back button of the next scene

Yes, you can edit the text of the button that appears in a scene you don't even have yet. By default, when you transition from one navigation controller scene to another, the "title" of the previous scene shows up as the title of the Back button in the next scene. Sometimes, however, the title may be long, or not necessarily appropriate. In these cases, you can set the Back button attribute to whatever string you want, and if the user drills down to the next scene, that text is displayed in the button that takes you back to the scene.

Editing Back button text does one additional thing: Because iOS can no longer use its default behavior to create a Back button, it creates a new custom bar button item within the navigation item that contains the title you wanted. You can customize this bar button item even more—changing its color and appearance using the Attributes Inspector.

So far, there is only a single scene under the navigation controller, so the Back button would never be displayed. Let's see how you can chain together multiple scenes to create the drill-down hierarchy that navigation controllers are known for.

Adding Additional Navigation Scenes with Push Segues

To add an additional scene to the navigation hierarchy, we follow the exact same process as adding a new modally presented scene to an application, as follows:

1. Establish the Root View Controller scene to be whatever you want, and include a control that will start the segue. If you want to trigger the segue manually, you don't need anything extra—you'll be connecting view controller to view controller.

2. Drag a new view controller instance into the Document Outline or Editor area. This creates a new empty scene with no navigation bar, no navigation item, just an empty scene.

3. Control-drag from the object that you want to trigger the segue to the new scene's view controller.

4. When prompted for a segue type, choose Push.

You'll see a new segue line added to the originating scene, as well as bunch of changes to the scene you just connected. The new scene shows the navigation bar and automatically has its own navigation item added and displayed. You can customize the title and Back button, add additional bar button items, the works.

What's even more important to realize is that you can keep doing this. You can add additional push segues—even branch from multiple segues to follow different paths, as shown in Figure 10.13. Xcode keeps track of everything for you.

Sharing Data Between Navigation Controller Scenes

Wondering how to share data between all the different scenes in a navigation controller-based application? The navigation controller instance itself provides a perfect place to share data. By creating and using a subclass of the `UINavigationController`, we can access this class using the `parentViewController` attribute from any of the scenes we create.

Understanding Tab Bar Controllers

The second type of view controller covered this hour is the tab bar controller (`UITabBarController`). Tab bar controllers, like navigation controllers, are prominently featured in a wide range of iOS applications. As the name implies, a tab bar controller presents a series of *tabs* at the bottom of the screen—represented as icons and text—that can be touched to switch between scenes. Each scene represents a different function in the application, or a unique way of viewing the application's information.

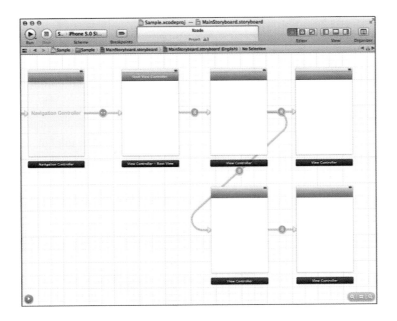

FIGURE 10.13
Create as many push segues as you need (even branches).

The Phone application on the iPhone, for example, presents different ways of sorting your calls using a tab bar controller, as shown in Figure 10.14.

FIGURE 10.14
A tab bar controller switches between unique scenes.

Tab Bars and Tab Bar Items

Like a navigation controller, the tab bar controller handles everything for you. When you touch a button to transition between scenes, it just works. You do not have to worry about programmatically handling tab bar events or manually switching between view controllers. The similarity doesn't end there.

A tab bar controller also contains a `UITabBar`—a UI element that resembles a toolbar, but in appearance only. Any scene that is presented with the tab bar controller inherits this navigation bar within its scene.

The scenes presented by a tab bar controller must contain a tab bar item (`UITabBarItem`) that has a title, an image, and if desired, a badge (a little red circle with a number in it).

> ### The Unused Tabbed Template
>
> Before you start building tab-based applications, I want to point out that Apple includes an iOS application template called the Tabbed Application. This template creates an application with two sample tabs already added, and a two view controller subclasses set up and associated with each tab. It also makes absolutely no sense (to me) to use.
>
> This template may get you up and running a few seconds faster than adding a tab bar controller to a storyboard, but for production projects, it has a fatal flaw: Apple has associated two view controllers with the two default tabs in the application and named them `FirstViewController` and `SecondViewController`. There's nothing wrong with this for learning exercises, but in a real application, you want to name these in a way that reflects their actual use (`MovieListViewController`, `TheaterListViewController`, and so on). You could certainly rename all of their references in Xcode, but by the time you did that, it would have been faster to just add and associate your own tab bar controller and view controller subclasses.

Using Tab Bar Controllers with Storyboards

To add a tab bar controller to an application, start with the Single View Application template. If you do not want the initial scene to segue into the tab bar controller, just delete the initial scene by removing its view controller, and then delete the corresponding `ViewController` interface and implementation files. When your storyboard is in the state you want, drag an instance of the Tab Bar Controller object from the Object Library into the Document Outline or the Editor area. This adds a controller and two sample tab bar scenes to the view, as shown in Figure 10.15.

The Tab Bar Controller scene represents the `UITabBarController` object that coordinates all the scene transitions. Within it is a Tab Bar object that you can customize slightly with Interface Builder, changing the color.

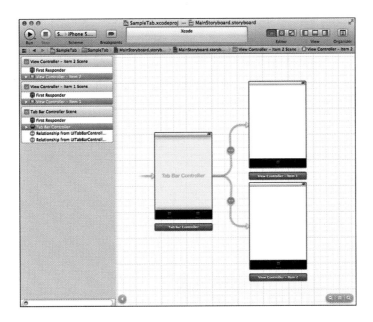

FIGURE 10.15
Adding a tab bar controller adds two default scenes to the application.

From the tab bar controller are two "relationship" connections to the two scenes that the tab bar will display. The scenes can be differentiated by the name of the tab bar button that is added to them: Item 1 and Item 2, by default.

Even though all the tab bar item buttons are shown in the Tab Bar Controller scene, they are actually part of the each individual scene. To change the tab bar buttons, you must edit the tab bar item added to a scene. The controller scene is left alone.

Did You Know?

Setting the Tab Bar Item Attributes

To edit the tab bar item (UITabBarItem) that is displayed for any scene, open that scene's view controller and select the tab bar item within the Document Outline area, and then open the Attributes Inspector (Option+Command+4), as shown in Figure 10.16.

Using the Tab Bar Item settings section, you can set a value to be displayed in the tab bar item badge. Typically, you want to set this via tab bar item's badgeValue property (an NSString) in code. You can also use the Identifier pop-up menu to choose from over a dozen predefined tab bar icons and labels. If you choose to use a predefined icon/label, you cannot customize it further because Apple wants these to remain constant throughout iOS.

FIGURE 10.16
Customize each
scene's tab bar
item.

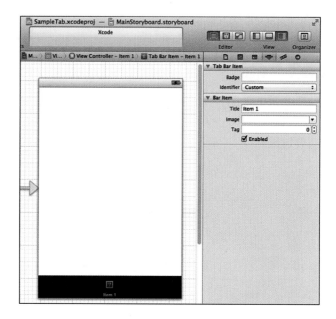

To set your own image and title, use the Bar Item settings section. The Title field sets the label for the tab bar item, and the Image drop-down associates an image resource from your project for the item.

That's everything you need to configure a scene for a tab bar controller. But what if you want to add additional scenes to the tab bar? We tackle that now, and as you'll see, it's even easier than adding a scene to a navigation controller.

Adding Additional Tab Bar Scenes

Unlike other segues that we've looked at, a tab bar has a clearly defined item (the tab bar item) that triggers a change in scene. The scene transition isn't even called a segue—it is a "relationship" between the tab bar controller and a scene.

To create a new scene, tab bar item, and the relationship between the controller and scene, start by adding a new view controller to the storyboard, as follows:

1. Drag a new view controller instance into the Document Outline or Editor area.

2. Control-drag from the Tab Bar Controller object to the new scene's view controller in the Document Outline.

3. When prompted, choose Relationship - viewControllers, as shown in Figure 10.17.

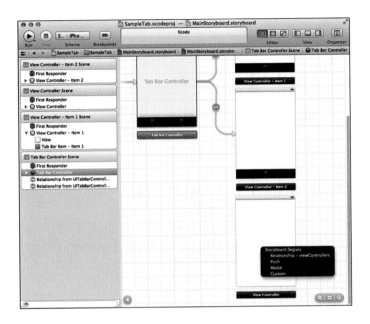

FIGURE 10.17
Create a
relationship
between
controllers.

Creating the relationship does everything we need—it automatically adds a tab bar
item to the new scene, ready to be configured. We can keep doing this to create as
many tabs and scenes as we need in the tab bar.

Sharing Data Between Tab Bar Scenes

Like the navigation controller, a tab bar controller presents us with an easy opportunity to share information. Create a tab bar controller (UITabBarController)
subclass that is assigned as the identity of the tab bar controller. Add properties
to the subclass that represent the data we want to share, then access those properties through the parentViewController property in each scene.

A Navigation Storyboard Example

To conclude this hour, we create an application that gives us a chance to practice
the skills discussed in this hour, and several of those introduced in the preceding two
hours. We build an application, LetsNavigate, that presents a series of three scenes
through a navigation controller (see Figure 10.18). Within each scene, we show a
Push button that increments a counter and then transitions to the next scene. The
counter is stored in a custom subclass of the navigation controller. In other words,
this provides both an example of building a navigation-based UI and of using the
navigation controller to manage a property that all the scenes can access.

FIGURE 10.18
Building multi-
scene naviga-
tion controller
example.

Implementation Overview

We start with a Single View application template, remove the initial scene and view controller, and then add a navigation controller and two custom classes—one a sub-class of a navigation controller that will enable each scene in the application to share information, the other a subclass of a view controller that will handle user interactions in the scenes.

We will remove the default table view root scene added with the navigation con-troller and add three additional scenes. A Push button is included in each scene's view with an action method to increment a counter—as well as a segue from that button to the next scene.

Setting Up the Project

Create a new Single View iPhone project called **LetsNavigate**. Before doing anything else, clean up the project so we only have the things that we need. Start by selecting the ViewController class files (ViewController.h and ViewController.m) and press-ing the Delete key. When prompted, choose to move the files to the trash, not just the references.

Next, click the MainStoryboard.storyboard file and then select the View Controller line in the Document Outline area (Editor, Show Document Outline) and again press Delete. The scene disappears. We now have the perfect starting point for our app.

Adding the Navigation Controller and Generic View Controller Classes

We need two additional classes added to the project. The first, a subclass of UINavigationController manages our push count property and is named **CountingNavigationController**. The second, a subclass of UIViewController, is named **GenericViewController** and handles incrementing the push count as well as displaying the count in each scene. To add these classes, follow these steps:

1. Click the + button at the bottom-left corner of the Project Navigator.

2. Choose the iOS Cocoa Touch category and the Objective-C class, and then click Next.

3. Name the new subclass **CountingNavigationController** (you will have to type the class name in), set it to be a subclass of UINavigationController, and click Next.

4. On the last setup screen, choose your main project code group from the Group pop-up menu, and then click Create.

5. Repeat this process to create a new UIViewController subclass named **GenericViewController**. Make sure you choose the right subclass for each of the new classes; otherwise, you'll have difficulty later on.

Adding the Navigation Controller

To add the navigation controller, follow these steps:

1. Open the MainStoryboard.storyboard in the Interface Builder editor.

2. Display the Object Library (Control+Option+Command+3) and drag a Navigation Controller object into an empty area of the Interface Builder editor (or into the Document Outline area).

   Your project will now show a Navigation Controller Scene and a Root View Controller Scene.

3. The Root View Controller scene is, by default, a table view controller-based scene. We don't want this, so select the table view controller in the Document Outline and press Delete. The scene disappears.

4. Now, concentrate on the Navigation Controller scene. We want to associate this controller with our CountingNavigationController class, so select the Navigation Controller line in the Document Outline and open the Identity Inspector (Option+Command+3).

5. From the class drop-down menu, choose CountingNavigationController.

Done.

Now let's add the three additional scenes we need and associate them with the generic view controller class we created.

Adding Additional Scenes and Associating the View Controller

With the storyboard still open, drag three instances of the View Controller object from the Object Library into the Editor area or the Document Outline. In a few minutes, these will be connected to the Navigation Controller scene to form a series of scenes to create a managed application workflow.

After adding the additional scenes, you want to do two things to each of them. First, set the identity of each scene's view controller. In this case, one view controller class is handling all of them, so the identity is set to GenericViewController. Next, it's a good idea to set a label for each view controller so that the scene has a friendlier name. To do so, follow these steps:

1. Start by selecting the first (whichever you decide is "first" is fine) scene's View Controller object and opening the Identity Inspector (Option+Command+3).

2. Use the Class drop-down menu to pick the GenericViewController.

3. Still within the Identity Inspector, set the Label field to **First**.

4. Move to one of the other scenes you added, select its view controller line, set its class to GenericViewController, and the label to **Second**.

5. Repeat the process for the last scene as well—setting its custom class and a label of **Third**.

When finished, your Document Outline should look like Figure 10.19.

Planning the Variables and Connections

I'm intentionally trying to keep these projects light so that there isn't a great deal of information that needs to be stored or actions that have to be defined. The CountingNavigationController will have a single property, pushCount, that contains the number of times we have pushed a new scene into view using the navigation controller.

The GenericViewController class will have a single property called countLabel that references a label in the UI displaying the current count of pushes. It will also have an action method named incrementCount that will increase the pushCount property in the CountingNavigationController by one.

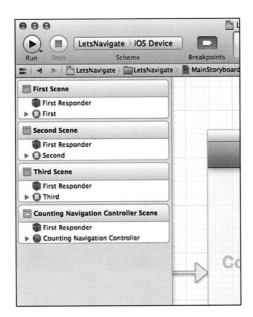

FIGURE 10.19
Your final
Document
Outline includes
a navigation
controller and
three scenes—
order is not
important.

Creating the Push Segues

To build a segue for the navigation controller, we need something to trigger it. Within the storyboard editor, add a button (UIButton) labeled **Push** to the First Scene and Second Scene, but not the Third Scene. Why not the Third? Because it is the last scene that can be displayed, there's nothing after it to segue to.

Now, Control-drag from the navigation controller (either in the Document Outline or in the Editor area) to the First Scene. When prompted for a segue, choose Relationship – Root View Controller. This sets the First Scene as the scene that is initially displayed by the navigation controller.

Next, Control-drag from the button in the First Scene to the Second Scene's view controller line in the Document Outline, or target the scene directly in the editor. When prompted for the segue type, choose Push, as shown in Figure 10.20. A new segue line, Segue from UIButton to Second, is added to the First Scene in the Document Outline, and the Second Scene inherits the navigation controller's navigation bar and gains a navigation item in its view.

Repeat this process, creating a push segue from the Second Scene's button to the Third Scene. Your Interface Builder editor should now contain a fully realized navigation controller sequence. Click and drag each scene in the view to arrange it in a way the makes sense to you. Figure 10.21 shows my interconnected views.

FIGURE 10.20
Create a push
segue.

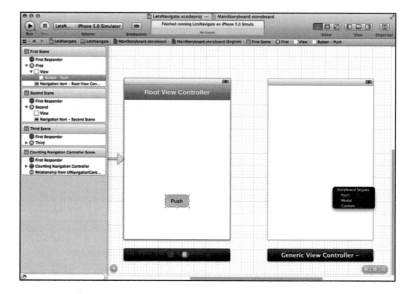

FIGURE 10.21
Connect all of
your views via
segues.

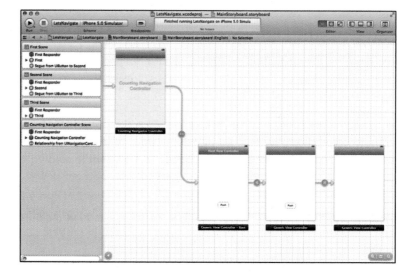

Creating the Interface

By adding the scenes and buttons, you have really just built most of the interface.
The final steps are customizing the title of the navigation item in each scene and
adding an output label to display the push count.

Begin by going through each of the scenes—First, Second, And Third—and double-
clicking the center of the navigation bar that now appears at the top of each view.

Title the first view **First Scene**, the second **Second Scene**, and the third... wait for it... **Third Scene**.

Finally, to each of the scenes add a label (UILabel) near the top that reads **Push Count:** and a second label (the output label) with the default text of **0** (and a large, center aligned font, if you want) to the center of each view.

Figure 10.22 shows the final interface design.

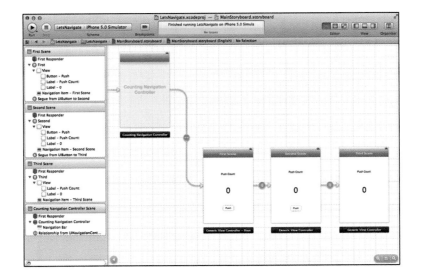

FIGURE 10.22
The final layout of the navigation application.

Creating and Connecting the Outlets and Actions

There is only one outlet and one action that need to be defined in this project—but they need to be connected several times. The outlet—a connection to the label displaying the push count (countLabel)—will be connected to each of the three scenes. The action, incrementCount, will only need to be connected to the button in the First Scene and Second Scene.

Position your display in the Interface Builder editor so that the First Scene is visible (or just use the Document Outline), click its push count label, and then switch to the Assistant Editor mode.

Adding the Outlet

Control-drag from the label in the center of the First Scene to the just below the @interface line in GenericViewController.h. When prompted, create a new outlet named countLabel.

That created the outlet and the connection from the First Scene; now you need to connect it to the other two scenes. Control-drag from the Second Scene's push count label and target the countLabel property you just created. The entire line will highlight, as shown in Figure 10.23, showing you are making a connection to an existing outlet. Repeat this for the Third Scene, connecting its push count label to the same property.

FIGURE 10.23
Create the outlet, and then connect the other scenes' labels.

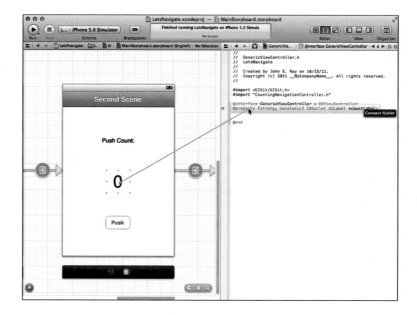

Adding the Action

Adding and connecting the action works in much the same way. Start by Control-dragging from the First Scene's button to just below the property definition in GenericViewController.h. When prompted, create a new action named **incrementCount**.

Switch to the second view controller and Control-drag from its button to the existing incrementCount action. You've just made all the connections we need.

Implementing the Application Logic

Most of our work is now behind us. To finish the tutorial, we first need to set up the pushCount property in the CountingNavigationController class so that it can keep track of the number of times we have pushed a new scene in the application.

Adding the Push Count Property

Open the CountingNavigationController.h interface file and add a property definition for an integer named pushCount below the @interface line:

```
@property (nonatomic) int pushCount;
```

Next, open the CountingNavigationController.m file and add a corresponding
@synthesize statement below the existing @implementation line:

```
@synthesize pushCount;
```

That's all we need to do to implement the custom CountingNavigationController
class. Because it is a subclass of a UINavigationController, it already performs all
the navigation controller tasks we need, and now it stores a pushCount property, too.

To access this property from the GenericViewController class that is handling the
content for all the scenes in the application, we need to import the custom navigation controller's interface file in GenericViewController.h. Add this line following the
existing #import statement:

```
#import "CountingNavigationController.h"
```

We're all set to finish our implementation, which is just a matter of adding the logic
to GenericViewController that increments the counter and makes sure it is displayed on the screen when a new scene is pushed into view.

Incrementing and Displaying the Counter

To increment the counter in GenericViewController.m, we use the
parentViewController property to access the pushCount property. The
parentViewController, as you have learned, is automatically set to the Navigation
Controller object within any scene managed by the navigation controller.

We need to typecast the parentViewController to our custom class of
CountingNavigationController, but the full implementation is just a single line.
Implement incrementCount as shown in Listing 10.2.

LISTING 10.2   The increment Count Implementation

```
- (IBAction)incrementCount:(id)sender {
    ((CountingNavigationController *)self.parentViewController).pushCount++;
}
```

The final step is to update the display to show the current count. Because pushing
the button increments the push count and pushes a new scene into view, the
incrementCount action is not necessarily the best place for this logic to fall. In fact,

it won't always be accurate because the count could be updated in another view and then the Back button used to "pop" back to the original view, which would now be showing an invalid count.

To get around this, we just add the display logic to the `viewWillAppear:animated` method. This method is called right before a view is displayed onscreen (regardless of whether it is through a segue or by a user touching the Back button), so it is a perfect place to update the label. Add the code in Listing 10.3 to the GenericViewController.m file.

LISTING 10.3   Update the Display in `viewWillAppear:animated`

```
1: -(void)viewWillAppear:(BOOL)animated {
2:     NSString *pushText;
3:     pushText=[[NSString alloc] initWithFormat:@"%d",
4:                 ((CountingNavigationController *)
5:                     self.parentViewController).pushCount];
6:     self.countLabel.text=pushText;
7: }
```

Line 2 declares a new string, `pushText`, that will contain a string representation of the counter. Line 3 allocates and initializes this string using the `NSString` `initWithFormat` method. The `%d` format string is replaced by the contents of the `pushCount` property, accessed using the same approach as in the `incrementCount` method.

In the last step, line 6, the `countLabel` is updated with the `pushText` string.

Building the Application

Run the application and test the navigation controller. Use the button to push new scenes on to the navigation controller stack, and then pop them back off with the Back button functionality that we get for free. The push count stays in sync through all the different scenes because we now have a central class (`CountingViewController`) managing our shared property for us.

Summary

The topics this hour introduced—multiple scenes and segues—are very important aspects of iOS development that can take your apps from being simple single-view "utility"-style programs to full-featured software. You learned how to visually and programmatically create modal segues and handle interactions between scenes.

In addition, the hour explored two new view controller classes. The first, the navigation controller, displays a sequence of scenes that are displayed one after the other—and are often used to "drill down" into detailed information about something. The second, the tab bar controller, is used to create applications with a single unifying bar at the bottom that can be used to switch between different scenes. The integration of these controllers with storyboard scenes and segues is a elegant and powerful feature of Xcode and iOS.

Q&A

Q. Why doesn't iOS just provide windows?

A. Can you imagine managing windows with just your fingers? The iOS interface is designed to be touched. It is not meant to model a typical desktop application environment, which was built around the mouse.

Q. Can I mix and match scenes and segues?

A. Yes and no. You cannot use a push segue without a navigation controller, nor create a working tab bar application without a tab bar controller. You can, however, implement a navigation controller that is used in conjunction with a tab bar controller, or display a modal segue that transitions to a navigation controller-managed series of scenes and so on.

Q. What if I want to share information between scenes that do not have a central controller class?

A. The fact that the tab bar controller and navigation controller have a nice place to implement shared properties is great, but not necessary. You can always create a custom singleton class in your application and reference it in other classes that need to exchange data.

Workshop

Quiz

1. Navigation controllers and tab bar controllers require extensive coding with the Storyboard feature. True or false?

2. All presentation and transition styles are compatible with one another. True or false?

3. There is no easy way to share data between scenes in a tab bar or navigation-based application. True or false?

Answers

1. False. The Xcode storyboard makes it possible to add these features almost entirely with drag-and-drop simplicity.

2. False. Some transitions will not work with some presentation styles. You can find the full guidelines in the developer documentation.

3. False. These controllers have a central controller class that offers a great place to share information between scene's view controllers.

Activities

1. Using the iOS Single View Application template, practice the storyboarding techniques described in this hour—from simple modal segues to navigation controllers and tab bar controllers.

2. Use the iOS Single View Application template (for the iPad) to test the different modal presentation styles available on Apple's tablet platform.

HOUR 11

Building and Executing Applications

What You'll Learn in This Hour:

▶ The terminology of the Xcode build tools
▶ How to create new project targets
▶ The types of per-target build settings you can modify
▶ The purpose and management of schemes
▶ How to use the iOS simulator to test iOS apps

Nothing is quite as grand as creating an application and running it for the first time. To run an application, however, Xcode must take into account how to compile the application, what dependencies (if any) it has, how to run it, whether to include debugging information, and many, many more possible variables. It is no exaggeration to say that an entire 24-hours book could be dedicated to tweaking and configuring the dozens of possible build settings Xcode presents us with.

In this hour, we take a step back and review the different components of the build system, what they are used for, ways they can be modified, and how it all ties together. This is not the most exciting hour in the book, but you'll thank yourself for learning the "language of the build" sooner rather than later.

The Language of the Build

Building a project usually produces an executable or a library. This seems simple enough, and is the ultimate outcome of most development projects. What lies beneath the surface, however, is anything but simple.

If you've been building sample code as you have read through the first several hours, you have likely been clicking the Run button and viewing the results, as shown in Figure 11.1. There is certainly nothing wrong with this; in fact, we encourage it. As you start to customize projects, however, you need to understand the terminology of the Xcode build system. What's a build configuration? An action? A scheme? Let's start this lesson by reviewing the many terms you'll encounter when you start delving deeper into the build process.

FIGURE 11.1
Clicking Run is simple. The Xcode build system is not.

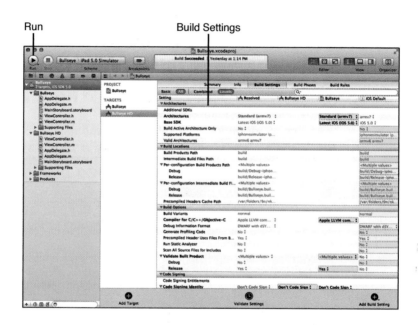

Targets

Targets are a collection of instructions that define how to build a project. Typically, a target is a framework or an application, but it can also be tests or other actions that are carried out against your project's code. Projects usually start with a single target (an application), but you can add others easily. You might, for example, start an iOS application with a single iPhone target, but later add an iPad target for a larger, more complex version of the app. You might also use a target to create a version of an application for a particular version of the OS.

To view the targets configured for your project, click the topmost project icon in the Project Navigator. The targets are listed in the column to the right of the navigation area, as shown in Figure 11.2.

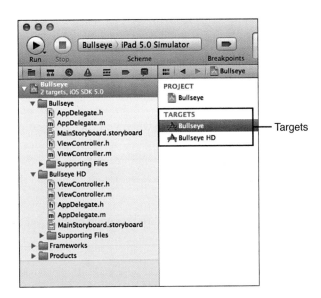

FIGURE 11.2
View the targets associated with your project.

Products

The files that are generated by following the build instructions in a target are called *products*. As you would expect, products are usually applications, libraries, or frameworks. In its initial state, a project has no completed products but, because of the target rules, knows the products that it will be producing.

You can look at the products that have been created (or are waiting to be built) by looking in the Products logical group within the Project Navigator, as shown in Figure 11.3.

Products that have not yet been created are highlighted with a red label. Those that are already built show in black. To find the actual files represented by a target (such as an executable), you can right-click the target and choose Show In Finder from the contextual menu.

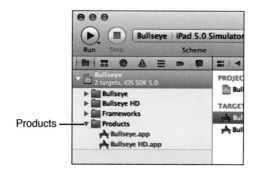

Products

Build Actions

A *build action* is what you are executing when you click the Run button on the Xcode toolbar. It builds the target (or targets), and then performs one or more predefined actions on them. The Run build action, for example, builds your target and launches it in OS X or installs it on an iOS device (or in the iOS simulator) and attaches a debugger to the process.

Five predefined build actions are configured for each project you create. The first step of each of these actions is to build one or more targets (You learn how it knows which targets shortly.)

Did You Know?

> The first step of any build action is to build the target. This makes "build" itself an informal and implied (but very important) build action.

▶ **Run:** The Run build action launches the application in OS X or installs the iOS application on a device or in the iOS simulator. A debugger process is attached to the running application for tracing/tracking its behavior. You learn more about debugging in Hour 19, "Getting the Bugs Out: Debugging with LLDB and GDB."

Watch Out!

> ### Debugging with Run
>
> Pay close attention to what I'm saying here about the Run build action. In its default configuration, it is intended for debugging an application, not simulating the application in a final release scenario. Applications that are built for debugging include symbol information that makes it possible to track/change variable contents on-the-fly and view the application's flow in relation to the source code in real time.

▶ **Test**: The Test build action is used to build and run any unit tests that you've created along with your project. Unit tests are pieces of code that execute the core functions of your application to verify that the proper results are being returned. This ensures that as you build your application out you do not introduce changes that break working code (a condition known as a regression). You learn about creating unit tests in Hour 18, "Test Early, Test Often."

▶ **Profile**: The Profile action is used in conjunction with an Xcode tool called Instruments. Instruments can analyze your running application for performance issues, memory leaks, and other problems that may not be detectable through simple debugging efforts. We walk through some of the basics of Instruments in Hour 21, "Advanced: Analyzing Code with Instruments."

▶ **Analyze**: The Analyze action performs a static analysis of your code, detecting logic issues that would not stop an application from building but might prevent it from running correctly.

▶ **Archive**: The Archive action creates a distribution-ready version of the application for uploading to the App Store or distributing to product testers. By default, it does not include any debugging information or unit tests that were initially added to the project. You can fine-tune the archive settings to deliver exactly the target or targets you intend to submit.

You can execute any of the build actions from the Product menu, or most of the actions (Archive being the exception) by clicking and holding on the Run button, as shown in Figure 11.4.

FIGURE 11.4
Choose the build action to execute by clicking and holding the Run button.

Build Configuration

As mentioned, you can build applications with debugging information using the Run build action or prepare an application that is devoid of any debugging symbols using the Archive build action. This brings up a question: How do these different actions build *differently*? The answer is that they use a different build configuration. Two build configurations are created with each project you create: a debug configuration and a release configuration. As their names suggest, one builds your project with debugging information included; the other doesn't. The build actions use one or the other build configuration, depending on what it is trying to accomplish.

You can verify these build configurations as follows:

1. Click the project-level icon in the Project Navigator.

2. Select the project icon in the column that appears to the right of the Navigator.

3. Click the Info tab in the top of the Editor area, as shown in Figure 11.5.

FIGURE 11.5
Each project includes a debug and release build configuration.

Build Configurations

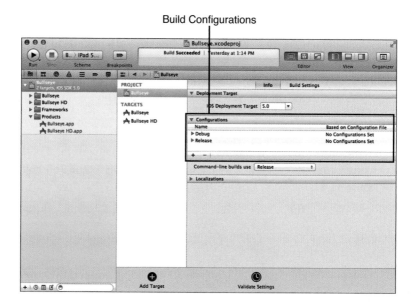

For most development projects, debug and release are all you need.

Schemes

If you are feeling an abundance of information overload by now, I don't blame you. Understanding how all the different pieces of the build system fit together can be like trying to solve a 5,000-piece puzzle of the sky on a clear day. That said, I introduce just one more component this hour: schemes.

If you have been building and running applications over the past few hours, you've seen your project name along with a destination for running the code (My Mac, iOS Device, iPhone Simulator, iPad Simulator) show up in a Scheme pop-up menu directly to the right of the Stop button, as shown in Figure 11.6.

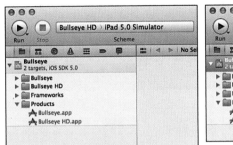 

FIGURE 11.6
The Scheme menu is directly to the right of the Stop button (shown here in unclicked/clicked states).

In reality, what you're seeing in the Scheme pop-up is not the name of your project but the name of a scheme that has been defined for your project. A scheme ties all the concepts that you have just learned about together. A scheme determines what targets will be built, what the various build actions will do when they are executed, and what build configuration are used for a given build action.

When you create a project, a scheme is automatically created and named for the project's target. It provides the default functionality that ties each of the build actions to the targe so that clicking Run will do what you expect.

Managing Targets

Although targets and schemes are not something you will change frequently (you see some examples in the later hours of this book), I wanted to give you an opportunity to start exploring these features on your own. In the earlier hours, you saw how to configure icons, launch images, and set entitlements for applications. What you were doing, in fact, was configuring your target. At that point in time, there was only a single target to look at, so it appeared that your settings were for a project. In actuality, however, they were for the target.

Creating a New Target

Creating a new target is nearly identical to creating a new project, but it occurs with an existing project. Click the topmost project icon in the Project Navigator, and then click the Add Target button that appears at the bottom of the Editor area, as shown in Figure 11.7.

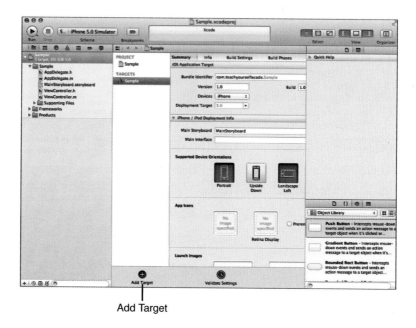

Add Target

You are then guided through the exact same project-creation assistant that you learned about in Hour 4, "Creating Projects with Xcode Templates." The result? A single project that contains two targets, and two sets of files for each of the targets, as shown in Figure 11.8.

To delete a target, just select it and press the Delete key. This removes the target, but it does not remove the target's files or any schemes that were defined for the target.

Managing Files Between Targets

A point of confusion with multiple targets is "which file belongs to which target." For targets to be useful, they should be able to share some files but not others. We look at one way to do this in the next section, but before we get there, I want to introduce the Target Membership tool, found within the File Inspector (Option+Command+1).

With a file selected in the Project Navigator, you can open the File Inspector and expand the Target Membership section to show all your possible targets for the project, as shown in Figure 11.9.

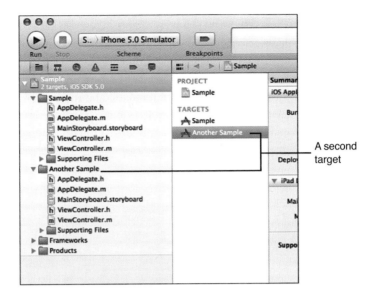

FIGURE 11.8
A single project with multiple targets.

A second target

Choose your Targets

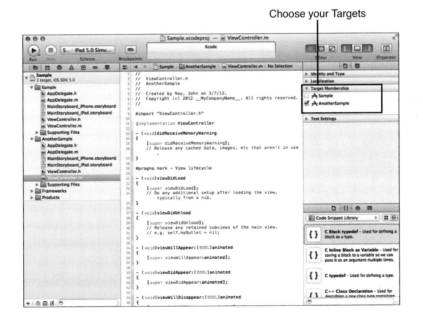

FIGURE 11.9
Associate a file with one or more targets.

Use the check boxes beside each target to determine whether the file is to be used when creating that target (or not).

A Targeted Case Study

When you add a new target to a project, it essentially creates another new project, with all the supporting files, inside your existing project. This is not necessarily what you want, so do not assume this default behavior is the way it "has to be." To see a simple example of a multitarget project that makes a bit more sense, open the Bullseye project included in the Hour 11 Projects folder. This is a very simple iOS project that, when a button is clicked, displays I'm SD (on an iPhone) and I'm HD (on an iPad), as shown in Figure 11.10.

FIGURE 11.10
A simple application that will make millions.

iPhone Target

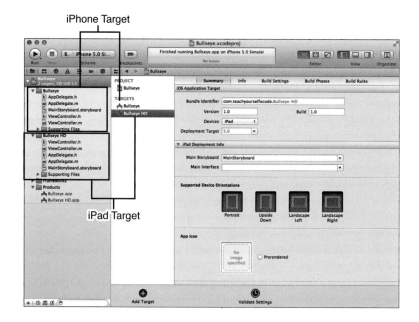

iPad Target

What makes this application unique is that it, like many iOS applications on the App Store, is not universal. There are both Bullseye HD and Bullseye targets within the project, shown in Figure 11.11. These create two distinct executables, one for the iPad and one for the iPhone.

To set up this project, I just created a basic iPhone app that worked the way I wanted it to, and then I added a new target. Using the project-creation assistant, I configured the new target to be iPad-specific. Xcode automatically added the new target in a group called Bullseye HD in my project. Even though the projects create separate executables, I wanted them to share the ViewController class that I developed for the original iPhone application (dramatically cutting down on my development time).

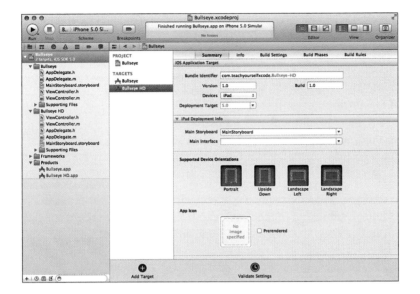

FIGURE 11.11
Multiple targets
for multiple
devices.

Unfortunately, because Xcode automatically adds all the files into the target that would be required for a brand new project, I needed to make two minor modifications. First, I deleted the ViewController class files that were added to the Bullseye HD group. Next, I dragged (from a Finder window) the existing iPhone Bullseye ViewController class files into the Bullseye HD group and told Xcode to add the files to the Bullseye HD target, and that it shouldn't create a new copy of the files, as shown in Figure 11.12.

> Remember, you can set which files are associated with which target by selecting the file in the Project Navigator and using the File Inspector (Control+Command+1). Just expand the Target Membership section, click the check box by each target the file should be considered a part of, and you are done.
>
> I could also add the ViewController.m implementation file to the Compile Sources section of the Build Phase settings to accomplish the same thing.
>
> For groups of files I can easily find in the Finder, however, I find this approach easier.

Did You Know?

As a final step, I edited the iPad version of the Mainstoryboard.storyboard file and created connections to the outlets and actions I had already defined in the iPhone version of the ViewController class. The end result? Two targets that have unique storyboards, share a ViewController class, and create two distinct executables.

FIGURE 11.12
Choose the target to associate with your files.

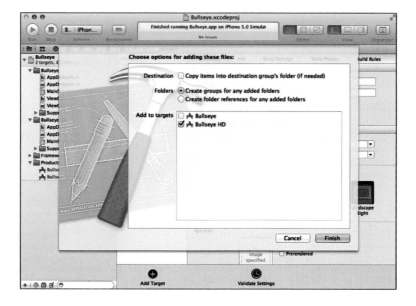

I can now execute my build actions on whichever target I want because the appropriate schemes were automatically added for each of the targets, as shown in Figure 11.13.

FIGURE 11.13
Choose the scheme that corresponds to the target you want to build.

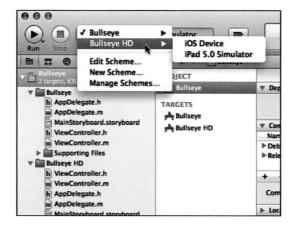

Target Build Settings, Phases, and Rules

Recall that a target defines the rules for a build. Therefore, for each target you create, you can modify how the build process is carried out. To do this, make sure the project icon is selected in the Navigator, and then choose the target you want to configure. The tabs at the top of the Editor area give you control over the build process for that specific target. The summary, as you have seen before, gives you easy access to basic settings, such as icons, supported device orientations, and resource requirements. The Info tab presents the information in a less friendly, but more inclusive manner—providing the opportunity to configure any of the dozens of possible project plist options that might apply to your application.

Build Settings

The more interesting settings are found under the Build Settings, Build Phases, and Build Rules tabs. The Build Settings tab, shown in Figure 11.14, makes it possible to choose things such as the base SDK for your project, the compiler being used, the permissions used for deployment, and much, much more. This is not a playground, so I highly recommend reviewing Apple's build documentation before touching anything here.

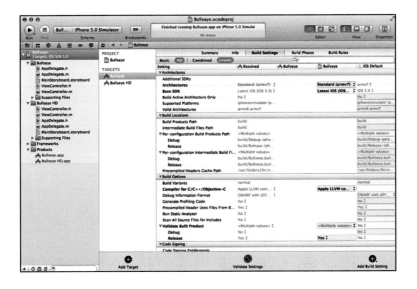

FIGURE 11.14
The Build Settings tab contains dozens of options and tweaks for your target's build process.

Build Phases

The Build Phases tab is essentially a list of steps, from top to bottom, of what happens during a build. For example, looking at the Bullseye Build Phases in Figure 11.15, you can see that the source code files will be compiled (Compile Sources), the resulting binaries will be linked with the necessary iOS frameworks included in the project (Link Binary with Libraries), and then the necessary resources will be copied into the executable (Copy Bundle Resources). The first step, Target Dependencies, is empty because this project is not dependent on anything else. If you need for another target to be built first (a library, for example), you can add it to this list by clicking the + icon at the bottom of the Target Dependencies section.

FIGURE 11.15
Customize each
step of the build
process.

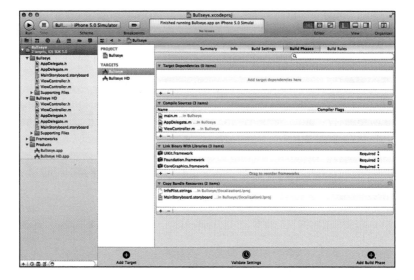

If the default phases are not enough, you can even add additional build phases using the Add Build Phase button in the bottom-right of the Editor area.

Build Rules

The final tab, Build Rules, is shown in Figure 11.16. This tab describes how certain types of files are handled when encountered during the build process. Rarely will you need to add any rules to this section, unless you are doing very specialized development.

Managing Schemes

Now that you understand how a project can have multiple targets, and how each target defines its own build rules, it is time to explore the glue that ties everything together: schemes. To view the schemes that are installed for a given project, click the left side of the Scheme pop-menu on the Xcode toolbar and choose Manage Schemes, as shown in Figure 11.17. You can also find this option under the Product menu. Use the Bullseye project to see these settings for yourself.

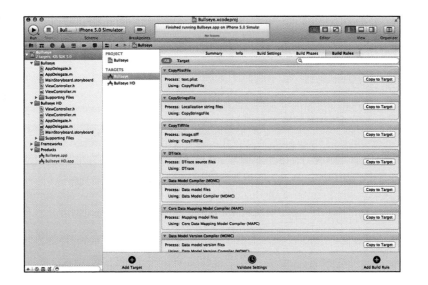

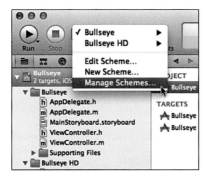

FIGURE 11.17
Manage the schemes that are attached to your project.

Because there are two targets in Bullseye (and the Autocreate Schemes check box is checked), you'll see two schemes: Bullseye and Bullseye HD. These define what happens when a build action is performed on the respective targets. Highlight the Bullseye scheme and click the Edit button to open the Scheme Editor.

Editing Schemes

The Scheme Editor provides a list of the build actions, including the action that is included (by default) with all other actions: Build. To edit a build action's settings, click the action in the left column. The right side of the window updates to display the options for that particular action. We start with the Build action and briefly cover what you can expect within each of the sections.

If you expand the actions in the left column by clicking the disclosure arrow, you can also edit pre-actions and post-actions. These are scripts (or email) that are executed before (pre) and/or (post) after the Build action. This isn't something you'll do often, but the capability is present should you need it.

Build

The Build action itself is used to define the targets that are built when each of the build actions are run. In Figure 11.18 you can see that only the Bullseye target is built when the Bullseye scheme's build actions are executed. If I wanted, I could click the + button at the bottom of the list of targets and add the Bullseye HD target, as well. This would enable me to build both applications simultaneously.

FIGURE 11.18
The build action settings.

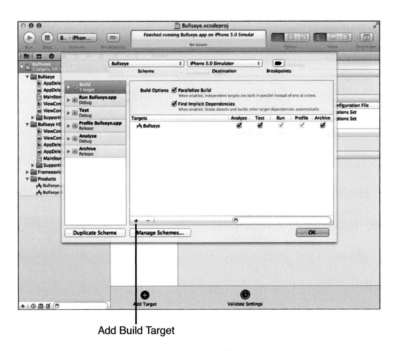

Add Build Target

You can only run (debug) one application at a time, regardless of how many targets you build during the Run build action.

Run

Within the Run build action settings, shown in Figure 11.19, you can choose whether Run launches a debug or release version of your application, what executable (if there are multiples) should actually be executed, and whether the application is launched automatically.

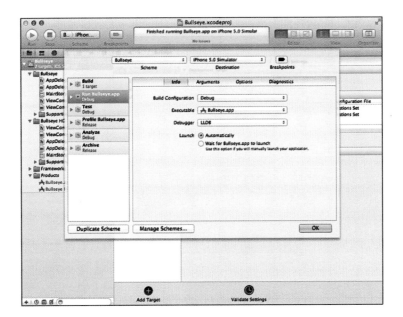

FIGURE 11.19
The Run build
action settings.

You can also use the other tabs within this section (Arguments, Options, and Diagnostics) to choose arguments and environment variables that will be passed to the application when it launches, set simulated location services, and activate additional debugging and logging settings.

Test

The Test build action settings, shown in Figure 11.20, set the build configuration to use (debug or release) when the Test action is executed, the debugger to use, and any unit tests that should be executed. There are no unit tests associated with the Bullseye project, so this configuration is mostly empty. You learn all about unit tests later in Hour 18.

By default, the Test action uses the Run action's arguments and environment variables, but you can also set them independently in the Arguments tab of the configuration.

FIGURE 11.20
The Test build
action settings.

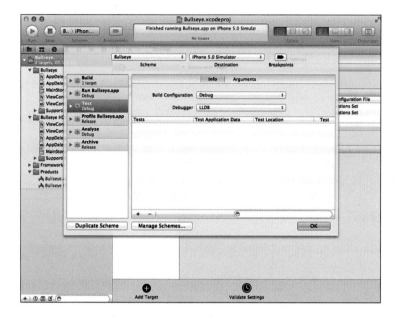

FIGURE 11.20
The Test build
action settings.

Profile

Recall that the Profile build action uses the Xcode Instruments tool to run tests against your running application. Use these settings, shown in Figure 11.21, to choose between a release or debug build configuration, which executable to launch, and which instrument (if you want to set a default) should be started when profiling begins. Again, the Arguments tab can override arguments and environment variables used during execution.

Analyze

The easiest of the build actions to configure, the Analyze action, shown in Figure 11.22, offers a choice between the release and debug build configurations. No other settings are required.

Archive

Last but not least, the Archive build action creates a "production-ready" version of your app that is ready to be submitted to the App Store. You can use this action's settings (see Figure 11.23) to set Archive to use a debug build configuration (but this really wouldn't make much sense), set a name for the archive it produces, and, finally, whether the Xcode Organizer launches when the action finishes, showing the archive.

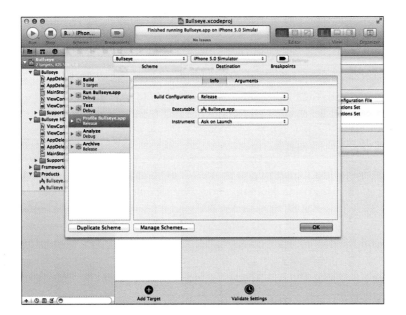

FIGURE 11.21
The Profile build action settings.

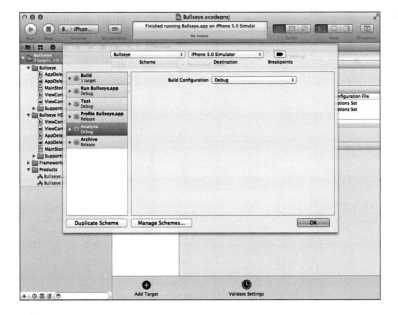

FIGURE 11.22
The Analyze build action settings.

FIGURE 11.23
The Archive
build action
settings.

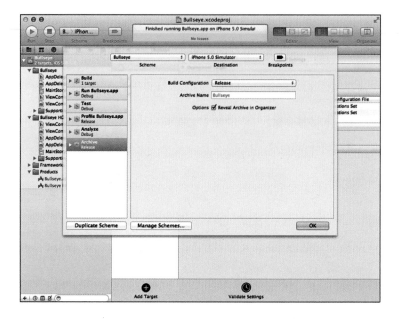

Adding New Schemes

In many cases, the default build setup (schemes, targets, and so on) that Xcode establishes for you when you create a project are all that you'll need. If you do decide you want to create a custom scheme, however, you can do that easily, as follows:

1. From the left side of the Scheme pop-up menu on the Xcode toolbar, choose Manage Schemes (or choose the menu item with that same name from the Product menu).

2. On the Manage Scheme screen, click + to add a new scheme.

3. You are prompted to name the scheme and choose a default target, as shown in Figure 11.24. Provide the requested values, and then click OK.

A new scheme appears in the Manage Scheme list, ready to be modified as described earlier.

To remove a Scheme you've added, select it in the management list and click the – button.

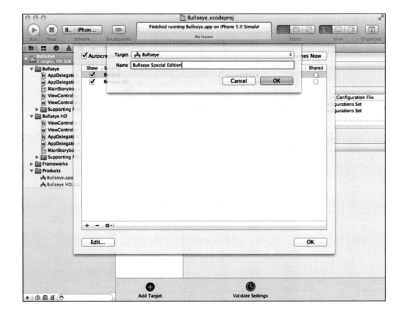

FIGURE 11.24
Add a new scheme to your project.

> If you accidentally remove one of the autocreated schemes in the Manage Scheme window, just click the Autocreate Schemes Now button to automatically re-create it.

Did You Know?

Using the iOS Simulator

The final topic we cover in this hour relates to what happens after you've chosen to build and run your application. If you are building for the Mac, you use the application exactly as you would any other. But what about for iOS apps? The answer is the iOS simulator. This tool, shown in Figure 11.25, is where you'll spend a great deal of your time after clicking Run in an iOS Xcode project.

Despite its fancy appearance, the iOS simulator is not a perfect iDevice. It cannot simulate complex multitouch events or provide readings from some sensors (gyroscope, accelerometer, and so on). The closest it comes on these counts is the ability to rotate to test landscape interfaces and a simple "shake" motion simulation. That said, for most apps, it has enough features to be a valuable part of your development process.

Simulation Versus Real-World Performance

One thing that you absolutely cannot count on in the simulator is that your simulated app performance will resemble your real app performance. The simulator
tends to run silky smooth, whereas real apps might have more limited resources
and not behave as nicely. Be sure to occasionally test on a physical device so that
you know your expectations are in line with reality.

Launching Applications in the Simulator

To launch an application in the simulator, open the project in Xcode, make sure
that the right side of the Scheme pop-up menu is set to the iPhone Simulator or iPad
Simulator, and then click Run. After a few seconds, the simulator launches and the
application displays. You can test this using the HelloSimulator project (available in
both iPhone- and iPad-specific versions) included in this hour's Projects folder.

Once up and running, the HelloSimulator app should display a simple line of text
and an image (see Figure 11.26).

When an application is running, you can interact with it using your mouse as if it
were your fingertip. Click buttons, drag sliders, and so on. If you click into a field
where input is expected, the onscreen keyboard displays. You can "type" using your
Mac keyboard or by clicking the onscreen keyboard buttons. The iOS copy and paste

services are also simulated by clicking and holding on text until the familiar loupe magnifier appears.

FIGURE 11.26
Click Run in Xcode to launch and run your application in the simulator.

Clicking the virtual Home button (or choosing Hardware, Home from the menu) exits the application but does not quit the debugger in Xcode. To completely stop execution, click the Stop button on the Xcode toolbar.

Launching an application in the simulator installs it in the simulator, just like installing an app on a real device. When you exit the app, it is still present on the simulator until you manually delete it.

To remove an installed application from the simulator, click and hold its icon until it starts "wiggling," and then click the X that appears in the upper-left corner. In other words, remove apps from the simulator in the exact same way as you remove them from a physical device.

To quickly reset the simulator back to a clean slate, choose Reset Content and Settings from the iOS Simulator menu.

Did You Know?

By default, your application will display on a simulated non-Retina screen. To switch to a different simulated device, choose from the options in the Hardware, Device menu.

By the Way

Generating Multitouch Events

Even though you have only a single pointer, you can simulate simple multitouch events, such as two-finger pulls and pinches, by holding down Option when your cursor is over the simulator screen. Two circles, representing fingertips, are drawn and can be controlled with your mouse or trackpad. To simulate a touch event, click and drag while continuing to hold down Option. Figure 11.27 shows the pinch gesture.

FIGURE 11.27
Simulate simple multitouch with the Option key.

Try this using the HelloSimulator app. You should be able to use the simulator's multitouch capabilities to shrink or expand the onscreen text and image.

Rotating the Simulated Device

To simulate a rotation on your virtual device, choose Rotate Right or Rotate Left from the Hardware menu (see Figure 11.28). You can use this to rotate the simulator window through all four possible orientations and view the results onscreen.

Again, test this with HelloSimulator. The app reacts to the rotation events and orients the text properly.

FIGURE 11.28
Rotate the interface through the possible orientations.

Simulating Other Conditions

You want to test against a few other esoteric conditions in the simulator. Using the Hardware menu, you can access these additional features:

▶ **Device**: Choose from the iPhone, iPhone Retina display, and iPad devices to simulate your application on each.

▶ **Version**: Check to see how your app behaves on earlier versions of the iOS. This option enables you to choose from many of the recent versions of the iOS. Note that you need to use the Xcode Component options (located in the Downloads section of the Xcode Preferences) to install simulator files for earlier iOS releases.

▶ **Shake Gesture**: Simulate a quick shake of the device.

▶ **Lock**: Simulates the condition of a locked device. Because a user can lock an iPhone or iPad while an application is running, some developers choose to have their programs react uniquely to this situation.

▶ **Simulate Memory Warning**: Triggers an application's low-memory event. Useful for testing to make sure your application exits gracefully if resources run low.

▶ **Toggle In-Call Status Bar**: When a call is active and an application is started, an additional line appears at the top of the screen (Touch to Return to Call). This option simulates that line.

▶ **Simulate Hardware Keyboard**: Simulates a connected keyboard (just use your Mac keyboard).

▶ **TV Out**: Displays a window that will show the contents of the device's TV out signal. We do not use this feature in this book.

Test a few of these out on the HelloSimulator application. Figure 11.29 shows the application's reaction to a simulated memory warning.

FIGURE 11.29
The simulator can react to a variety of different simulated conditions.

Summary

It's always difficult for me to try to define the vocabulary for a system when a large number of the terms start the same way: build, build actions, build phases, build configurations, build rules, and so on. The Xcode build system is not something that can be mastered in a single sitting. This hour's lesson provided an introduction to the terms you'll encounter when reading about the build system, the role of targets and target build settings, the purpose of build actions, and the use of schemes to tie everything together. You should have a sense of how all of these things work together to produce your Xcode products, but don't worry if it's all a bit overwhelming. Many of these options will never need changed, and we revisit them with some examples later in the book.

As a final step, you also learned about the iOS simulator as a tool for testing and debugging iOS applications—a critical piece of the iOS build/run workflow that is not necessary for native OS X apps.

Q&A

Q. *I built a release copy of my OS X application. Where can I find it?*

A. To find any of your projects products, just right-click the target and choose Show in Finder.

Q. *My sample projects have always included multiple targets. Why do yours only have one?*

A. You have likely been including the unit tests during your project-creation step. There's absolutely nothing wrong with this. I tend to leave the unit tests out in early tutorials to avoid any unnecessary clutter.

Q. *Can I develop a full application for iOS without ever testing it on a device?*

A. You certainly can, but I do not recommend it. The iOS simulator is good, but it is not a replacement for a real device. You'll be missing most hardware events, a sense of the true execution speed/performance, and a full real-world test of your UI. In Hour 1, "Xcode 4," you learned about basic iOS device provisioning for development, and you will learn even more in Hour 22, "Managing and Provisioning iOS Devices."

Workshop

Quiz

1. What does a target do?

2. A project only has one scheme. True or false?

3. The iOS simulator cannot respond to rotation events. True or false?

Answers

1. A target defines a product that your project will build. It does this by tying files to build settings, phases, and rules.

2. False. By default, a project has one scheme for every defined target. You can, however, define as many schemes as you need for your particular project.

3. False and true. The simulator can handle simple rotation, such as entering landscape mode, but it cannot simulate complex rotations or acceleration that would be useful for testing accelerometer or gyroscope-driven applications.

Activities

1. Following the steps described in the "A Targeted Case Study" section earlier, and what you've learned in the previous hours, create a simple "Hello World" OS X or iOS application that includes two related but distinct targets. One might generate Hello World, whereas the other states Hello Earth, for example.

2. Use the Xcode iOS project templates, or a sample project found in the Xcode documentation, to test the iOS simulator. Be sure to test both iPhone and iPad modes of the simulator, and see what happens when you run an iPhone app in the iPad mode.

HOUR 12

Using Source Control

What You'll Learn in This Hour:

▶ The source control features offered in Xcode
▶ How to create and restore project snapshots
▶ The language of source control systems
▶ How to connect to remote Subversion and Git repositories
▶ The tools available for working with Subversion and Git

As projects grow larger, it becomes more and more important to keep track of the changes that you make and be able to identify modifications to your code. A change can sometimes cause unintended behaviors that, without a good way to audit your coding, might be difficult to track down. This is especially true for projects where one or more people need to access and modify the same project.

The answer to this problem is to use source control—a term that refers to a system that keeps track of changes to source code files. Xcode offers a number of source control options, from creating simple project snapshots, to integration with two of the most popular source control systems currently available: Subversion and Git. This hour's lesson walks through these options and helps you get started using the tools Xcode provides.

Using Xcode Snapshots

If you're planning to make many changes to your code and you're not quite sure you'll like the outcome, you might want to take advantage of the Xcode "snapshot" feature. A code snapshot is, in essence, a copy of all your source code at a particular moment in time. If you do not like changes you have made, you can revert to an earlier snapshot. Snapshots are also helpful because they show what has changed between multiple versions of an application.

Snapshots are a limited form of source control. Later in this hour, you learn about the full source control features offered in Xcode and how to take advantage of them. For many small projects, however, snapshots are likely all you will need.

Creating Snapshots

To take a snapshot of an open project, choose File, Create Snapshot. You are prompted for a name of the snapshot and a description, as shown in Figure 12.1. Provide appropriate input, and then click Create Snapshot. That's all there is to it.

FIGURE 12.1
Create a snapshot of your project at any point in time.

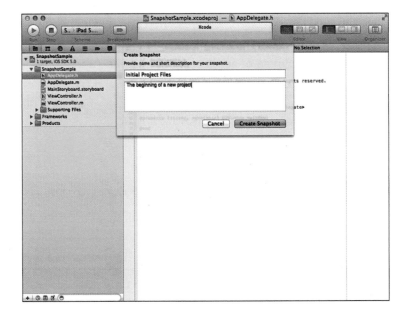

Viewing and Restoring Snapshots

To view (and possibly restore) an available snapshot, choose File, Restore Snapshot. The snapshot viewer displays available snapshots for the project. Choose one and then click Restore, as demonstrated in Figure 12.2. Don't worry. Xcode won't restore just yet; you still have a chancel to cancel.

Notice that at the top of the snapshot selection list you can choose from All Snapshots or just User Created Snapshots. Xcode can automatically generate some snapshots for you (more on that in a minute), so if you want to see only the snapshots you have created, click the User Created Snapshots button.

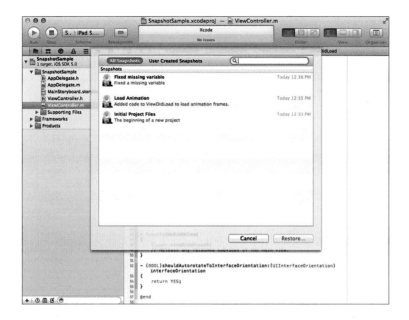

FIGURE 12.2
Choose the snapshot to (potentially) restore.

The display updates to show the files that changed between your current code and the chosen snapshot. Clicking a filename shows the snapshot code on the left and the current code on the right—highlighting changes between the different versions of code, as shown in Figure 12.3.

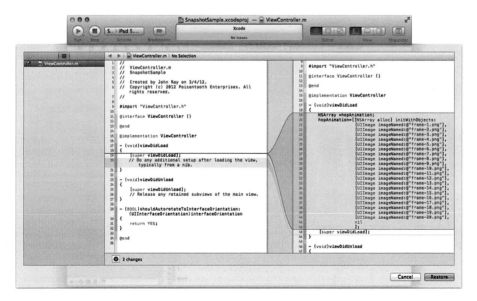

FIGURE 12.3
Use a snapshot to figure out what changes you have made among different versions of your application.

If, after viewing the changes, you still want to restore to the selected snapshot, make sure the files you want to restore are checked in the file list and then click the Restore button. Click Cancel to exit the snapshot viewer without making any changes.

Managing and Exporting Snapshots

You can manage all your project's snapshots as well as export a snapshot as a new copy of your project by accessing the Projects section of the Organizer. Open the Organizer using the Organizer button on the far right of the Xcode toolbar, or by choosing Window, Organizer from the menu. Click the Projects icon to switch to the Projects section.

Projects are listed down the left side of the window, as shown in Figure 12.4. Clicking a project shows the snapshots associated with it. You can select individual snapshots and click the Delete Snapshot button to remove it, or the Export snapshot button to export all the files into a new folder of your choosing.

FIGURE 12.4
Manage and export your snapshots.

Xcode Auto Snapshots

Xcode can (and will) automatically take snapshots for you when you complete an action that makes changes across all (or many) of your files, such as a find and replace. To control this behavior, choose File, Project Settings, and then click the Snapshots check box in the dialog that appears, as shown in Figure 12.5. You can also use the Snapshots Location field to choose where project snapshots are saved.

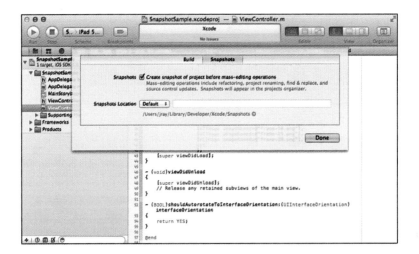

FIGURE 12.5
Enable or
disable auto
snapshots.

A Brief Introduction to Source Control Systems

Snapshots are a great way to keep copies of your projects as you make enhancements or bug fixes. However, they pale in comparison to the features provided by a dedicated source control system. For the rest of this hour, we look at features in Xcode that, although similar to snapshots, go far beyond this simple functionality.

Xcode includes support for two popular version control systems: Subversion, also known as SVN (http://subversion.apache.org/), and Git (http://git-scm.com/). Like any version control system, the purpose of these products is the same, but the implementation in Xcode is different enough to be confusing. Before trying to use Xcode with SVN or Git, you need a bit of background in the philosophy and terminology of each system.

Repositories and Working Copies

Both Git and Subversion can provide server-based repositories. These act as very lightweight file servers that include the files for a project, along with a log of all the changes that have been made over the life of the project.

To edit code that is stored in a repository, you create what is called a working copy from all, or a portion of, the repository. The working copy is a local copy of a project that is edited on your computer (often pulled from a Git or SVN repository). The initial creation of a working copy is called a *checkout* in SVN terminology and a *clone* in Git terminology.

A checkout creates a copy of the code in an SVN repository along with the information SVN needs to track your changes. A clone of a Git repository, however, creates a full local Git repository that is no longer reliant on a server at all. The local repository contains a "remote" entry that links back to the originating server, but you do not have to use it if you don't want to.

Committing Changes

One of the biggest differences between your use of Git and SVN in Xcode is saving changes to your code. You edit your projects exactly as you always have, editing the working copies of your code. When you decide you want to save a change to the repository, you execute a *commit* action. The commit notes the change and gives you an opportunity to annotate the change, as well.

In Subversion, a commit stores the updated file back to the repository immediately. In Git, however, your local copy *is* the repository, so nothing is updated on the remote repository. To push your changes back to a network repository, you must execute a Push command, as discussed later in this hour.

Downloading Changes

As you commit and, in the case of Git, push changes to a central repository, you'll also want to download changes that other users have added to the repository. To do this, you execute an Update command on the SVN repositories and a Pull on Git repositories. In either operation, if there are conflicts with the code occur in your working copy, you are given the opportunity to reconcile the conflicting code.

Branching and Merging

Developers often need to maintain a release version of a product while working on new features. The base/release version of a project in Git/SVN is the *trunk*. New versions of the trunk are developed in branches off of the trunk or off of another branch. In Subversion, you work on branches in a new working copy of your code. Git maintains a single working copy and enables you to switch branches at will.

When changes are complete, and a branched version is ready to become the release version, it is merged with another branch (or the trunk) to create a unified code base. Conflicts are dealt with, and then the finished code is committed to the repository and pushed (with Git) to the remote server, if desired.

Did You
Know?

You might, in your SVN/Git travels, encounter references to the term *tags*. Tags are simply named copies of a repository. You might maintain a tagged copy of each release of your software (version 1.0, version 2.0, and so on).

These are the basic operations that you learn about in the rest this hour. We cover just the tools necessary to make this work in Xcode. Entire books are written about using Git and Subversion, and the feature set exposed in Xcode is much smaller than what is available from the CLI. If you're interested in learning more about these tools, I highly recommend reading the resources on their respective websites.

By the
Way

If you want to experiment with server-hosted Git/Subversion repositories, sign up for an account at Beanstalk (http://beanstalkapp.com/), Assembla (https://www.assembla.com/), or Github (https://github.com/). The first two sites offer low-cost (and trial) accounts with access to both Subversion and Git. The third option (Github) provides free Git repositories for open source projects and low-cost options for private Git repositories.

Working with Subversion and Git Repositories

Xcode's integration of Subversion and Git features directly into the UI make working with these systems quite simple, even if you have never touched a version control system before. In fact Xcode even enables you to create local Git repositories that you can use to track your own changes on a project or share, via a file server, with other individuals working on a project.

In this part of the hour, we create a local repository, and then cover the process needed to connect to remote SVN or Git servers. Because these topics do not necessarily flow together as well as I would like, do not feel bad about jumping around to find the information relevant to you.

Watch
Out!

Finding the Elusive Source Control Settings

Xcode's source control features are generally easy to use but are spread out through the application in a way that does not seem very intuitive. In general, you should focus your attention on two places if you are looking for something: the Organizer's Repositories area and the Source Control submenu under the File menu.

Creating Local GIT Repositories

If you're a small developer with a good backup system and only a few people work-ing on a project, you can probably do just fine with a locally hosted Git repository that Xcode can create for you when you start your project.

To create a project that includes its own Git repository, follow these steps:

1. Begin the project-creation process, as you learned in Hour 4, "Using Xcode Templates to Create Projects."

2. When prompted to save the project, be sure the Source Control check box is checked, as shown in Figure 12.6.

FIGURE 12.6
Make sure you
have checked
the option to
use source
control.

3. Click Create. The project is created and opened.

Within the main project group in the Project Navigator, you'll see a status icon, probably M, as demonstrated in Figure 12.7. This shows the status of the project's source control and demonstrates that your new project is within a repository. You learn more about the source control status icons in the section "Managing a Project in Source Control," later this hour.

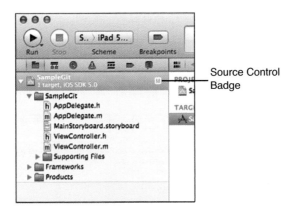

Source Control
Badge

FIGURE 12.7
A source control
icon appears in
your main
project group.

If you want to start working with files in your repository, skip ahead to the
"Managing a Project in Source Control" section. If you think you would like to con-
nect your new repository to a Git server, read the upcoming section "Loading a
Project into a Repository."

Connecting to Remote Repositories

If you have already established a hosted repository outside of Xcode, you can connect Xcode to the repository by walking through a simple setup assistant. This
enables Xcode to download and work with copies of the stored code—or upload new
code to the server. You manage access to your repositories through the Xcode
Organizer's Repositories section (Window, Organizer), as shown in Figure 12.8.

To add a new repository, follow these steps:

1. Click the + button in the lower-left corner of the Repository view within the
   Organizer, as shown in Figure 12.8.

2. When prompted, add a name for the repository and the URL that describes its
   location, as shown in Figure 12.9. This information is available from your
   repository provider (and is usually displayed front and center when a repository is created).

3. The repository type is autodetected, but if it isn't, use the Type pop-up menu to
   choose between Subversion and Git.

4. Click Next to continue.

Repositories

FIGURE 12.8
Use the
Organizer to
manage your
repositories.

Add Repository

FIGURE 12.9
Enter the infor-
mation for the
new repository.

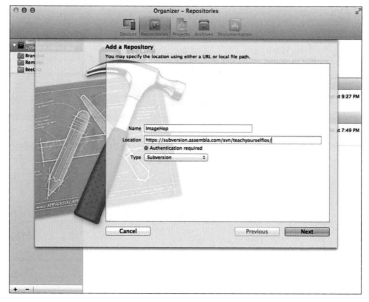

5. If prompted for authentication information, enter it in the dialog box shown in Figure 12.10 and then click OK.

FIGURE 12.10
Provide authentication information if requested.

6. Subversion repositories may prompt for additional information—the paths to the Trunk, Branches, and Tags directories, as shown in Figure 12.11. Enter these if you have them. These are special folders within the repository and are not necessary for creating your connection.

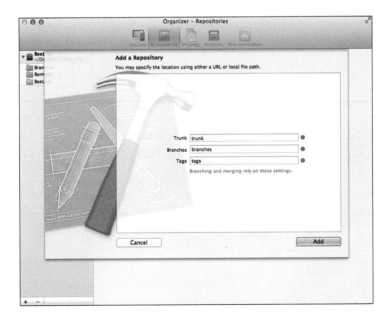

FIGURE 12.11
Enter the paths for Subversion repository directories.

7. Click Add, and the repository is added to the repository list within the Organizer. Selecting the repository enables you to review the type of the repository and its configuration information at the top of the organizer.

As you work with the repository setup assistant, notice the little green, yellow, or red indicators by some of the fields you fill in. These indicate, in real time, whether Xcode has been successful in creating a connection. Yellow or green is usually good. Red means you are probably entering the information incorrectly.

The Xcode welcome screen includes an option to connect to a repository. This actually starts the Checkout or Clone Repository function (also accessible from the Organizer). Instead of just creating a link to a remote repository, it also gives you the option of checking out (Subversion) or cloning the repository (Git) once the connection is in place. The assistant, despite serving largely the same function, collects your information in a different manner than the standard repository setup.

My preference is to just set up the repository (as done here) and then use the other available tools for a clone or checkout. This approach gives you more control and a more consistent interface.

Some Connection Advice

Subversion and Git are not insignificant tools; there are plenty of things that cannot be covered in this hour. I would, however, like to cover two important pieces of information you may find helpful.

First, Git repositories authenticate you by a Secure Shell (SSH) key. You'll do this through whatever interface is provided for your server before connecting with Xcode. You can create a new key for your OS X account using the this command and following the prompts that display:

```
ssh-keygen -t rsa -C "email@youremailaddress.com"
```

When finished, your public key is stored in the file ~/.ssh/id_rsa.pub. This is the file (or the contents of the file) that the Git repository needs you to provide before updating.

Second, Xcode's Subversion interface has an annoying tendency to fail because it automatically accepts an SSL certificate on the hosting provider. To correct this, initiate a checkout of the repository from the OS X command line using the command svn co <your repository URL>, like this:

```
$ svn co https://yourrepositoryurl
Error validating server certificate for 'https://yourrepositoryurl:443':
 - The certificate is not issued by a trusted authority. Use the
   fingerprint to validate the certificate manually!
Certificate information:
 - Hostname: yourrepositoryurl
 - Valid: from Tue, 28 Jun 2011 00:00:00 GMT until Wed, 27 Jun 2012
23:59:59 GMT
 - Issuer: InCommon, Internet2, US
 - Fingerprint: e8:36:95:15:7a:a0:05:b9:1d:c2:bc:c0:fd:dd:78:7d:98:bb:da:31
(R)eject, accept (t)emporarily or accept (p)ermanently? p
```

When prompted, accept the certificate, cancel the checkout, and then retry your connection in Xcode. It should work.

Loading a Project into a Repository

After creating a repository and connecting to it, you either want to pull code from it or add code to it. If you already have a project in the repository and want to download a working copy of it, skip ahead to the "Creating a Working Copy" section.

If you're still reading, you want to add code to the repository, right? In that case, there are a number of different approaches you can take. Regardless of whether you're using Subversion or Git, you can create a working copy of the repository and copy your existing project folder into it, and then commit those changes back to the repository. That said, there are methods specific to both Git and Subversion that might make getting your first code files in a bit easier.

Subversion

Subversion repositories have a special import tool to simplify the import process. To populate a subversion repository for the first time, follow these steps:

1. Open the Organizer and switch to the Repositories view.

2. Expand the SVN repository that you want to perform your initial upload to.

3. Select the Trunk folder, as shown in Figure 12.12.

FIGURE 12.12
Select the trunk to import your initial code files.

4. Click the Import button in the lower-right corner of the window.

5. When prompted, choose your project folder, as shown in Figure 12.13.

6. Enter a comment for your initial upload to the repository, as shown in Figure 12.14, and then click Import.

FIGURE 12.13
Choose the project to import.

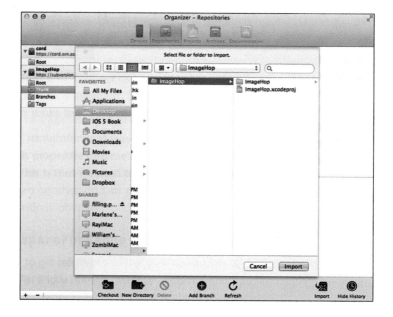

FIGURE 12.14
Enter a comment for the import.

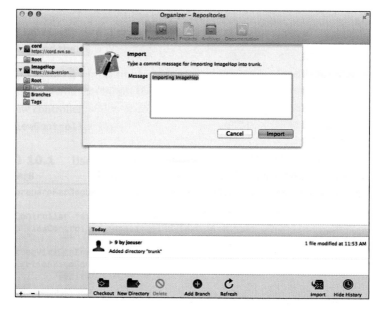

Your project is then imported into the Trunk directory. Be aware that depending on how large the project is, this can take quite some time. Xcode provides almost zero feedback during this process, so be patient. Figure 12.15 shows a project, ImageHop, showing up under the Trunk directory after a successful import.

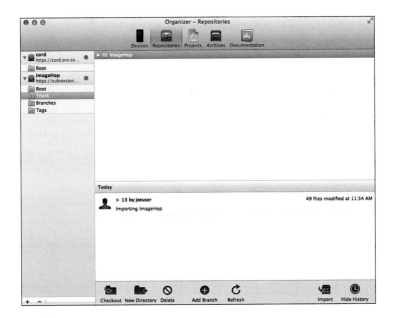

FIGURE 12.15
After the import is complete, the project folder should be visible.

Subversion repositories typically have Trunk, Branches, and Tags directories located under the Root directory. If your repository doesn't have these, you can select the Root folder, and then click the New Directory button at the bottom of the Organizer window to add these directories. Once added, click the icon for the repository within the list on the left side of the organizer and make sure the paths (usually just trunk, branches, and tags) are filled in for each of these locations.

By the Way

Git

For Git projects, you need to either copy your project into a local Git working copy, or if you have already set your project up under local Git source control, you can push the entire project to a repository very quickly.

Git repositories are self-contained. So, instead of pushing a local Git project into a repository you define in Xcode, you instead "tell" your local Git project about the presence of a remote Git repository and provide it with the information it needs to access it. Your repository can then automatically push to the remote server.

When you create a working copy of a Git repository from a remote server, the information we are about to enter is transferred along with it. So your local copy, even if you move it to a completely different machine, always knows how to connect to the repository it came from.

Did You Know?

To configure a remote repository for a local Git-based project, follow these steps:

1. Open the Organizer and switch to the Repositories view. All your local repositories are listed.

2. Expand the repository you want to work with and click the Remotes folder within it.

3. Click the Add Remote button at the bottom of the Organizer window.

4. When prompted, enter the name and location for the remote repository, as shown in Figure 12.16.

5. Click Create.

FIGURE 12.16
Enter the name and location string for the repository.

6. Close the Organizer and switch back to your project.

7. From the File menu, choose Source Control, Push.

8. When prompted, choose the repository you configured and then click Push, as shown in Figure 12.17.

Your project is pushed to the remote Git repository. You have effectively just converted your local Git project into one that is connected to a hosted Git repository.

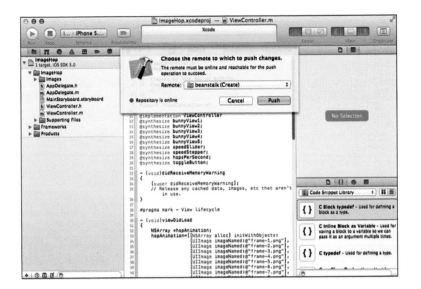

FIGURE 12.17
Click Push to
upload your
changes.

Creating a Working Copy

Before you can start working with code that is under source control, you need to create
a working copy. For Git projects, you may have already done exactly that by creating
a local repository. The local repository is your working copy and can be connected
back to a hosted repository using the steps described in the previous section.

Subversion users always, after having created an initial import, need to create a
working copy to use in Xcode. Regardless of the route you took to get here, this section walks through the steps of using one of your defined repositories to create a
working copy of a project that you can then use in Xcode:

1. Open the Organizer and switch to the Repositories view.

2. For Git repositories, click in the column on the right to select the name of the
   repository. For Subversion repositories, expand the repository by clicking the
   disclosure arrow, and then click the Trunk, Branches, or Tags directory within,
   depending on where the code you want to check out is located.

3. The content area to the right of the repositories list refreshes to show the possible directories that you can check out (Subversion) or clone (Git), as shown in
   Figure 12.18.

4. Select the directory and click the Checkout button (Subversion) or Clone button
   (Git) at the bottom of the Organizer.

5. When prompted, enter a name to use for saving the working copy.

Xcode downloads the code and prompts you whether to open the project and begin working. The working copy is shown with a blue folder under its repository in the Organizer.

Did You Know?

> When you create a Git working copy by cloning a repository, the working copy shows up with its own repository entry in the Organizer, *not* under the original remote repository. It is still aware of the remote repository, but not reliant on it.

By the Way

> I have had limited success when I tell Xcode to open a project immediately after checkout. I find that checking out the project then opening it from the Finder is more reliable than just waiting for Xcode to decide whether it wants to behave.

Managing a Project in Source Control

Once you have a project under source control, you work just as you normally would, but you now have some additional options at your disposal. You'll also notice some changes in how the files display in the Project Navigator. In this, the last part of the hour, we review many of the common activities you will perform with your Subversion or Git repository.

Status Codes

When working with a project that is under source control (that is, your working copy), you'll notice that a number of badges appear beside the files listed in your Project Navigator, as shown in Figure 12.19.

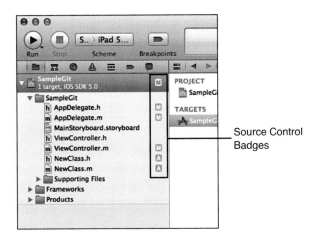

FIGURE 12.19
The Project Navigator now contains badges indicating source control status.

Source Control Badges

Table 12.1 lists the badges you might encounter, as provided by Apple.

TABLE 12.1   Badges You Might Encounter

Symbol	Meaning
M	Locally modified file
U	Updated in repository
A	Locally added
D	Locally deleted
I	Ignored
R	Replaced in the repository
–	The contents of the folder have mixed status; display the contents to see individual status
?	Not under source control

You can click the tiny repository icon (shaped like a filing cabinet drawer) at the bottom of the Project Navigator to filter your Project Navigator files to show only the files that have an updated source control status.

Did You Know?

Commits and Pushes

The most common type of change you need to make when working with source control is a commit. A commit is used to add a finished collection of code to the repository. You might, for example, perform a commit at the end of every day or commit any changes you have made after you have tested them thoroughly.

To perform a commit, follow these steps:

1. Choose File, Source Control, Commit.

2. The Commit dialog appears, as shown in Figure 12.20.

FIGURE 12.20
Commit the
check files to
the repository.

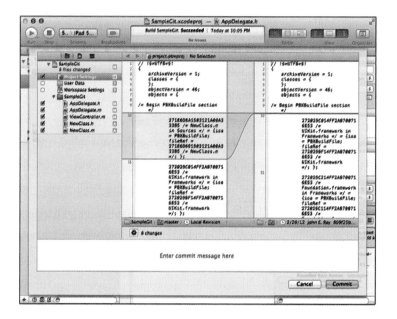

3. Click to check the check boxes beside each of the modified or added files that you want to commit.

4. Enter a message to describe your changes in the text area at the bottom of the dialog.

5. Click Commit to commit your changes to the repository.

> You might want to commit only related files at the same time—not everything all at once. This gives you an opportunity to document your changes more fully than applying a single commit comment to every changed file in your project.

After you have completed a commit on Subversion, you're done. Your file is sent back to the hosted repository. With Git, however, your changes are sent to the server only after you execute a Push command. To push your changes, select File, Source Control, Push from the menu. After a few seconds, you should see a list of the possible remote destinations you can choose from, as shown in Figure 12.21. Choose the destination and then click Push. Your changes are transmitted to the remote repository.

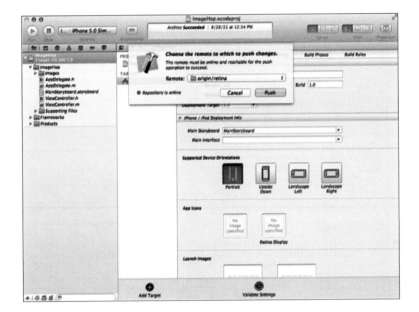

FIGURE 12.21
Choose where the files should be pushed.

Don't Commit (Everything)!
You do not have to commit files just because they have been modified. You can discard your changes within the Project Navigator, or from the commit screen by right-clicking the file and choosing Discard Changes from the Source Control menu. Using this same menu, you can also choose to ignore files that you do not want to commit or manage in your repository or commit a selection of files immediately.

Updates and Pulls

While you're making changes to your project in your local working copy, others might do the same in their copy, committing changes back to the repository. The end result: Your version of the project might become out of sync with the central repository. This is not a problem. In fact, it's a guaranteed outcome of a distributed source control system.

To update your working copy of a project to the latest version held in a repository, you use the Update command (Subversion) or Pull command (Git). Strangely, only the Pull command is available from the File, Source Control menu, whereas Update is available under the contextual menu. To keep things consistent, I recommend these steps:

1. Go to the Organizer's Repositories area

2. Select the blue folder (the working copy) of the project you want to update/pull.

3. Click the Update or Pull button that appears below the content area of the screen, as shown in Figure 12.22.

FIGURE 12.22
Click the Update or Pull button (shown here) to get your code in sync.

Pull (or Update)

Did You Know?

During a commit, update, or branch merge, you might get a warning about conflicting changes in your code. If this is the case, you are given a UI to correct any conflicts before proceeding. Conflicts occur when there is not a clear path to merge heavy changes across a file—often when two people have modified the same method in the same file.

Viewing Revisions

Using source control enables you to go back through your code and see what changed and when. You can get a quick view of all the commits that have been made to a repository, working copy, or any directory of a repository by selecting it in the Organizer, as shown in Figure 12.23.

FIGURE 12.23
Use the Organizer to get a quick view of the history of your changes.

You can even expand each item in the history and can click the View Changes button to see the changes that have been made to a specific file. As you browse the history, you'll notice that the names associated with changes are not necessarily helpful. To make reviewing the history easier on the eyes (and brain), Apple allows you to tie source control users to individuals in your OS X Contacts application. To do this, just click the silhouette of a person in the history. A popover appears, as shown in Figure 12.24.

Use the popover to enter the pertinent information about the person, or click Choose Card to pick a card from your contacts.

Using the Version Editor

In addition to the Organizer, you can also view the changes that have been made to a file through the Version editor in the main Xcode interface. This works on the current file you have selected, so it is a bit easier to target and identify individual changes.

FIGURE 12.24
Choose a person to tie to the repository changes

To display the Version editor, click the third icon in the Editor section of the Xcode toolbar. The screen refreshes to show one of three modes (Comparison, Blame, and Log), controlled by the three icons in the lower-right corner, as shown in Figure 12.25. Here, the Log mode is visible.

In the Log mode, a chronological list of changes is shown to the right of the current file. Clicking the arrow beside each entry displays the changes.

The Blame mode is similar to the Log mode, but displays the change entries next to the code that was changed, as shown in Figure 12.26. Click the gear icon beside each name to show a popover with the full details about the change, and then click the arrow within the popover to view the changes.

The final view, Comparison mode, shown in Figure 12.27, displays revisions side by side in the Editor area.

Use the pop-up file paths under each side of the view to choose the revision you want to see. Alternatively, you can click the clock icon to show a Time Machine-like view of both files. In this view (visible in Figure 12.27), you can use the arrows on either side of the black bar to position the point in time you want to display on either side.

Version Editor

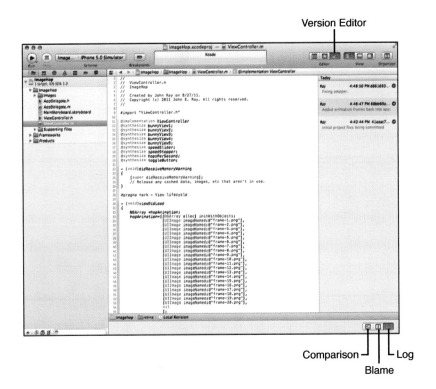

FIGURE 12.25
Use the Version editor to target changes to a specific file.

Comparison — └ Log

Blame

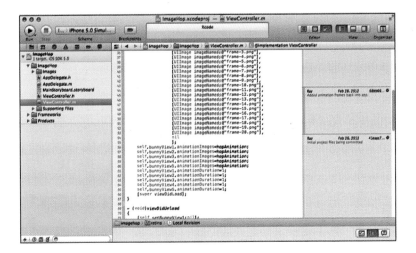

FIGURE 12.26
Blame mode makes it easy to assign blame to your team.

FIGURE 12.27
Use the
Comparison
view to see
changes
side-by-side.

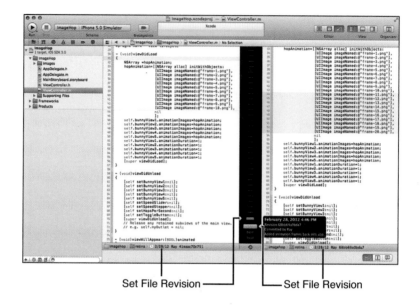

Set File Revision ⎯⎯⎯   ⎯⎯ Set File Revision

What's Missing?

Do you notice something missing from this discussion? Like the ability to revert to a previous version of a file? That's because this feature is not yet integrated into Xcode. If you need to revert to a previous commit, you either view the differences between the files and copy and paste or drop to the command line and issue Git/Subversion commands directly.

Learn more about how to do this in Git at http://book.git-scm.com/4_undoing_in_git_-_reset,_checkout_and_revert.html and in Subversion at http://svnbook.red-bean.com/nightly/en/svn.tour.cycle.html#svn.tour.cycle.revert.

Branches and Merges

When writing code, you'll finally reach a point (I hope) where you are ready to release a product. At that point, you will likely want to create a new branch of your code that will contain any future work (feature additions, for example). You can still continue to work on the existing copy for bug fixes and so on, but the new branch represents your next release.

Creating Branches

To create a branch in Subversion or Git, follow these steps. (Apple has made the process mostly identical regardless of your repository choice).

1. Open the Organizer and switch to the Repositories view.

2. Navigate to the Branches folder within the repository where you want to create a branch.

3. Click the Add Branch button at the bottom of the window.

4. Provide a name for the branch and choose a starting point (an existing branch, or the trunk copy of your code) to copy, as shown in Figure 12.28.

5. In Subversion, this is committed back to the repository immediately, so enter a message to go with the branch action.

6. Choose whether to check out the branch and make a new working copy. In Git, this option is called Automatically Switch to This Branch because instead of creating a new working copy, it switches the existing working copy to the code contained in the branch.

7. Click Create.

FIGURE 12.28
Create a new branch.

Xcode now churns away for a while and, if you have chosen to create a new working copy or switch branches, opens the new branch ready for editing. You then work within the branch until you reach a point where you are ready to merge it back to your main code base, such as a new release. At that point, you perform a merge.

Did You Know?

Although Subversion allows you to check out multiple working copies from any branch you want like, Git makes it very simple to switch between branches on-the-fly. To switch your Git working copy to a new branch, choose the working copy folder within the Xcode Organizer Repositories view, and then click the Switch Branch button in the lower-right corner of the window. You are prompted for the branch you want to switch to, and then Xcode makes the switch and opens the branch for editing.

Performing Merges

To merge a branch back to another branch or to the trunk of your repository, first open a working copy of the code that you want to merge into. This would be your first release, the trunk, or the branch you used to make the branch you're currently working on. Now, with the project open, follow these steps:

1. View the project in the main Xcode workspace (not the Organizer).

2. Choose File, Source Control, Merge.

3. Pick the branch that you are merging with your code, as shown in Figure 12.29.

FIGURE 12.29
Choose the branch to merge with your code.

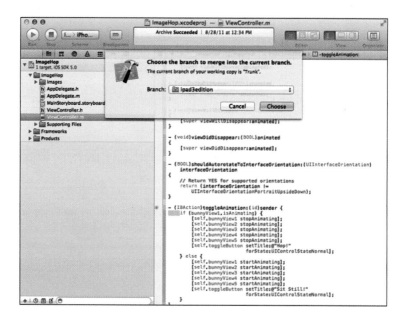

Xcode merges the branches together, identifying any conflicting code along with way, as shown in Figure 12.30. At this point, you must resolve any conflicts before proceeding.

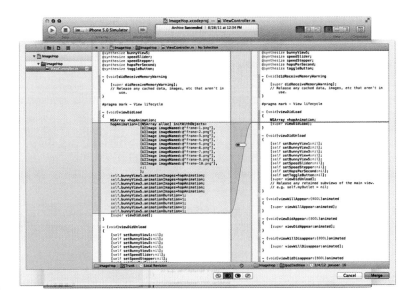

FIGURE 12.30
Fix any conflicts
in your files.

Work through each file listed on the left side of the display. Using the buttons at the bottom of the screen, choose whether to use the code from the file on the right or the file on the left. When satisfied with your selections, click the Merge button to merge the changes into your repository. You should then perform a commit (and a push, in Git) to sync the merge to the remote source control servers.

Summary

In this hour, you learned how to use the different source control options in Xcode. Snapshots, the easiest to employ, can be used on any project at any time and create a view of your code at a specific point in time. You can even export a snapshot to a new project if you choose to split your development at some point. In addition to snapshots, Xcode integrates access to Subversion and Git repositories, including local Git repositories that require no additional servers. Using these options, you can easily work with teams to collaboratively code. Although a few options are missing, and the interface is not as consistent as I would like, the Xcode source control tools do provide most of the features you need to manage large, distributed projects.

Q&A

Q. *Aren't snapshots just as good as using Git or Subversion?*

A. If they fulfill the source control need you have, absolutely. Git and Subversion are useful for projects with multiple developers and multiple branches. These tools also put source control front and center, making you aware of the status of your source files at all times.

Q. *Why doesn't Xcode provide the ability to revert to a previous revision within a repository?*

A. I wish I knew. You can right-click a changed source file and copy the differences from one file to another, but as of the time of this writing, reverts are still not possible.

Q. *Source control sounds like a hassle. Should I bother?*

A. I recommend working with a local Git repository. If you see value in this, expand your horizons by looking at a hosted repository in the future.

Workshop

Quiz

1. Snapshots are implemented using Subversion. True or false?

2. Using the Versions editor, you can easily revert to an earlier copy of a file under source control. Yes or no?

3. How do you upload a local Git repository to a remote server?

Answers

1. Snapshots are a feature of Xcode outside of Subversion or Git.

2. No. You can view the differences between files, but not revert. This is currently not a feature provided with Xcode, but can be handled by using the Subversion and Git tools directly at the command line.

3. Use the Organizer to redefine a remote for the repository, and then use the File, Source Control, Push command to push the existing code base into the remote.

Activities

1. Create a project and experiment with the various source control options. Use the snapshot feature to create and restore snapshots. Use a local Git repository to create branches, merges, resolve conflicts, and so on.

2. Sign up for a Subversion or Git repository at one of the hosting providers mentioned in this hour. Practice connecting to the repository in Xcode and importing projects and creating working copies.

HOUR 13

Xcode-Supported Languages

What You'll Learn in This Hour:

▶ The strengths and weaknesses of different language options under Xcode
▶ How to choose and use the right language
▶ How to add third-party language templates to Xcode

Xcode ships with built-in support for projects written in C, C++, Objective-C, and AppleScript. However, you might want to use one of the many other available programming languages, and it is quite convenient to stick with one development environment for all your programming projects. Thankfully, although Xcode has clearly been optimized for Apple's Objective-C programming language, it is also easily extendable for other programming languages. In fact, if you can provide Xcode with an external program that understands your favorite language and does the right thing when handed a file containing code in it, you can adapt Xcode to any language that can be written in a text file.

This hour provides an overview of the built-in languages and some other popular languages that Xcode can be used for, such as Perl, Python, and Ruby. You also learn how to install and use third-party language templates that can extend Xcode capabilities, and you learn how to adapt external build components if these are not already easily available.

> **By the Way**
>
> Why might you want to use anything other than Objective-C? As good as Objective-C is, most languages have specific tasks for which they're particularly well suited. Objective-C happens to be particularly well suited for many Cocoa and general OS X tasks due to the underlying libraries, but it is a fairly general-purpose language. Other languages are particularly well suited for graphics programming, processing text files, and doing math. Still others are particularly good for quick and easily adaptable utilities for the command line, for interfacing with databases, or for generating web content.

> Sometimes the decision to use a different language stems from the availability of existing code. Millions of lines of scientific algorithms were written in Fortran, and if you can use them instead of rewriting them, you can save years of development effort. The same goes for business algorithms and Pascal (or COBOL). I hope I never, ever, have to write another line of COBOL in my life; but if you need to, Xcode can do that, too.

Choosing the Right Language

The right language for solving a problem depends on of a number of things (for example, the language's base capabilities, your familiarity with it, and the pre-existing code or libraries that are available to perform specific tasks). The right language for processing a text file and extracting simple strings that match a pattern is unlikely to be the same as the language that's right for writing a video game, and neither is probably the right language for constructing a web interface to a database.

If you're familiar with (or fluent in) only a single language, you're stuck using that language as a hammer, with every programming project necessarily looking like a nail to you. Most people get good enough with that big hammer that they can work well enough this way for years, despite the accompanying frustration and inefficiency. Take the time to learn the capabilities of different languages, find out what libraries are already written for it to handle complex tasks, and spend some time working with the one that seems most appropriate for each project you undertake. The effort and time you invest in learning new languages will be quickly repaid when you start realizing that you can write in just five lines (with one of your shiny new languages) the five pages you would have had to write to solve a problem with your big old hammer.

By the Way

> Xcode syntax checking and Xcode support for compiling and debugging in a language are independent of each other. Xcode actually knows at least a little bit about the syntax of a large number of languages (and even beyond languages, formal formats for text files). For example, Xcode understands HTML syntax, but has no idea what to do with it. This means that out of the box you could use it for editing HTML files and get syntax highlighting and other convenient editing features, but you could not *do* anything with the HTML pages you edit in it.
>
> If you configure an external build system project, however, you can explain to Xcode that it should use Safari to display the HTML. Figures 13.1 and 13.2 show the build system configuration and the result of running a project containing an HTML file and an image using this configuration. You'll learn more about how to configure external build system components later in this hour.

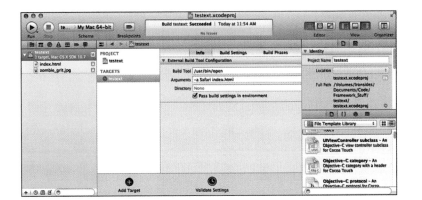

FIGURE 13.1
A build system configuration that uses Safari to display an HTML page.

FIGURE 13.2
The result of using this configuration to run a project containing an HTML file and an image.

As mentioned previously, you can use Xcode for languages that it does not natively support (including those already installed in the system, such as Perl, Python, and Ruby). In addition, you can download other languages and use Xcode for them. As long as the language is installed on your system, you can use Xcode to build your project.

Built-In Languages

C

C is, quite likely, the most important programming language in existence. It is the language on which UNIX was built, on which the Internet was built, and on which countless end-user applications have been developed for the past 30+ years. Your Mac, Linux, the Internet, none of them would be the same without C. (Microsoft probably even uses it somewhere.) When they weren't programming in Assembler, or directly in machine code, the gods programmed in C. Compared to other modern languages, C is much less forgiving, much more terse, and generally much more ill tempered. However, it is about as close to programming on the bare metal as you can get while still using a well-supported language with good library support for everything from numeric calculations to graphics.

C doesn't hold your hand. If you write an assignment statement that reads the value of an integer and you accidentally give it a variable holding a string rather than an integer to read from, C is happy to assume that you know exactly what you're doing and grabs the memory contents from the string and interprets them as though they had been stored as an integer. If you try to store a 4-byte value in a 1-byte container, C happily stores the first byte in the target and the next 3 bytes over the top of whatever happened to be in memory after that location. If you're not extremely careful about how you write your code, C will bite you. And although that kind of behavior sounds a lot like a misfeature, it is also some of the stuff that has made C so powerful and pervasive over the years. If you know what you're doing, you can store a pile of different variables containing arbitrary data in memory and then dance around that memory accessing it and writing to it using pure pointer math, without ever referencing the variables directly. Because C operates just barely above the assembly/machine-code level, you can make optimizations such as aligning array storage so that it fits the physical indexing and addressing schema of the RAM in your machine. If speed is important, these kinds of tweaks can speed memory access up by an order of magnitude.

Did You Know?

Learn C. Unless you really need to squeeze every last bit of performance out of your machine, you are unlikely to actually need to use it on a regular basis, but the skills and discipline you develop will significantly improve your programming in practically any other language. It will also prove useful if you need to glue together C++ code, with which the Internet is riddled, and Objective-C code. As the lowest-common-denominator (but better standardized than either), C is better at talking to both of these higher-level languages than either are at talking to each other.

The canonical reference book for C is *The C Programming Language*, although most programmers know it only by the names of its authors, Kernighan and Ritchie. Although not a particularly long book, it is such a definitive reference that much of the standard C language functionality was designed so that it worked the way that this book says it should, rather than the book being written to match the language. Get it. It's good.

By the Way

Best Uses

C is best used for programs that require speed or brute strength or those that require intricate memory manipulations. C is particularly ill suited for processing text, but it handles large volumes of binary data effortlessly.

C++

C++ was one of two early attempts to bring the concept of object-oriented programming to the C language. It is powerful, but in many respects is overly complex. Although the entire C language was defined and stabilized at only a few pages of parser code quite early in its life, C++ has undergone several rather convulsive revisions, the most recent occurring in 2011. This complexity has not prevented it from being used for an amazing variety of software, and in fact has probably facilitated C++'s application to the wide range of tasks where it has been used. However, it is a source of some annoyance for many programmers; after all, it is reasonably easy to begin to program in C++, but quite difficult to master it sufficiently to be sure that one has chosen the best solution from the options available.

One of the most controversial features of C++ is that it lets you get away with things that it probably should not. C++ can deal with both the procedural and object oriented. In fact, it can deal with both paradigms in the same code, in the same project. This mixing and matching is great if you're writing for yourself and just need something that works. You can attack the problem in whatever fashion fits your thinking at the moment. It is a real problem for maintenance and reuse, though, because it is often quite difficult to tell what's going on without a deep study of the code.

Did You Know?

Get a C++ book. Unless you plan to develop cross-platform applications that need to compile on Linux and other UNIX platforms, you are probably going to be doing more of your real-work programming in Apple's preferred Objective-C. You want to be able to reference C++ constructs and occasionally tweak code that you collect from open source repositories or other C++ developers, so a good reference to the language is going to prove really helpful, but you probably do not need to invest the effort to actually master the language. The definitive reference for C++ is *The C++ Programming Language* by Bjarne Stroustrup.

Best Uses

C++ is best used for large programs that require many interrelated, cooperating parts. Its multiple-inheritance object model enables quite sophisticated class development, but its complexity means that it is poorly suited for small or infrequent programming tasks where a programmer might not develop and maintain mastery.

If you need to make pre-existing C++ code work in an Objective-C project, look into Objective-C++, which is compiler front-end that enables you to combine C++ and Objective-C syntax in the same file.

Objective-C

Objective-C was the other early attempt to objectify C, but it stayed largely hidden from public view until it was adopted as the platform for building the NeXT operating system. Now it is Apple's workhorse object-oriented language. Its syntax differs slightly from the C++ syntax, with C++ tending toward slightly more "talky" and Objective-C tending toward slightly more terse.

Originally inspired by the object messaging model from SmallTalk, Objective-C lacks a number of the complex class-inheritance mechanisms that are present in C++, and it omits some classical object-oriented paradigms, such as class variables, private methods, and operator overloading. C++-style namespaces are also missing. In return, Objective-C implements its object model using messages and adds reflectivity (or introspection)—that is, the ability for a program to observe and modify itself, which enables numerous convenient features that are not possible with languages that strictly segregate executable code and data. For example, Objective-C enables the creation of weakly typed objects that can be queried at runtime to determine what messages they can respond to, enabling a single class definition to operate across a plethora of data types without needing masses of per-case code.

The power of messages combined with reflectivity should not be mistaken to be as simple as those two words appear. Instead of *calling functions* or *calling methods*, Objective-C *sends messages*. This is not just a semantic distinction. If your program that "calls functions" tries to call a function that does not exist, the program has no idea what to do next. The function it is supposed to be running in is not there, so it breaks. If Objective-C sends a message, and nothing is listening, well, the message gets lost, but unless you've decided to trap that behavior and act on it, that's no reason to bring everything to a screeching halt. The message paradigm and the associated code-is-data reflectivity allow Objective-C programs to defer to runtime many decisions that would have to be compiled-in in C++ or C. Learning to take advantage of this flexibility takes some unlearning for old C/C++ programmers, and a bit of time to sink in, but once mastered, it enables code elegance that cannot be accomplished in many other languages.

You need Objective-C books, and to use Objective-C productively on the Mac or iOS device, Cocoa books. There's no way around it. Hour 2, "Just Enough Objective-C and Cocoa," introduces you to the language; but for complex projects, you should invest in a book or two.

Unfortunately, because Apple is both the primary developer and primary user of Objective-C, there are few original, definitive works such as are available for C and C++. The best current reference is Aaron Hillegass's *Objective-C Programming: The Big Nerd Ranch Guide*.

You can also read through Apple's documentation, starting with: http://developer.apple.com/library/mac/#referencelibrary/GettingStarted/Learning_Objective-C_A_Primer/_index.html.

And more good resources are available from http://cocoadevcentral.com/d/learn_objectivec/ - where you can also learn a bit about the Cocoa libraries, which are almost inextricably linked with Objective-C on Apple systems.

Best Uses

Objective-C is an almost absolute requirement for Cocoa programming, and is clearly the preferred choice for development under OS X. Implemented as a lightweight layer on top of C, it has most of C's strengths, while providing useful frameworks that make things like text processing less painful.

AppleScript

AppleScript is Apple's ridiculously useful but incredibly poorly promoted scripting language, useful for everything from renaming a bunch of files in a directory to tying together numerous large commercial applications into a single-click workflow for processing data. AppleScript has access to many components of the Cocoa user interface (for example, file-picking dialogs) and to any functionality that any Mac application exposes through an Apple Events interface.

AppleScript enables users to construct a script that, for example, can ask for a directory, collect the files from the directory, launch Photoshop and apply croppings and preprogrammed manipulations and filters to each of the files, change their resolutions to a standard size, make thumbnails of all of them, create an HTML page containing the thumbnails and link it to the modified versions, and finally package the whole thing up and upload it to deploy on a web server. As a scripting language, all of this functionality can be developed incrementally, and because the "work" is done by external applications, all you really need to put in the AppleScript is the smarts necessary to talk to the applications and pass the results around between them.

Although the ever-present AppleScript Editor application is limited to building fairly simple scripts that are entirely self-contained, Xcode enables the development of integrated AppleScript/Objective-C/Cocoa applications, letting you leverage the strength of each environment to deal with the tasks in which it excels. It currently seems easiest to retrieve the AppleScript dictionary from a program using the AppleScript Editor, as shown in Figure 13.3. After you've identified the features you want to use in your Cocoa-AppleScript application, you can create a project in Xcode (Cocoa-AppleScript Application, under the Applications group) and add your AppleScript calls. The default project that's created by the template is a little less helpful than many of Apple's other default templates, in that it does not call your attention to the correct wrapper section for adding your code with a commented block and appropriate message receiver.

To get started, you can try adding a listener method for `applicationDidFinishLaunching` between the demarcated initialization and cleanup blocks. Figure 13.4 shows a simple example that opens a Finder dialog for you to pick a folder and then sends the files in the folder off to Photoshop to build them into a contact sheet. Because the point of using the Cocoa-AppleScript mechanism was to leverage the Cocoa features, you probably actually want to build some interface functionality in to the NIB file and catch messages from that, instead of running straight from the launch as this example does.

FIGURE 13.3
Using the AppleScript Editor to retrieve the AppleScript dictionary from a program.

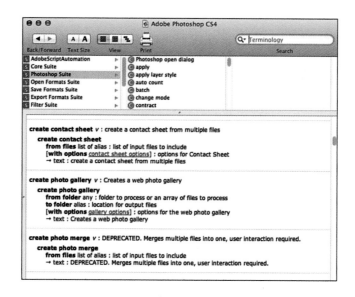

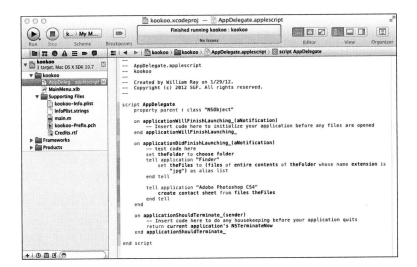

FIGURE 13.4
AppleScript can accomplish complex behaviors (such as prompting user input through a file-browser dialog and such as feeding entire folders of files through an application-processing pipeline) with very few lines of code.

Although AppleScript is enormously useful, it seems like Apple and the application vendors both enjoy fiddling with it enough that what works today often needs tweaked tomorrow. The tweaks usually are not too difficult, but given the frequency of changes to the application interfaces, and seemingly to Apple's end of things as well, you are better off using the documentation on your system than relying on any printed reference. Between the developer documentation available in Xcode and the documentation every application provides through its AppleScript dictionary, you should be good to go.

Did You Know?

Best Uses

AppleScript is application glue. It is best used for coordinating and connecting functions from the Finder and other OS X applications. It has severely limited functionality for any type of data processing or manipulation within itself.

By the Way

Java

Java is the darling of the modern and trendy object-oriented programming crowd, and as an incredibly verbose language with numerous features to protect the programmer from carelessness, it generally annoys old-school C programmers to no end, while simultaneously amusing more modern programmers who think the C programmers are silly for *liking* to walk uphill to school, both ways.

Java has the quite interesting feature that, at least theoretically, you can write your application once in Java and then run it, without modification, on any platform that has a *Java Virtual Machine* (JVM). There is, admittedly, some performance penalty induced by the requirement that the JVM has to sit between the program and your real hardware, but the intention is that the extreme portability of the language makes the performance hit worth it. The intentions and theories are, perhaps, a bit optimistic. Practically every Java application you can find on the Internet is distributed with special versions for each operating system because things are not quite identical enough. Practically every Java application also feels like it is running on a machine that is 10 years older than the rest of the software on your system.

Originally envisioned as a way to deploy software interfaces over a network (actually not the Internet), Java was quickly adopted as a way to deliver write-once, run-anywhere software from a web server and run it within a web browser. As such, it has a significantly enhanced set of security features to help prevent a malicious remote server from negatively affecting a client computer that is running its code. Some of these security features also induce impediments that are peculiar to Java. For example, the JVM operates in a restricted memory region, and it is entirely possible (and quite common) for Java programs to run out of memory within the JVM, even though the computer's RAM is mostly free. Java was also quickly adopted as the object-oriented training language of preference for a great many university computer science programs. This has fostered the development of quite a large library of utility applications written in Java, so it is a useful language to have around for the purpose of avoiding reinventing the wheel. Unfortunately, this is also probably a significant factor in the dismal performance of many Java applications, as many of the programmers who have worked in the language are still at the stage in their careers where paradigm overrides practicality and so they write like they were taught, instead of using the "dirty tricks" that experienced programmers use to squeeze performance out of code.

Did You Know?

Even Apple doesn't think you should use Xcode for Java projects. It is "supported," but not well. Apple recommends Eclipse (http://www.eclipse.org/), NetBeans (http://www.netbeans.org/), or JetBrains IntelliJ IDEA (http://www.jetbrains.com/idea/) as better IDEs for large Java projects.

By the Way

Best Uses

Java is best used for developing small cross-platform applications, especially those that run within web browsers. It places severe limitations on program memory, and its performance might cause users to feel that their machines are sluggish.

Perl

Perl is Larry Wall's Pathologically Eclectic Rubbish Lister (or, *Practical Extraction and Report Language*, if you prefer). Its overwhelmingly most significant feature is its treatment of regular expressions. Regular expressions are a way of describing patterns in strings and the allowable variation in the patterns. If you're familiar with wildcards at the command line, you're familiar with a very primitive form of regular expression. The type of regular expressions that Perl supports can model much more complex patterns in data.

Combined with a C-like syntax for general utility programming, Perl makes for a very convenient language for processing text files, finding patterns within them, and acting on the pieces of the patterns. For example, a Perl program to read an HTML document and extract all the links to image files would, if you were feeling verbose, take three lines of code. If you wanted to download all the image files, as well, that would add one more. Perl's regular expression engine is so powerful that it is even possible to (*easily*) write a regular expression to grade math problems. And it only takes three lines!

Don't believe me? Put the following code in a file named grademath.pl and make the file executable. (Kudos to Tim Conrow of comp.misc.lang.perl for pointing me to this solution more than a decade ago.)

```
#!/usr/bin/perl
use re "eval";
print $ARGV[0] =~ m@(\d+)\s*([+*%-])\s*(\d+)\s*=\s*(??{eval "$1 $2 $3"})@ ?
                                            "pass\n" : "fail\n";
```

Run it from the command line like this:

```
ray% ./grademath.pl "6 + 5 = 19"
fail
ray% ./grademath.pl "6 + 5 = 11"
pass
ray% ./grademath.pl "3 * 9 = 27"
pass
```

Perl's great strength, its regular expression engine, is also probably its greatest weakness. In addition to complex regular expressions looking much like the result of your cat taking a nap on your keyboard, if you spend much time working in Perl, everything starts to look like a problem to be beaten with a clever application of regular expressions. A surprising lot of tasks can be addressed that way, but sometimes it is good to take a step back and see whether that graphical adventure game you're writing might be better written in something that doesn't believe that the whole world is made of text.

Xcode supports Perl syntax highlighting, but because Perl is an interpreted rather than compiled language, there's nothing to "build" for a Perl script. You could, if you wanted, set up an external build system rule to run the script from the command line when you click Run. However, Perl scripts are more often useful from the command line, with data piped in or with files and arguments provided at a shell prompt.

Get yourself a copy of the Camel book, otherwise known as *Programming Perl*. It is the definitive reference and will ease you on your way to appreciating the wonders of regular expressions.

Best Uses

Perl is ideally suited for processing textual data, breaking it into manageable chunks, and manipulating those chunks. It is not a particularly high-performance language, but the rapidity with which sophisticated processing procedures can be developed often more than offsets what Perl lacks in speed. Perl is almost never the right language for working with binary data.

Adding Support for Other Languages

In addition to being useful for languages that are "all there" but that just need special consideration in the way that their projects are set up, such as Perl, Xcode can be extended using third-party add-ons. These add-ons can supplement Xcode capabilities with anything from additional templates and appropriately customized build settings to completely new compilers for languages that the default Xcode is not even aware of. Two of the most popular languages supported by third-party add-ons for Xcode are Python and Ruby. Add-ons for other languages, such as Fortran and COBOL, are available, but functional updates to them usually lag considerably behind Xcode releases.

Python

Python is one of a new breed of languages that manage to combine quite high-level language constructs and direct execution without (obvious) compilation with significant performance. Python is object oriented without being too talky, and has both a large following of loyal users and an amazing collection of utility libraries.

Among Python's other admirable traits, complex math (in both senses of the word) is quite easy to implement. Matrices, for example, can be first-class objects, letting you write canonical algebraic notation to perform matrix manipulation, instead of requiring that you write two pages of nested for loops, as would be required in

C-derived languages. This flexibility is a result of the ease of extending Python's default classes and overloading Python operators.

Python's syntax is generally C-like, with some notable exceptions, the most significant of which is that it does not use any type of block delimiter to demarcate the code blocks under the control of, for example, conditional expressions. Instead, Python uses indentation. Whether this is a good thing or a bad thing is the subject of an ongoing battle of epic proportions in online discussion groups. Regardless of whether it is good or bad, however, this feature of Python absolutely requires a Python-aware editor for development.

Xcode understands Python syntax as shipped, but can additionally be extended by the inclusion of useful project templates. Available from https://github.com/chenhait-eng/Python-Project-Template-for-Xcode-4, these templates provide preconfigured default projects for both the Apple-provided system Python and for MacPython (http://wiki.python.org/moin/MacPython) if you have that version installed. Both templates available at the link can be installed in either ~/Library/Developer/Xcode/Templates/ for your personal use, or in /Applications/Xcode.app/Contents/Developer/Library/Xcode/Templates/Project Templates/Mac/Other/ to make them available systemwide. When selected as an Other project type for a new project, both configure an external build system build, with most of the required trivia filled in.

Did You Know?

That bit of fine print that flashed by when you were clicking through to create your Python project after installing these templates said that you needed to edit the build scheme to run your script and that there were instructions in a ReadMe file in the Supporting Files directory.

The brief summary is that you need to select Edit Scheme from the Product menu, and then edit the properties for the Run phase. Under the Info tab, the Executable needs to be set to the same Python path as is configured for the external build system. The Debugger should be set to None. Under the Arguments tab, turn on Base Expansions for your target, and add a new item to Arguments Passed on Launch. Fill this argument in with $(SOURCE_ROOT)/*targetname*/ followed by the name of the Python file that should be executed when you click Run.

By the Way

Best Uses

Python is extremely well suited for use in scientific and mathematical applications, especially those where its SciPy and NumPy libraries bring in highly optimized solutions to common mathematical tasks. Fortran programmers are likely to find Python appealing. In other contexts where libraries are available to support a given task, Python's implementations tend to be quite good. Python's lack of block delimiters make it nightmarish to use if the code is transported back and forth between different developers with editors that mix tabs and spaces.

Ruby

Ruby is another modern, high-performance, high-level language. Like Python, it has a dedicated following of loyal users and a number of useful libraries. It is also an object-oriented language, although it is simultaneously more thoroughly object oriented in its general approach and less pushy about being object oriented in actual use.

Like Objective-C, Ruby is reflective, enabling dynamic metaprogramming and modification at runtime. Unlike Python, which supports private methods that are truly private, Ruby exposes every class method to running programs, enabling full subclassing of any class, and thereby overriding and replacement of class methods.

In Ruby, everything is an object. Everything. Classes are objects, variables are objects, even (what look like static) numbers are objects. Combined with reflection, this means that you can do things like ask the number 5 what methods it supports. Seriously. If you put the command `5.public_methods;` in a Ruby file, what you're doing is asking the numeral 5 what methods it understands. And if you really want, you can extend the methods and teach 5 new tricks.

Another significant feature of Ruby, although it sounds silly to say, is that Ruby somehow inspires the creation of clean code. Where Perl frequently looks like random noise, and Python starts to all run together with its lack of block delimiters, Ruby code just somehow looks neat and tidy. I have no idea why, but I'm not the only person to have observed this. Give it a try, and I bet you'll agree with me.

Xcode understands Ruby syntax as shipped, but it can also be extended to support full Cocoa-Ruby application types by adding a (semi) third-party add-on. This particular add-on is a bit peculiar because Apple actually supports its development and ships its framework with Lion, but for some reason they currently make the shipped version of the framework private, thereby disabling Xcode software builds against it. By installing the MacRuby package available from http://www.macruby.org/, you give yourself not only a usable Cocoa-Ruby framework, but also add a new Cocoa-Ruby application type to Xcode's list of application projects that you can create. Like the Cocoa-AppleScript project, the default Cocoa-Ruby project creates a Ruby-powered Cocoa application underlying a NIB-based UI.

Did You Know?

You should study Ruby for a bit to see whether some of its unique features might be magic bullets to solve your programming problems. Although far too varied to begin to detail here, Ruby provides access to some very powerful programming constructs, with surprisingly simple invocation. For example, it is quite easy to tie a Ruby program to a SQL database, such that whenever you manipulate variables in the program it changes values in the database, and vice versa. It is also quite

> easy to pass chunks of code around as anonymous functions, to let other bits of code execute them elsewhere. This might not sound like it is very useful, but when you manage to wrap your head around the idea, it opens up whole new worlds for code cleanliness and clarity.
>
> If you like Python, there is a good chance you won't like Ruby. If you like Ruby, there is a good chance you won't like Python. Try them both, and then stick with the one you find most comfortable.

By the Way

Best Uses

Ruby is well suited for numerous general-programming tasks, and with its Cocoa interface, you can use it to develop high-quality OS X applications. Where Ruby libraries fit a particular task, they tend to be quite well thought out and well written (like with Python).

Other "Unsupported" Languages

The configuration and build steps for the Perl and Python languages are prototypical of what you must do to use Xcode for development in any language that it does not natively know how to compile. As demonstrated by this hour's very first example, using Xcode on HTML, "running" what you've written doesn't even have to mean running it in the sense of executing it as a program. As long as you can configure the external build system with an appropriate build tool and arguments, and configure the scheme executable and arguments correctly, Xcode really can become a code-editing and code-maintenance tool from which you can automatically deliver your project files into any external application.

Summary

This hour covered the general characteristics and flavor of the main languages supported by Xcode and some other languages that can be supported either through the external build system paradigm or through the addition of third-party components. You learned some of the strengths and weaknesses of each language and the types of uses that each is best suited for. Keep these in mind when you reach Hour 15, "Putting It All Together: Building a Mac OS Application," and start to think about putting everything into practice to build a complete working application.

The language you choose should be guided by both the capabilities and suitability of the language for the task at hand and by how comfortable you are in the language (or how interested you are in learning it). You can complete nearly any programming task with practically any programming language, although the effort required will probably differ significantly. Most people, however, will gladly take a lot of fun learning over a little bit of drudgery.

Q&A

Q. *Do the external build system build tool and the scheme run executable really have to be the same?*

A. No. These actually serve two different purposes. The build tool is actually intended to transform your files into something that's ready to run, and the executable in the Run component of the scheme is what's supposed to be used to run your program after it has been built. This difference is somewhat nonobvious in these examples because the external build system has been used on scripting languages that are executed directly, rather than "built" before running.

Q. *Are these all the languages that can be used in Xcode?*

A. Heavens no. They aren't even all the ones that Xcode knows syntax for.

Q. *Is JavaScript the same thing as Java?*

A. Not even close. JavaScript is a completely different language that uses some of the same keywords as Java. It was originally intended as a lightweight, quick-to-implement scripting language for adding in-web-browser functionality. Exactly why it was renamed from LiveScript to JavaScript remains shrouded in some controversy, but the naming has certainly caused some confusion. And yes, Xcode knows JavaScript syntax, too.

Workshop

Quiz

1. What are the best references for learning about Objective-C?

2. Order the languages discussed from slowest to fastest in terms of how quickly they could multiply every element in a matrix by 2.

3. Which language will cause you the most headaches if you're careless?

Answers

1. Apple's developer and online documentation.

2. This is a trick question. For a straightforward implementation, the order is AppleScript or Java, Perl, Python and Ruby tied, C++, Objective-C, and C. However, remember that Python has some real smarts built around things like matrices as first-class objects. This lets you write A*2 to multiply matrix A by scalar 2. The underlying implementation can split that task across cores, so this can yield speeds far beyond what C's closer-to-the-metal implementation can do looping iteratively through the whole matrix on one CPU core.

3. C, or perhaps Perl, depending on your version of *careless*. C causes headaches because it is unrelentingly literal. Perl causes headaches because it is overly helpful but not overly careful itself.

Activities

1. Update the template for the Cocoa-AppleScript project so that it includes default cases to catch `applicationDidFinishLaunching` and `awakeFromNib` messages.

2. Build a new external build system project that supports sh/bash shell scripts. This will prove useful to you when you start building more-complex projects where some steps of the build process require running a script to move or modify files within the project.

HOUR 14

Planning for Reuse: Frameworks and Libraries

What You'll Learn in This Hour:

▶ The purpose of libraries and frameworks

▶ The difference between libraries, frameworks, and just plain code

▶ How to build static libraries and frameworks

▶ How to deploy a framework so that it can be shared with other programmers or applications

▶ How to adapt library code from other sources

This hour begins a series of four lessons that put everything you have learned together into common development tasks in Xcode 4. Hold tight. These hours might take a bit longer than an hour because you can put the pieces together in so many different ways. In the end, you want to make sure you have chosen the best combination for the development project you have planned.

This hour starts by introducing the role of libraries and frameworks in development, walks you through building a static library and a reusable framework, and then illustrates how you can adopt library code from libraries developed on other platforms into Xcode.

Understanding Frameworks

Frameworks and libraries are both ways of packaging compiled copies of reusable code so that it can be used in multiple projects. Frameworks are primarily used for dynamic components—that is, components that are not built in to the software when it is compiled, but rather are loaded in each time it is run. Libraries can be either dynamic (loaded at runtime) or static (included in the compiled application when it is built), though Apple discourages the use of bare dynamic libraries, and instead prefers them to be packaged into frameworks.

> If you're already familiar with the idea of dynamic libraries, you can think of frameworks as a more completely featured version of the dynamic library idea. Whereas dynamic libraries package only executable routines and associated symbols, and are instantiated as a single versioned file, a single framework can encapsulate any number of independent dynamic library files, all the header files that define the routines for the dynamic libraries, and also associated resource files such as images, documentation files, or other data used by the libraries.
>
> If you are not familiar with dynamic libraries, you probably do not really need to worry about writing your own frameworks for a while anyway. You're welcome to keep reading, but if this reusable components business is confusing, don't worry; when you need it, it'll all make sense.

Static libraries are used to dump their object contents directly into your project, as though the source is there, when you build your project. The necessary objects are linked, the necessary executable modules are copied into your application, and it all gets collected together in a single executable file where all the necessary pieces (and if your compiler is good, none of the unnecessary pieces) are included.

You can think of the difference between static and dynamic libraries as much like the difference between DVDs and streaming copies of a movie. You link the static library at compile time, which includes its executable object code into your application. You buy the DVD, which becomes part of your personal collection. If you move the application, the compiled-in executable components copy with it. If you move apartments, you take the DVD with you. If you copy the application, you duplicate the compiled-in executable components, thereby using disk space to store the same thing twice. If your friend wants to own a copy of the DVD, he buys his own copy, and the two of you now have two physical copies between you. If the static library gets updated and a new version becomes available with new features, your application doesn't know anything about this and keeps on using the compiled-in code it has always been using. If you want the new features, you recompile the application. If the studio releases a new version of the DVD, you're stuck with the old one you already own. If you want the new one, you buy another copy.

However, if you bought a streaming copy of the movie from the iTunes Store, you do not get a copy of the movie until (and only while) you're watching it. This is like using a dynamic library. Your application knows that it can use the library, but it doesn't actually have the executable code on hand. When you launch the application, it has to load the content, just like you have to download the movie to watch it. When you move apartments, you do not take a copy of the movie; you just download it again when you want to watch it again. When you run your application a second time, it has to load the dynamic library all over again. When your friend wants a copy of the movie, she gets pointed to the very same downloadable content that you use. When you duplicate your program, it doesn't duplicate the dynamic library, the new copy just also knows where to ask to use the library at runtime. When the studio updates the movie in iTunes to correct some damaged footage, you see the updated version automatically the next time you watch it. When the dynamic library is updated to fix a bug or function more efficiently, those changes are automatically available to your application when it loads the updated dynamic library the next time it runs.

Making the Choice

If a routine in your project could also be useful in some other project, placing that routine in either a framework or a static library is a way to let you maintain the reusable routine independent of either project, while making sure that it can be used in both.

If the routines that you're considering putting into a framework really do not have any use outside your current project, it is often pointless, and usually actually counterproductive, to put them into libraries or frameworks.

If the reusable bits are going to be completely finished and never need updated, putting them into a static library makes sense.

If the reusable bits might need to be updated often, especially if they need to be updated without recompiling the entire application project, a framework is appropriate—this is even true if the bits are not really all that reusable.

If the code has a significant memory footprint, and multiple programs might need to use that code at the same time (multiple different programs or multiple running copies of the same program), a framework is appropriate because every running program shares access to the same loaded instance of a framework.

However, if you want to use the same reusable code bits in both a Mac OS X application and an iOS application, you may want to target a static library. Apple doesn't allow the use of third-party frameworks on iOS devices yet, so if you use framework-specific features when building the OS X version, you'll have additional work to do when adapting those routines to a static library for your iOS deployment.

Did You Know?

There is also a new automagic way to deal with code/data reusability with Xcode 4. Workspaces, covered in Hour 20, "Keeping Things Organized: Shared Workspaces," promise to automatically address issues of code and data reuse across multiple projects, simply by maintaining those projects within a single shared workspace environment.

Unfortunately, although this will undoubtedly become a much more streamlined and convenient way to handle reusable components as Xcode continues to mature, a) some of the workspace features are not quite ready for prime time, and b) workspaces are an Xcode-specific feature. In contrast, libraries and frameworks are uses and adaptations of standard software development/distribution mechanisms that are almost universal. So, the workspace-specific mechanisms limit your ability to share your work with users of other development environments on OS X or on other platforms such as Linux.

For example, consider developing a video game. If your game uses physics, it is probably important to you that your game and its physics run as fast as possible. If you're just developing one video game, forget libraries; compiling the physics code directly into your game makes the most sense. It'll start faster, and the optimizer will be able to reject unused portions of the code, appropriately defer execution, unwrap loops, and so on more efficiently.

If you're developing a suite of games all based around the same physics engine, consider using a static library that gets linked with all your games. You lose a little bit of efficiency because some optimizer tricks cannot be applied to the library when it is compiled independent of the final applications, but the linker will still do its best to eliminate unused bits. If your physics code is finished, though, and you're never going to touch it again, and no one else will need to either, a single static library that just gets linked to each of the games makes life easy and nearly maximizes performance.

However, if you're developing a game or a suite of games, all of which use the same communication engine to facilitate network play, and you're continuously updating the communication engine as you think of new tricks to optimize the communications stream, using a dynamic library in a framework makes good sense. You lose a bit of efficiency because each time the game starts it has to load the dynamic library, figure out what symbols are where, and coordinate all of that with your existing program, and optimization cannot make nearly as much an improvement in execution speed. However, you get the significant benefit of being able to tweak the communications code and deploy new variations on it under your game, or all of your games, just by recompiling the framework, without having to rebuild your game or games.

An amazing amount of bad advice exists on the Internet regarding using frameworks. In addition to everyone and his brother recommending that you put oodles of code that has no business being in a framework into frameworks, Internet programming mavens have another favorite chestnut that many of them seem quite eager to offer: embedded frameworks.

They just love embedded frameworks. Embedded frameworks are frameworks that you build and then include inside your application bundle so that your application always uses its own, self-contained private copy of the framework that is always exactly the version it expects and is always exactly where it expects it to be. This provides quite a lot of convenience, and in fact you learn how to set up a framework for this purpose in this hour of the book.

Stop and think about this for a minute, though. If the purpose of a framework is to encapsulate reusable, independently updatable routines, is it really a big advantage to hide it privately inside an application bundle, where it cannot be reused and where it cannot be updated? Usually, the answer is no. In fact, usually the answer is that if an embedded framework will work, linking the code directly as a part of your application works better.

Embedded frameworks are really best used for situations where you either want to distribute the framework conveniently bundled inside your application and then let the application install it for systemwide usage or when it's impossible to properly install the framework in /Library/Frameworks/ because of system security issues. They also prove useful when you are co-developing a piece of software and a support framework for it, because embedded frameworks limit the amount of trouble that errors or test code in the framework can cause for the rest of the system (because their effect is limited to the application bundle that contains them). Other than those situations, however, embedded frameworks are usually the lazy way of accomplishing something that could better be done some other way.

Making a Static Library

Making a static library is much like making most other projects in Xcode. In short, you tell Xcode that you want to build a project, select Static Library as the type of project to build, add some code, and build away. You can then include the result as a component in other projects that need to use the routines you have built within the library. The only real trick to this process is that you also need to specify the parts of the library that should be exposed to programs that want to use the library. Internal parts of the library (bits that the library requires for functionality but that the applications that use the library shouldn't be fiddling with) need to be declared to be private to the library (peculiarly, Apple uses the term *project* for these), and bits that need to be available for the external application's use need to be declared public. The following section walks you through the process of building a static library for a simple library that provides a doubly linked list class.

To build a static library, follow these steps:

1. Tell Xcode that you want to create a new project by selecting File, New, New Project from the menu.

2. Select the Framework & Library collection from the left pane and the Cocoa Library item from the right pane, as shown in Figure 14.1.

FIGURE 14.1
Creating a new
Cocoa Library
project.

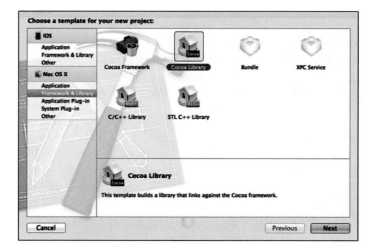

3. Decide on a product name and provide a company identifier.

You should decide on a uniform company identifier and use it for all of your work, but it doesn't much matter what that identifier is as long as it is likely to be unique. As mentioned previously, Apple recommends a reverse-domain-name string for your company specifier. For your own personal use, any arbitrary string is fine.

4. For the project name, choose something meaningful related to the functionality of the library you're building.

We are building a doubly linked list library, so I am calling my project Lists. The value you supply here also gets used for the default class name in the generated project files, so it is probably best to avoid spaces, although you can modify this value in the files if it turns out you prefer to have your classes named something else.

5. Unless you have a good reason to do otherwise, fill in the rest of the dialog box as shown in Figure 14.2.

6. Select Static for the type. After all, although you can build a dynamic library this way, there's little point; frameworks do it better.

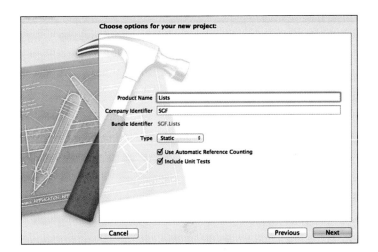

FIGURE 14.2
Choosing
options for your
project.

7. Turn on Use Automatic Reference Counting.

   Unless you really want to manage freeing all allocated memory yourself, just let Automatic Reference Counting deal with freeing memory whenever the last reference to an object is removed.

8. Turn on Include Unit Tests.

   This is up to you. I prefer to include them in case I want to use them later. You might consider them as extraneous to the project.

9. Finally, navigate to where you want to store the project and create it.

Leave the Source Control box checked, as shown in Figure 14.3, to create a local version-control repository for the project, unless you want to exclusively connect the project to a remote version control server. If you leave it on, you can enable both local and remote version control. So unless disk space is seriously tight, leaving local version control turned on does not hurt.

Xcode populates your project with a collection of directories and likely culprits that your project may depend on. You land in a full Xcode project window, as shown in Figure 14.4, with two targets in the Navigator panel (your library and its test suite), several tabs of useful details (some of which you might want to customize in the main Editor area), and compact interfaces to some likely utility functions you might need in the Utilities.

FIGURE 14.3
Navigating to where you would like to store your project.

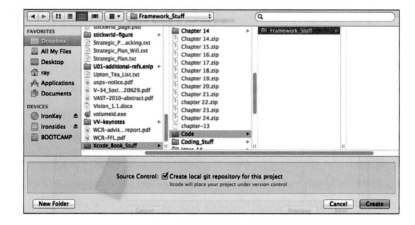

FIGURE 14.4
Your Xcode project window.

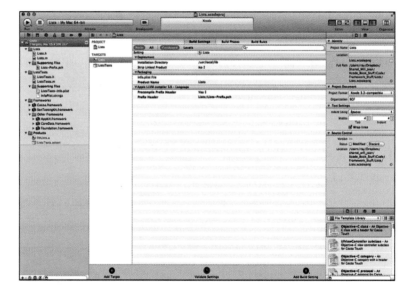

Note that you have a library (starting with lib and ending in .a) and a test suite that appear under Products in the Navigator panel. They are both red because neither has been successfully built yet. Under the Build Settings tab, you can modify the intended deployment directory (although this value is overridden by another setting in the Xcode Preferences Locations tab, discussed in more detail later in this hour), as well as numerous other configurable settings that affect details of the way that your target is built.

Under the Build Settings tab are more configuration options for your project. In this panel, shown in Figure 14.5, you can configure deployments for other versions of the operating system, set up multi-architecture builds, and adjust several features of the debugging system.

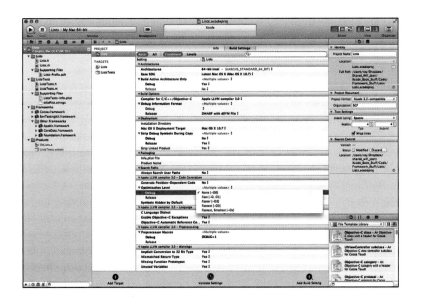

FIGURE 14.5
The Build Settings panel.

Pay attention to the Optimization Level setting. Setting this to more optimized levels can make a significant difference in how fast your program runs. It is not uncommon to see speedups of 3x or more when optimization is turned on. However, optimizing compilers are tricky things. In addition to just eliminating wasted space in your executable, they can also figure out certain situations where your code would have been more efficient if written somewhat differently, and they'll use their more efficient version for building if optimization is turned on. This can lead to quite bizarre effects when debugging because what you see in the debugger is your code, but what is running is the optimized version.

When debugging optimized software, you will often see the program seemingly ignoring simple explicit statements and internally producing values that are entirely inconsistent with the logic of the code as you have written it. This is not an error, but rather an instance of the compiler recognizing, for example, that it would have been much more efficient if you had compared i to 6 instead of incrementing i and comparing it to 7. This behavior is doubly confusing when you're building libraries because they are often dissociated from the code that will eventually use them, which makes debugging more difficult.

Listing 14.1 shows the prepopulated contents of the .h file.

LISTING 14.1   Prepopulated Contents of a default .h File

```
//
//  Lists.h
//  Lists
//
//  Created by William Ray on 1/28/12.
//  Copyright (c) 2012 SGF. All rights reserved.
//

#import <Foundation/Foundation.h>

@interface Lists : NSObject

@end
```

Listing 14.2 shows the prepopulated contents of the .m file.

LISTING 14.2   Prepopulated Contents of a default .m File

```
//
//  Lists.m
//  Lists
//
//  Created by William Ray on 1/28/12.
//  Copyright (c) 2012 SGF. All rights reserved.
//

#import "Lists.h"

@implementation Lists

- (id)init
{
    self = [super init];
    if (self) {
        // Initialization code here.
    }

    return self;
}

@end
```

Add your header code to the .h file by clicking in the Navigator and editing it in the Editor (in my case, that's Lists.h) and add your implementation code into the .m file (my Lists.m). Click the Run button, and you should be rewarded with a successful build, as shown in Figure 14.6. Note that my libLists.a product has now turned black, indicating a clean build.

Select the library (*.a) product and look at the File Inspector in the Utilities. You'll see, under Identity and Type, shown in Figure 14.7, that the build has placed your library in a fairly bizarre directory. This library is what you need to distribute to other people to let them use your code or to place in your /usr/local/lib directory if you want other projects of yours to be able to link against it. You can click the small arrow next to the path to reveal the file in the finder and then copy it somewhere more obvious, or you can change your Xcode preferences to control this behavior.

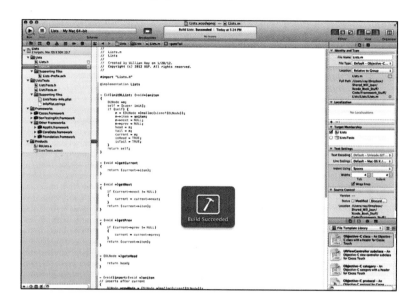

FIGURE 14.6
A successful build.

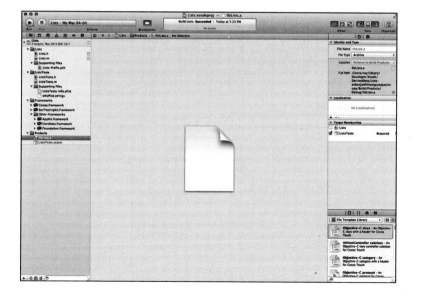

FIGURE 14.7
Identity and Type in the Utilities panel shows where your library has been placed.

Open your Xcode preferences and go to the Locations tab. On the pane that appears, shown in Figure 14.8, you'll see that derived data (things like the .a file you built) is going to go into the Default directory, which is buried in ~/Library/Developer/Xcode/DerivedData/. You can change that Default value to Relative, in which case it switches to using a DerivedData directory within your Project directory, or you can change the value to Custom, which lets you specify an explicit path. The Relative setting is a bit more sane than the Default setting.

FIGURE 14.8
Under the Locations tab in the Xcode preferences, you can change the default locations for the derived data, as well as for snapshots and archives.

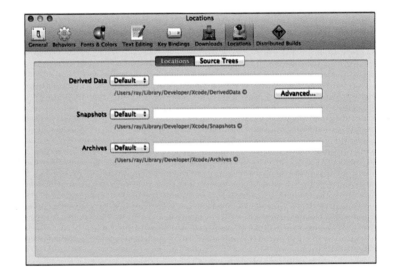

You have another option, too, hidden under the Advanced button. This button brings up another dialog, shown in Figure 14.9, where you can set the build location to either the default or the locations specified by targets. The Locations Specified by Targets setting generates a behavior that is probably more like what you were expecting. It creates Debug (or other appropriate target) directories within the Project directory and puts the output files there, as shown in Figure 14.10. This is essentially the behavior you have come to expect from earlier versions of Xcode.

FIGURE 14.9
Clicking the Advanced button for the derived data brings up this dialog to set the build location to either the default or locations specified by targets.

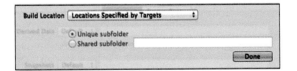

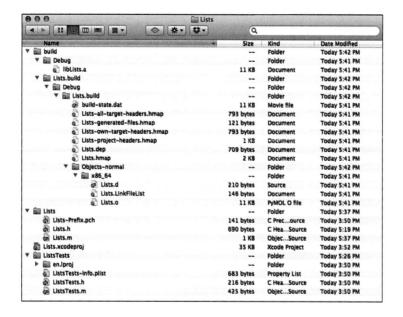

> **By the Way**
>
> Consider this an Xcode bug. If you change the Build Location option to Locations Specified by Targets in the dialog shown in Figure 14.9, and then look at the dialog shown in Figure 14.8, it'll look exactly the same. This dialog does not update to reflect the fact that the files now are not going to land in the Default directory.

If you want to validate that your library does what its supposed to do, and do a bit of debugging without writing a proper application around it, you can use the Unit Test testing suite that Xcode has already begun to populate for you. Under the Tests directory, you have another .h file and .m file. These are supposed to be used for building unit tests so that you can continually monitor the functionality of your code as you build it (as covered in detail in Hour 18, "Test Early, Test Often"), but they are also useful for quick-and-dirty debugging.

As shown in Figure 14.11, add some simple calls to your library functions and add diagnostics with NSLog(). Select Test from the Product menu, and the code you have added will be run, linked against your library. This can give you a rapid readout of functionality without you ever needing to write a main() routine.

Making a Framework

To make a framework, you follow much the same process as when making a static library. The biggest difference, other than telling Xcode that you are building a framework, is that you can include noncode components inside frameworks. Because frameworks are really directory structures like any other bundle, they can contain not just the compiled executable code, but also the header files defining the routine interfaces, image files, and other components that the library, or applications using the library, might need. Setting up these additional components requires a few steps beyond what a static library requires.

FIGURE 14.11
Showing a successful test run generated by adding some simple calls to the library, adding diagnostics with NSLog() and running Test from the Product menu.

To build a framework, follow these steps:

1. Tell Xcode that you want to create a new project by selecting File, New, New Project from menu.

2. Select the Framework & Library collection from the left pane and the Cocoa Framework item from the right pane, as shown in Figure 14.12.

3. Fill in your project name and company identifier as was done for a library and leave the Automatic Reference Counting and Unit Tests options turned on.

4. Pick a place to put it.

5. Again, leave the Git repository turned on.

    You are then presented with a prepopulated Navigator panel with much the same content as was present for your library, and similar build options in the main Editor panel.

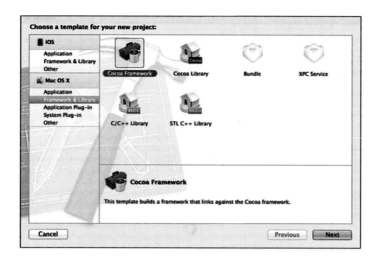

FIGURE 14.12
Selecting
the Cocoa
Framework item
to start a frame-
work project.

6. Fill in your .m and .h files.

7. The same content as you used for your library will do, although you probably
   want to use a different class name, just to reduce confusion.

Here comes a big difference between frameworks and libraries.

If additional resources would be convenient for your code to carry around with it,
such as images it will use in NIB files, you can drag them into the Navigator and
drop them in the Supporting Files folder that's with your framework implementation and header files now. Any data files that would be good to keep with your
code after it has been distributed can be included here, either directly in the
Supporting Files folder or in a directory structure of your choosing beneath it.

After you drop the items, tell the resulting dialog that you want to copy the items
and to create groups for Folders. Make sure that any target that might need
access to the files is selected before clicking Finish.

With the library, all you got was the output .a file and the header .h file that you
wrote for it. Frameworks are bundles of related resources, and the files you add
are included in your framework when it is built.

---

8. Fill in your test suite, too.

9. Build your project by selecting Build from the Product menu, and then test it
   by selecting Test from the Product menu.

If you have your build configuration set to Debug in your build scheme (see
Hour 19), everything will probably work just fine. However, if you have your build

configuration set to Release, you are likely to get an error when your test suite tries to #import your framework header file. This is due to a subtle difference in how the compiler looks for header files when it is using frameworks as compared to when it is using libraries. Specifically, frameworks are supposed to carry their headers around with them, and for some reason, Xcode does not default to copying the headers into the build directory.

By the Way

Consider this another Xcode bug. Sometimes, for reasons I don't understand, Xcode will produce correct output from your test routine, as shown in Figure 14.13, and simultaneously complain that it cannot find the header file that it needs to compile.

FIGURE 14.13
Sometimes Xcode produces correct output from your test routine even while complaining that it cannot find the header files that it needs to compile.

When you look in the Build directory, shown in Figure 14.14, you see the source of the trouble. Under the ListsToo.framework directory, there are proper Versions and Resources directories, but no Headers directory. Things trying to use this framework cannot find them because the directory and the headers it is supposed to contain are missing.

To fix this, follow these steps:

1. Select your project in the Navigator.

2. Display the Build Phases tab in the main Editor panel.

   Here, you find a section called Copy Headers, conveniently denoted as having no items.

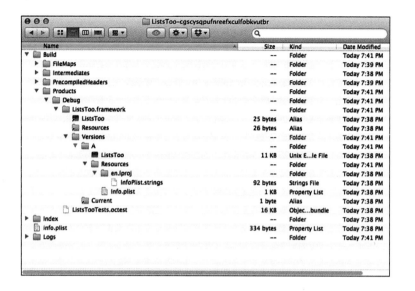

FIGURE 14.14
The Build directory for this framework is missing the Headers directory.

3. Open the Copy Headers section so that you can see the Public, Private, and Project headers subsections and the + button beneath them, as shown in Figure 14.15.

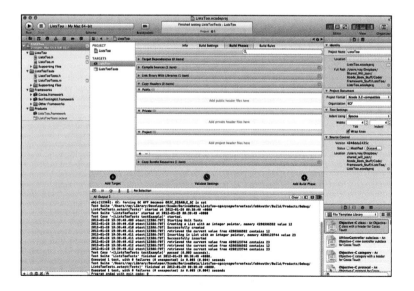

FIGURE 14.15
Under the Build Phases tab of the Navigator panel, you can copy the missing header files.

4. Click the + button.

You are then presented with a dialog like that in Figure 14.16.

FIGURE 14.16
Select the
header file that
you want to
copy from this
dialog that
appears after
clicking the +
button.

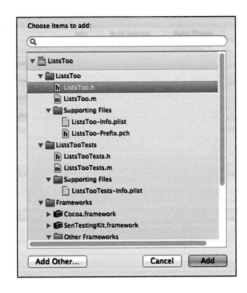

5. Select your .h header file and click Add.

Annoyingly, you'll find that the .h file lands in the Project headers section, as shown in Figure 14.17. This is not helpful. Project headers are, semi-intuitively, private to the project and are not exported. Private headers are, counterintuitively, private to the project but will be exported, although they cannot be used by external applications. Public headers are exported and are available for use by external code. This is where you want your .h file to go.

FIGURE 14.17
The header file
gets copied to
the Projects
section.

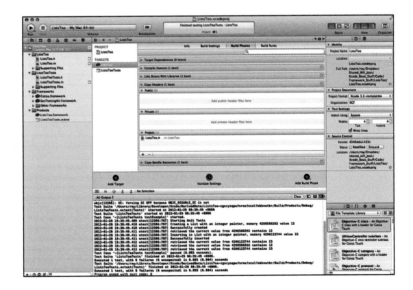

6. Select your header .h file where it has landed in the Projects section and drag it to the Public section so that your configuration looks like Figure 14.18.

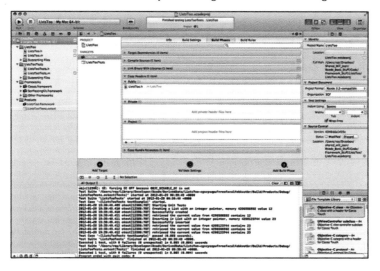

FIGURE 14.18
The header file has now been moved from the Projects section to the Public section.

7. Select your framework in the Navigator again and use the Project menu to build it.

Your Build directory should change to include a Headers directory within the Versions section and a link to it from the top level of the Framework directory, as shown in Figure 14.19. Now if you go back and run your tests, they can find your header files correctly.

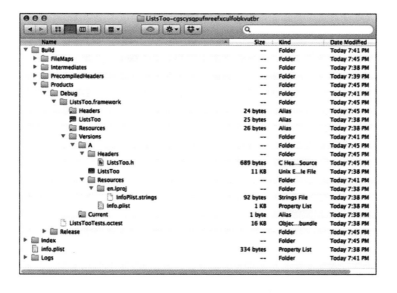

FIGURE 14.19
After building, the Build directory includes a Headers directory within the Versions section and a link to it from the top level of the Framework directory.

Deploying a Framework

You learn how to include your framework in applications that you write in Hour 15, "Putting It All Together: Building a Mac OS Application," but sometimes the point of a framework is just to have the framework. If you need to share the framework, or test it in place in /Libraries/Frameworks/, the easiest way to do this is to archive your framework project, as follows:

1. Under the Product menu, select Archive. This creates an archive of your project and opens the Organizer.

2. Select your project from the archives, as shown in Figure 14.20, and then click the Share button. A dialog like that in Figure 14.21 opens.

FIGURE 14.20
Selecting your project from the Archives in the Organizer.

FIGURE 14.21
Clicking the Share button brings up this dialog, where you can select the Built Products option.

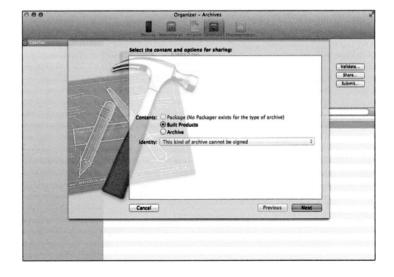

3. Select the Built Products option, click Next, and give it some place to save the archive.

It creates a folder in that location, and if you check the contents of the folder, you'll see that it is a complete copy of your framework, ready to be copied into /Library/ Frameworks/ or ~/Library/Frameworks/.

Reusing Code from Existing C/C++ Libraries

Most existing C and C++ libraries can be built using Xcode with little difficulty. These traditional libraries are simply collections of concatenated object files, and Xcode can compile and concatenate them using simple project templates designed for this task. Figure 14.22 shows the result of attempting to build a simple C program that is trying to call three functions (libfunc1(), 2, and 3) that are not defined within it. Not only does the Editor window flag the implicit declarations of these functions when the program tries to call them, but the error messages highlight the fact that there are no definitions that it can find for libfunc1(), libfunc2(), and libfunc3().

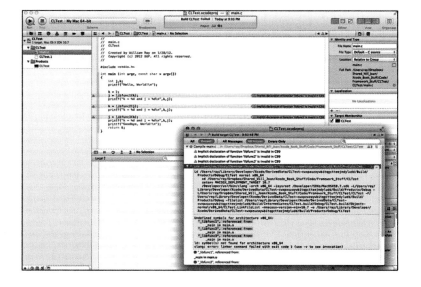

FIGURE 14.22
Showing what happens when trying to build a simple C program that calls functions that are not defined in it.

To remedy this, follow these steps:

1. Create a new project, selecting the C/C++ Library project template.

2. Add C language files and define your functions in them.

3. Add a header file with prototypes for your functions.

   Listings 14.3 and 14.4 show a very simple header file defining libfunc1(), libfunc2(), and libfunc3(), and the entire contents of the C file defining libfunc1(). There are two additional, almost identical C files defining libfunc2() and libfunc3() that are not shown.

LISTING 14.3   Header File Defining `libfunc1()`, `libfunc2()`, and `libfunc3()`

```
//
//  libstaticC.h
//  StaticC
//
//  Created by William Ray on 1/28/12.
//  Copyright (c) 2012 SGF. All rights reserved.
//

#ifndef StaticC_libstaticC_h
#define StaticC_libstaticC_h

int libfunc1(int);
int libfunc2(int);
int libfunc3(int);

#endif
```

LISTING 14.4   Contents of the C File Defining `libfunc1()`

```
//
//  libfile1.c
//  StaticC
//
//  Created by William Ray on 1/28/12.
//  Copyright (c) 2012 SGF. All rights reserved.
//

#include "libstaticC.h"

int libfunc1(int inval)
{
    return inval * 3;
}
```

The libfile2.c and libfile3.c files contain essentially identical code, with the appropriate function definitions.

4. Build the project by selecting Build under the Product menu. The three.c files are compiled into .o files and aggregated into a single .a file. This .a file is your C language library.

5. Open the project that failed in Figure 14.22 and position its Xcode window behind the project where you built the static library.

6. Then drag the .a file and the .h file over into the Project directory of the failed application, as shown in Figure 14.23.

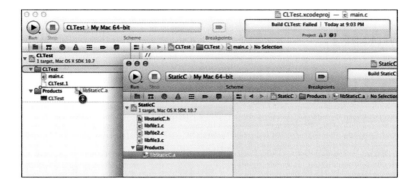

FIGURE 14.23
Adding the static library containing functions that the failed C project needs.

> **By the Way**
>
> Non-Xcode build systems usually aggregate object files using a program called ar, called from within a file named Makefile. Use a text editor (the Xcode Editor will do) to look in the Makefile for a line that starts with ar. It should contain a bunch of files ending in .o, and one that starts with lib and ends with .a. That line is responsible for creating the library archive. Collect all the .c files that correspond to those .o files and add them to your C/C++ library project. The output from the build will be an equivalent .a file to that built by the Makefile.

7. In the dialog that opens after you drop the .h and .a files, select the option to copy items into the destination group's folder.

Copying the files does require you to copy the library again if you update it, but if you do not tell it to copy the files, Xcode instead inserts dependencies on the full paths to the library and header. With full paths, if you move between machines or otherwise try to build in a new location, Xcode cannot locate the files at that full path, and your build will fail.

After you have copied the library and header file over, you should get a clean build from your C language application.

Did You Know?

Although it is quite easy to compile C and C++ libraries using Xcode, and quite easy to use them in C and C++ programs written in Xcode, it is a bit of a trick to call C++ library functions in application code written in Objective-C. The most straightforward solution is to write C language interface code to sit between the Objective-C application and the C++ library. Objective-C can speak to a C library easily enough, and the C++ code can be induced to generate a C-compatible calling interface by including `extern C` in front of function declarations. A more elegant but somewhat more involved solution is discussed at http://www.philjordan.eu/article/strategies-for-using-c++-in-objective-c-projects.

Summary

Libraries and frameworks are an excellent way to both compartmentalize your code and facilitate reusing it for other projects. In this hour, you learned the differences between libraries, which are single-file collections of compiled code, and frameworks, which are special bundles that can contain libraries and additional resources such as image or data files, localization strings, and documentation. You learned how to make the decision between building a library or a framework or just compiling your code straight into your application. You also learned how to build your reusable code into a library and into a framework and how to test the results without writing a large application to use the functions and how to package the library up to deploy on other systems or share with other users and programmers. You also learned how to construct and use Xcode library targets for building C and C++ libraries out of code that others provide for libraries in these languages.

Q&A

Q. *What runs faster, bare code in an application, that code in a library, or that code in a framework?*

A. Everything else being the same, code compiled directly in an application is at least fractionally faster than any of the other options.

Q. *I'm looking at some open source software, and it builds and then uses a dynamic library. Should I use a dynamic Cocoa library or a framework?*

A. Really, you can do either, although the framework option is cleaner if you are willing to do the little bit of extra work to set it up, beyond the "just drag in the files" procedure necessary for the plain dynamic library.

Q. *Is passing around void pointers like you did in your linked list really kosher?*

A. Well, it's cheap. If you're comfortable with C-style typecasting, it is a convenient way to abstract a library interface, such as for a linked list, so that it doesn't matter what data type it is actually working with. If you are not comfortable with C-style typecasting, this way lie monsters.

Workshop

Quiz

1. Is there ever a good reason to use an embedded framework?

2. Where does Xcode store by default the components that it is building for your project?

3. Why does software that you're trying to build, using your new framework complain that it cannot find the header files?

Answers

1. Yes, there are several, although most of them are fairly specific cases where, for example, you need to be able to rebuild part of your application without rebuilding it all (such as for a plug-in system). Where frameworks really shine, though, is for sharing your libraries with others by putting it in /Library/Frameworks/.

2. In a DerivedData directory buried in ~/Library/Developer/Xcode/.

3. Because you still need to add a Copy Headers build phase to your project and tell it which headers to add to the framework Headers directory.

Activities

1. Download the project for the Doubly Linked List Framework from http://teachyourselfxcode.com/ and build it.

2. Add the code necessary to implement the rest of the doubly linked list functionality. Add error checking on returned values.

3. Add testing code to the test suite to make sure that your new functionality produces the expected results.

HOUR 15

Putting It All Together: Building an OS X Application

What You'll Learn in This Hour:

▶ How to use a shared framework in your project

▶ How to add a second view component with a controller independent from the application delegate

▶ How to incorporate an embedded framework project into your application to accommodate interproject dependencies

So far in this book, you've learned all about the Xcode interface and how to use it to construct the necessary component pieces of an OS X application. In this hour, you refresh what you've learned about the interface and the tools for building components, while going through the process of building a complete Objective-C-based Cocoa application. The application we build in this hour is kind of like a very simple Etch A Sketch. It takes X and Y coordinate values as input, plots the points and draws lines between them in a graphical view, and lists the coordinates that you've entered in a browser. This hour does not cover every possible functionality, but by the time you have finished, you should have a good idea of how to add features like editing the points list in the doodle or connecting it up to more interesting sources of coordinate data than just what you can enter from the keyboard.

Like Hour 14, "Planning for Reuse: Frameworks and Libraries," this hour is a bit longer than some of the others. This is partly because what you have already learned is somewhat involved and requires a thorough walkthrough here. And, it is partly because even though Xcode keeps getting better and better, Apple still needs to smooth out some rough spots. After all, it doesn't take wandering too far off the path to end up with an application that looks all right but works all wrong.

Getting Started

Let's start at the very beginning:

1. Launch Xcode, and then choose File, New, New Project to create a new project. The familiar new project dialog opens, as shown in Figure 15.1. Because we're building an Objective-C/Cocoa application, select the Cocoa Application template and click Next.

2. In the next dialog, shown in Figure 15.2, fill in your application name, company name, and a class prefix.

   The company name is covered in an earlier hour. The class prefix should be a few capital letters, and by prepending it onto all of your class names and methods, it is used to disambiguate between the SuperAwesomeClass that you wrote and the decidedly less-super-awesome SuperAwesomeClass that some other guy coincidentally named his class, as well. Apple uses NS (from NextStep) as the prefix for all of their class and method names. You can use your initials; how likely is it that the guy who stole your class name also has the same initials as you? Unless you have a good reason not to, use the same class prefix in all your work. That way, you can readily recall it, and you will not have to try to remember what prefix went with what class, and you can always easily identify your class methods among the other calls in the code you write.

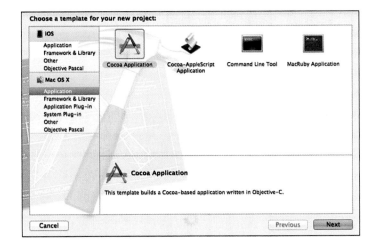

FIGURE 15.1
Selecting the
Cocoa
Application
template.

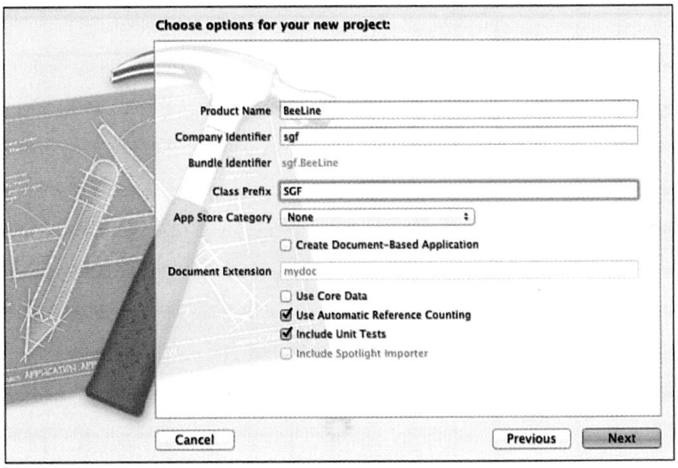

FIGURE 15.2
Setting options,
including class
prefix.

I'm naming my application BeeLine, and I have chosen SGF for my class prefix. Unless you plan to submit your application to the Apple App Store, you can leave the App Store category set to None.

3. Leave the Create Document-Based Application check box unchecked (because we build a single-window application in this hour). A document-based application is the type that, similar to Preview, opens multiple independent windows, each containing a different document, and each using the same menu and control structure.

4. Uncheck (if it is checked) the Use Core Data check box. Our demo application does not use Core Data, although we extend it to use Core Data for storage in Hour 17, "Attaching Big Data: Using Core Data in Your Applications."

5. Select Automatic Reference Counting and also select Unit Tests, if not already selected.

6. Click Next, find a good place to store your project, select the option to create a local Git repository, and then click Create. After a few moments as things are set up on disk, the main Xcode interface opens. You're now ready to roll.

Figure 15.3 shows the almost-default configuration of the interface after it launches. I dragged a PNG image of one of my bees into the App Icon box. I used a PNG with a transparent background so that the bee shows in the shape of the bee, instead of as a square with a bee in it.

FIGURE 15.3
The default interface with the App Icon filled in.

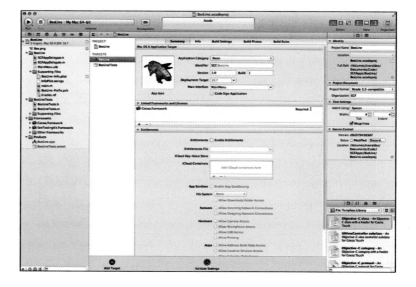

Because we're just starting, the rest of the configurable information in the Editor area can be left alone. Once your app is famous and it is time to release version 2, this is where you return to update things such as the version setting. We also leave the Entitlements section alone. The Entitlements section is where you can configure settings to restrict your application to a "sandbox," limiting its access to other applications and peripherals on the computer, and where you can configure access and limitations to iCloud-based data storage.

If you browse the groups and files with which Xcode has populated the Navigator, you'll see that it has created an Application Delegate class prepended with the class prefix you specified, as well as a default NIB file for your interface, the required main.m file, some unit-test skeleton code, and the basic plist files needed to get up and running. If you were to build and run your application at this point, it actually would run successfully, but it would not do much interesting.

Unless you plan to adopt test-driven development, which we cover in Hour 18, "Test Early, Test Often," the first thing you need to do is create the elements of your user interface. Of course, you can change these later if you decide that they're not quite what you need. Unlike traditional programming environments, however, where you start with some sort of "main" routine and insert code to tell it which routines to call, with Cocoa, you start with an interface and you tell the interface elements which methods to invoke.

Creating the Interface

Select the NIB file, and the Interface Builder editor will load in the Editor area. Front and center is a mostly blank window with a graph-paper background, and along the left is a dock with a few less-than-helpful shapes. The shapes in the dock are representatives and proxies for certain elements of your code and for elements of your user interface. They're necessary because you connect things in the interface with things in the code by Control-dragging from elements in one onto the other. From top to bottom, the items that appear in the default Interface Builder editor dock are a wireframe cube, solid red cube, and default application icon that represent the file's owner, first responder, and the application, respectively.

These are followed by a sort of pull-down menu icon that represents the application's default menu, a window-like icon that represents the main window, and two transparent blue cubes, the first a proxy for the application delegate, and the second representing the Font Manager. We do not use the Font Manager in this project.

At the top of the Interface Builder editor, you see the menu for your application, and if you hover your cursor over items in the Interface Builder editor dock, they identify themselves for you, as shown in Figure 15.4.

Note the tiny dot to the left of the Main Menu proxy in the dock in Figure 15.4. This dot indicates that that interface element is currently displayed. You have to use the X (close) icon on an item that is displayed to hide it again.

FIGURE 15.4
To find out what the items are in the Interface Builder editor dock, hover your cursor over them.

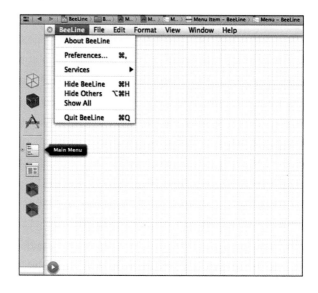

If you click the next proxy down, the Window proxy, it opens in the Interface Builder editor window, as well, as shown in Figure 15.5. If you previously had one of the menus dropped from the menu bar, as I did in Figure 15.4, you need to click its title in the menu bar again to close it; otherwise, it will be open and might hide the application window you're trying to edit.

FIGURE 15.5
The Window proxy also opens in the Interface Builder editor.

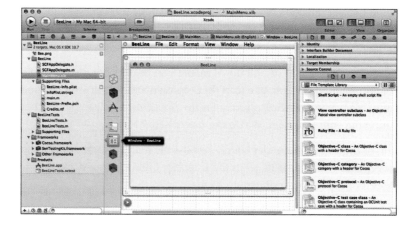

Now that you have the window displayed and ready to edit, you can start adding interface elements, as follows:

1. In the Utilities, click the little box icon, shown in Figure 15.6, to show the Object Library.

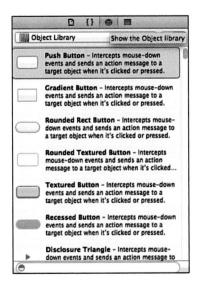

FIGURE 15.6
When you click
the box icon,
the Object
Library displays.

2. We use a custom view in this project, so scroll down the Objects list until you see the Custom View item. Drag an instance of it into your interface. If you choose Layout Views from the Object Library drop-down list, you can find the Custom View somewhat more easily.

3. Position it in the interface as shown in Figure 15.7, and drop it there.

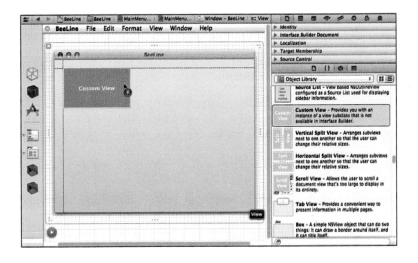

FIGURE 15.7
Position the
Custom View
item in your
interface.

4. Drag the lower-right corner down to size it appropriately within the window, as shown in Figure 15.8. I am making mine 320x320.

FIGURE 15.8
Sizing the
custom view.

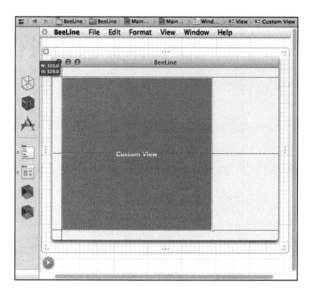

> Do not worry about ultimate precision in placing items in this view. The automatic guides and the notifier indicating the size are useful, but you can configure exact pixel-positioning values from a different panel in the Utilities. We look at that one when Xcode messes up the size on one of our text fields, later in this hour.

By the Way

5. Now we need two Text Field and two Label controls, a Push Button control, and a Browser data view. You can find the Text Field, Label, and Push Button controls under Controls in the Object Library drop-down, and you can find Browser under Data Views. Find each of these and drag them in to the interface and position them as shown in Figure 15.9.

6. Select your first text field, and find the Attributes Inspector in the Utilities (also shown in Figure 15.9). The Attributes Inspector icon, if not obvious, looks a bit like a superhero's utility belt. Use View, Utilities, Show Attributes Inspector as an easy way to make it visible.

7. In the Text Field area, enter a value into the Title field. While you are in this area, you can also assign text alignment, text color, and other properties for the text to be displayed.

When you press Return with your value in the Title field of the Text Field area in the Attributes Inspector, the Interface Builder updates its version of the text field to match the value. You might think that you should probably be able to edit this value directly in the Interface Builder editor itself. After all, you can click in the text field and enter a value. You probably should be right.

Unfortunately, however, at least some of the time, if you try this, you'll either end up editing the Text Field Cell rather than the text field itself, or you'll edit the Text Field properly, but Xcode will decide to shrink your text field to fit your default value. Figure 15.10 shows the difference in the Interface Builder highlighting when you have accidentally selected the Text Field Cell, and Figure 15.11 shows what happens if Xcode shrinks your text field to match your default value.

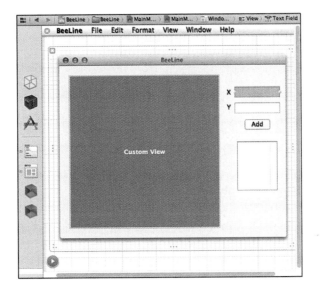

FIGURE 15.9
Adding two text fields, two labels, a push button, and a browser to the interface.

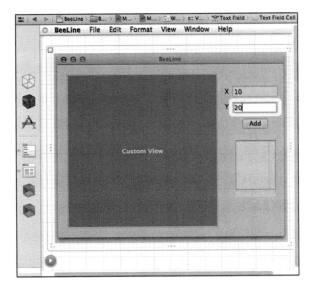

FIGURE 15.10
At least some of the time, when you click the text field in the Interface Builder editor, you end up editing the Text Field Cell rather than the Text Field.

FIGURE 15.11
Xcode often
automatically
shrinks your
text field to fit
your default
value when you
edit the Text
Field directly in
the Interface
Builder editor.

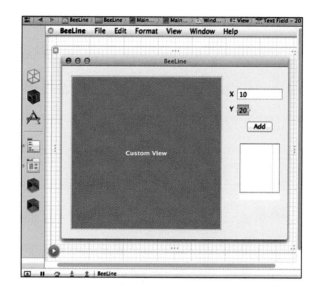

If Xcode messes up your nice layout like this (or if you need to apply finer control to your interface layout than you can accomplish by drag and drop), you can fix it using the Size Inspector, by clicking the icon in Utilities that looks a little bit like a Band-Aid (or by choosing View, Utilities, Show Size Inspector), as shown in Figure 15.12. Once in the Size Inspector, you can adjust the width of the field that Xcode accidentally shrunk to match the size of the remaining correct field.

FIGURE 15.12
In the Size
Inspector, you
can adjust the
width of the text
field that Xcode
previously
adjusted.

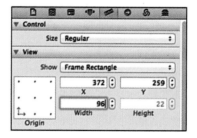

Attaching Code

Now it is time to start building and assigning functionality to the interface elements. Because Cocoa interface components serve as the initiators of most of the functionality in Cocoa applications, you attach this functionality by creating Objective-C classes for each interface component that has complex functionality. For BeeLine, we start with the custom view, as follows:

1. In the Utilities, click the icon for the File Template Library, as shown in Figure 15.13. Somewhat surprisingly, it looks a bit like a file icon. You can also make this easier by choosing OS X from the File Template drop-down.

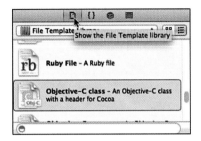

FIGURE 15.13
Opening the File
Template
Library.

2. Scroll down in the list of file templates until you find the Objective-C class template, and drag a copy of it over into the Navigator.

3. Drop it in the main application group, beneath your application proxy, as shown in Figure 15.14.

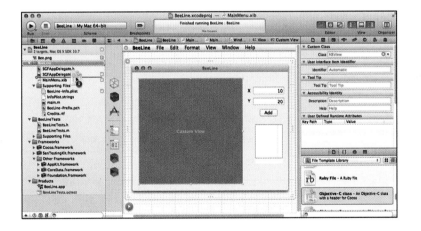

FIGURE 15.14
Dragging the
Objective-C
class template
to the main
application.

4. A dialog pops up, as shown in Figure 15.15, in which you assign a name under which to save your file, the group in which to assign it, and the targets to which it belongs. I named my class QuartzGrough.

FIGURE 15.15
Assigning a
name, group,
and targets to
the file that you
just dragged in
to the main
application.

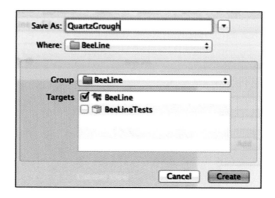

Did You Know?

If you're paying attention, you've just caught me ignoring the "always use your unique private class prefix" mantra that I suggested you adhere to earlier. Partly I'm doing this because you're going to meet lots of lazy code where that naming best practice hasn't been obeyed, so you ought to get some experience seeing the mishmash, and partly I'm doing this because Xcode has some nice tools for helping you fix this kind of sloppiness (which you learn how to use later).

5. Select the .h file for your class in the Navigator. It will open for editing in the main Editor area. By default, it is going to #import Foundation.h, and it will declare an NSObject class. We're going to attach this class to our custom view, so we need the class declaration to match.

6. To find out the appropriate class, select your NIB file in the Navigator, click the Window proxy in the Interface Builder editor dock if it is not already visible, and then select Custom View on the main window of the interface.

7. Now go to the Utilities and click the Identity Inspector icon, as shown in Figure 15.16. This icon looks a little bit like an application window. In the Class field under Custom Class, you'll see that the custom view is specifically an NSView (also shown in Figure 15.16). Or, choose View, Utilities, Show Identity Inspector.

8. Use the Navigator to return to editing your new class .h file, and change the NSObject declaration for the class to an NSView declaration.

9. Also change the #import to load Cocoa.h rather than Foundation.h, as shown in Figure 15.17.

10. Switch back to editing the NIB file and select Custom View again.

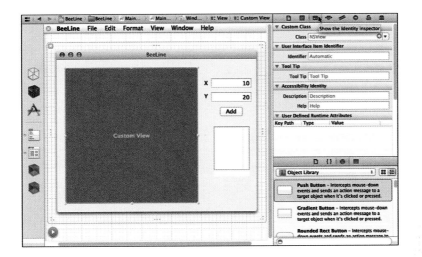

FIGURE 15.16
In the Identity Inspector, we see that the custom view is an NSView.

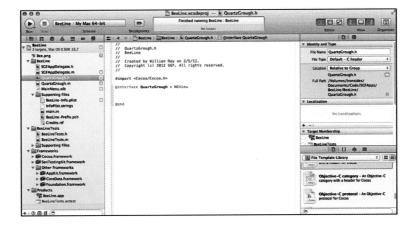

FIGURE 15.17
We have changed the NSObject declaration to NSView and the Foundation.h #import to Cocoa.h.

11. Bring up the Identity Inspector in the Utilities. Remember that the Custom View region is an NSView, and you've just declared your class to inherit from NSView, so you can use your class to run the custom view.

12. To attach the custom view to your class, change the class for the custom view so that it uses your class rather than the default NSView. Click in the Class field under Custom Class and find your new class in the list. Select it, as shown in Figure 15.18, and you should see the custom view change name to match the class you're writing.

FIGURE 15.18
Changing the default NSView class to our custom class.

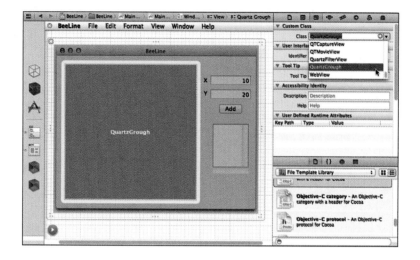

Build and run your application, and you should see a surprisingly functional replicate of the interface you just designed. The menus are there, you can edit text in the text fields, and the button "clicks." Of course, nothing happens when you click the button because you have not written the code to add functionality yet. But, quite a lot of your application is already working, and all via just for a couple lines of code and dragging some icons around.

Despite everything that's going right with your application so far, if you try to resize your application's window, you'll see that some issues are still left to address, as shown in Figure 15.19. Specifically, the interface components are where they belong at the default window size, but they do not move and scale appropriately when you resize the window.

FIGURE 15.19
Interface components are not where they should be if we resize the window.

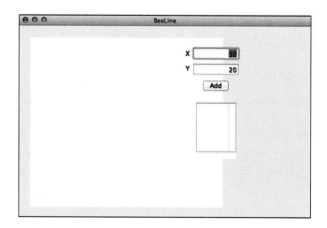

So, return to the Size Inspector in the Utilities, and under the View heading, adjust the autosizing parameters as appropriate for where you've positioned your interface elements.

With where I positioned my X and Y coordinate text fields I want them to stay glued at a fixed distance from the right side of the window and at a fixed distance from the top of the window. I do not want them to resize, just move with the window boundaries. This configuration is applied to both my X and Y coordinate text fields in Figure 15.20, and the result on the interface is shown. You should apply similar settings to the other interface elements so that they behave more appropriately.

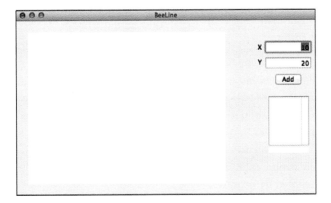

FIGURE 15.20
After we adjust settings in the Size Inspector, the text fields stay a fixed distance from the window boundaries.

Inserting Interface Object References into the Code

Now that we have the class types in agreement between our new class and the custom view, it's time to give the code a handle on the interface object:

1. Select the NIB file in the Navigator to open your interface in the Interface Builder editor once again.

2. Click the Assistant Editor icon in the top icon bar of the main Xcode interface. You can find the Assistant Editor icon in the group of three editor icons at the top right; it looks either like a butler's shirt or one of those gigantic pay-per-view binoculars that line scenic vistas at tourist traps. The source editor opens beside the Interface Builder editor. Both are cramped in the central main Editor area in Xcode, so you might want to hide the Navigator and Utilities to win some extra room to work. Alternatively, choose View, Assistant Editor, Show Assistant Editor.

In the source editor, you should see the header file for your application delegate. This is where you need to declare the (in-code) objects that will correspond to the interface objects you have created in the Interface Builder editor. You can do this by writing all the associated code yourself, but it is much easier to simply Control-drag your interface elements into the application delegate header file, positioning them after the @property declaration for the window.

3. Add a #import "QuartzGrough.h" line, and a @class QuartzGrough; line following it, after any other #import statements in the app delegate header.

4. Starting with the QuartzGrough view, Control-drag each of the interface components from the interface into the application delegate header file in the Assistant Editor.

Figure 15.21 shows the beginning of this process for the QuartzGrough view. To help you remember which interface component you're working with, as you drag, a blue line connects the interface component you're connecting and your current drop target. After you drop the connection into the .h file, a mini-dialog opens, requesting additional details, as shown in Figure 15.22. For the view, we're creating an outlet, which is to say an element from which data can be read and written. I'm calling it myGroughGraph. The QuartzGrough type is assigned by default.

5. Leave Storage set to Strong unless you know when and why not to.

6. After you have the details filled in correctly, click Connect. An @property for your new outlet will appear in the header file.

FIGURE 15.21
You can declare interface objects in code by Control-dragging to the appropriate interface component.

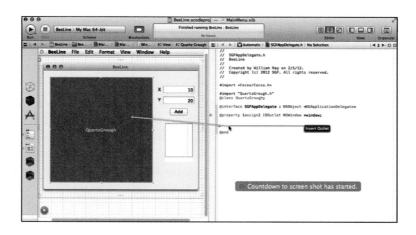

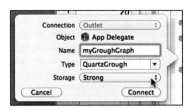

FIGURE 15.22
Providing Xcode additional details for the interface object code.

7. Unless you want to do something fancy, the default functionality of the NSTextFields in your text fields will suffice, so just Control-drag those over to the application delegate header without creating new classes for them. Figure 15.23 shows the settings I used for one of my text fields. The other one is the same, except it is named YCoord.

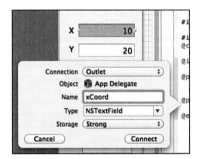

FIGURE 15.23
For the X and Y coordinate boxes, the default NSTextField should be fine.

Pay attention when selecting the text fields. Just like when you entered default values for the text fields, it is easy to end up selecting the NSTextFieldCell rather than the NSTextField. If this happens to you, you'll see something similar to Figure 15.24 when you drop the connection in the header. The highlighting around the text field in the interface is distinctly different, and if you're paying attention you'll see that the outlet dialog also reflects that you're creating a connection for the wrong type.

Did You Know?

We're going to ignore the browser for now and come back to create a connection for that later, so the last thing you need to connect is the button. The button interface object differs from the view and the text fields, in that it is a direct-acting object that needs to invoke a method immediately when you click it, rather than a passive object that simply sets or displays the contents of a variable.

8. Control-drag and drop the button into the header, as you have for the view and text field elements.

FIGURE 15.24
Be careful when selecting the text fields, because you could end up selecting the NSTextField Cell rather than the NSTextField.

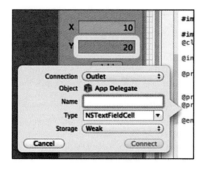

9. In the mini-dialog that appears, you need to change the Connection type from Outlet to Action and specify a name, as shown in Figure 15.25.

   The name you provide corresponds to the message that the button will send to the application delegate when the button is clicked, so I'm calling my action plotPoint.

10. Click Connect. Note that it creates the declaration for an instance method of type IBAction in the application delegate header.

FIGURE 15.25
When setting up the button, choose the Action connection type and name it whatever message you want to appear when the button is clicked.

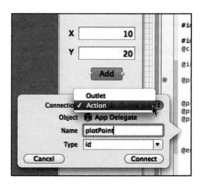

11. Select the implementation (.m) file for the application delegate in the Navigator.

   You will see that a number of @synthesize directives have been added at the top to match the outlets you declared in the header. At the bottom of the file, you see that Xcode has inserted a default method implementation for your action.

12. To finally achieve some not-so-instant gratification that all this clicking and twiddling is actually doing something, add an `NSLog()` call as something for the plotPoint action to do. It is not quite plotting a point, but it will be gratifying to see that clicking the button actually can do something other than make the button turn blue. The code added to the plotPoint action, the BeeLine interface during a button click, and the resulting output in the Debug area are shown in Figure 15.26. Houston, we have click-off.

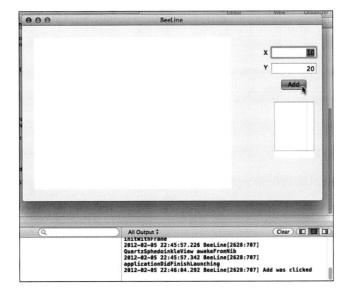

FIGURE 15.26
With the addition of `NSLog()` to the code, when we click the button, it not only turns blue, but also provides output that we have clicked the button.

Tying Things Together

Now we want to make our main interface actually do something with the interface components that it knows about. Right now, the application delegate knows the contents of the text fields and knows that the View area belongs to a QuartzGrough named myGroughGraph.

To communicate these values from the application delegate into our QuartzGrough, and invoke a method there when the push button is clicked, we need additional code. In QuartzGrough.h, we need to declare some properties that can move Cartesian coordinates in and out of myGroughGraph and a method that can be called to ask myGroughGraph to take action. We can do that that by adding properties to QuartzGrough named anX and anY, and an instance method plotUpdate. In QuartzGrough.m, we need to implement that function so that it can do something when asked. Finally, in the application delegate, within the IBAction method for the button, we need to collect the values from the text fields and assign these values into our QuartzGrough variables, and then we need to set up a call to ask the QuartzGrough method to do something. The code snippets for each of these steps are shown in Listings 15.1, 15.2, and 15.3, respectively.

LISTING 15.1   The Header Additions That Enable External Code to Communicate with a QuartzGrough Instance

```
@property (assign) float anX;
@property (assign) float anY;

- (void) plotUpdate;
```

Did You Know?

In Listing 15.1, you can see that I've added anX and anY properties, but that I immediately assign those into other variables in Listing 15.2. Although some additional code is necessary to make this design completely useful, I'm doing this to separate the "interface" to the QuartzGrough from the internal variables it uses for calculations. I only want anX and anY to function as an interface that other classes can write data into and that QuartzGrough can read data from. I assign these into internal instance variables normX and normY as soon as plotUpdate gets them, to free up the interface.

LISTING 15.2   An Implementation of the **plotUpdate** Method

```
-(void) plotUpdate
{
    normX = anX + 1.0;
    normY = anY + 1.0;

    [self update];
}
```

To use these interface variables and methods, the application delegate communicates with the QuartzGrough instance by setting the anX and anY instance variables in the QuartzGrough and then sending a message to the QuartzGrough's plotUpdate method.

LISTING 15.3 The App Delegate Code Necessary to Communicate Coordinates and a Request to Plot to the QuartzGrough

```
- (IBAction)plotPoint:(id)sender
{
    myGroughGraph.anX = [[xCoord stringValue] floatValue];
    myGroughGraph.anY = [[yCoord stringValue] floatValue];
    [myGroughGraph plotUpdate];
}
```

Once again, it is time to test the application. So, click Run. When the interface opens, type some values into the text fields and click the Add button. As shown in Figure 15.27, the Debug area output demonstrates that the application delegate is receiving the button-click and reporting it ("Add was clicked"), and it is then immediately calling the QuartzGrough method in myGroughGraph (AnX = …). My variables appear to be arriving in the QuartzGrough intact, as the values it is reporting are what I entered.

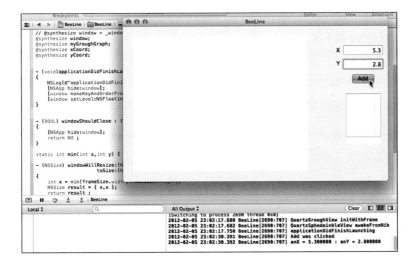

FIGURE 15.27
Testing shows that the variables are working correctly, as the values agree with what was entered.

Without detailing the rest of the code here (you can find a copy in the Hour 15 (V1) subdirectory of the code available at http://teachyourselfxcode/), if you add graphics-drawing code to the GroughGraph.m implementation, and call it from plotUpdate, you'll actually have a program that takes user input from you and plots it in the view, as shown in Figure 15.28. Okay, so it is not quite App Store material yet, but when you stop to consider just how much functionality this represents, and how few lines of code are required to produce the results, it is really quite impressive.

FIGURE 15.28
Our application
can now draw
some graphics.

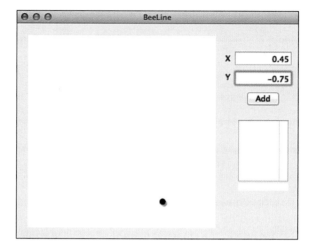

Increasing Functionality with a Framework

Plotting a point at some coordinates we specify is neat, but just one point in the display gets kind of boring. What we have at the moment is essentially a view and a controller, with no underlying model to hold data. To enhance functionality, we need a storage mechanism for the data we enter. It should support adding items and traversing through an ordered list of items from start to finish. Functions to insert and delete items would probably be nice, too. We could write a custom class for that model right here in our code, but coincidentally, in the last hour we built a framework that supplies a linked list class, and it provides exactly the sort of functionality we need.

Adding a framework to a project so that you can use its functionality is fairly simple (although, again, Apple has not quite yet pulled all the loose ends together in Xcode, so it is not as simple as it could be), but you can accomplish this in a couple of different ways, and the process differs depending on what kind of framework you have.

Adding a Shared Framework

If your framework is a shared framework (that is, one that is available for all installed software to use; for example, in /Library/Frameworks), the process for adding it to your project begins in the Summary tab for your project. I previously installed the doubly linked list we created in Hour 14 as a shared library in /Library/Frameworks as the framework ListsToo.framework.

To add a shared framework, follow these steps:

1. To add ListsToo.framework to the BeeLine project, select the top-level Project icon in the Navigator.

2. Select your application from the Targets list in the Editor area.

3. Click the Summary tab. Beneath the version and icon details for your application target, you'll see a Linked Frameworks and Libraries section with a + icon beneath it to add items.

4. Click the +, as shown in Figure 15.29. A dialog opens, like that shown in Figure 15.30.

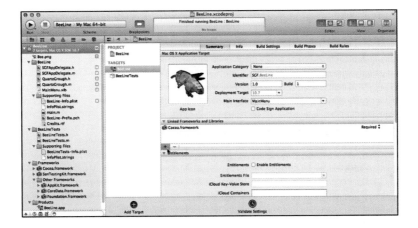

FIGURE 15.29
Clicking the + to add our shared framework to the project.

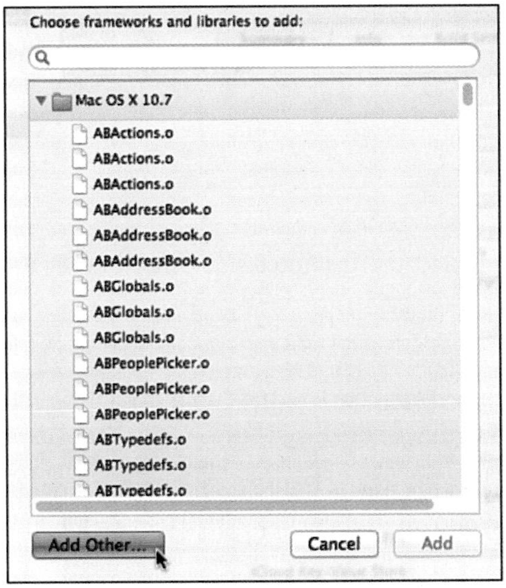

FIGURE 15.30
In the dialog that appears, click the Add Other button.

Did You Know?

Unfortunately, frameworks that are not either default Apple frameworks or ones that are actually present in your project will not show up in the list, so instead of being able to simply select from this list, you must navigate to where your framework is located.

5. Click the Add Other button. When you do so, a file-browser dialog opens. Again, unfortunately, Apple has made the /Library folder hidden by default, so you cannot easily browse to it.

6. Press Command-Shift-G to open a path-entry field.

7. Type **/Library/Frameworks** into the Go to the folder: field, and then click Go, as shown in Figure 15.31.

FIGURE 15.31
After typing Command-Shift-G, enter the path to your shared framework.

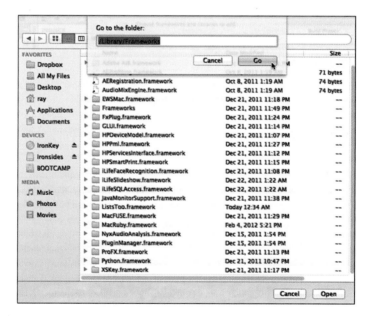

8. Navigate to and select the ListsToo.framework from the file browser.

9. Click Open.

If you've done everything right, back in the Summary tab, you'll find ListsToo.framework has been added to the list of Linked Frameworks and Libraries

Next, we need to connect the functionality from ListsToo into our application code. This is quite easy. Just add an #import for <ListsToo/ListsToo.h> to the

GroughGraph.h header file, and all the exposed method interfaces in ListsToo become available to BeeLine. A simple declaration of a pointer to a ListsToo object at the top of the GroughGraph.m implementation, and Beeline now has a handle to ListsToo that can be populated by a ListsToo instance.

To utilize this instance, we just need to treat it as we previously did for testing ListsToo in its testing module. We need to create objects that store our data, in this case X and Y coordinates for Cartesian points, acquire pointers to those objects, and populate the ListsToo item void* storage with these pointers.

Listing 15.4 shows the code necessary to start using the ListsToo framework for storing the pair of values from our X and Y text fields each time we click the Add button. The only real complication beyond what you saw when implementing ListsToo in Hour 14 is that we cannot initialize the first ListsToo item until after we have received our first Add click.

To accomplish this delay, I added a Boolean-valued "plotting" variable to QuartzGrough that is initialized to false when an instance is created. The plotUpdate method (which eventually is invoked when Add is clicked) checks that variable, and if it has not yet been flipped to true, it initializes the ListsToo list with the incoming X and Y values, and then flips the plotting variable to true. Subsequent clicks on Add (and calls to plotUpdate) find "plotting" to be true and append to the ListsToo list instead of initializing it.

Figure 15.32 shows the result after entering two different pairs of values and clicking Add twice. Note that you now see output from the ListsToo walkList method in the Debug area, as well, and that it is reporting that we have a list with two items in it.

LISTING 15.4   Enabling QuartzGrough.m to Use the ListsToo Framework

```
typedef struct myPointType myPointType;
struct myPointType {
  float myX;
  float myY;
};

ListsToo *pointsList;
bool  plotting = false;


-(void) plotUpdate
{
    void(^pointsPrinter)(void*) = ^(void* toPrint)
    {
        NSLog(@"point at %f, %f",((myPointType*)toPrint)->myX - 1.0,
((myPointType*)toPrint)->myY - 1.0);
    };

    normX = anX + 1.0;
```

LISTING 15.4   Continued

```
normY = anY + 1.0;

myPointType *aPoint = malloc(sizeof(myPointType));
aPoint->myX = normX;
aPoint->myY = normY;

if(!plotting)
{
    plotting = true;
    pointsList = [[BetterList alloc] initDLList: aPoint];
}
else
{
    [pointsList append:aPoint];
}

[self update];
[pointsList walkList:pointsPrinter];
}
```

FIGURE 15.32
Here we have entered two different pairs of values and clicked Add twice.

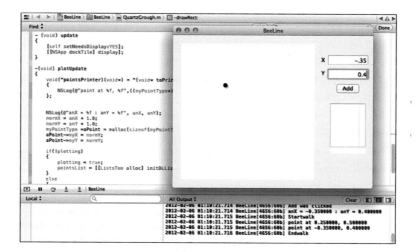

BeeLine is still only plotting one of the points, but that's only because the QuartzGrough drawRect method does not know anything about the list of points yet. It's still working from the current normX and normY variables that are passed in from the text fields. If we update the drawRect code as shown in Listing 15.5, fancier things will happen, as shown in Figure 15.33.

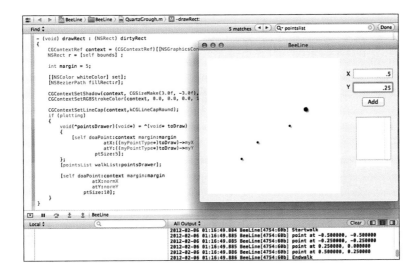

FIGURE 15.33
After updating the drawRect code, we now have four dots in this instance.

In Listing 15.5, you see that you can update the drawing code to plot all points in the pointsList by just using the ListsToo walkList iterator and handing it an anonymous block that renders the points. Note that this is a fairly subtle change to the code. Where before drawRect used a single invocation of doaPoint, sending the current values of normX and normY, we now build a strikingly similar invocation of doaPoint into an anonymous code block, and we hand that block off to the ListsToo walkList method. When the list iterates over itself, it calls our anonymous block for each point for us (quite a convenience). We're invoking doaPoint one extra time after traversing the entire list of points, using a different point radius, just to provide some visual context to our point display.

LISTING 15.5　Using the ListsToo walkList Iterator and Handing It an Anonymous Block

```
- (void) drawRect : (NSRect) dirtyRect
{
  CGContextRef context = (CGContextRef)[[NSGraphicsContext currentContext]
➥graphicsPort];

  NSRect r = [self bounds] ;

  int margin = 5;

  [[NSColor whiteColor] set];
  [NSBezierPath fillRect:r];
```

LISTING 15.5   Continued

```
CGContextSetShadow(context, CGSizeMake(3.0f, -3.0f), 2.0f);
CGContextSetRGBStrokeColor(context, 0.0, 0.0, 0.0, 1.0);
CGContextSetLineCap(context,kCGLineCapRound);

if (plotting)
{
  void(^pointsDrawer)(void*) = ^(void* toDraw)
  {
    [self doaPoint:context margin:margin
               atX:((myPointType*)toDraw)->myX
               atY:((myPointType*)toDraw)->myY
          ptSize:5];
  };
  [pointsList walkList:pointsDrawer];

  [self doaPoint:context margin:margin
             atX:normX
             atY:normY
        ptSize:10];
}
}
```

Just a few more lines of code and you can have BeeLine drawing lines between the points, as well. If you want to experiment with the project at this stage, you can find a copy in the Hour 15 (V2) subdirectory of the code available at http://teachyourselfxcode.com/.

Adding a Second View

Right now, you have an application with an underlying data model (an instance of ListsToo) that holds and manipulates a list of points, a view (our QuartzGrough subclass of NSView) that plots those points, and a controller instantiated in your application delegate. When you built the interface, however, you included a browser component that we have not yet discussed. The browser component is there to provide a second view of the model, but it still needs to be connected.

As was the case for the QuartzGrough, connecting this view requires a fair amount of flipping between items in the Interface Builder editor. We do it slightly differently this time, however. When we connected the QuartzGrough, we only intended for it to be used as a display for the data, and it was our only view in the application. Therefore, subclassing the NSView in QuartzGrough and connecting it through the application delegate was an adequate solution. For our new view, we want to develop additional interaction functionality beyond using it as a simple display, and adding that code to the app delegate would be inelegant. So for this interface component, we create a separate delegate class and that requires a few more steps.

Just as you did with the QuartzGrough, you first need to add a class to handle the view, as follows:

1. Follow the same steps you used to create the QuartzGrough header and implementation files and create a new PointsBrowser class.

2. Select your NIB file in the Navigator. Because interface elements are connected to code by Control-dragging, we need a representative for our new class in the Interface Builder editor, but there isn't one provided by default.

3. Reveal the Utilities if they're hidden, and select the Object Library (again, the little box) icon.

4. Find the object proxy for an NSObject; it looks like the other blue proxy object box icons that are in the Interface Builder editor dock.

5. Drag it over to the dock, as shown in Figure 15.34.

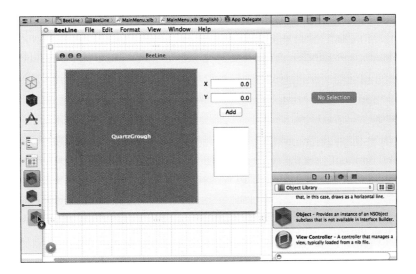

FIGURE 15.34
Adding the NSObject proxy to the Interface Builder editor dock.

6. Leaving that proxy icon selected in the dock, select the Identity Inspector in the Utilities, and find the new class you just created, as shown in Figure 15.35.

7. Control-drag from the Browser component in the interface and drop it onto the new proxy you just created in the Interface Builder editor dock. In the tiny dialog that appears, indicate that this connection is for a delegate.

Back in your app delegate, you need to add appropriate @properties and @synthesize lines to the header and implementation, but these need to be created for your PointsBrowser delegate object, not for the NSBrowser it represents.

FIGURE 15.35
Finding the new class in the Identity Inspector while selecting the proxy icon in the dock.

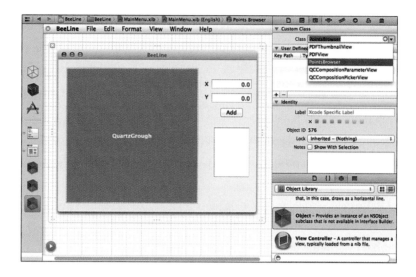

8. Open the NIB file in the Editor area, and open the Assistant Editor window. The app delegate header should open beside the Interface Builder editor.

9. Control-drag the blue-box proxy icon for your `PointsBrowser` class over to the app delegate header and drop it below your other `@properties` directive lines.

10. The familiar connection-property dialog pops up, where you provide a name and optionally set the storage type. In this case, either weak or strong storage is fine. I named the property `ptsBrowser` and set the storage type to strong.

By the Way

Although a much better topic for an Objective-C book, a weak storage type indicates that the Automatic Reference Counting (ARC) memory-cleanup magic should treat this property as owned by some other object than the application delegate. The strong type indicates that the app delegate is the owner. Because the program cannot run after the application delegate is deallocated, it really doesn't matter whether ARC thinks that something else owns the browser object. If, however, you were attaching the browser to, for example, a window that might close, while another window adopted the same browser, the weak storage would let you manage the allocation and deallocation of the browser separately from the creation and destruction of the windows.

11. While you're looking at the app delegate header, add an `#import` for the header for your new class (`#import "PointsBrowser.h"`).

12. Also add the class to the `@class` directive for the App delegate.

13. Right-click the proxy icon for the PointsBrowser class in the Interface Builder editor dock.

14. In the heads-up dialog (HUD) that appears, click and drag from the open circle in the New Referencing Outlet line up to the app delegate proxy in the dock, as shown in Figure 15.36.

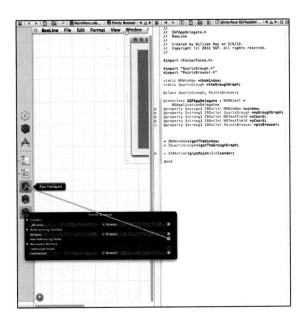

FIGURE 15.36
Clicking and dragging the New Referencing Outlet to the app delegate proxy in the HUD.

15. Another HUD appears. In it, select the name of the property you just added to the app delegate for this object (in this case, ptsBrowser).

Finally, you need to set up the outlet connection between the NSBrowser and the PointsBrowser delegate itself.

16. With the Interface Builder editor and the Assistant Editor still open, click in the jump bar above the display of the app delegate header and navigate your way to the PointsBrowser.h header.

17. Control-click and drag from the NSBrowser component in the interface into the PointsBrowser.h header to create an outlet connection.

18. Give the outlet a name and choose a storage type. (I chose _aBrowser and strong storage.)

After all of this fiddling, which is certainly more involved than what we did to get the NSView working, but which also gives us more flexibility, we are finally ready to start connecting data and actions to our browser.

19. Use the Navigator to open the PointsBrowser.m implementation file.

20. Scroll down to just above the @end directive and define a new IBAction method as shown in Listing 15.6. This method explicitly declares an Interface Builder action type that we can then connect things to using the Interface Builder editor.

LISTING 15.6   Declaring a Method with an **IBAction** Type Makes It Available as a Connectable Action Method in the Interface Builder Editor

```
- (IBAction) rowSelected: (id)sender
{
    NSBrowserCell *cell = [_aBrowser selectedCellInColumn: 0];
    NSLog(@"ptsBrowser: selected <%@> at %d",cell.stringValue,
[cell.representedObject intValue]);
}
```

21. Navigate to the PointsBrowser.h header and add the declaration for the rowSelected method so that it can be called by other classes.

22. Select the NIB file in the Navigator and return to the Interface Builder editor.

23. Right-click the proxy for PointsBrowser in the Interface Builder editor dock. You'll see that you now have an available Received Action for the new rowSelected IBAction you just created.

24. Click in the empty circle in the rowSelected line.

25. Drag a connection to the browser component of the interface and drop the connection there.

The code necessary to actually program the behavior of the NSBrowser requires more Cocoa expertise than possible to cover in this book. However, if you want to experiment further, you can find a copy in the Hour 15 (V3) subdirectory of the code available at http://teachyourselfxcode/. When you run it, you'll find that the NSBrowser populates itself with points as you add them, as shown in Figure 15.37, and the Debug area properly reports selections from the NSBrowser, as shown in Figure 15.38.

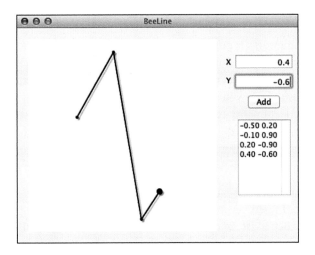

FIGURE 15.37
NSBrowser has been pro-grammed to populate itself with points as you add them.

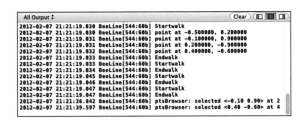

FIGURE 15.38
Debug output reports the cor-rect points from the NSBroswer.

Did You Know?

One thing to pay attention to in the sample code is how the PointsBrowser class gets access to the ListsToo instance being used by the QuartzGrough. Although not the most elegant solution, the app delegate has access to both the myGroughGraph instance of QuartzGrough, and the ptsBrowser instance of PointsBrowser. By adding a bare pointer to a ListsToo object in the PointsBrowser class, and exposing an instance method to set this pointer to an already extant ListsToo object, we enable the app delegate to extract the pointer of myGroughGraph's ListsToo object (myGroughGraph->pointsList) and send that into ptsBrowser for its use.

From a code-elegance perspective, it is probably better if the app delegate itself owns pointsList and hands that variable off to both the graphical view and the browser view. Hindsight is the mother of refactoring!

Switching to an Embedded Framework

Using shared frameworks is great when a systemwide one is in place to do what you want to do. However, using shared frameworks places a lot of restrictions on what you can do. For example, you cannot conveniently distribute your application to anyone who doesn't have your shared framework installed. Nor can you conveniently edit the functionality of the framework if it does not do exactly what you want. If you have access to the framework project, as in this case, you can insert the framework project within your application project as a subproject, and then set it up to incorporate the built framework within the application bundle so that it is always available with your application when you distribute it.

For this example, I use a version of the ListsToo framework we built previously, renamed here to BetterList. To add BetterList to the BeeLine project, I deleted ListsToo from the BeeLine project and opened a Finder window so that I could see the BetterList project. You can find a copy of the files for starting at this point in the Hour 15 (V4) subdirectory of the code available at http://teachyourselfxcode/. I've already made all the in-code changes to BeeLine to reference the `BetterList` class rather than the `ListsToo` class. To add BetterList as an embedded framework, follow these steps:

1. Open the BeeLine project in Xcode.

2. Switch to the Finder and navigate to the directory that contains the BetterLists.xcodeproj project file.

3. Position this Finder window so that you can see the Navigator for the BeeLine Xcode project behind it.

4. Drag the BetterList project into the BeeLine project and drop it immediately beneath the BeeLine project, as shown in Figure 15.39. It should appear as an indented blue project group, beneath the BeeLine project group.

5. Under the File menu, click Project Settings and change the derived data location. Unless you know exactly what you're doing, click the Advanced button and change the build location to Locations Specified by Targets, as shown in Figure 15.40.

   I expect that in future versions of Xcode the default derived data location option will become much more useful. For now, though, it induces one more layer of confusion with Xcode as to where you should look for header files and libraries, and life is much easier if you simply let the projects assert control.

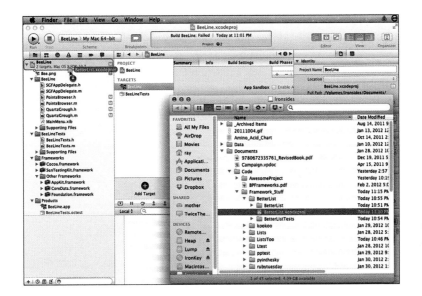

FIGURE 15.39
Inserting a
framework
project into the
current project

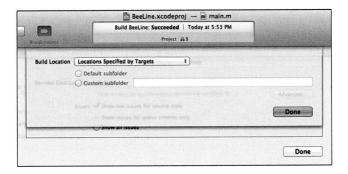

FIGURE 15.40
Changing the
derived data
location to
Locations
Specified by
Targets makes
it easier for your
project to find
header files and
libraries.

Linking up this embedded framework is a bit more involved than linking to a shared framework. For one thing, we want changes to the BetterList framework to automatically appear for the BeeLine application, so the BeeLine project needs to know that it should try to rebuild the BetterList framework if that framework needs rebuilt. To accomplish this, we need to configure the dependencies portion of the build process to indicate the dependency between BeeLine and BetterList.

6. Select the BeeLine project in the Navigator and the BeeLine target in the Editor area.

7. Display the Build Phases tab at the top of the Editor area.

8. Open the Target Dependencies item if it is not already open, and then click the + icon (Add Items button) for dependencies, as shown in Figure 15.41.

FIGURE 15.41
Including our
framework proj-
ect, BetterList,
as a depend-
ency for our
BeeLine project.

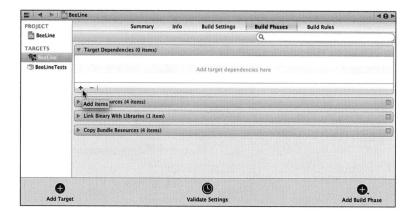

9. A drop-down dialog appears. Select the BetterList framework.

10. Click Add.

If you cannot select the framework under BetterList, or if it doesn't appear, or if the BetterList.xcodeproj group in the Navigator appears as just a single line with no group-reveal triangle, it is because you have the BetterList project open somewhere else (for example, in another Xcode window). Close it and just work with it from within this project. Likewise, if you have BetterList open from within this project, and you also try to open it by double-clicking its icon in the Finder, Xcode will say unpleasant things. Best to only open each project in one place at a time.

Next, you need to add a new build phase.

11. Still in the Build Phases tab of the Editor area for the BeeLine target, click the large + icon above New Build Phase at the bottom of the editor.

12. A pop-up menu appears. Select the Add Copy Files option, as shown in Figure 15.42.

13. A new build phase group, titled Copy Files, appears at the bottom of the list of build phases. Click the + icon in it to add files.

14. In the dialog that appears, navigate to the BetterList.framework in the BetterList products group, select it, and click Add.

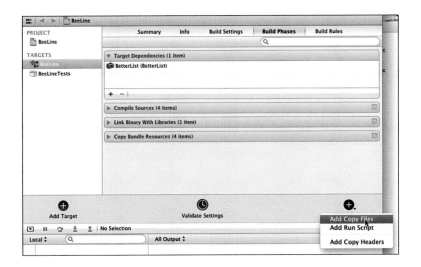

FIGURE 15.42
Adding a new
Build Phase
that copies
files.

15. Back in the Copy Files build phase, change the destination to Frameworks.

When you have finished, the new build phase should appear as shown in Figure 15.43.

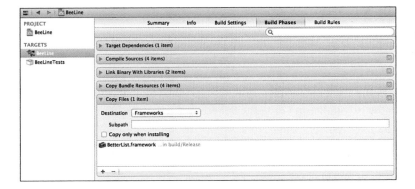

FIGURE 15.43
A new build
phase that
copies files to
the BetterList
framework has
been success-
fully added.

16. Now, click the disclosure triangle for the Copy Files phase to collapse the list under it.

17. Then click and drag the Copy Files phase up until it is just beneath the Target Dependencies phase, as shown in Figure 15.44.

FIGURE 15.44
Moving the Copy
Files build
phase to just
below the Target
Dependencies
phase.

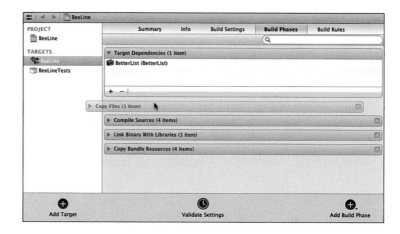

18. Drop the Copy Files phase there.

    You still need to tell BeeLine that it needs to link with the BetterList frame-
    work. You might think that you could open the Link Binary with Libraries
    phase and just add BetterList from there. However, you currently have about
    even odds that although the BetterList.framework appeared under the
    Workspace when you added it to the Copy Files phase it won't appear there if
    you click Add for the Link phase. This is probably an Xcode bug.

19. To work around an apparent bug in the Link section of the build phases,
    return to the Summary tab for the BeeLine target. Clicking + to add
    BetterList.framework to the Linked Frameworks and Libraries group, may or
    may not work here, either. Instead, open the Products group under BetterLists
    in the Navigator and drag the BetterLists.framework from the Project
    Navigator into the Editor area. Locate the Linked Frameworks and Libraries
    group in the Editor area and drop the BetterLists.framework under
    Cocoa.framework. If you go back and check the build phases, you'll find that
    it's been added to the correct group there, too.

    A tiny bit of additional configuration needs to be completed, and you'll be
    back up and running, only now using an embedded framework that you can
    edit conveniently and directly in your main project and that itself gets inserted
    into your application bundle so that everything gets copied when you distrib-
    ute your application.

20. Select the BetterList project in the Navigator, and the BetterList framework
    target in the Editor area.

21. Open the build phases for the BetterList framework target.

22. Verify that the BetterList.h file is in the public headers group, or add it back if it has disappeared. You can do this as was shown in Hour 14, or if Xcode is feeling particularly helpful, you can drag it straight from the Navigator into the Public header group.

At this point, you should be able to run BeeLine again, and it should function as before. Even better, if you go into BetterList.m and comment out those annoying NSLog() lines that report the beginning and end of a walkList traversal, and then click Run for BeeLine, it rebuilds BetterList for you, before building Beeline, with results as shown in Figure 15.45.

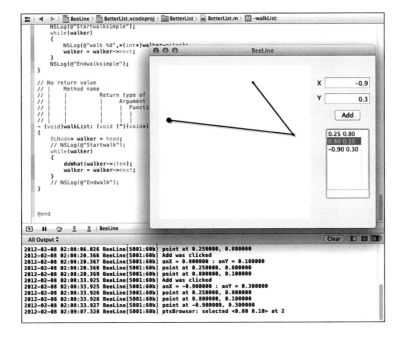

FIGURE 15.45
Now clicking Run for BeeLine also rebuilds BetterList before rebuilding BeeLine.

Finally, just to wrap up, if you want to distribute your application (and who doesn't), you need to make one more tweak, this time to the BetterLists build configuration. When Xcode runs your application, it applies some magic to make the embedded framework functional, no matter where the framework itself specifies that it should be installed. If you try to run your BeeLine application from the Finder at this point, however, it complains that it cannot find the required framework. This behavior seems peculiar, because the complaint you'll get is actually generated *by* the framework, regarding its installation location. Your app is in fact finding the framework where it thinks it belongs, and is then being directed to where the framework isn't, by the framework itself. It seems that the entire world outside of Apple thinks that this ought to be a bug, whereas Apple thinks that this is perfectly logical. I'm a big fan of Apple, but I vote with the rest of the world on this one: I cannot think of any reason that the framework, which the application has clearly already found, cannot run in place without modification. Apple disagrees, so we have one more thing to do: We need to inform BetterList that it is expected to live within an application instead of in the default shared library location.

23. Select the BetterLists subproject in the Navigator, and the BetterList framework target in the Editor area. Open the BetterList framework's build settings. Select the All option and dig around for the installation directory value. If it helps, you can use the Search field with a search such as "directory" to limit the displayed options.

24. The Installation Directory option for BetterLists will, by default, be set to /Library/Frameworks. Double-click the /Library/Frameworks value, and (depending seemingly on the phase of the moon) you will either be able to edit it directly in place or a small editor dialog will appear where you can change the value.

25. Change the installation directory from its current value, which probably will not appear as literally /Library/Frameworks in the editor dialog, but instead as a macro-substitution variable that expands to /Library/Frameworks in use, to **@execution_path/../Frameworks**, as shown in Figure 15.46.

    This directive is a "magic value" that tells the framework that it is okay to look for itself in a Frameworks directory that is in parallel to the path of any executable that is trying to use it.

    Also pay attention to values of the Deployment Location, Deployment Postprocessing, and Skip Install options. These values interact in some completely nonintuitive ways, but thankfully, to make things work the way you want them to work, they should all be set to No.

26. Make the setting change to the installation directory and click Done. Then, because Xcode currently displays some difficulty in getting this setting to actually stick the first time it is set, select the BeeLine project in the Navigator, and

then reselect the BetterList project and the build settings for the BetterList target again, and verify that the installation directory really shows up as @execution_path/../Frameworks. If it does not, just repeat the previous steps to set it, until Xcode finally gives in.

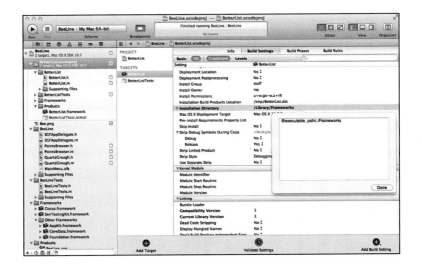

FIGURE 15.46
Changing the Installation Directory option so that the framework knows to look for itself in a directory parallel to the path of any executable that it tries to use.

27. Reselect the BeeLine project and choose Product, Build For, Build For Running from the menu. Back in the Finder, you'll find your BeeLine application in the Release subdirectory of the build directory that is in parallel to the BeeLine.xcodeproj file. Launching it in the Finder should now give you the same experience as running it within Xcode (although all those annoying log messages are now going into your console logs).

Summary

In this hour, you practiced the skills you learned in previous hours, putting them all together to build a working OS X application. You learned how to build a single-window, single-view application, and then updated it with a second view with an independent controller. You also learned how to use shared frameworks and how to embed frameworks for those times when you need to edit and test the framework at the same time as the application. Keep the workflow you practiced in this hour in mind as you work through the following hours in the book. Being able to construct a working OS X application is a prerequisite for each of them.

Q&A

Q. *Could the* NSView *component of the interface be handled by an independent controller, as was done for the* NSBrowser?

A. Yes. In fact, that is the preferred way to do things. Many OS X applications, however, are built with the controller for one or more views embedded in the application delegate. That does not mean that this is a good way to do things, but it was important for you to see both styles (and you get to fix it in the next hour, when you convert this OS X application into an iOS app).

Q. *Is a project limited to building one executable application?*

A. No. You can incorporate subprojects for additional applications using the same method we used for incorporating the embedded framework, or you can just add additional targets to your existing project. Subprojects have the convenience that they carry around their own individual build environments and can be worked on independently from the main project. Additional targets, however, handle code completion and argument checking better (although this advantage is possibly due to a bug in the symbol processing for subprojects) and can be better controlled for compiling subsets of executables by using schemes.

Workshop

Quiz

1. Why does the framework subproject you just included in your application refuse to let you access its contents?

2. Where can you find your finished .app application?

3. Where do your NSLog() messages go when you're running your application from the Finder rather than in Xcode?

Answers

1. Because you still have the framework project open in another, independent Xcode window.

2. If you set the project to use derived-data directories as specified by targets, you'll find a build directory inside your project directory, and your application will be in either the Debug or Release subdirectory of this build directory. If you left the derived-data location at the default, your application is in a pseudo-randomly named subdirectory of ~/Library/Developer/Xcode/DerivedData/. If you want to find it, try reading the final lines of the most recent build entry in the Log Navigator tab of the Navigator.

3. They are sent to the system console device. You can browse these logs using the Console.app application in /Applications/Utilities.

Activities

1. Modify the PointsBrowser class so that when an item is selected in the NSBrowser the list insertion point is moved from the end of the list to after the selected item.

2. Refactor the code so that the QuartzGrough does not own the point list model, but instead receives it from its parent.

HOUR 16

Building an iOS Application

What You'll Learn in This Hour:

▶ How to set up a project to build an application that can run on the iPhone, iPod touch, and iPad

▶ How to add a Cocoa Touch static library target to an existing framework project, to enable its use on iOS

▶ The kinds of things to watch out for when porting code between OS X and iOS

▶ How to implement singleton classes to handle data passing between different controllers in your iOS MVC schema

In this hour, you rebuild the OS X application that you built in the preceding hour into a universal iOS application. Because OS X and iOS are converging, this gets easier with every new release of OS X, iOS, and Xcode, but for a number of reasons it is still not as seamless a process as one might hope, as follows:

▶ **UI manipulability**: At the most basic, iOS devices require some adjustments to programming simply because of the practical difference in the iOS/Cocoa Touch and OS X/Cocoa user interfaces. For example, if your program responds to users hovering their cursor over an interface element in your OS X application, you must find an alternative for this for your iOS application because iOS does not have a cursor to hover.

▶ **Library differences**: Annoyingly, differences at the library level must also be addressed, differences beyond those required by differing hardware. These are primarily the result of iOS using different, simplified libraries to replace some functionality that's available in OS X, requiring that you rewrite some method calls for iOS.

▶ **UI element availability**: There are also some differences in the suite of standard user interface elements available on iOS. So, if you have used elements that are unique to OS X/Cocoa, you must replace those and change your underlying code to support the iOS elements available.

▶ **MVC design constraints**: In addition, developing for iOS requires you to adhere to the *model-view-controller* (MVC) design pattern much more closely than does OS X. Whereas it is not at all uncommon for the application delegate to end up carrying around the majority of the functionality in small OS X applications, in iOS applications the app delegate's job is solely management of the application life cycle, and functionality is embedded in or below view controllers that are responsible for instantiating each scene or "full-screen" display.

▶ **User expectations**: Finally, although not a strict requirement for porting an application to iOS, users of iPhones, iPods, and iPads have high expectations for interactivity in their iOS applications. So, you will probably want to build new features to provide natural navigation and interaction via familiar iOS gestures.

Because good iOS interface design and appropriate use of iOS technologies is a better subject for a standalone book, this hour focuses on the changes necessary to port the functionality of a OS X application to the iOS environment. We leave the decisions about how to wrap additional and appropriate iOS functionality into the application up to your creative genius.

Assessing What You Already Have

When adapting an OS X application to iOS, you must first consider the pieces that you have in your OS X application and determine how they might work best work under iOS. You need to perform this analysis for both your interface and your underlying driving logic.

In the case of your application's UI, your main window, if you have one, probably needs an entire iOS scene devoted to it. If you have dialogs in your OS X application, they probably need individual dedicated scenes. If your main interface combines both display elements and UI elements, you might need to split those off into separate iOS scenes.

You also need to consider the possible routes that a user can take through your application interface. In OS X, you are probably used to designing free-form user experiences where users can open multiple windows and wander as they choose between them. With the exception of a few special cases where users need to be taken linearly through a complete series of steps to complete some task, it is generally considered bad practice to put users on rails and only allow one path through your OS X interface. In iOS, however, your users are limited to a single scene at a time, and can only switch between that scene and the specific other scenes that you enable the interface to guide them to. In iOS, it is just as bad form to give them too many options as it is to guide them too carefully in OS X.

You also need to carefully study your application logic. You will likely have logic and data that you must split out of the application delegate and move into either an appropriate controller or model component. You also might need to break up some of your view logic. If you have previously instantiated what are really two independent views in the same OS X window by conflating their code under the same controller, you might be sharing data between them through that shared parent controller in a fashion that cannot be easily replicated when you split the views apart in iOS.

Looking at BeeLine from Hour 15, "Putting It All Together: Building an OS X Application," we have a window that contains a graphics subview and an NSBrowser subview that are displaying the same data and user-entry text fields and a button. For purely screen-space reasons, an iOS version, especially an iPhone version, will probably need to have the graphics subview and NSBrowser subview split onto separate scenes.

Because we were working in the direction of connecting the NSBrowser functionality with the user-input functionality (to support changing the insertion point in our list of points and deleting points from the list), keeping the coordinate-entry text fields together with the NSBrowser component makes sense. We also previously used the app delegate as the controller for the graphics subview, and because we did this, we could get away with passing data between the graphics subview and the NSBrowser using the app delegate as an intermediate.

For iOS, both of these things must change. The controller for the graphics view must be pulled out as a separate class. The pointsList data, which previously was owned by the graphics subview and was communicated to the NSBrowser by the app delegate, must be managed by a separate class and some additional magic invented to communicate it to both controllers that need to use the data. (We accomplish this using a design pattern known as a *singleton*, discussed in more detail later in this hour.)

Finally, looking carefully at the interface elements available in iOS, we can see that the NSBrowser class that we used for listing points in the OS X version is not available in iOS. So, we need to replace that component. Although not hierarchical, the iOS-compatible TableView class is a reasonable substitute. If we had extended BeeLine to support multiple lists of points using the NSBrowser to select among the list hierarchy, we would need to invent some functionality here because iOS does not provide a similar hierarchy browser class.

In addition, we have been using our BetterList framework to provide the underlying data model, and Apple currently reserves dynamically linked frameworks for themselves in iOS, requiring that application authors use statically linked libraries instead. So, we need to create a static version of BetterList to support our iOS application.

All together, for our iOS conversion, we need to do the following:

1. Create an iOS application with two scenes.

2. Update our BetterList framework to create a static library for iOS and incorporate it into our iOS app.

3. Update our application logic to support iOS-specific library calls.

4. Create a singleton class to hold our point list data and pass it between the scenes.

5. Replace the `NSBrowser` support logic with `TableView` support logic.

6. Populate the primary scene with our graphics view.

7. Populate the secondary scene with a `TableView` (to replace our `NSBrowser` view), and with the X and Y coordinate input boxes.

8. Connect the UI elements in the primary and secondary scenes with the application logic.

9. Add UI tweaks to support iOS features such as rotation.

Throughout the rest of this hour, we walk through the steps necessary to complete each of these items. However, because you are now getting more experience with the specific actions required to perform these steps, you will find in this hour just general instructions for activities with which you are already familiar. If you need to refresh your memory on specific tasks, refer back to Hour 14, where each step is explained in greater detail.

Hour 4, "Using Xcode Templates to Create Projects," covered the various iOS design patterns (types) that Xcode supports. Remember, though, that you are not locked into just one design. Your application can incorporate aspects of different types as necessary or desired. For example, it is entirely possible to have a tabbed application with one tab presenting a master-detail view of some data, enabling the user to select from a list of items and peruse high-level details, and another tab presenting a page-based opportunity to browse through the contents of the selected item in depth. If you need to review the various design types available, see Hour 4.

Building from the Template

To re-implement BeeLine, we need a main view for the graph, and we need a secondary view where the user can add data and interact with the list of points. We build this using a Utility Application template. To get started, follow these steps:

1. Create a new project in Xcode. Under iOS, select Application and choose the Utility Application template, as shown in Figure 16.1.

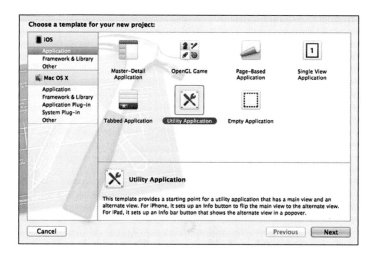

FIGURE 16.1
Selecting the Utility Application template from the iOS choices.

2. Fill in the details for your project as shown in Figure 16.2. So that we can use the same application on both iPhone and iPad devices, make sure that the Device Family setting is Universal. Select Use Storyboard and Automatic Reference Counting. We won't be using Core Data with iBLine, so leave that option un-checked (although if you think you might need to add Core Data support at a later date, selecting this and working around the extra code it adds until you need it is much easier than gluing in the bits you need in the future). As a matter of principle, check the Include Unit Tests check box.

FIGURE 16.2
Choosing options for the project.

3. Click Next, choose a place to store your project, and click Finish.

After working for a few moments, Xcode presents you with your bare Utility Application template. As shown in Figure 16.3, you are already provided with header and implementation files for the application delegate and with view controllers for both the main view and the "flipside" view. In the Editor section of the interface, you can configure numerous options for device features you want to support, such as what rotations your application needs to know about and standard things like application icons.

FIGURE 16.3
Xcode provides header and implementation files for the application delegate, as well as for the main and flipside view controllers.

Adding a Static Library Target

Now that you have your basic application project created from the template, it's time to add a Cocoa Touch-compatible static library to the BetterList framework project we've been using. To do this, follow these steps:

A really careful programmer would have realized that BetterList needed some tweaks and worked on them before even bothering to start on the iBLine project. If you're like me, though, you will inevitably end up in the situation we have set up here, where you have a new project started and another that you need to incorporate that requires additional editing. I have left the major steps in this order to show you the few extra things you need to do to succeed if you find yourself in this situation.

1. Close your iBLine project and open your BetterList project.

Only Open Projects Once

Closing iBLine isn't strictly necessary, but Xcode currently gets confused sometimes when you have a project open directly and it is also included as a sub-project in another open project. To avoid situations where Xcode cannot decide which open project is really in control of a file, it is safer to have one open project and to make sure any others that have potentially overlapping content are closed.

2. Select the BetterList project in the Navigator and again in the Editor area. Click the Add Target button (+) at the bottom of the Editor area, as shown in Figure 16.4.

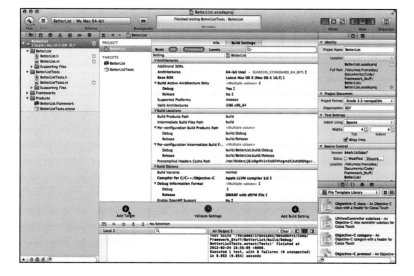

FIGURE 16.4
Adding a target.

3. In the dialog that appears, select the Framework & Library option in the iOS section of the project templates. The Cocoa Touch Static Library template is currently the only option available. Select it, and then click Next.

4. Choose a name for your static library target. It would be nice if you could just re-use BetterList here so that your BetterList project could create both a BetterList.framework framework distribution and a libBetterList.a static library, but Xcode does not let you use an identical base name, even thought it is going to add prefixes and suffixes that would make them distinct for the actual targets. Because Xcode prepends *lib* to the name provided here, I'm not adding that myself. Instead, as shown in Figure 16.6, I call the new target BetterListlib.

FIGURE 16.5
Selecting the
Cocoa Touch
Static Library
template.

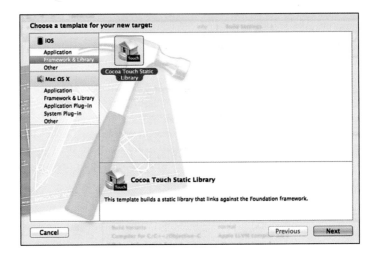

FIGURE 16.6
Choosing
options for
the target.

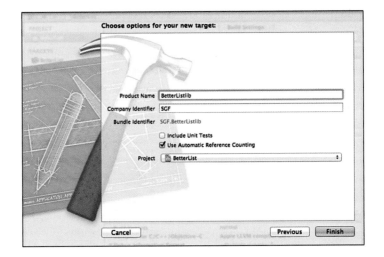

5. Uncheck the Include Unit Tests check box. Unless something new and different is going to happen that is unique to your new library, the unit tests of logic already instantiated in the framework should suffice to make sure that the BetterList functionality remains stable.

6. Make sure that the project to which you want to add the target is selected, and then click Finish.

Xcode populates your project with a new target and with new header and implementation files to implement your target. Because the new target in this case is just a differently stored version of our existing functionality, we do not need any new implementation files. We just need to convince Xcode to build a static library target with our existing one.

7. Open the new group that Xcode has created for BetterListlib in the Navigator, and select the new implementation and header files. Right-click and select Delete, as shown in Figure 16.7. When prompted, tell Xcode to go ahead and delete the files from disk.

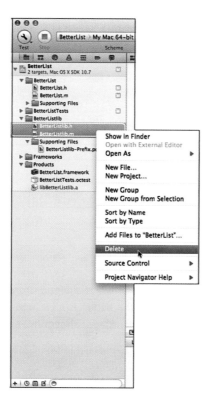

FIGURE 16.7
Deleting the new implementation and header files for BetterListlib.

8. Select your original BetterList.m implementation file in the Navigator and reveal the Utilities area. Under the Target Membership heading, you'll find the BetterList framework (toolbox icon) check box already selected. Check the check box beside your new target BetterListlib (Acropolis-looking classical architecture icon), too, as shown in Figure 16.8.

9. Select your original BetterList.h header file from the Navigator, and likewise, in the Utilities, select it as a target member for BetterListlib. After doing so, change its membership setting from (the default) Project header to Public, as shown in Figure 16.9.

FIGURE 16.8
Adding
BetterList.m
as a target
member for
BetterListlib.

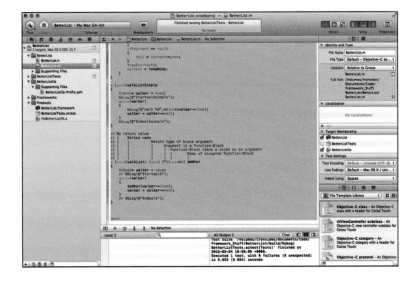

FIGURE 16.9
Adding
BetterList.h
as a target
member for
BetterListlib and
setting its
membership
to Public.

10. From the Product menu, choose Edit Scheme and, from the pop-up at the top of the dialog, switch to editing the BetterListlib scheme. Under the Build options, uncheck the Test build phase, as shown in Figure 16.10.

11. Display the Run options for the BetterListlib scheme, and under the info tab, switch the build configuration to Release, as shown in Figure 16.11, and then close the Scheme Editor.

12. (Optional) From the file menu, choose Project Settings, and then click the Advanced button to set the derived data location to Locations Specified by Targets.

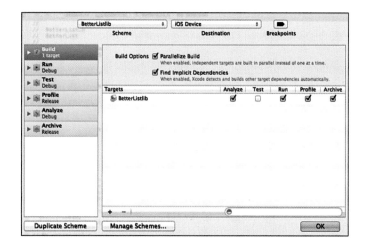

FIGURE 16.10
Deselecting the Test build phase for BetterListlib.

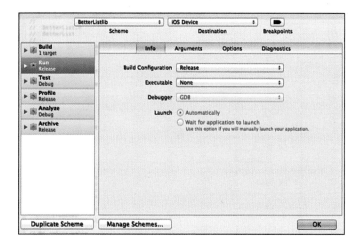

FIGURE 16.11
Setting the build configuration for the BetterListlib scheme to Release.

Everything can be completed with the default directories selected for the derived data location, but in the interim as Apple works out some of the kinks with projects, automatically finding the right paths for dependency data in subprojects, it is often, especially in small projects, much easier to be explicit with these settings rather than to rely on the sometimes-flakey automatic settings.

13. Back at the main Xcode window, from the Scheme pop-up menu on the toolbar select BetterListlib, iOS Device, as shown in Figure 16.12.

FIGURE 16.12 Setting BetterListlib to test iOS device architecture.

14. From the Product menu, choose Build For, Build for Running.

You should be rewarded with a Build Succeeded notification, and if you check your BetterList directory in the Finder, you should find that its build subdirectory has now been populated with a Release-iphoneos subdirectory. In that subdirectory, you should find your static library (libBetterListlib.a) and a distribution hierarchy for the header, /usr/local/include/BetterList.h, as shown in Figure 16.13. If you do not see these things, check your steps and try again.

FIGURE 16.13 The static library and header file should appear in a Release-iphoneos subdirectory of your BetterList directory in the Finder.

By the Way

If things are not working out quite as expected at this point, the information available from the Log Navigator (little speech-bubble icon) under the Navigator can be invaluable. The most probable source of difficulty, if you're getting a Build Succeeded notification and aren't seeing any errors, is Xcode putting the file somewhere other than where you wanted it. If you look at the detailed log entries for the last steps of your build process, you can usually identify the trouble and either correct it or, as is often easier, just move the files somewhere more useful by hand.

After you have succeeded in getting the BetterList project to build a libBetterListlib.a
static library, it is time to incorporate it into iBLine. To do so, follow these steps:

1. Close the BetterList project. If you don't, you'll drive yourself nuts when it adds
   itself to iBLine but you can't interact with its components.

2. From the Finder (or from the File menu in Xcode), open the iBLine project.

3. Select the iBLine project in the Navigator and right-click it. Choose Add Files
   to iBLine from the pop-up menu that appears, as shown in Figure 16.14.

FIGURE 16.14
Getting ready to
add files to the
iBLine project

4. In the file selection dialog that opens, navigate to wherever your BetterList
   project is located. Just in case you're a bit disorganized and work in multiple
   locations, you might want to expand the folders under it to make sure that
   you're really looking at the directory that contains the static library you just
   built. Select the BetterList.xcodeproj file and make sure it is going to be added
   to the iBLine target, as shown in Figure 16.15. Click the Add button.

5. The BetterList.xcodeproj project should now show up as a subproject of the
   iBLine project in the Navigator. Select the iBLine project in the Navigator and
   select the iBLine target in the Editor area. Open the tab for the iBLine build
   phases. Using either the + buttons at the bottom of each build section listing,
   or dragging the files from the Navigator area, add BetterListlib as a target
   dependency, and libBetterListlib.a to the list of libraries for linking, as shown
   in Figure 16.16.

FIGURE 16.15
Selecting the
BetterList.xcode
proj file to add
to the iBLine
target.

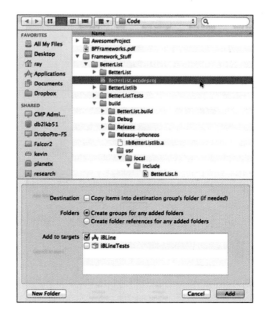

FIGURE 16.16
Updating the
BetterList.xcode
proj project
by adding
BetterListlib as
a target depend-
ency and
libBetterListlib.a
to the list of
libraries to be
linked.

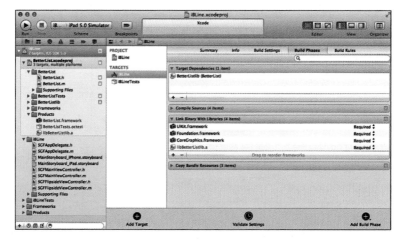

By the
Way

Remember that the BetterList project is now a child of both your original BeeLine
OS X application and your iBLine iOS application. This is convenient from the point
of view of making sure that when you add functionality to BetterList in either it's
available to both. However, it can cause problems if you do something to
BetterList in one that breaks functionality in the other, because you won't find out
about this until you have the other project open in Xcode, and if that's six months
in the future, you are likely to have forgotten exactly what you changed.

It is also difficult to work on both BeeLine and iBLine at the same time with this configuration because only one of them can actually have the BetterList project open at a time. Whichever of the BeeLine and iBLine projects is opened second will complain about "project integrity" because it cannot open BetterList itself. Because of this, if you were to complete all your BetterList functionality and wouldn't be touching it again, it would be better to just include the finished static library and header rather than the project. Alternatively, you could configure both BeeLine and iBLine to be peers within the same workspace (which you learn more about this in Hour 20, "Keeping things Organized: Shared Workspaces"), so that you could fiddle with BetterList from either of them without confusing Xcode when you open the other project.

To wrap things up so that the code in your iBLine project can find the headers defining the functionality available in BetterList, you need to complete one more step. (This will probably change as Xcode matures and the workspace functionality improves.)

6. Display the Build Settings tab for the iBLine target and choose to show all the settings. Look for the Search Paths section. You can use the search function to search for "header" or "path" to make things easier. Find the line for Header Search Paths. If you're not going to install your BetterList.h header in its intended final /usr/local/include location, you must configure the header search path so that the compiler can find it. The correct setting for the header search paths depends on where you put your BetterList directory.

In my case, I have a Framework_Stuff directory parallel to my applications directory SGFApps. My BeeLine and iBLine project directories are in the SGFApps directory, and the BetterList directory is in the Framework_Stuff directory. Therefore, I added a line to header search paths that contains `${SRCROOT}/../../Framework_Stuff/ BetterList/build/Release-iphoneos`. That is to say, include headers from a path starting in the current source directory, go up two levels (to the SGFApps directory, and then to the one above it), then back down into the Framework_Stuff directory, the BetterList directory under it, and the build directory and Release-iphoneos directories that we previously identified as where the BetterList project was storing the finished libBetterListlib.a static library. Your configuration should look similar to that shown in Figure 16.17.

If you select your iBLine scheme and iPhone simulator from the Xcode toolbar and run your iBLine project now, you should be greeted by not only a Build Succeeded notification but also by an onscreen iPhone running your app. The front side displays a blank view with an Info button icon (little italic *i*). You can flip this to the alternative view, which has a title bar and a Done button, which flips back to the main view, as shown in Figures 16.18 and 16.19. If you have gotten this far, you're all set to start building your logic and connecting it to the interface.

FIGURE 16.17
Adding a header search path so that the iBLine project can find the headers in BetterLists.

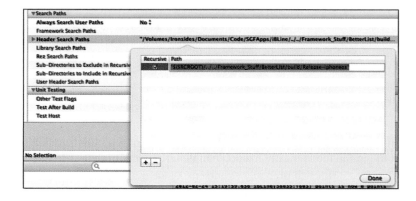

FIGURE 16.18
The front view with the Info button in the iPhone simulator.

FIGURE 16.19
The alternative view with a title bar and a Done button in the iPhone simulator.

Updating Application Logic and Library Calls for iOS

There are surprisingly few modifications that must be performed in the application logic in BeeLine to make it work under iOS. However, OS X and iOS are still too distant for this to be a simple single-click process. As a result, you must dig through your application logic by hand and find places where library routines differ or where differences in iOS require a modification of approach. The specific issues that you need to deal with for any given application are sufficiently diverse that you really need a book on Cocoa Touch and additional references for Objective-C to complete this process for a general application.

For the purposes of converting BeeLine into iBLine, we just hit some of the highlights that are typical of the issues you'll encounter with other applications. The full source for iBLine, appropriately converted for iOS, is available in the Hour 16 folder of the book source files, available from http://teachyourselfxcode.com/.

BeeLine's `QuartzGrough` class translates rather directly into a graph-drawing class for iOS. In iBLine, I call the analogous class `iGrough`. Some of the specific differences are as follows:

- Because we need to break out the `Model` component more cleanly for our data, `iGrough` is not going to own the `BetterList` instance, as was done in `QuartzGrough`.

- QuartzGrough was an `NSView` and used `NSPoints` and `[self size:[self bounds]]` to identify the current drawing region. It also used `NSColors` and filled a filled `NSBezierPath` to draw the graph background. `iGrough` is a `UIView` and doesn't know about `NSPoints`, `NSColors`, or filled `NSBezierPaths`. It also doesn't respond to a bounds message. Instead, `iGrough` needs to use `CGPoints`, a `CGColorSpace`, and a `CGContextFillRect`.

> Note that the Core Graphics CG* routines and variables are C language functions and structs rather than Objective-C methods and objects. Keeping this in mind often helps when trying to figure out what the appropriate translation is between some of the analogous-but-not-identical OS X and iOS functionality.

- The `UIView` context vertical axis is reversed compared to the `NSView` context vertical axis. In the `UIView`, the 0,0 origin is at the upper left rather than the `NSView` location of the lower left. As a result, we need to invert the Y coordinate of our plot to cause it to draw right-side up.

- In BeeLine, the application delegate set the `QuartzGrough` anX and anY instance variables and then invoked the `QuartzGrough` instance method `plotUpdate` directly in response to the user clicking the Add button. This will not work for iBLine for two reasons: First, because the Add button will be in a different scene (the flipped view), invoking the `iGrough` plotting routine when Add is clicked doesn't make any sense; we want the graphics to be plotted when the view flips back to the main view, not when Add is clicked. Second, because the Add button belongs to the FlipsideViewController, and the FlipsideViewController is a peer of the MainViewController, rather than its parent, we do not have convenient access to the iGrough instance variables from any method that the Add button can invoke. Part of this problem we alleviate by changing the QuartzGrough plotUpdate method into a sendPoints method in iGrough and passing in the whole list of points to be plotted. The other part of the problem we overcome by implementing a single-ton class to facilitate communication between the FlipsideViewController and the MainViewController.

> See the provided code in the Hour 16 folder for this book, for specific code changes to address these and other issues in converting QuartzGrough into iGrough.

Creating a Singleton to Hold Data and Share It Between Scenes

Singleton classes are an extremely powerful design pattern that seem to generate an unwarranted amount of confusion, especially given that they are actually exceed-ingly straightforward in implementation. A singleton class is simply a class that only allows an individual instance of itself to exist at any time. You can use such a class to provide access to single-copy hardware devices, such as the accelerometer in the iOS devices (and Apple uses the singleton design pattern for similar purposes extensively), but it can also be used to provide a way to communicate shared data and resources between other (potentially peer) classes.

No matter which class instantiates the singleton first, a single instance of it comes into being, and every other class that attempts to instantiate it just gets back a refer-ence to the same already-instantiated copy. As a result, any data that that one copy contains is available to all the classes that have (attempted to) instantiate the sin-gleton, and with appropriate setter and getter methods, each class that needs to communicate via the singleton can store data into it and retrieve data out of it.

To pass our BetterList around so that it can be stored into by methods in the FlipsideViewController, and accessed by methods in the MainViewController and the iGrough view, we create a singleton to carry around a BetterList, and each class that needs to access the BetterList can do so by addressing it through the sin-gleton. Our singleton class, named DataPhile, has a header file (DataPhile.h) that contains the code shown in Listing 16.1.

LISTING 16.1   **Header File DataPhile.h for the DataPhile Singleton Class**

```
#import "BetterList.h"

typedef struct myPointType myPointType;
struct myPointType {
        float myX;
        float myY;
};

@interface DataPhile : NSObject

+ (id)getSharedDataPhile;
+ (BetterList*)setupPointsList: (void*) theThing;

- (NSMutableArray*) getDataPhileArray;
- (BetterList*)getPointsList;

@end
```

DataPhile also has an implementation file (DataPhile.m) that contains the code in Listing 16.2.

LISTING 16.2   **Implementation File for DataPhile.m for the DataPhile Singleton Class**

```
#import "DataPhile.h"

@implementation DataPhile

static id dataPhile = nil;
static NSMutableArray *points;
static BetterList *pointsList = nil;

+ (void)initialize
{
    if(self == [DataPhile class])
    {
        dataPhile = [[self alloc] init];
        points = [NSMutableArray arrayWithCapacity:1];
    }
}

+ (id)getSharedDataPhile
{
    return dataPhile;
}

+ (BetterList*)setupPointsList: (void*) theThing
{
    pointsList = [[BetterList alloc] initDLList: theThing];
    return pointsList;
}
```

LISTING 16.2   Continued

```
- (NSMutableArray*)getDataPhileArray
{
    return points;
}

- (BetterList*)getPointsList
{
    return pointsList;
}

@end
```

You might at first find the logic behind the class methods confusing, but it will quickly become second nature after you discover how useful this pattern is for coordinating between your views without needing to pass lengthy lists of always-the-same parameters around explicitly. The first thing to note is the class method initialize. The initialize class method is invoked once, and only once, during the first attempt to invoke an instance of the class. Inside initialize, we set the class variable dataPhile to the return of our instance allocation and init procedure, and the class variable points to an NSMutableArray initialized to be large enough to contain a single item.

Did You Know?

The astute reader will wonder why I'm talking about setting "class variables" when Objective-C ostensibly does not provide class variables. While technically true that Objective-C lacks a specific class variable idiom, that doesn't mean that it is impossible to use the existing functionality to implement something that works like a class variable. The static global variables dataPhile, points, and pointsList can only be set through class methods in DataPhile, and their contents are available (identically) to any instance (although we can only have one instance here). Because it looks like a duck, walks like a duck, and quacks like a duck, I'm calling it a class variable as shorthand.

Did You Know?

The assignments in initialize are wrapped in a conditional that checks whether self is actually a literal DataPhile class. This is boilerplate. The initialize method is invoked once, regardless of whether it is the class or a derived class that is instanced first. If for some reason I want to do something different if a derived class is instanced first, I can catch that with this conditional. Because I have no derived classes for DataPhile, the conditional is completely redundant, and I've left it in the code only as a reminder in case I need it for something later.

The next features worthy of mention are the class methods getSharedDataPhile and setupPointsList:

▶ `getSharedDataPhile` does nothing more than return the value of the `dataPhile` "class" variable. Because this is a static global value settable only by the `initialize` method, any class that messages `DataPhile`'s `getSharedDataPhile` method is going to get exactly the same response: a reference to the single instance of `DataPhile` that was created when the `initialize` method was called for the class.

▶ The `setupPointsList` class method is used to fill in the `pointList` "class" variable. It doesn't strictly need to be a class method because the `pointsList` is global and there is only going to be one instance of the `DataPhile` class, but in the service of self-documenting code, there's an elegance to having methods that affect class variables be class methods.

Finally, we have a pair of instance methods, `getDataPhileArray`, and `getPointsList`, that retrieve the "class" variables `points` and `pointsList`. These do not strictly need to be instance methods, and there's at least one coherent argument to be made for making them class methods instead, that being that they interact with class variables and therefore are more transparent as class methods. However, a counterargument can be made that code looks cleaner if the routines that use your singleton retrieve an instance of your singleton class (always the same instance) and then retrieve values from the instance instead of always talking to the class itself. Maintaining `getSharedDataPhile` as a class method remains sensible here because it makes it explicit in the application code that the `DataPhile` instance is singular and belongs to the class rather than a unique instance created by the application code that is using it.

Finally, note that we've moved the definition of `myPointType` into the DataPhile.h header. This is purely for convenience. Every class that needs to access the points from our BetterList is going to need to include the DataPhile.h header, so moving that definition here, instead of keeping it with `iGrough`, keeps things neater.

All together, it takes much more effort to describe the singleton pattern than to use it. This might be its one negative aspect. After singletons stop looking peculiar and you become fluent with them, you'll likely start seeing many situations where they could make your life easier. If you're like most programmers, you'll probably find more places where they look like they might fit than are actually good places to use them. An application that is using singletons to store all of its data is probably doing something wrong or is likely to have areas where its functionality could be significantly expanded if it weren't limited to single-instance copies of data. Beware of painting yourself into a corner by overusing singletons, but don't be afraid to use them judiciously if passing values between the components of your application would just add redundancy to your code.

Swapping iOS Components for OS X Components

This bit is a little tricky. Both the NSBrowser and the TableView are very powerful classes with many options, and neither the display nor the options translate directly between them. With the NSBrowser for BeeLine, we could subclass the NSBrowser class, set the interface element to be a member of our subclass, and add methods to populate it to that subclass. This is not how UITableViews are used. UITableViews are simply UITableViews, and they self-populate themselves with data by being linked, rather than subclassed into, a class that contains specifically named methods, and they achieve added functionality by specification of a delegate.

To attach a class to a UITableView as its data source, the class needs to implement specific instance methods. A minimalist set includes a numberOfSelectionsInTable View method and tableView:numberOfRowsInSection and tableView:cellFor RowAtIndexPath methods. The UITableView also needs a delegate containing at a minimum a tableView:didSelectRowAtIndexPath method in which to implement some action when a tableView row is selected. The Hour 16 folder of this book's source files contains the minimal code necessary to support a TableView embedded in the FlipsideViewController. In a more complex application, where a UITableView could be afforded a scene of its own, it is better to create an independent class to serve as the UITableView data source and delegate. With the two-scene Utility Application template, however, using the FlipsideViewController is easier.

Populating the Primary Scene

Now that our code is in place, we can get on with building the UI and connecting all the pieces. Although you do not have to write all the code before adding the UI components, you might find doing so easier because if you do build the UI first, you'll end up repeatedly going back and forth between the Interface Builder and the code. When you add interface elements, they often need code to support them. If the code is not already present, you must write it and then return to the Interface Builder and try to remember what you want to connect it to. By putting the code in place first, you can then place interface elements and immediately connect them with their appropriate classes without having to constantly flip back and forth.

Because we're replicating the BeeLine project, the first thing we need to add to the main scene is a view area where we can plot our data. Doing this requires much the same sequence of actions with which you're becoming familiar in Interface Builder:

1. Select the MainStoryboard_iPhone.storyboard in the navigator and maneuver the storyboard editor area until you can see the entire main view controller.

2. Open the Utilities area and show the Object Library.

3. Find the View item (a UIView) and drag it onto the Main View Controller scene in the storyboard, as shown in Figure 16.20.

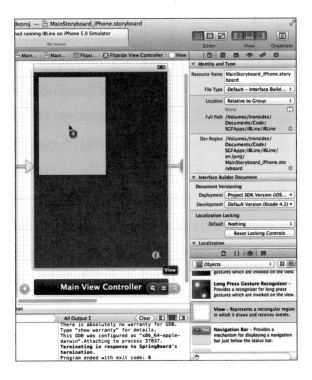

FIGURE 16.20
Dragging the View item into in the Main View Controller scene in the storyboard.

4. Resize the View item you have placed to suit your preferences, and then show the Identity Inspector in the Utilities area and change the class for the View item from the original UIView class to our UIView-derived iGrough class, as shown in Figure 16.21.

FIGURE 16.21
Changing the
class for the
View to our
iGrough class.

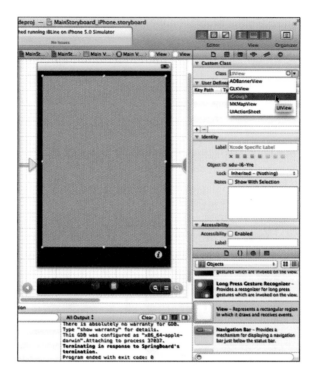

Populating the Secondary Scene

Populating the secondary scene with the rest of the UI elements is no more difficult:

1. Move the storyboard view until the FlipsideViewController scene is fully visible in the Editor area.

2. Drag in a pair of text fields for the X and Y coordinate entries and a pair of labels.

   We did not need to change the default color of the labels in BeeLine because the default OS X application background is light gray and the default label color is black. Unfortunately, the default iOS background is dark gray, while the default label color remains black (note to Apple: that's not insanely great), so you must change it.

3. Select both of your labels in Interface Builder by clicking on the first one and Option-clicking the second. Then show the Attributes Inspector in the Utilities. Near the bottom of the Label fields, you'll see a Text Color pop-up. Click it.

Don't click and hold. A standard color picker will appear. Select the color you want for your text, as shown in Figure 16.22. Notice that your labels change color as you adjust the setting in the color picker, although they remain tinted with your highlight color until you click elsewhere in Interface Builder to deselect the labels.

Text Color Field

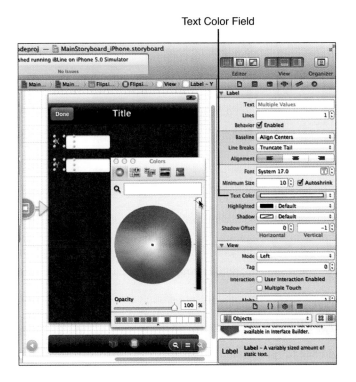

FIGURE 16.22
Selecting color
for the text.

4. Complete the interface by adding a Round Rect Button for the Add function and a TableView to display the list of points, as shown in Figure 16.23.

> We are just filling out the iPhone interface components here. Setting up the iPad interface follows an identical procedure, the only difference being that you need to select the MainStoryBoard_iPad.storyboard to begin working on it.

Did You Know?

Finally, it is time to connect the code functionality and the interface elements to complete our iOS application.

FIGURE 16.23
Finishing the
interface
with an Add
button and a
`TableView` to
display the list
of points.

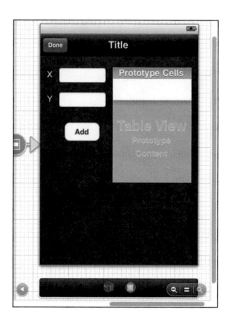

You will find most of this familiar from the procedure we followed to build the OS X application. As usual, though, Xcode provides more than one way to approach the problem, so we use a slight variation from the previous method. To connect the user interface components, follow these steps:

1. Select the MainStoryboard_iPhone.storyboard in the Navigator and open the Scene List sidebar. (If it's not open, the right-pointing triangle at the bottom of the Interface Builder opens it.)

2. In the Main View Controller Scene group in the sidebar, reveal the contents of the main view controller, and then reveal the contents of the view contained in it.

3. Click the Assistant Editor button on the toolbar. If your Assistant Editor mode is set to Automatic, the MainViewController header file should appear in the Assistant Editor. If it does not, navigate to that file using the jump bar.

4. Control-click the iGrough in the sidebar (which peculiarly is only named Grough in the sidebar list, despite being properly an iGrough) and drag a connection from it over to the MainViewController header, as shown in Figure 16.24. Drop it below the last @property declaration and above the @end.

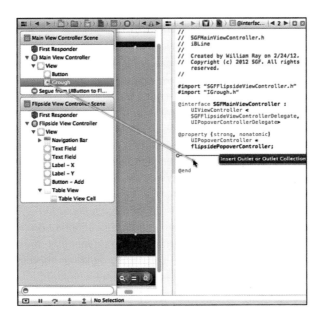

FIGURE 16.24
Connecting the iGrough in the sidebar list to between the last @property and to the @end in the MainView Controller.h.

5. Create an outlet connection and name it. As shown in Figure 16.25, I'm using aGroughGraph, carried over from the BeeLine implementation.

FIGURE 16.25
Creating an outlet connection and naming it.

6. Switch to FlipsideViewController. Select it in its sidebar group and expand it and also expand the view within it. If you need to manually point the Assistant Editor to the FlipsideViewController header, do so now.

7. Create outlets for both text fields by Control-clicking and dragging from each into the FlipsideViewController header. Name them **xCoord** and **yCoord** as previously done in BeeLine. Also create an action for the button. As you're proceeding, things should look like Figure 16.26.

FIGURE 16.26
Creating outlets for the text fields and an action for the button.

8. When it comes time to configure the action for the button, you'll find that you have an additional configuration parameter for the event that's not available for OS X applications. iOS, of course, lacks a cursor. As a result, traditional OS X events like MouseDown and MouseUp cannot be completely replicated, and probably shouldn't mean the same things in iOS even if they could. Instead, they're replaced by "touch" events. The most intuitively appropriate of the available options, for most button operations, is the Touch Up Inside option, so select this, as shown in Figure 16.27, for your button action.

FIGURE 16.27
Configuring the action for the button to be a Touch Up Inside event.

9. Control-drag an outlet for the UITableView into the FlipsideViewController header. Configure it as shown in Figure 16.28.

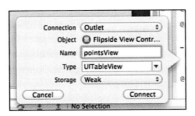

FIGURE 16.28
Configuring a
UITableView
outlet into the
FlipsideView
Controller.

10. Now hide the Assistant Editor and show just the main Interface Builder editor again. Position the storyboard so that you can see the entire `FlipsideViewController`.

11. Control-click the `UITableView` in the Interface Builder. A Heads Up Display (HUD) dialog appears with some available fields that you probably haven't seen before. Control-click the open outlet for the `dataSource` and drag and drop on the `FlipsideViewController` proxy in the dock beneath the scene, as shown in Figure 16.29. This tells Interface Builder and Xcode to use the canonically named methods found in the `FlipsideViewController` to provide data for the table.

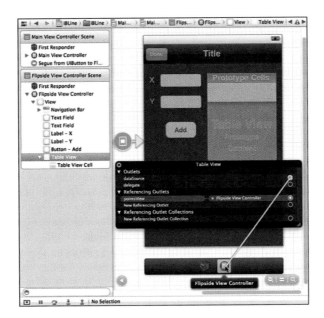

FIGURE 16.29
Setting the data
provided to the
table to use
canonically
named methods
found in the
FlipsideView
Controller.

12. Repeat this for the open outlet for the `UITableView` delegate, as shown in Figure 16.30. This tells Interface Builder and Xcode to set up the appropriate message delegation so that the table functionality can be enhanced by adding delegate methods to the FlipsideViewController.

FIGURE 16.30
Adding delegate
methods to the
FlipsideView
Controller to
enhance table
functionality.

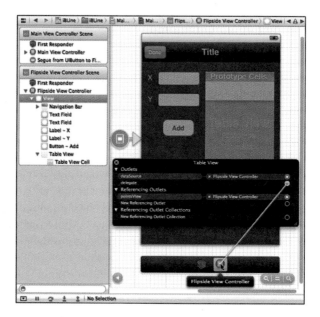

13. Finally, within Table View in the Interface Builder sidebar, select the Table View Cell or click the white bar just beneath the Prototype Cells header in the Table View, open the Attributes Inspector in the Utilities area, and change the identifier to **freeCell**, as shown in Figure 16.31. This connects the cells in the placed tableView with the cell allocation performed in the FlipsideViewController.

Did You Know?

If you have set up an iPad version of the interface, you must repeat these connections for the iPad version.

The FlipsideViewController now needs a bit of extra code added to it to complete the plotPoint method for the Add button and to connect it to the singleton that carries our BetterList instance. The MainViewController also needs these connections added. The code for both is in the Hour 16 folder of the source code.

Change the identifier here

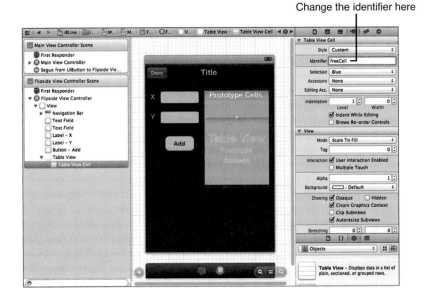

FIGURE 16.31
Changing the
Table View Cell
identifier to
freeCell.

And now you should have an application that works on the iPhone with essentially identical functionality to the BeeLine application you constructed for OS X. If you click the Run button on the toolbar, you should be greeted (after a bit of compiling) by a virtual iPhone running your new application. Considerably more gratifying than before, your main view should now contain a white graphics view, as shown in Figure 16.32. If you click on the Info button (the italic *i*) to flip to the alternate view, you will see your X and Y coordinate entry boxes and your empty table view. Fill in a few values (between -1.0 and 1.0) and it should look like Figure 16.33. Tap the Done button to flip back to the main view, and the application will flip back to the main view and plot a graph of the points you have entered, as shown in Figure 16.34.

Adding iOS Specialty Features

Although you're technically done with the job of literally converting the application functionality from BeeLine to iBLine, you could still do plenty of things to make the user experience better on iOS (for example, supporting rotation). To get you started, the version of iBLine that's in the Hour 16 folder of this book's source files includes the logic and the modification of the notifications received by the `MainViewController` that are necessary to receive rotation events and to redisplay the graph interface as appropriate for rotated displays.

FIGURE 16.32
The main view
now has white
graphics (left).

FIGURE 16.33
The alternate
view has the X
and Y coordi-
nate entry
boxes and your
table view with
the entries
(middle).

FIGURE 16.34
After tapping
Done, we return
to the main
view, which has
the graph of the
points that were
entered in the
alternate view
(right).

Summary

In this hour, you converted an OS X application into an iOS application, including some tweaks to the functionality to support iOS and Cocoa Touch-specific features. The steps you followed here are typical of what you must do any time you face this task.

OS X applications tend to use dynamic frameworks, so converting these to iOS static libraries is always necessary. Most of your code will translate, with the occasional minor annoyance of discovering, for example, that the graphics coordinate systems are inverted between the two platforms. You'll probably have a few UI features in your OS X application that don't have exact analogs in what iOS provides. Still, reusing the pieces from an OS X application on iOS should not be difficult, and if you have done a good job of separating the model, view, and controller aspects of your application, the specific features that you need to address should be well compartmentalized, enabling you to address each of them as discrete programming tasks.

As you become more familiar with both OS X and iOS fundamentals, you'll find that these conversions become easier, both because of your increased skill and because you'll find yourself favoring easily converted interface idioms when doing initial development on either platform. With Apple's clear intent to unify the OS across desktop and palmtop platforms, getting into this habit is probably a great way to prepare for Apple's next big thing.

Q&A

Q. *Is there a better way to handle the Header Path setting so that the iBLine code can find the BetterLists header?*

A. I sure hope so. We cover one improved alternative in Hour 20, but there should be other solutions that are better than setting an explicit path, as well. Unfortunately, none of them seem completely stable at the moment. For example, if go back and look at the Search Paths section of the Build settings, you'll see an option to Always Search User Paths. Setting this to Yes produces the tempting behavior that the code editor thinks that the BetterList header can be found even without an explicit header search path. Unfortunately, although the code editor can find it, the compiler still can't. Let's hope this bug is resolved soon.

Q. *What other iOS-specific features would be good to implement for iBLine?*

A. Wow, lots of them. How about pinch/zoom on the iGrough? Shake to erase the entire plotted graph? Tie the point collection into either the accelerometer or the GPS so that users can play with drawing by waving the phone in the air or by walking around with it? The more iOS bells and whistles you can *usefully* add to your mobile application, the better it will fit with the other applications on the user's device. This makes the user experience more seamless and makes users happy. Don't go down the road of adding iOS fluff just to have more bells and whistles, though. Just as surely as users like appropriately applied iOS features, they react with visceral disgust when you misuse one. Please, please, please, don't set up push notifications to send all your friends updated coordinate lists every time you add a point. They'll hate you for that.

Q. *Will this really run on an iPhone as well as in the simulator?*

A. You bet. We cover provisioning actual iOS hardware devices and getting your application into the App Store in Hours 22 and 23 ("Managing and Provisioning iOS Devices" and "Distributing Your Applications," respectively).

Q. *I think I did everything right, but whenever I try to run my project, I get an error about something being undefined. I vaguely remember creating an outlet with that name a while ago, but I deleted those bits. What's up?*

A. The Storyboard and Interface Builder features are great for what they do well, but really annoying for what they do poorly. When you drag connections into pieces of code, you're not just adding @property and @synthesize lines to your header and implementation files. You're also telling Interface Builder to add some other things behind the scenes (If you enter the text-editing mode, rather than the graphical-editing mode for a NIB or storyboard, you'll see what I mean). Unfortunately, when you delete the @property and @synthesize lines from your header and implementation files, this does not tell the Interface Builder or the Storyboard feature to delete those bits of internal magic. The error you're seeing is because some interface element still thinks it has an outlet or action connected. Bring up the Interface Builder or Storyboard feature and right-click each interface element to bring up its HUD of connections. You'll eventually find one that references the no-longer-existing @property that Xcode is complaining about. Click on the little X button beside that item, and it should disappear from the HUD. Now you should be good to go.

Workshop

Quiz

1. What does the storyboard editor use instead of the Interface Builder dock for holding proxies?

2. How many different ways are there to add an outlet connection for an interface element?

3. What code belongs in the application delegate?

Answers

1. It uses a little bar beneath each scene that holds the name of the scene (derived from the controller for that view) when the scene is not the active selected one and holds the proxy object/file representations for the scene when it is active.

2. At least four. You can Control-drag from the item in the Interface Builder or storyboard itself. You can Control-drag from the item in the expanded component list beside the storyboard or Interface Builder editor. You can right-click the item to show its Heads Up Display and drag from an existing outlet to a target or from the New Referencing Outlet item to a target. Finally, you can use the Connections Inspector in the Utilities to access the same list of outlets as you get from right-clicking the interface element. There are probably more.

3. Only what is necessary to manage the application life cycle. If it doesn't have to do with setting up or tearing down the application, it doesn't belong there.

Activities

1. Build the iPad interface for iBLine.

2. Implement pinch and zoom on the iGrough so that it changes the plotted coordinate range to something larger or smaller than the [-1,+1] range that it currently supports.

3. Split the dataSource and delegate for the UITableView out so that they aren't embedded in the FlipsideViewController any more. Attach them to the DataPhile and remove the dependence on BetterLists from the iGrough.

HOUR 17

Attaching Big Data: Using Core Data in Your Applications

What You'll Learn in This Hour:

▶ The terminology of Core Data
▶ How to create Core Data models
▶ How to access Core Data through Managed Objects
▶ How to Bind OS X interfaces to Core Data entities

Way back in Hour 3, "Understanding the MVC Design Pattern," you learned about the model-view-controller design pattern as we walked through an application (Library) that demonstrated the principles of this pattern. That example showed a Core Data model that provides data to the views within an iOS application—linking authors with their books.

Why, now, are we returning to Core Data for an hour's lesson? Because your authors believe that Core Data—although a large topic—is important enough to warrant a full formal introduction. Core Data can change the way you think about application design and the way you code. Instead of you having to laboriously write methods to interact with a database, Core Data can abstract the process for you, and, coupled with the Interface Builder editor, even create rather complex application functionality without you ever touching a line of code. This hour demonstrates exactly that.

Introducing Core Data

Core Data is a large, rather-intimidating framework that is easier to learn through use than from sitting down and reading a large reference manual. If you recall, Core Data provides high-performance persistent storage to your applications. The default implementation of this storage is through SQLite, but that, aside from being an interesting fact, is irrelevant. The back-end storage is abstracted from the user, and from you, the developer. In fact, the less you try to apply your knowledge of relational database systems to Core Data, the further ahead you'll be.

Why Core Data?

Small iOS and OS X applications are well suited to use the defaults system available for storing simple key-value data. This approach does not scale well, however. It also does not allow (without tons of programming) a representation of real-world data. Core Data fills this need without the developer having to re-invent the wheel.

Did You Know?

> OS X and iOS provide a system for storing key/value pairs called the *defaults sys-tem*. It is accessed through the `NSUserDefaults` class and provides persistent data storage for application preferences, settings, and other simple data structures.

Core Data also provides some speed-of-development benefits. Using the Xcode Core Data model editor, you can define, visually, what your data model looks like. No coding, no initializing and allocating: Just point and click. You can also create classes that map directly to that data model, which makes accessing information as easy as accessing a variable. Even more impressive, you can create OS X applications that display, sort, add, modify, and delete data without writing one single line of code. Not one.

Speaking the Core Data Language

If you have worked with databases, it isn't hard to make the leap to using Core Data. What you have to do, however, is stop thinking about manually defining the bits and pieces that tie pieces of data together. Instead, you concentrate on the model itself, not how it is implemented. Let's quickly review some of the language you'll often encounter when working with Core Data. This will help you get away from the SQL mindset and start thinking in Core Data terms:

▶ **Entity**: A unique unit consisting of pieces of related data—like a company, a person, an address, and so on—similar to a database table. A Core Data entity can be mapped to an object.

▶ **Attributes**: The "pieces of related data" that make up an entity. Consider these the properties of the entity object. A person entity might have attributes like first name, last name, email address, and so on. In database terms, these are the columns within a table.

▶ **Relationships**: The defined connections between two entities. A person and address entity might be defined by a relationship that states "a person can have multiple addresses." Unlike a database where columns are used to relate data, relationships are defined between entities and the implementation is handled behind the scenes.

▶ **Properties**: The attributes and relationships of an entity.

▶ **Schema**: The combination of entities, attributes, and relationships that make up a Core Data model.

▶ **Object store**: The "back-end" storage for a Core Data model. The object store maintains your data between application executions.

▶ **Object graph**: A representation of the relationship between objects as a directed graph.

▶ **Managed object**: An instance of the objects within a schema (NSManagedObject). Although roughly equivalent to a database record, you work with managed objects like other Objective-C objects and can walk the object graph using dot notation to deference across entities and attributes. You also use standard methods for modifying information within the model. Multiple objects (think the results of a search) are managed in an NSSet of NSManagedObjects.

▶ **Managed object context**: Working with a managed object requires a managed object context. The context ensures integrity within the managed object and the underlying object store (NSManagedObjectContext).

▶ **Fetch request**: An object that describes data to be retrieved from an object store. Fetch requests define the entity that will serve as the starting point in the object graph that is created by the request, the sort order for when multiple objects are returned, and a filter (called a predicate) to narrow the results.

▶ **Predicate**: A string that describes a means of limited the data returned by a fetch request. A predicate to select all Person objects with a last name of "Smith" might look like this: Person.lastName="Smith".

▶ **Configuration**: Core Data configurations provide a method of defining sets of entities so that you can define a master set of entities that you need and then use different configurations to target specific subsets of these entities.

▶ **Fetched properties**: A weak one-way relationship that is defined using a fetch request rather than a true defined relationship. You might define a relationship to "other people with the same last name" as fetched property for a Person entity. Made available as an array rather than a set.

▶ **Binding**: A defined relationship between an object and a Core Data entity or attribute. You learn how to bind UI objects directly to Core Data entities a bit later this hour.

Unfortunately, getting into the full scope of Core Data possibilities is beyond the scope of this book, but we do look at enough of the tools and functionality for you to gain an appreciation this valuable framework and toolset.

By the Way

> At the time of this writing, Core Data does not support any UI bindings in iOS applications. Although I hope this changes, a great many of the *wow* features of Core Data are available only when doing OS X development.

Using the Xcode Core Data Model Editor

Your Core Data work begins with a Core Data model. The model is the Core Data schema, and is developed directly in Xcode with the Core Data model editor. Models get into your apps in one of two ways: You either add them during the project-creation process by clicking the Use Core Data check box, as shown in Figure 17.1, or you add a Data Model file (.xcdatamodeld) from the Core Data iOS/OS X file template categories in Xcode.

FIGURE 17.1
Add a Core Data model to your project during creation (or afterward).

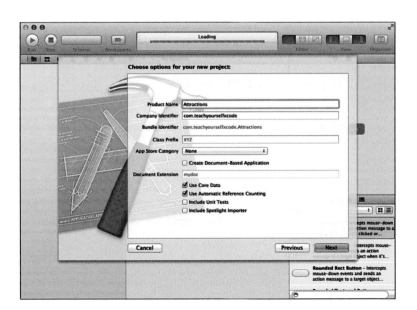

In this hour, the walkthrough example creates a simple Core Data model and application that collects information about cities, and notable attractions within each city. If you want to follow along, create a new OS X Cocoa application named **Attractions** now. Be sure to choose to use Core Data during the project-creation process. If you would rather just read, don't worry; the project files are included in this hour's Projects folder.

The first step in creating a Core Data model is to open the model file for editing. To do this, select the .xcdatamodeld file in the Project Navigator. Your screen refreshes to show the Core Data model editor, as shown in Figure 17.2.

Model File

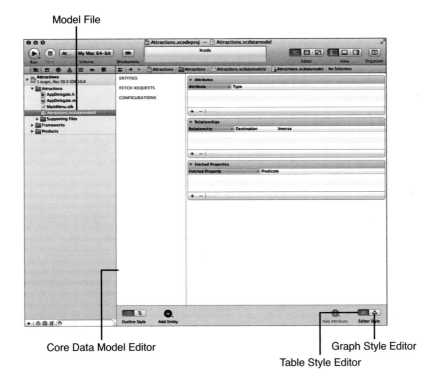

FIGURE 17.2
Click the model file to load the editor.

Core Data Model Editor

Table Style Editor

Graph Style Editor

Use the editor style buttons in the lower-right corner of the Editor area to switch to the table-style display. The graph displays a visual representation of your data, but is not nearly as easy to use as the table style. This example demonstrates use of the editor with the table style.

In the left column of your editor, you'll see headings for entities, fetch requests, and configurations. Because you haven't created anything yet, these are empty—with the exception of a default configuration. To the right of the column are three sections titled Attributes, Relationships, and Fetched Properties. These contain information that describe/define your entities, once they are defined. Speaking of which, let's create some entities.

Adding Entities

Everything in a model ties to an entity. To add an entity, follow these steps:

1. Click the Add Entity button.

2. A new entity with the name Entity is added to the entity list in the column on the right of the model editor.

3. The entity name is made available for editing. Begin typing to set it, as shown in Figure 17.3. You can double-click the name of the entity to change it at any time.

FIGURE 17.3
Add a new entity to your model.

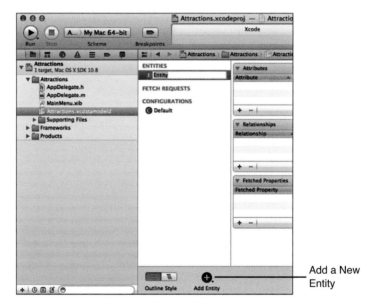

Add a New Entity

Watch
Out!

The Mysteriously Changing Interface

The Add Entity button is really a pop-up menu. If you click and hold, it has options for creating Fetch requests and configurations as well as entities. If it has been changed from the default, it will not show Add Entity in its label. Just click and hold to set it back to the Add Entity default.

This example shows two entities: Attraction (something fun to do) and Location. They are linked by two relationships: a one-to-many relationship between location and attraction (a location can have multiple attractions) and a one-to-one relationship between attraction and location (a specific attraction can only exist in one location.)

Using these steps, add two entities named **Attraction** and **Location**. They do not need to contain anything; they just need to exist. Once added, your display should resemble Figure 17.4.

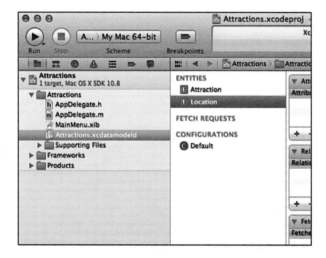

FIGURE 17.4
A model with two empty entities.

Obviously, entities are not much use without attributes that can store information. So, your next step is to add the attributes.

Adding Attributes

Attributes have two basic identifying properties: an attribute name and a type. To add an attribute to an entity, follow these steps:

1. Click to highlight the entity in the left column of the model editor.

2. Click the + button at the bottom of the Attributes section.

3. A new attribute is added to the list with the name attribute—ready to be edited. Type to change the name to whatever you want.

4. Finally, set the attribute type by clicking the pop-up menu immediately to the right of the attribute name, as shown in Figure 17.5.

FIGURE 17.5
Add attributes
to your entities.

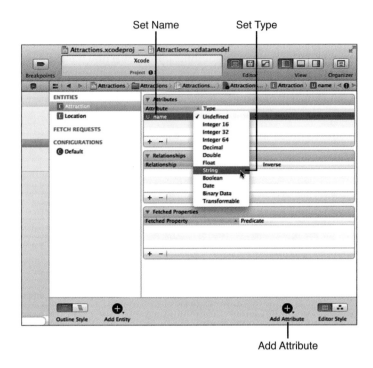

Add Attribute

For the Attractions project, I established a name attribute and an info attribute for
the Attraction entity; and, for the Location entity, I established city, state, and
zipcode. All of these are strings.

My Location entity, with all defined attributes, is shown in Figure 17.6.

FIGURE 17.6
The Location
entity with
city, state,
zipcode
attributes.

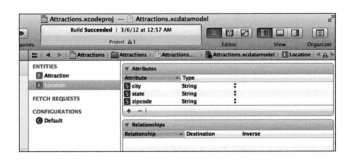

By the
Way

In addition to names and types, you can use the Data Model Inspector
(Option+Command+3) to set attributes as indexed values, optional, and other esoteric settings. The Apple Guide "Getting Started with Core Data" in the Xcode documentation is a good place to begin exploring the options we cannot cover in
depth here.

Defining Relationships

The last step in most data models is defining the relationships between entities. Relationships, although a very powerful part of a data model, are surprisingly simple to create. They are defined by the entities involved in the relationship, an arbitrary name of your choosing, and the cardinality of the relationship.

Relationships can also have an *inverse* relationship, which is nothing more than a second relationship that defines the reverse of any given relationship. In the case of the Attractions data model I'm working with, one relationship is that a location can have multiple attractions (a one-to-many relationship). The inverse of that relationship is that an attraction can have one location (a one-to-one relationship). Complicated terms for concepts that are common sense.

To add a relationship between entities, complete this process:

1. Select the entity that you want to relate to another from the left column of the editor.

2. Click the + button at the bottom of the Relationships section.

3. A new relationship is added to the list with the name `relationship`. Change the name to whatever you want.

4. Use the Destination pop-up menu to set the destination entity (the other side of the relationship). This is demonstrated in Figure 17.7.

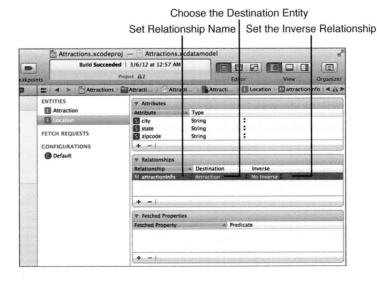

FIGURE 17.7
Name and set the destination for your relationship.

5. Use the Inverse pop-up menu to choose another relationship that has been defined (if any) that represents the reverse of the relationship you just created. If this is the first relationship you have added, you must add the second (inverse) relationship and then come back and set the inverse here.

These steps set the relationship between entities, but it defaults the cardinality of the relationship to one-to-one. To set a one-to-many relationship, you must open the Data Model Inspector (Option+Command+3) and check the Relationship settings Plural check box, as shown in Figure 17.8.

FIGURE 17.8
Check the Plural check box to configure a one-to-many relationship.

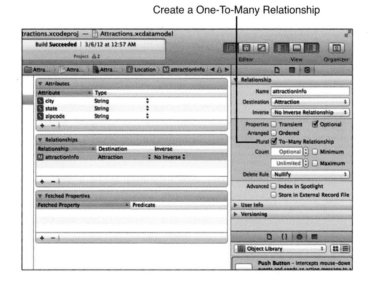

For the Attractions data model, define two relationships. The first, from the Attraction entity to the Location entity should be named **locationInfo** and set as a one-to-one relationship. The second, from Location to Attraction, named **attractionInfo**, should be configured as a plural (one-to-many) relationship. After both relationships are in place, they should be set to be each other's inverse (the inverse of locationInfo is attractionInfo, and vice versa).

> **By the Way**
>
> You might also want to look at the options for the delete rule for the relationship. A cascading delete rule, for example, ensures that when an object in a data set is deleted, the deletion cascades across the relationship to the related objects. Often, this is the preferred behavior across related entities.

Using the Graph Editor Style

Creating your entities, attributes, and relationships using the table style of the Core
Data model editor is great for focusing on a single entity at a time. The graph style,
however, can give you a nice overview of all the entities, attributes, and relationships you have defined, as shown in Figure 17.9.

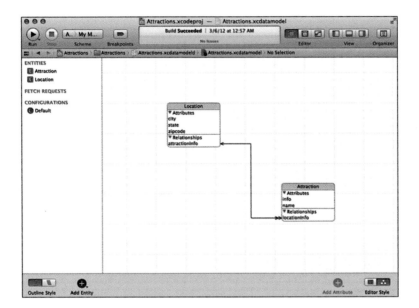

FIGURE 17.9
The graph style
view of the
Attractions data
model.

In the graph view, you can drag individual entities around to arrange them in a way
that is logical to you. Each entity lists its attributes and relationships, and connections are drawn between each entity to visually demonstrate the relationships.
Cardinality is communicated by the number of arrowheads on a relationship connection. One arrowhead = a one-to-one relationship, two arrowheads = a one-to-
many relationship.

Did You Know?

The graph style is actually a full editor for your model. You can click to highlight an
entity, and then click the Add Attribute button (a pop-up menu with Add
Relationship and Add Fetch Property options, as well) to add a new attribute to the
entity. You can edit the names within the visual representation of the entities, and
use the Data Model Inspector (Option+Command+3) to set the type. You can even
define relationships by clicking and dragging from one entity to another.

I find this to be an extremely inefficient way of defining a data model, but if you
want to give it a try, be aware that the tools are there, even if they are not readily
apparent.

Binding a Data Model to a User Interface

After you have built a data model, you'll want to do something useful with it. You can take two approaches when working with the data. First, you can write code to read and manipulate information. This is obviously an important skill, but, to be frank, it is also a bit boring. The second approach is to *bind* the data model to interface components, enabling quite advanced application functionality without writing a line of code. We start with the second approach in this part of the lesson, and then finish up with some code that can access the data model.

Because you can bind information to controls in Xcode in dozens of different ways, what we look at in this section is one approach for a small set of controls and a very simple data model. Core Data creates immense opportunities for your applications, but you need to spend more time with the Xcode documentation to familiarize yourself with all the intricacies of the binding system.

For this tutorial, we bind the Attractions data model to a user interface that enables the users to see, add, edit, and remove information from the `Location` and `Attraction` entities—all without typing one line of code. If you want to continue building the project from scratch, you can—but the UI might take a few minutes. If you want to get a quick start, open the Attractions (Disconnected) version of the project from this hour's Projects folder. This contains the finished data model and a complete UI with no bindings in place. Otherwise, make sure your data model is wrapped up before continuing on.

Implementation Overview

The Attractions application presents, when complete, two windows: Attractions and Locations. The Locations window contains an interface for collecting and managing information about the cities that contain attractions. The Attractions window enables the user to create a new attraction and tie it to an existing location. Figure 17.10 shows the finished application in action.

To get our Core Data model connected to the interface, we need to add two Array Controller objects (`NSArrayController`) to the XIB file. These are special objects that manage collections of information and selections within these collections. For our purposes, the collections will be the Core Data entities we defined (`Attraction` and `Location`). After the array controllers have been configured, they can be bound to the interface elements. We use special *controller keys* to ask the controllers for information:

► **selection**: The selected objects within the collection. When the user clicks an attraction in the list, for example, it is represented by the selection key.

► **arrangedObjects**: An array of sorted objects. The arrangedObjects key populates our interface with the entity attributes for our entire entity, or for the selection.

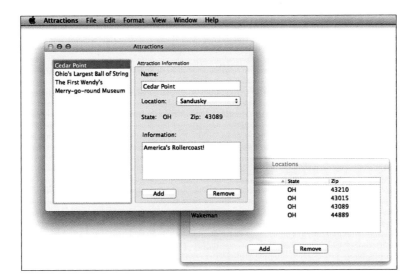

FIGURE 17.10
Manage attractions and locations.

The app delegate will serve as the managed object context, and we'll use the array controller's built-in actions of add and remove to add and remove data from the underlying data store. Let's get started.

Creating the Interface

Open the XIB file in your new project or in the Attractions (Disconnected) project. Figure 17.11 shows the interface I created for the application.

If you want to create the interface as an exercise in using Interface Builder, these are the elements you want to add to the default Cocoa application XIB before moving on.

► **For the Attractions window**

A single-column table view to contain the list of attractions. In my example, the headers are turned off.

A text field to enter or edit an attraction name.

A pop-up button to choose from the locations that have been defined.

A wrapping text field to enter or edit a description of the attraction.

Two labels, initially set to NA, for the state and zip data. This will be populated when the user chooses a location.

Two push buttons (Add and Remove) for adding and deleting attractions.

You should add any labels that you want to help describe the UI elements (such as Name, Location, and so on). I placed most of my UI inside of a box element, but that is strictly a superficial design decision.

▶ **For the Locations window**

The second Window object itself; the default XIB has a single window.

A three-column table view with headers set to City Name, State, Zip.

Two push buttons (Add and Remove) for adding and deleting locations.

FIGURE 17.11
A potential interface for the application.

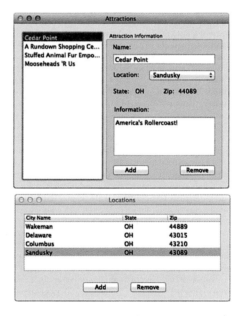

That's it. There is nothing particularly special about the UI. Just add your objects and tweak them using the Attributes Inspector (Options+Command+4).

Adding Array Controllers

Once the interface is built, we're ready to get down to work. As mentioned earlier, we need two Array Controller objects to provide our interface to the Core Data entities. Using the Object Library, drag two Array Controller objects into the Objects list for the application. They will appear as shown in Figure 17.12.

FIGURE 17.12
Add two array controllers to the XIB objects.

Labeling the Array Controllers

Now, to make it easy to tell the controllers apart, rename them. Select the first array controller and, using the Identity Inspector (Option+Command+3), set its label to **Attractions**, as shown in Figure 17.13.

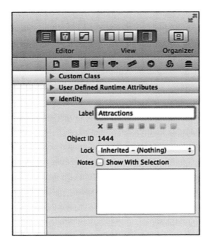

Repeat this process for the second array controller, labeling it **Locations**. Xcode, for some reason, doesn't seem to like updating the object list to show the labels until you save the XIB file and click off of it and then click back on. Do that now, and you should see the array controllers labeled after the Core Data entities we want them to represent.

Setting the Managed Object Context

Next we need to set the managed object context for the controller. Select the Attractions controller, and then open the Bindings Inspector (Option+Command+7).

Expand the Parameters section of the inspector and set the Bind To value to App Delegate and the Key Path value to **managedObjectContext**, as shown in Figure 17.14.

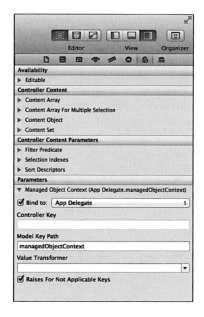

Do the exact same thing for the Locations array controller object. Just one more step and we'll be ready to bind data to the UI.

Setting the Controller Entity

The last thing we need to do with the array controllers is tell them what entity is going to be providing them with data. To do this, select the controller (starting with Attractions) and open the Attributes Inspector (Option+Command+4). Expand the Object Controller section and set the mode to Entity Name. Next, in the Entity Name field, type **Attraction**. Finally, check the Prepares Content check box, as shown in Figure 17.15. The array controller is now successfully configured to work with the Attraction entity.

Rinse and repeat for the Location array controller. Congratulations, you have completed the steps to make the Core Data model accessible to the application UI.

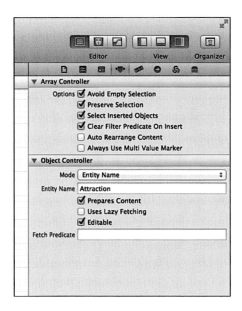

FIGURE 17.15
Configure the
entity for each
controller.

Binding Data to the Attractions Window UI

To bind the data to the UI, we work through each UI element and various settings under the Bindings Inspector (Option+Command+7). Because this application has a number of different UI components, it is easy to overlook a step, so be sure to follow along closely until you get the hang of the process.

The Attractions Table Column

Let's start with the single-column table that will list the contents of the Attractions entity. Expand the Scroll View—Table View object until you get to the entry for the Table Column. Select the Table Column object and open the Bindings Inspector. For this element, we want to set the bindings for its value, so expand the Value section of the inspector.

Click the Bind To check box and choose Attractions from the pop-up menu. Provide the controller key of **arrangedObjects**, and the model key path of **name**, as shown in Figure 17.16.

This translates to "fill the table column with the name attribute from the Attraction entity" (by way of the Attractions array controller).

FIGURE 17.16
Set the bindings
for the attrac-
tions table
column.

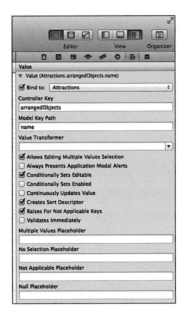

The Name and Information Fields

The name and information fields in the Attractions window should be used to edit the currently selected attraction. To set this functionality for the Name text field, select it and open the Bindings Inspector. Again, expand the Value section and set the Bind To option to bind to the Attractions array controller. This time, however, set the controller key to **selection** because we are interested in editing the currently selected item in the array controller. Set the Model Key Path field to **name** because the field should be changing the name attribute data in the Attractions entity. Figure 17.17 shows the completed configuration for the Name field.

Do the exact same thing for the wrapping text field, but instead of setting the model key path to name, set it to **info**—the entity attribute that will hold a description of the attraction.

The Location Pop-Up Menu (Pop-Up Button)

The pop-up menu of locations is a bit different because it requires that we access data from another source: the Locations array controller. Let's walk through this setup.

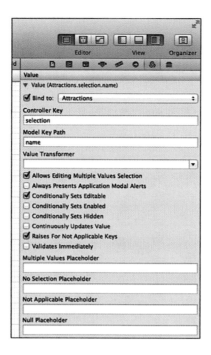

FIGURE 17.17
Set the bindings for the Name field.

Select the pop-up menu and open Bindings Inspector. You set your binding options in the Value Selection section of the inspector, but you need to make three separate settings, as follows:

1. Expand the Content entry. Bind the content to the Locations array controller, and set the controller key to **arrangedObjects**, as shown in Figure 17.18.

2. Expand the Content Values entry and also bind it to the Locations array controller, using the controller key **arrangedObjects** and the model key path **city**.

   This tells the pop-up menu to display the values from the city attribute of the Location entity—by way of the Locations array controller. Figure 17.19 shows the finished configuration.

3. Expand the Selected Object entry, and this time bind it to the Attractions array controller using the controller key **selection** and the model key path **locationInfo**, as shown in Figure 17.20.

   Why are we now dealing with the Attractions array controller again? Because we want to store the selected location *for the attraction* using the locationInfo relationship established in the Core Data model.

FIGURE 17.18
Set the content bindings.

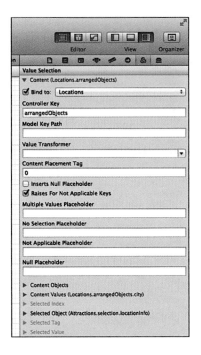

FIGURE 17.19
Set the content values.

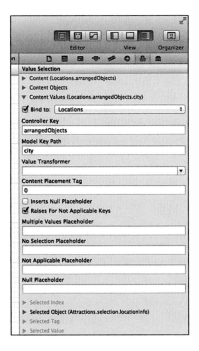

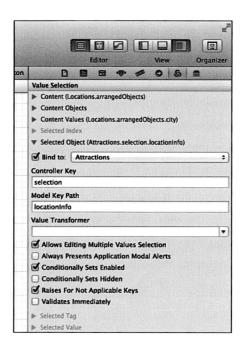

FIGURE 17.20
Set the
selected object
bindings.

Congratulations. This is the most complicated step you'll encounter this hour, and you have made it through.

The State and Zip Labels

The state and zip labels are easy to configure, but will reveal a bit more of the power behind data bindings, because we will grab their values by traversing the relationship from Attributes to Locations. For example, select the label that should show the state, and then open the Bindings Inspector.

Expand the Value section, and bind the element to the `Attractions` array controller. Next, set the controller key to **selection**. Now, enter **locationInfo.state** for the model key path. What this tells the system is that for the currently selected Attraction in the array controller, use the `locationInfo` relationship to grab the Location attribute `state` that has been related to the attraction. Figure 17.21 shows this setup.

The zip label should now be configured the same way, but using the model key path of **locationInfo.zipcode**.

FIGURE 17.21
Traverse the
relationship to
access data
across entities.

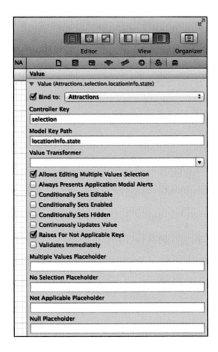

The Add and Remove Buttons

The final two UI features of the Attractions window are the Add and Remove buttons. These need to be connected to the add and remove actions on the Attractions array controller. To do this, Control-drag from the Add button to the Attractions array controller in the Objects list. When prompted, choose the add action. Do the same for the Remove button, connecting it to the remove action. Because this Control-drag process is almost certainly getting old by now, I'll spare you the screenshots.

If you want, you should now be able to build and run the application and create new attractions. Use the Window menu to show the Attractions window if it is not visible. You won't be able to choose any locations (because we haven't added a way to do that yet), but everything else should "just work."

Binding Data to the Locations Window UI

After what you have accomplished with the Attractions window bindings, the Locations window bindings are going to be a piece of cake. Each of the three table columns needs a binding, and the Add and Remove buttons need to connect to the add and remove actions on the Locations array controller.

The Table Columns

Start by selecting the city column within the table (the first column). Open the Bindings Inspector and expand the Value entry. Set the column to bind to the Locations array controller with the controller key **arrangedObjects** and the model key path **city**, as shown in Figure 17.22.

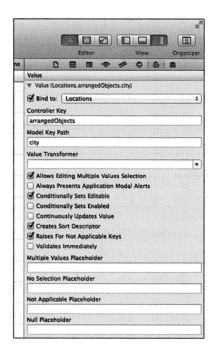

FIGURE 17.22
Bind the table columns.

Repeat this for the second column (state), but using the model key path of **state** and the third column (zip) with the model key path **zipcode**.

The Add and Remove Buttons

Finish up the application by connecting the Add and Remove buttons using the same procedure you followed for the Attractions window. The Add button should connect to the add action on the Locations array controller and the Remove button to the remove action.

Building the Application

The application is now complete. You should be able to build and run the application, add locations, add attractions, modify locations and attractions, and so on. If you did not build the application by hand, just use the Attractions (Complete) project to see the results.

After putting in a few values, try quitting and restarting the application—the data stays put. You have just created a simple database application that didn't require any coding by hand.

Accessing Data Through Code

Now that you have seen the glamorous side of Core Data, let's take a look at how you can work with the data directly in code. Using the data model that we created earlier for the Attractions application, let's review some of the methods you can use to read and write data.

Open the Attractions (Code) project file to view the completed examples or just follow along with Attractions project that you finished in the preceding section.

Creating NSManagedObject Subclasses

One of the nice things about Core Data is that after you have created a model you can map the entities of the model directly to objects in your code. You do this through the creation of NSManagedObject subclasses—typically one for each entity. The best part? This is something that Xcode does for you.

To create a managed object class for each of the entities in Attractions, follow these steps:

1. Click the .xcdatamodeld file to open the Core Data model editor.

2. Select the Location and Attraction entities in the left column by pressing Shift and clicking each.

3. Choose File, New, New File from the menu.

4. Select the NSManagedObject subclass from the Core Data file template category, as shown in Figure 17.23.

5. Click Next.

6. Make sure the Attractions code group is specified and the Options check box is unchecked.

7. Click Create.

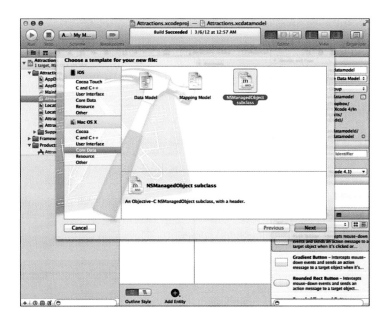

FIGURE 17.23
Choose the NSManaged Object subclass when prompted.

Notice that classes Attraction and Location are added to your project, as shown in Figure 17.24. You use instances of these classes to work with data in the Core Data model.

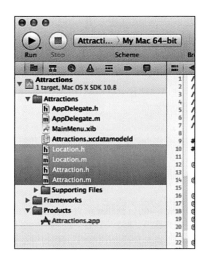

FIGURE 17.24
Classes for each of your entities are added to the project.

> When you add entities to your Core Data model, they are, by default, instances of the class NSManagedObject. When you use this technique to create your NSManagedObject subclasses, the entities are automatically set to the appropriate subclass name. You can check this by selecting an entity in the model editor and viewing the Entity section of the Data Model Inspector (Option+Command+3).

Writing Data

Now that you have created classes to represent the Core Data entities you want to work with, storing data is as simple as initializing and populating new Attraction and Location objects. To initialize a new object that will be added to the data store, you use the NSEntityDescription class method insertNewObjectForEntityForName:inManagedObjectContext:.

To see this in action, let's add some code to the AppDelegate class's applicationDidFinishLaunching method to store a new city and attraction. Before we can write the code, we need to update AppDelegate.m to import the interface files for the Attraction and Location classes. Add this code to the top of the file, after the existing line #import "AppDelegate.h":

```
#import "Location.h"
#import "Attraction.h"
```

Now, update applicationDidFinishLaunching by adding the code in Listing 17.1.

LISTING 17.1   Write Data to the Core Data Store

```
 1: - (void)applicationDidFinishLaunching:(NSNotification *)aNotification
 2: {
 3:
 4:     NSManagedObjectContext *objectContext = [self managedObjectContext];
 5:
 6:     Location *location = [NSEntityDescription
 7:                         insertNewObjectForEntityForName:@"Location"
 8:                         inManagedObjectContext:objectContext];
 9:     location.city=@"Birmingham";
10:     location.state=@"OH";
11:     location.zipcode=@"44889";
12:
13:     Attraction *attraction = [NSEntityDescription
14:                         insertNewObjectForEntityForName:@"Attraction"
15:                         inManagedObjectContext:objectContext];
16:
17:     attraction.name=@"Woolly Bear Drive-in";
18:     attraction.info=@"A tiny restaurant with great burgers";
19:     attraction.locationInfo=location;
20:
21:     NSError *error;
```

LISTING 17.1 Continued

```
22:     [objectContext save:&error];
23:
24:     // Insert code here to initialize your application
25: }
```

In line 4, we grab the `managedObjectContext` object that we can use to work with our data model. Recall that an object of this type is required for accessing a Core Data model. If you scroll through the AppDelegate.m file, you'll see how this object comes into existence. Because this application is based on a Core Data template, *lots* of supporting setup code is added to the app delegate, including an instance of a managed object context.

Line 6 creates a new `Location` object named `location` based on the `Location` entity.

Lines 9–11 populate the new object with data.

Lines 13–18 create and populate a new `attraction` object.

Line 19 sets the relationship between the `attraction` and the `location` objects; notice that it uses the `locationInfo` relationship that we defined in the model.

Line 22 saves the data back to the store.

As you can see from this example, writing data is not difficult. In fact, it is almost as easy as assigning values to variables/properties.

Reading Data

Reading data is actually easier than writing it—even across relationships. To read data, we must create an `NSFetchRequest` object and use it to execute a fetch request. From that, we are given an array of results that we can loop through. Consider the code snippet in Listing 17.2.

LISTING 17.2 Loop Through All the Locations, Outputting All Their Attractions

```
 1:    NSFetchRequest *fetchRequest = [NSFetchRequest
 2:                            fetchRequestWithEntityName:@"Location"];
 3:    NSArray *fetchedLocations = [objectContext
 4:                            executeFetchRequest:fetchRequest
 5:                            error:&error];
 6:    for (Location *aLocation in fetchedLocations) {
 7:        for (Attraction *anAttraction in aLocation.attractionInfo) {
 8:            NSLog(@"%@ %@",anAttraction.locationInfo.zipcode,anAttraction.name);
 9:        }
10:    }
```

Here, we start in lines 1 and 2 by creating a fetch request using the `NSFetchRequest` class method `fetchRequestWithEntityName`.

The results are stored in the `fetchedLocations` array in lines 3–5.

Lines 6–10 loop through each of the `fetchedLocations`, declaring each item as a `Location` object stored in the variable `aLocation`.

Because a location can contain multiple attractions, we know that `aLocation.attractionInfo` points to an `NSSet` of `Attraction` objects. This means we can loop over that set (as we do in lines 7–9), accessing each successive attraction object through the variable `anAttraction` and outputting its attributes with `NSLog()`.

By the Way

> Note that you insert this code at the end of the method defined in Listing 17.1. It depends on the declarations in lines 4 and 21.
>
> If you want to run it by itself, make sure you declare the `objectContext` and `error` variables at the top of the listing.

As you know, this is not a book that is intended to teach you how to code. I have included these examples, however, so that you get a sense of what working with Core Data is like, beyond just defining a model.

Summary

This hour introduced a powerful framework—Core Data—that can greatly expand the capabilities of the applications you develop and the speed at which you develop them. Core Data provides persistent data storage that you can use in iOS and OS X applications. Xcode includes visual tools for defining Core Data models as simple as a single entity or consisting of dozens of entities and relationships.

Accessing data from a Core Data model can be done through code or by way of interface bindings (currently OS X only). You can create interfaces that add, delete, and update data without ever writing a single line of code. Even when code is required, you can access your data through `NSManagedObject` classes, which is very similar to working with any other collection of objects. The use of Core Data does entail a learning curve, but the benefits to your applications make it worth the effort.

Q&A

Q. *If Core Data, by default, sits on top of SQLite, why can't I just use SQLite directly?*

A. The benefit of Core Data is that you do not have to worry about the underlying implementation—it manages your data for you. Stop thinking in relational database terms and *let* Core Data do its job.

Q. *Why would I use Fetched Properties rather than a real relationship?*

A. Fetched Properties are used when a real relationship is not important. Your data model should be as lean and structured as possible. Defining relationships that you may not need or that are rarely used is unnecessary overhead.

Q. *Why can't I use data binding in iOS?*

A. Apple just hasn't implemented it yet. In the meantime, read the documentation for the `NSFetchedResultsController` class. It can streamline the use of Core Data with iOS table views.

Workshop

Quiz

1. Core Data is a requirement for OS X and iOS applications. True or false?

2. iOS and OS X support UI data bindings. Yes or no?

3. In a one-to-many relationship that is dereferenced, how do you access the objects on the "many" side?

Answers

1. False. Core Data is a great feature for working with large or complex data sets. For simple key/value data storage, using the application defaults system is a perfectly acceptable solution.

2. No. Only OS X supports UI data bindings at this time. It is possible (as you learned in this hour) to build functional applications using Core Data and no code. In iOS, this is not yet an option.

3. When you dereference across a one-to-many relationship, you are handed an NSSet of the "many" objects. You can then loop through the set to work with each individually.

Activities

1. Build the Attractions (or a similar) app from scratch. I know it was easy to follow along with the same project, but doing this from scratch exposes you to Core Data and many aspects of the Interface Builder editor—important skills to practice.

2. Return to the BeeLine application and create a data model to store the points used in the application. Update the application code to read the points from a Core Data implementation.

HOUR 18

Test Early, Test Often

What You'll Learn in This Hour:

▶ The wrong way (adding unit tests to an existing application)

▶ The right way (test-driven development and testing before code)

▶ How to use the available OCUnit testing macros to validate your application logic

▶ How to give the OCUnit framework a handle into your running app to test live application features

All the examples so far have focused on the aspects of Xcode necessary to complete the steps, and this has led to us displaying some fairly shoddy practices in terms of code development, testing, and debugging. Code littered with NSLog() calls, although convenient to use as an example (of something other than good code), is difficult to maintain and is quite unlikely to be well tested. Fortunately, Xcode integrates the SenTesting OCUnit Unit Testing framework, making it easy to use a well-principled testing methodology and enabling you to continually validate functionality in a manner that is much easier than reading NSLog() output.

The OCUnit Unit Testing framework, and all unit-testing frameworks in general, is intended to support a very specific testing paradigm that has emerged from recent advances in programming practices. This paradigm, known as *test-driven development*, is a software development method in which tests that validate functionality are written before the code that implements the functionality. If you're not familiar with the idea, this might sound odd, or even a bit crazy, but done well, the result can be code that is much easier to maintain and much less time spent in the debugger trying to figure out why something stopped working. However, if you are like most people, you are coming at unit testing with some code already written and a need to implement testing into that existing code for quality control. The OCUnit framework can help with this goal, as well, but it is much harder to make sure that you have tests written to validate every aspect of your software if you start late in the game.

Adding Unit Tests to an Existing Application

How you go about adding unit tests to an existing application depends on whether you were thinking ahead back when you created the project for the application. If you indicated that unit tests should be included when you initially created the project, even though you haven't been using them while coding, almost everything is set up, and you just need to start adding code to the unit-test target to start reaping the benefits of unit testing.

If you did not originally tell Xcode to include the Unit Test module, or if the project is coming from an earlier version of Xcode where unit testing wasn't integrated, you have a bit more work to do. If you're lucky enough to have created your project with tests enabled, skip ahead to the "Implementing Tests for Existing Code" section; otherwise, complete the following section before starting to implement tests. We use Apple's OpenGL demo code, available from https://developer.apple.com/library/mac/samplecode/GLEssentials/GLEssentials.zip, for this example. As delivered, the example's code does not include the unit-testing framework or any instantiated tests.

If this does not compile properly for you out of the box, it is probably because they are updating operating systems and Xcode versions much faster than they can keep up with updating their example project files. If you run into this difficulty on the GLEssentials project from Apple, you can probably get past it by changing the Base SDK to match your current operating system. You can find the Base SDK setting under the Build Settings for the project.

To add unit tests to an existing application, follow these steps:

1. Open your existing unit-test-less project in Xcode. You can tell that it is testless because it does not include any Tests group for files within the project nor any *target*.octest product in the Products group, as shown in Figure 18.1.

2. Select the project in the Navigator.

3. Click the + (Add Target) icon at the bottom of the Xcode window.

4. Select the Other category of templates (for either OS X or iOS, as appropriate for your environment), select the Cocoa Unit Testing Bundle, as shown in Figure 18.2, and then click Next.

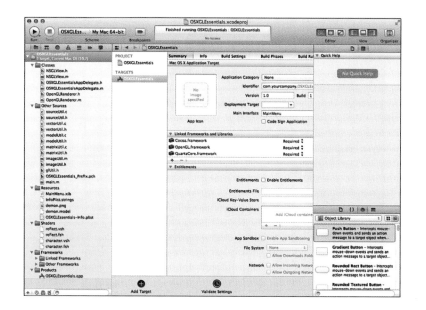

FIGURE 18.1
You can tell that
this project is
unit-test-less
because it does
not have any
Tests group for
files nor a
target.octest
product in the
Products group.

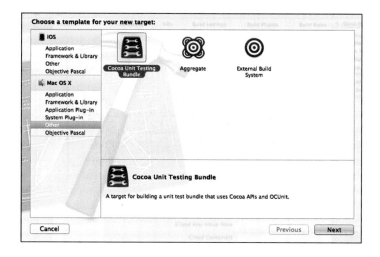

FIGURE 18.2
Selecting the
Cocoa Unit
Testing Bundle.

5. Enter a product name for your tests. It probably makes the most sense to give your testing suite for an application a name similar to the application. I named mine GLEssentials. A smarter name to pick might be GLEssentialsTests.

6. Enable Automatic Reference Counting. Make sure the Project is still set appropriately. Enter your company identifier or abbreviation and click Finish. As fully filled out, the target options should appear as shown in Figure 18.3.

FIGURE 18.3
Filling out the
target options
for the test
suite.

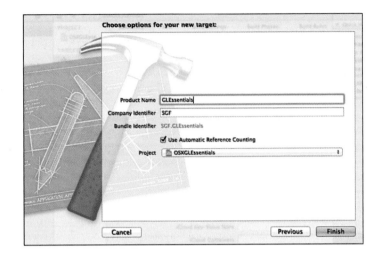

After completing these steps, return to the Xcode window that appears in
Figure 18.4. A new GLEssentials.octest product should exist in the Products
group in the Navigator. A new GLEssentials group, containing an implementation file and a header file, should now appear in the Navigator, just above
the Frameworks group. A new GLEssentials Target, with an icon that looks like
a Lego block should appear under the Targets list in the Editor area. The
SenTestingKit and Cocoa frameworks should have been added in the
Frameworks group, below Linked Frameworks.

FIGURE 18.4
The Xcode inter-
face just after
adding our test
suite.

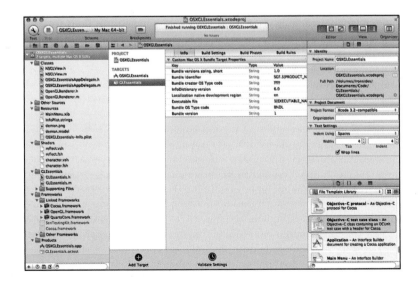

You're getting closer, but you still have more work to do. If you try to run tests right now, as shown in Figure 18.5, Xcode helpfully reminds you of what you still need to do.

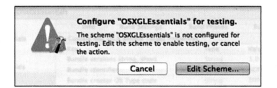

Configure "OSXGLEssentials" for testing.

The scheme "OSXGLEssentials" is not configured for testing. Edit the scheme to enable testing, or cancel the action.

Cancel   Edit Scheme...

FIGURE 18.5
When trying to run tests now, Xcode tells us that we must first configure the project for testing.

7. If you tried that, just to be contrary, click the Edit Scheme button. If you're not the contrarian, under the Product menu, select Edit Scheme.

8. The Scheme Editor opens. Select the Test scheme, as shown in Figure 18.6. Configure it for testing the debug or release versions of the application, as needed.

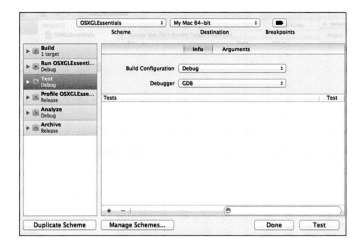

FIGURE 18.6
Select the Test scheme and configure it for use with either the debug or release versions of the application.

Although there "shouldn't" be any differences in application behavior between debug and release versions, typical differences in the way that debugging and optimization flags are set for these two types of builds means that memory usage and traversal is rather different between them. If you have a hidden bug in your code where an off-by-one error results in a single-character buffer overrun, it is quite possible for this code to never fail when compiled for debugging, yet always

By the Way

crash when compiled for release. Situations like this, where something like the presence of the debugging symbols is enough to make the difference between completely functional and completely dead code, are more common than you probably think. So, test both debug and release configurations. Doing so will save you headaches later.

9. Click the + button below the (empty) list of tests.

10. In the dialog that opens, open the project, and select the testing bundle you created, as shown in Figure 18.7. Then click Add.

FIGURE 18.7
Selecting the testing bundle created earlier.

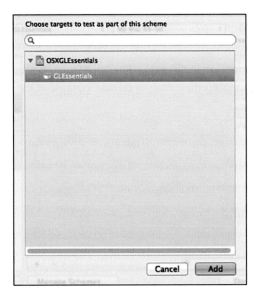

11. Back in the Scheme Editor, you should now see your testing bundle. If you click its reveal triangle, you'll see your testing class, with an additional reveal triangle, and if you open it, you'll see a single test method. Each of these has a checked check box next to it, indicating that it is enabled for testing with the current scheme setting, as shown in Figure 18.8. Close the Scheme Editor by clicking OK.

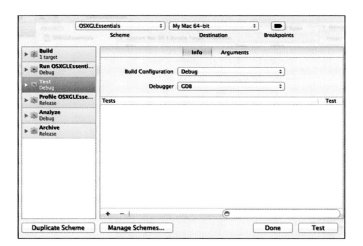

FIGURE 18.8
Then testing
bundle now
appears in the
Scheme Editor
and includes a
testing class
with a single
test.

12. Click the Run button in the upper-left corner of the Xcode interface and wait until a pop-up menu of run options appears. Select Test, or under the Product menu, select Test. A short time will pass. If you watch the build status, you'll see reports of compiling code flashing by, and then your build will... fail.

But, this is a *good* thing. If you look in the Navigator, you'll see your GLEssentials test class with a red error icon, as shown in Figure 18.9. Click its disclosure triangle to see the source of the error and you'll see that it is something in your GLEssentials class implementation that produced the error. Reveal the details under the GLEssentials.m implementation file and you'll see a bit more (cramped) detail. Click the red error icon beside the brief error details, and the source of the error will open in the Editor area. As you can see from Figure 18.10, the actual "failure" in the build is that the test case example (named testExample) successfully ran. And success, in the case of running the example method provided by Apple, is for it to throw an STFail message, complaining that you have not actually implemented any tests, which probably means it is time to add some.

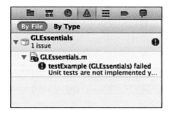

FIGURE 18.9
In the Navigator
panel, the red
error icon is
showing.

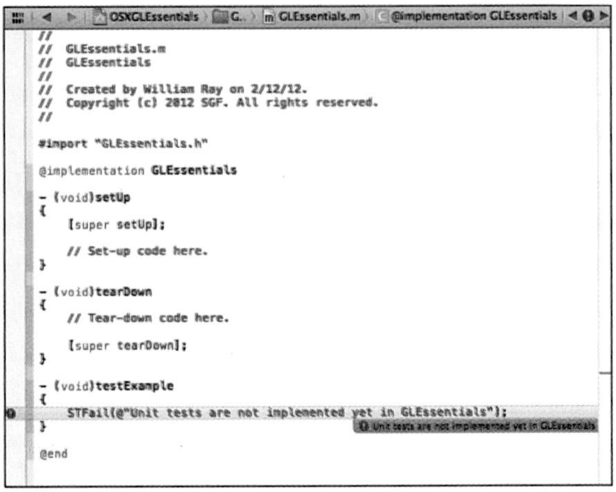

FIGURE 18.10
In the Editor
area, we
see that
testExample ran
but did not have
any tests
implemented.

Implementing Tests for Existing Code

Implementing tests for existing code usually sounds easier than following the test-driven development (TDD) mantra of implementing tests before functionality. In fact, though, it is usually rather difficult to figure out exactly what to test and how to test it. If you follow the TDD mantra and implement tests first, your code tends to be designed in modules that can be tested. If you implement code first and add tests later, it is quite often the case that the functionality that you want to test is buried in methods that because of their reliance on user interaction, network access, or other complicated behavior are quite difficult to test in an automated fashion.

If you are faced with this situation, you must put on your thinking cap and identify components within the application that can be tested and components that cannot. For those that can, you can implement tests as follows:

1. In the Navigator, select your testing class implementation file and open it in the source editor.

2. Delete Apple's `testExample` method.

3. Create a new instance method with a `void` return type. Make sure its name starts with *test*. The rest of its name should reflect what it is going to test for you. For instance, let's test Apple's vector math addition routine, found in the vectorUtil.c source file. So, we name our test method **testVec4Add**. The bare method should look something like Listing 18.1.

LISTING 18.1   Bare Method for Testing vectorUtil.c

```
- (void)testVec4Add
{

}
```

4. To get access to the method (vec4Add is a function in this case), we need to add its code to our test case target. So, select the vectorUtil.c file from the Other Sources group in the Navigator, open the Utilities, and select the testing bundle GLEssentials for Target Membership, in addition to the already selected OSXGLEssentials application target, as shown in Figure 18.11.

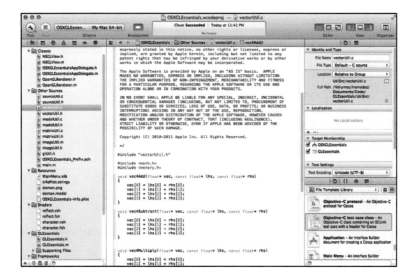

FIGURE 18.11
Setting up vectorUtil.c so that the test method can access it.

5. Up at the top of the implementation file, add an #import line for the vectorUtil.h file.

6. Now add code to test the Vec4Add routine to your testVec4Add testing method.

Exactly how you choose to test this method is up to you; in fact, if this were your project, you would probably want to test several different features of it, possibly with several different testing method implementations. For example, it is, of course, appropriate to test whether it properly adds two vectors and produces the correct mathematical result. It is also appropriate to test whether it handles null pointers, or vectors containing non-numeric values, or vectors with different storage sizes properly. Looking at Apple's implementation, I'm guessing the answer is no.

You can put any "generic" setup code that you think you're going to need for more than one test in the setUP method for your testing class. For example, if you are going to need a set of standard variables with known values for each of your tests, initializing them here, rather than in each test individually, makes your test cleaner. Another common thing to include in the setUp method is the invocation of network connections, initialization of databases, and instantiation of necessary classes. Put any necessary code to cleanly remove, deallocate, or tear down anything that you initialize in setUP in the tearDown method.

Did You Know?

The setUp and tearDown methods are run separately for each test case method that you include in your class.

To actually test the method (function, in this case) under consideration, you need to build the appropriate parameters to pass to the method (or function), invoke the method with the parameters, and then examine the result. The SenTesting suite provides a number of STAssert macros that perform the "examine the result" part of that process for you; you just have to pick the right one.

The primary macros you'll want to choose from are probably from the highly useful subset of the complete bunch shown in Table 18.1.

TABLE 18.1   The Most Useful STAssert Macros for Testing Code Unit Functionality

STAssertNil(a1, format_string, args...)	Fail if a1 is not nil.
STAssertNotNil(a1, format_string, args...)	Fail if a1 is nil.
STAssertEquals(a1, a2, format_string, args...)	Fail if a1 is not equal to a2.
STAssertEqualObjects(a1, a2, format_string, args...)	Fail if a1 and a2 are not equal objects, based on a1's isEqualTo method.
STAssertEqualsWithAccuracy(a1, a2, accuracy, format_string, args...)	Fail if a1 and a2 differ by more than accuracy.
STAssertTrue(expr, format_string, args...)	Fail if expr evaluates to false.
STAssertFalse(expr, format_string, args...)	Fail if expr evaluates to true.
STFail(format_string, args...)	Always fail.

Others, for more specialized uses, are defined and documented in /Developer/ Library/Frameworks/SenTestingKit.framework/Versions/A/Headers/ SenTestCase_Macros.h.

In each case, the macro takes a return value or values from your tests, compares them to expected values or each other, and if they don't pass whatever variety of assertion the macro applies, the format_string (an NSString) is used to produce a printf-type formatted string from the remaining args... values, a failure exception is thrown for the build, and the formatted result is logged.

Putting this together for the Vec4Add function, and planning to test whether it properly adds two proper vectors, we come up with a testVec4Add method that looks something like Listing 18.2.

LISTING 18.2 testVec4Add Method for Adding Two Proper Vectors

```
- (void)testVec4Add
{
    float *vecA, *vecB, *vecC, *vecD;
    int i;

        NSLog(@"Testing vec4Add");
    vecA = malloc(sizeof(float)*4);
    vecB = malloc(sizeof(float)*4);
    vecC = malloc(sizeof(float)*4);
    vecD = malloc(sizeof(float)*4);

    vecA[0] =  1.2; vecA[1] =  3.4; vecA[2] =  5.6; vecA[3] =  7.8;
    vecB[0] =  9.9; vecB[1] =  7.8; vecB[2] =  5.7; vecB[3] =  3.6;
//  vecC;
    vecD[0] = 11.1; vecD[1] = 11.2; vecD[2] = 11.3; vecD[3] = 11.4;

    vec4Add(vecC, vecA, vecB);

    for(i=0;i<4;i++)
    {
        STAssertEquals(vecC[i], vecD[i],
                    @"vec4Add index %d Exp %f Rec %f",
                    i, vecD[i], vecC[i]);
    }

    free(vecA); free(vecB); free(vecC); free(vecD);
        NSLog(@"Done Testing vec4Add");
}
```

Now, if you run your tests, the result will be yet another fail, as shown in Figure 18.12. This time, however, it is not such a good thing that it is a failure because the test is actually telling you that the vec4Add routine is producing incorrect results. Examined more closely, the specific errors are as follows:

```
GLEssentials.m: error: testVec4Add (GLEssentials) failed: '11.099999' should be
➥equal to '11.100000': vec4Add index 0 Exp 11.100000 Rec 11.099999
GLEssentials.m: error: testVec4Add (GLEssentials) failed: '11.200001' should be
➥equal to '11.200000': vec4Add index 1 Exp 11.200000 Rec 11.200001
GLEssentials.m: error: testVec4Add (GLEssentials) failed: '11.299999' should be
➥equal to '11.300000': vec4Add index 2 Exp 11.300000 Rec 11.299999
```

FIGURE 18.12
The tests fail because vec4Add is producing incorrect results.

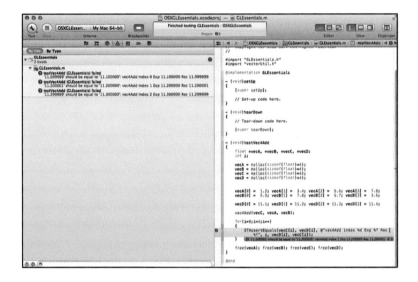

Because I added some helpful debugging code in the return message format string, I can see that the problem looks like a floating-point precision error. For example, we're supposed to be receiving 11.1 back in the 0th vector component of the summed vector, and instead we're receiving 11.099999 (and probably some more repeating 9s after that).

Chances are, this is not really an error but simply a limitation on the precision of the variables we are using. So, let's try updating the STAssert macro we're using, to compare the values with some tolerance for error. Changing the STAssertEquals macro invocation and replacing it with STAssertEqualsWithAccuracy, with the accuracy tolerance set at 0.000001, results in the long-hoped-for behavior of the testVec4Add method passing its test, as shown in Figure 18.13.

If you examine the Debug area, you'll see that the SenTestingKit framework reports when it starts the test case testVec4Add, the NSLog lines I added to validate that my test was running appear, and then the SenTestingKit reports the successful conclusion of the test and the time it took to complete. Parsing the NSLog()-based output from the OCUnit testing module is not the easiest task in the world, but because it is tightly integrated into Xcode, failures come back to the GUI, and you really only have to look at the log if you want more information about your successes.

FIGURE 18.13
After you adjust the accuracy tolerance, the tests pass.

Finally, to verify that the test case actually catches real errors, we induce an actual error in the vec4Add routine. As delivered from Apple, the routine is as appears in Listing 18.4.

LISTING 18.4   vec4Add Routine from Apple

```
void vec4Add(float* vec, const float* lhs, const float* rhs)
{
        vec[0] = lhs[0] + rhs[0];
        vec[1] = lhs[1] + rhs[1];
        vec[2] = lhs[2] + rhs[2];
        vec[3] = lhs[3] + rhs[3];
}
```

Edit it so that the third vector component assignment reads as follows:

```
vec[2] = lhs[1] + rhs[3];
```

Now run your test case again. You should first see a report that the build succeeded. Because the edit is legal C code, this is expected. Xcode should be able to build the application; it just shouldn't run properly anymore. Immediately after, you should see a message that says "Tests Failed" and the dreaded red error icon appears in the Status field, and the Navigator switches to a view showing you the cause of the error. In this case, a received value of 7.0 should be equal to an asserted value of 11.3. Because we broke the vector adder, it did not correctly add 5.6 + 5.7, and instead added 3.4 + 3.6. The test fails (correctly) when the adder does not work. All is well, but fix the bug you introduced in the vec4Add function and retest it, just for good measure.

> Who watches the watchers? The `NSLog()` calls in `testVec4Add` seem gratuitous because the testing framework already reports that it is starting the test and finishing the test. However, those calls are there to give me more confidence that my `testVec4Add` method actually runs top to bottom. One of the most annoying mistakes that can happen in unit testing is the implementation of a test that doesn't actually run completely. Portions of tests that do not run cannot fail, and it is only failures that get reported back to the interface for you to check.

Unit testing the rest of the application logic proceeds from here in an iterative fashion, as follows:

1. Identify a method, function, or other component of your code that needs tested.

2. Figure out how to test it.

3. Add a test method to your testing class.

4. Add code to implement you test.

5. Tweak the code that implements the test until it passes for correct output from the application code.

6. Tweak the application code so that it produces incorrect output so that you can be sure the test properly fails.

7. Fix your application code again and retest.

8. Repeat as necessary.

If you find that you need to implement conceptually distinct subsets of unit tests—for example, a group that tests vector math functions, and a different group that tests image rendering, or a group that tests vector math with floats and a different group that tests it with integers—you can facilitate this by adding additional testing classes. This approach lets you segregate your testing methods so that they can be grouped with appropriate setup methods so that only the correct and necessary setup values and variables are created. It also facilitates enabling and disabling groups of related tests, in cases where you want to focus on specific features of the code and not waste time on regions where you either know that things are currently correct or know that they are currently broken but not a priority.

If you want to add additional test classes, you can do this by dragging test class templates out of the File Template Library in the Utilities, into the group for the testing bundle in the Navigator. To add a class, follow these steps:

1. Show the File Template Library in the Utilities and drag an Objective-C Test Case Class template and drop it into your Tests group in the Navigator, as shown in Figure 18.14.

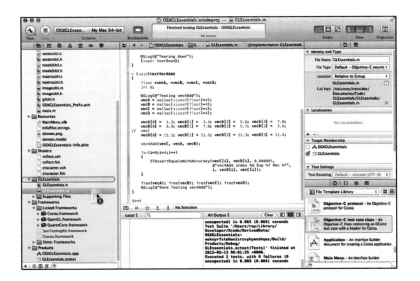

FIGURE 18.14
Dragging a test class template into the project.

> Make sure that your Objective-C test class matches the OS target you're building for. There are two, identical-looking Objective-C Test Class templates. One of them is for iOS and Cocoa Touch; the other is for OS X and Cocoa. You can make your life a little easier by using the File Template Library drop-down to select the appropriate subgroup of templates (OS X or iOS) for your project. Read the description of the template carefully to make sure you have the right one.

Watch Out!

2. In the dialog that opens, shown in Figure 18.15, name your test class and optionally create a new directory for it. Do *not* click Create yet.

3. Deselect the application target from the targets and select the building-block iconed testing bundle that you created in the first steps of this hour. Now click Create. Back in the main Xcode interface, you should see that a new pair of files, one implementation and one header for your new class, has appeared in the group for your testing bundle.

Test your application again and examine the contents of the Debug area. You'll see that a new test has been added and passed. This is the default `testApp` test method from the class you just added. You can add more test methods to this new class, and you can add `setUp` and `tearDown` methods copied from your original testing class to initialize specific items that the tests in this class need to function.

If you look at the demonstration code provided in the Objective-C Test Case class that you dragged in, you will find something interesting. This class invokes itself in such a fashion that it acquires a handle to the application delegate. This should give you some hints about other things you might be able to do with the OCUnit testing framework.

With a little more tweaking of settings, you can actually give your test cases access to the running application itself. Although this is a bit more dangerous than just testing discrete bits of the logic by linking specific classes from your application's code and testing their methods, it is actually the default setup that Xcode creates when you start off with a project that includes unit tests.

Accessing the Rest of an Application Through the Bundle Loader

In the preceding example, we followed the canonical unit-testing path of linking the source for the methods we want to test with the unit-testing class we're implementing. This is clean, neat, and significantly reduces the running time and memory overhead for your tests, but it does not provide a way for you to test your methods *in situ*, only in the "clean room" environment of the unit-testing framework.

Fortunately, Xcode provides a convenient way to work around this limitation, in the form of the Bundle Loader, which, with only two tweaks to the build settings for your project, can give your unit-test classes full access to the application internals. Formally, many tests that you can write this way are not actually unit tests but are rather integration tests, but you will probably be happy with the functionality no matter what it is called.

To enable the Bundle Loader, follow these steps:

1. Select your project in the Navigator and your testing target from the Targets in the Editor area.

2. Open the Build Settings tab for your testing target.

3. Select All rules, Combined.

4. Enter the word **bundle** (no quotation marks required) into the Search field. The giant list of cryptic settings should condense down to what is shown in Figure 18.16.

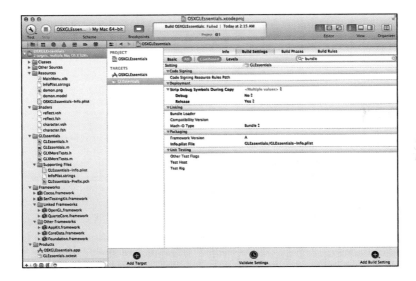

FIGURE 18.16
Searching for bundle.

5. Double-click the Bundle Loader field. A pop-up editing field appears.

6. Enter $(BUILT_PRODUCTS_DIR)/OSXGLEssentials.app/Contents/MacOS/OSXGLEssentials into the editing field, and then click Done.

7. Cancel the search for *bundle* and search now for *host*. A setting for Test Host should appear.

8. Double-click the Test Host field. A pop-up editing field appears.

9. Enter **$(BUNDLE_LOADER)** into the editing field and click Done.

10. Select your application target (not your testing target) in the left column of the Editor area.

11. Open the Build Settings tab for it. Select All rules, Combined.

12. Enter the word **symbols** into the Search field.

13. Find the setting for Symbols Hidden by Default.

14. Click the (default) Yes setting and change it to No, as shown in Figure 18.17.

FIGURE 18.17
Changing the
Symbols Hidden
by Default set-
ting from Yes
to No.

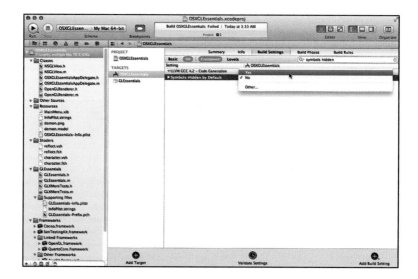

Now you have access to the symbol space of your application. If you run your tests, you'll probably notice that the application window briefly appears. With this setup, you can access methods from the application without explicitly linking specific source files with the testing target. Moreover, and more usefully, if you add appropriate getter and setter methods to expose application internals like the NSWindow pointer, you can send messages to the instantiated methods in the running application.

For an iOS app, the Test Host setting controls whether the tests will run within the simulator or standalone outside it as pure logic tests. If it is configured as recommended here, the tests run in the simulator.

For example, if you use this technique to enable the Bundle Loader for Unit Tests in BeeLine (Hour 15, "Putting It All Together: Building an OS X Application"), you can add a test case with code like Listing 18.5, and it will automatically draw a list of points into the QuartzGrough view, just as though you entered the X and Y values and clicked the Add button yourself.

LISTING 18.5 Test Case Code That Automatically Draws a List of Points into the QuartzGrough View

```
- (void)testPointAddingPipeline
{
    NSRect testRect;
    testRect.origin.x = 10;
    testRect.origin.y = 20;
    testRect.size.width = 200;
    testRect.size.height = 100;

    QuartzGrough *aGroughGraph = [SGFAppDelegate getTheGroughGraph];

    aGroughGraph.anX = 0.4;
    aGroughGraph.anY = 0.6;
    [aGroughGraph plotUpdate];

    aGroughGraph.anX = 0.6;
    aGroughGraph.anY = 0.8;
    [aGroughGraph plotUpdate];

    aGroughGraph.anX = -0.3;
    aGroughGraph.anY = 0.2;
    [aGroughGraph plotUpdate];

    [aGroughGraph drawRect:testRect];
}
```

If you want to experiment with BeeLine with the Bundle Loader enabled, and a test case configured to drive the interface, you can download the project from the hour 18 source code at http://teachyourselfxcode.com.

Summary

In this hour, you learned about unit testing and how to apply the SenTesting framework (OCUnit) to develop unit tests for your application logic. You learned how to add the testing framework to an existing application and why it is a better idea to start building unit tests immediately from the beginning of your project. You learned how to write test methods and how to make them correctly pass when they should pass and fail when they should fail. Finally, you learned how to access the running application bundle, enabling the use of the unit-testing framework for some types of integration testing, as well.

Q&A

Q. *How could you handle unit-testing the* `plotPoint` *method of the BeeLine application delegate? It relies on user input and receiving UI events from a sender.*

A. One possible answer is that unit testing of complex code often requires the implementation of components called *mocks, fakes,* and *stubs.* Each of these (and there is some disagreement in the community exactly what is meant by the different terms) is a variety of stand-in bits of code that in some fashion pretends to be an interface or a connection to a database or other complex connection. Used properly, they can pretend to be the UI and send event messages in to your application as though a user clicked an interface component. There are rapidly evolving libraries available on the Internet to aid you in developing mocks for your unit tests. Because they are changing so rapidly, we recommend an Internet search to find the most recent, but http://www.ocmock.org/ is probably a good place to start.

Another possible answer is that the difficulty in figuring out how to test this call should suggest to you that the implementation is less clean than might be desired. This is probably an opportunity to refactor the code and separate out the functionality of what to do with the results of a UI action and the receipt of the UI action itself.

Q. *How in the world does the test-driven development paradigm of writing tests before you write code work?*

A. Usually painfully, at first. The TDD paradigm requires that you be able to articulate what a method should do before you implement it. This is probably a good idea overall. It does not lend itself to organically growing applications, but it does drive a workflow where you know how to test every step of an implementation because you know what to expect from a method before you write it.

Q. *What if I expect the wrong thing from the code?*

A. That is one of the downsides to TDD. When the same person is writing the tests and the code, the tests and the code may be subject to the same blind spots. This is why debugging, which we cover in the next hour, is still required even when you are using TDD methods.

Workshop

Quiz

1. Why can you just start adding testing methods to some of your projects, invoking methods out of your application and frameworks without doing any further configuration, while other projects complain with linker errors claiming they cannot find the application methods?

2. How can you test whether two pointers point to the same memory location in a unit test?

3. What can you do if what is required for "passing" a particular test cannot be encoded into any of the STAssert comparisons?

Answers

1. Projects that were initially set up with unit testing turned on have the Bundle Loader configuration already set up and therefore do not require you to explicitly link the source files for the methods you want to test with the testing framework target.

2. STAssertEqual, using the values of the pointers, will accomplish this. Make sure you do not use the targets of the pointers because then STAssertEqual will not fail when you hand it different pointers that point to different variables that have identical values.

3. Write your test case to carry out whatever conditional evaluation you require, and invoke STFail() directly if your evaluation indicates test failure.

Activities

1. Implement unit tests for each of the BetterList framework methods. Exercise as many of the STAssert macros as you can.

2. Add a new method to the BetterList framework using the TDD "tests before code" paradigm. Make the new method roll the list down—that is, have it move the tail of the list before the head, making the former tail into the new head, the former head the second item, and the former next-to-last item into the tail. Implement the unit tests for this method before implementing the method, and then develop the method implementation to satisfy your tests. Test and develop until your tests pass.

HOUR 19

Getting the Bugs Out

What You'll Learn in This Hour:

▶ How to use the debugger to find out why your program crashed
▶ How to use the debugger to find out how your program is working
▶ How to manipulate your running program to test ideas and potential fixes for problems

In the preceding hour, you learned about using unit tests, which are a great tool for validating that everything is still working right when it's working right. However, they are only so helpful when something is working wrong. When your code is not behaving as planned, you need to be able to dig into it and check the values that variables are holding and verify that execution is following the path through your code that you were planning.

So far in this book, we have been using NSLog() to write debugging output to the console to keep an eye on these internal behaviors of applications. Variations on this theme, adding output statements to code so that it can self-document the process of its execution and the states of its variables as it goes, are the universal route by which everybody comes to debugging. It's easy, it's intuitive, and it's a huge time-eating productivity killer.

Completely ignoring the fact that NSLog() is intended for logging purposes and not for debugging, and that you have almost certainly looked at your console logs and cursed other programmers whose products blather reams of useless (to you) debugging output into the log where you're trying to find a critical system fault, using log output for debugging output is still a poor idea. Each NSLog() call can output only a predetermined collection of data from a single point in your program, and it's almost never the case that you get exactly the right output, from exactly the right location, on the first try. And then there's the annoyance of having to clean the useless NSLog()s back out of the code again once you're confident that a routine is working properly.

Thankfully, there is a better way: using a proper debugger.

> Make sure to remove no-longer-necessary NSLog() statements before distributing
> your application. This output lands in the system log on your users' machines,
> and filling their logs with unnecessary debugging is impolite at best and a route to
> poor feedback in the App Store and other public venues if users actually start
> to notice.

Debuggers are a programmer's best friend. When you're running your program
through a debugger, you can pause your program anywhere, examine the contents
of all the variables, and step through your code one line at a time to observe how
values are being calculated and stored.

The only downside of debuggers is that they look scary to use. This appearance—
and it's only an appearance; after all, using a debugger under Xcode is, if anything,
easier than using NSLog()—prevents many programmers from even trying to use
debuggers. Don't be one of those programmers. If you can write code, you can use a
debugger, and if you can use a debugger, writing code gets easier.

> If you are sitting there reading this and thinking, "Ah, well, the debugger might not
> be that bad, but I'm getting on okay with NSLog(). I'll worry about the debugger
> later." *Reconsider.* If you look at the debugger and think "that's a little intimidat-
> ing," don't panic. Really, the debugger is "hard," the same way "computers are
> hard." Everyone thinks that when starting out, so you're in perfectly good com-
> pany. Everyone quickly discovers that those concerns were misplaced. You will,
> too, and be a better programmer in the end with the debugger.

Getting Started with the Debugger

You have almost certainly been using the debugger already even if, perhaps, you
weren't aware of it. Unless you fiddled with things earlier and have only been building for release when following instructions in this book so far, every time you have
run your projects, you have been running them in the debugger. So, no need to be
shy; you've been introduced.

Load up iBLine (use the version from the Hour 19 folder in the source available from
http://teachyourselfxcode.com/—I've added one more feature to it to support the
exercises in this hour) and run it by clicking the Run button on the toolbar. Check
the output section in the Debug area. Yours should look like what's shown in Figure
19.1. Notice our NSLog() lines down at the bottom and how it says GNU gdb... at the
top? gdb is the debugger. You're already using it. See, that was easy.

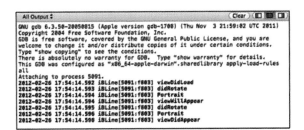

FIGURE 19.1
The Debug area
shows NSLog()
output lines
with gdb as
the debugger.

Associating Debuggers with Targets

If the output section in the Debug area doesn't inform you that you're using gdb or
lldb, the build action that's currently configured for your target doesn't have a
debugger associated with it. To fix this, choose Edit Scheme from the Product menu.
In the scheme editing dialog, display the Info tab for the Run action and configure
the Run action for debugging and select a debugger. As of Xcode 4.2 and iOS 5, you
must select the gdb debugger for iOS. You can select either gdb or lldb for OS X
applications. Your settings should be similar to those shown in Figure 19.2.

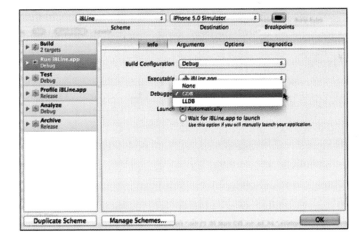

FIGURE 19.2
Selecting GDB
from the debug-
ger settings.

The current external functionalities of gdb and lldb are very close. Their internal
functionalities, and what will probably be possible in the future, are rather
different.

gdb is the GNU debugger, from the Free Software Foundation. It's very powerful,
well supported, and has stood behind the creation of pretty much every piece of
complex software in the OS X and UNIX world for the past several decades.
Unfortunately, as a GNU General Public License application, some severe

limitations apply as to what Apple can do with it. To alleviate the difficulties caused by these limitations, Apple has recently been developing their own debugger, lldb. Lldb will be much more tightly integrated into Xcode, and will eventually provide enhanced functionality that's not possible with gdb.

Unfortunately, they're not there yet. Apple recommends using lldb for OS X applications, but lldb is not yet available for use with iOS architectures. Rather than including support for the enhanced lldb features in the limited cases where it's applicable, Apple has currently only exposed the lldb functions that are common with gdb. Therefore, at this point, as long as the debugger is supported on the architecture for your target, it makes little difference which you select. In the future, as lldb matures and Apple exposes more of its functionality in Xcode, it will certainly become the debugger of choice, and in all likelihood, support for gdb will be dropped entirely.

Putting the Debugger to Work

Of course, while you're now over that hurdle of starting to use the debugger, it hasn't done anything much for you yet. This is because you haven't asked it to. The debugger's job is to watch your application for you, grab its collar if it messes up, and let you poke around in the running application internals to figure out if and why the application is misbehaving. If your application hasn't misbehaved, and you haven't asked the debugger to intervene, the debugger sits there in the background minding its own business.

The easiest way to get the debugger to step out of the background is to cause your application to do something untoward (for example, to try to use memory that doesn't belong to it). As a matter of fact, as you have been working through examples and developing your Xcode skills, you have probably even seen it do this but didn't realized what was happening.

I've added some code to iBLine so that you can intentionally run the program off the rails and see what gdb does about it. To herd iBLine into generating an error, follow these steps:

1. Make sure you're using the project version from the Hour 19 folder in the source available from http://teachyourselfxcode/.

2. Make sure your scheme is set up to build a debug version for the Run action and that the gdb debugger is configured for the Run action.

3. Run iBLine from the toolbar.

4. Add three points, and then click Done to make sure that they're plotted.

5. Click the Info button (the italic *i*) to go back to adding more points.

6. Before you add a new point, click-drag across the second point listing in the UITableView. It should display a standard iPhone-style Delete option, as shown in Figure 19.3.

FIGURE 19.3
The UITableView about to send a delete message for an entry.

7. Click Delete. Click Done to return to the graph to verify that the middle point has actually been removed.

8. Click the Info button again. Add another point and check the graph to verify that the new point has been appended.

9. Return to the FlipsideViewController and click-drag-swipe across each of the points listed in the UITableView, deleting each of them.

10. Once the UITableView is empty, enter another pair of values into the X and Y coordinate boxes and click the Add button again.

Whoa. Something's wrong. The iPhone application didn't respond as expected, and the Xcode interface jumped back to the front. There's some unfamiliar content in the Navigator, and a green bar is highlighting a line of code in BetterList.m in the Editor area. It probably looks like what's shown in Figure 19.4.

You have probably seen this before. That green bar, and the cryptic comment "Program received signal EXC_BAD_ACCESS." When you have hit this previously, you knew something was wrong and probably went in and added some NSLog()

statements to try to figure out where the application was going sideways. Without knowing it, here, too, you have been using the debugger. It's the debugger that highlighted that line of code for you, and although EXC_BAD_ACCESS might seem cryptic, the debugger is trying to tell you something useful about what went wrong.

FIGURE 19.4
The debugger highlighted the line where the application received the EXC_BAD_ACCESS signal.

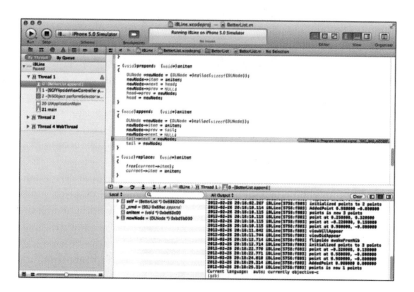

By the Way

Documenting every response and return code from gdb and lldb would require an entire book (or two). EXC_BAD_ACCESS is one you'll see often, and it means that your program tried to access a location in memory and for some reason it could not. Usually that reason is because the memory it is trying to access does not belong to it.

To make the fullest possible use of the debugger, we strongly recommend that you buy a book on gdb, or if Apple has gotten lldb completely integrated by the time you read this, a book on lldb. You don't need to read and learn the material, but a reference book to consult when the debugger says something cryptic will prove mighty handy.

EXC_BAD_ACCESS means that your program failed (at the command line this would be a segmentation fault), because the operating system caught it trying to access memory that it wasn't allowed to access. This can happen for a number of reasons, including logic errors where some variable has been corrupted and points off into the wilderness. However, the most common cause is attempting to do something with a nil (or Nil, or NULL) pointer. nil, Nil, and NULL pointers all point to memory location zero, and nothing should ever be living at memory location zero, so your program shouldn't be trying to either read or write to it.

Useful information from the debugger, indeed, but don't go writing NSLog() statements into the surrounding code to try to catch that zero pointer just yet. Along with telling you where the problem happened, gdb also tells you about all the variables in the current scope. Yes, you get that for free, too. Look on the left side of the Debug area shown in Figure 19.4. Notice the list of items there? self, _cmd, anitem, newNode? This area is the Variables View. Look more closely at the routine where that EXC_BAD_ACCESS fault occurred. Yes, the appropriately named Variables View is listing the variables in the routine where execution is currently paused.

Try expanding the listing for newNode and for self. The list should now look similar to that shown in Figure 19.5. Notice that the head, tail, and current variables for self, all DLNode pointers, are pointing to location 0x0? You have just found a bug that's been hanging around in BetterList since we first wrote it. If you call the remove method when there's a single item in the list, the item gets deleted but the BetterList instance hangs around, pointing to a nil current item and to nil head and tail items. The append method, however, assumes that its instance has at least one node in it and dutifully tries to add the new list item that it creates, after the previous list tail. How long would it have taken you to find that bug using NSLog() statements? Unless you have seen that bug coming since we implemented BetterList back in Hour 14, "Planning for Reuse: Frameworks and Libraries," I bet the answer is "a lot longer than it took to click the reveal triangle by the self variable."

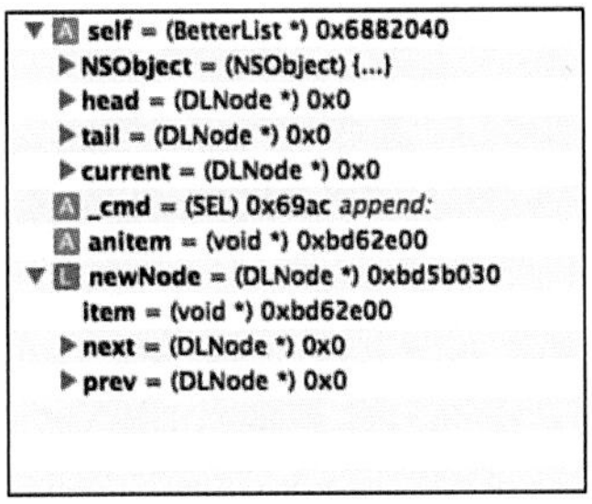

FIGURE 19.5
After expanding the listing for newNode and self, we discover that all the DLNode pointers point to 0x0.

Proactive Debugging

Of course, waiting until your program goes off the tracks and only looking at the debugger when it does isn't the most efficient way of programming either. Pleasantly, debuggers are just as adept at letting you browse around the innards of an otherwise healthy program. This lets you verify how your program is running and check that everything is going to plan. Before we get started, let's take a step back and become familiar with the debugging interface as presented in Xcode. Figure 19.6 labels the important areas and controls.

FIGURE 19.6
The debugging
interface in
Xcode.

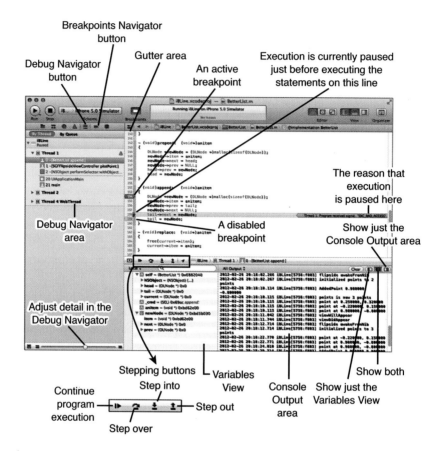

In the Debug Navigator, you'll find a list of threads. Until you're up to programming threads, most of this information will be irrelevant to you. However, under the primary thread, you can find the call stack for your application. This lists the methods currently running. Examining the call stack can give you insight into how your program arrived at the routine its in and whether there are peculiarities, such as your method being invoked from somewhere unexpected. If you look closely at the Debug Navigator shown in Figure 19.6, you can see that the top (most recent) method invoked is the BetterList append: method. This method was messaged from the FlipsideViewController plotPoint method, which was messaged from something in the NSObject class. Twenty-one methods further up the stack, the grand-daddy C main routine is still running. If you want more detail about the methods between the originating main and the location where your program is currently stopped, you can adjust the available detail in the Debug Navigator by sliding the detail slider at the bottom of the Debug Navigator area.

▶ A Breakpoint Navigator can also be displayed in the Navigator area. The Breakpoint Navigator lists all the breakpoints you currently have set for the target and lets you toggle them on and off as needed. You learn more about breakpoints and how to use them in the next section.

▶ In the main Editor area, the debugger shows the region of the code where your program is currently paused, with the current line highlighted. If you want to have line numbers displayed in the gutter as shown in Figure 19.6, you can enable them by opening the Xcode preferences from the Xcode menu and checking the Show Line Numbers check box in the Text Editing tab. If you have breakpoints set in the region, they show up as blue flags in the gutter. Line 154 has an active breakpoint, and line 159 has an inactive breakpoint in Figure 19.6. You learn about breakpoints and how to use them in the next section.

If you hover over variables in the code shown in the main Editor area, Xcode displays pop-up datatips. Figure 19.7 shows a typical example. Here, we're paused in BetterList's append method, just after the newNode has been allocated, its item assigned, and its previous and next pointers filled in. Because all the members of the DLNode structure are pointers, the values you're seeing here are hexadecimal memory locations. If you were to hover over a simple variable, or a structure or object with simple variable components, you would see their integer, float, and so on values displayed in the datatip.

FIGURE 19.7
Hovering over variables in the main Editor area causes pop-up datatips to appear.

Having line numbers displayed in the gutter makes it a lot easier to figure out which breakpoints in the Breakpoint Navigator go with which lines in code displayed in the Editor area.

By the Way

▶ At the bottom-left of the main Editor area is a small panel of Step buttons that give you control over what the debugger does next. Your options are as follows:

Continue: The Continue button instructs the debugger to release its control over the application and let the application get on with business. Of course, if the application just crashed because of an EXC_BAD_ACCESS fault, it's not going to accomplish anything else even if you ask it to continue.

Step Over: The Step Over button has a slightly confusing name. In most cases, it really means "do the next step" in the program. If the next step is a simple statement, that statement is executed, and the debugger pauses again. If the next step contains a method invocation, the entire method invocation is executed as "a step," and the debugger pauses after the method returns.

Step Into: This button behaves identically to Step Over for simple statements, but instead of stepping over method and procedure invocations, Step Into enters the called method and pauses on the first statement in it.

Step Out: This button does not really mean step, as the Step Over and Step Into buttons do. Instead, it means "finish up everything in the current method, and then pause again once control returns to whatever routine called this one." This behavior is not contextually dependent on whether the next step is a method invocation or a simple statement.

Did You Know?

Beside these, there's an icon to set up a simulated location. This lets you test location-aware code, but doesn't have anything to do with the debugger. We're not sure why that functionality is wedged in there.

▶ At the bottom-right of the main Editor area is a jump bar where you can browse through the calling stack that has gotten the program to this point and examine variables and memory content in any frame of the stack, in addition to the immediate line where your program is paused.

▶ The Console log output section with which you're already familiar is beneath the main Editor area on the right.

▶ The Variables View, which you were briefly introduced to earlier, is beneath the main Editor area on the left. This view shows current variables and their values. It has a search window so that you can limit the variables to only those most relevant, and it has options to restrict itself to only local scope variables, all variables including global and static variables accessible from the current scope, and an Auto setting that tries to make intelligent guesses about what variables are most relevant.

Compound variables (structures and objects) are hierarchically expandable in the Variables View, to let you browse child variables or to collapse them and reduce clutter.

Each top-level variable shown includes a small icon to indicate its scope: *A* for argument variables, passed in to the current scope; *L* for local variables defined in the current scope; *S* for static variables; and *G* for global variables.

Unfortunately, as of Xcode 4.2, global variable display is broken when using gdb. If you can switch your project to use lldb, the global variables show up properly. If you can't, keep your fingers crossed that Apple fixes this bug. Global variable display worked just fine in earlier versions of Xcode, so the difficulty here is not an inherent limitation of gdb.

Working with Breakpoints

Now that you're familiar with where to find all the tools to use the debugger, it's time to start actively using the features. Every debugger's big hammer is its ability to set breakpoints, and gdb and lldb are no different. You set breakpoints to tell the debugger where you want it to pause the program, and then you use the other tools at your disposal to study the state of the application while it is paused.

You can set as many breakpoints in your code as you like, anywhere that you need one. Every time that your running program tries to execute any of the statements marked with a breakpoint, the debugger interrupts it and brings control back to you and Xcode, where you can examine the state of the program, and even edit some aspects of the running program on-the-fly.

Setting Breakpoints

To set a breakpoint, simply find the location in your program where you want to interrupt the program and click in the gutter. A blue flag icon will appear, and the next time you run your program, it pauses at that statement. To experiment with this, set a breakpoint for the remove method, in BetterList. Follow these steps to set it:

1. Navigate to the BetterList.m file included in the BetterList subproject in your iBLine project. Display BetterList.m in the main Editor area.

2. Click in the gutter beside the line that defines the (void) remove instance method. A blue flag will appear; it should be on line 168 if you have line numbers turned on.

3. Now run iBLine in the iPhone simulator by selecting the iBLine iPhone simulator scheme and clicking the Run button on the Xcode toolbar.

4. Add two points, and then swipe to delete the first. Click Delete.

5. The iPhone simulator should pause, and Xcode should immediately pop to the foreground, with the entry point for the remove method highlighted, as shown in Figure 19.8. The highlighted line is line 170, the creation of the tempNode, because this is the first executable statement after the method entry point.

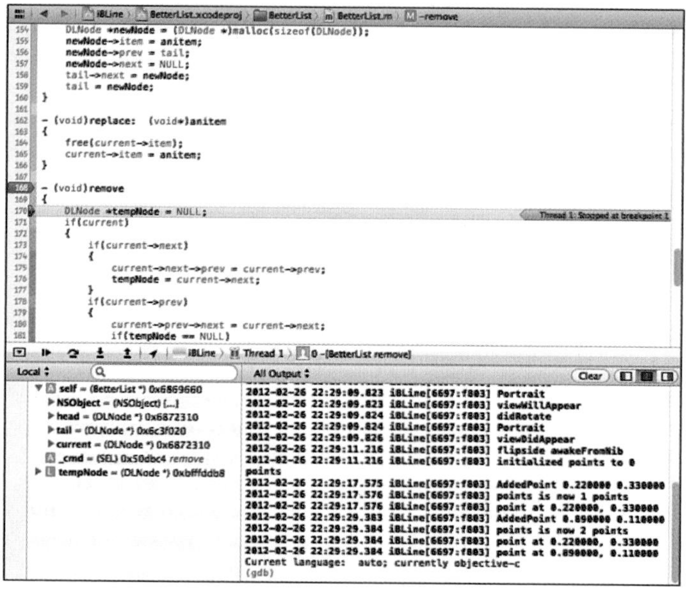

FIGURE 19.8
Xcode has
appeared in the
foreground with
line 168, the
entry point for
the remove
method, high-
lighted, as well
as line 170, the
first executable
statement after
the method
entry point.

Did You Know?

The line hasn't executed yet. You can tell this by looking at the Variables View, where the tempNode currently actually has a nonzero value. This value is random bits lying about in the memory where the tempNode variable lives. It's not zero because C languages know that initialization costs time and assume that you'll deal with initialization if and when you need to.

Maneuvering a Paused Application

iBLine is now paused at the first step of the remove method, letting you examine the variables and the calling stack, but you're not just limited to sitting here or jumping to the next breakpoint. You can also continue your program's execution in baby steps and follow its progress in the debugger. The details of the baby steps your program will take are controlled by the Step buttons at the bottom of the main Editor area (labeled in Figure 19.6) or by tiny icons that replicate those on the stepping buttons and that appear next to the gutter as you cursor-over lines of code.

The simplest stepping action is simply to Continue Program Execution, which causes the program to run either until it hits another breakpoint or to completion, or a crash, whichever comes first. This is probably the most common action to take after a program has paused at a breakpoint.

The next stepping action is the Step Over action. This is probably the next most common action, and clicking it will proceed through the current method, one line at a time, remaining at the level of the method where the breakpoint occurred until it reaches the end of the method (or the return call). After hitting the end of the method, it steps up into the parent calling method and proceeds in a similar fashion. At no point does it step down into methods that are called.

The third option is the Step Into action. This action performs the same task as the Step Over action, except it always steps down into methods that are called, instead of executing them completely in a single step.

The fourth option is the Step Out action. This action completes all the remaining steps in the current method and pauses the program again after control returns to the method that invoked the one containing the breakpoint.

Continuing Program Execution

You can now start exploring the program control functionality. From where we paused earlier (at the end of step 5 in the preceding section), proceed as follows:

1. Click the Continue button. Control should return to the iPhone simulator. The second point you created should still remain in iBLine's UITableView.

2. Click the Project Navigator in the Navigator area so that you can see the files for your project. Select the FlipsideViewController implementation file.

3. Scroll down to the tableView method that is listening for an editingStyle message (it should be line 173) and set a breakpoint for the method. You should now have a breakpoint set for the remove method for BetterList and for the tableView dataSource method that handles deleting cells from the UITableView.

4. Back in the iPhone simulator, add another point, and then delete the first one on the list again.

The iPhone simulator pauses, and Xcode comes to the front with the debugger again. This time it should be paused in the FlipsideViewController method where we just set the breakpoint. Your display should look something like what is shown in Figure 19.9. Remember that the line that the debugger is paused on hasn't executed yet.

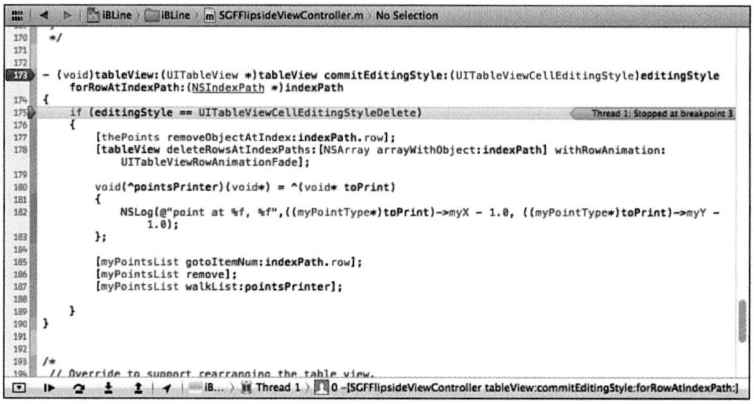

FIGURE 19.9
Xcode has appeared in the foreground again, paused in the `FlipsideView Controller` method, where we set our breakpoint.

Stepping Forward One Line

Sometimes you really want to know about what the program is doing at other lines near your breakpoint, and setting individual breakpoints for all of them seems silly. The Step Over action is here to solve that problem. From where the debugger is paused in step 4 in the preceding section, do the following to single step through your program:

1. Pay attention to the line where Xcode is currently paused and to the contents of the Variables View.

2. Click the Step Over icon at the bottom of the main Editor area. The current line updates, stepping into the conditional statement and pausing on `[thePoints removeObjectAtIndex:indexPath.row]`.

3. Practice stepping forward a few more times. Note that each time you do you move one statement further in the execution of the current method, whether that statement is a simple variable assignment or a complex method invocation. When you try to step over `[myPointsList remove]`, however, you'll find that you're interrupted down in the `remove` method for BetterList. This is because you have left a breakpoint for the `remove` method. Go ahead and Continue Program Execution after you hit the breakpoint at `remove`, and then add another point or two in `iBLine`, and delete another one to get back to the breakpoint in the `FlipsideViewController`.

Stepping Forward Several Lines

If you want to continue for several lines, but not uncontrollably to the next breakpoint, you can set a one-time Continue to Here breakpoint. From where Xcode paused in step 3 in the preceding section, we are probably more interested in the activity around [myPointsList remove] than at the top of the function. To jump directly there without having to click Step Over several times, just do this:

1. Right-click the line containing [myPointsList gotoItemNum:indexPath.row].

2. In the pop-up menu that appears, select Continue to Here, as shown in Figure 19.10. Xcode restarts iBLine and leaves it running until it is ready to execute the line you just indicated, where it pauses again.

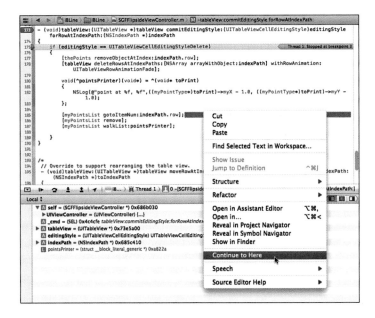

FIGURE 19.10
To continue for several lines, but not as far as the next breakpoint, set a Continue to Here breakpoint.

Using the Step Into Action

So far, we've been using the step actions to step over method invocations without going down into them to see how they're working. We can get into the remove method because we've set a breakpoint there. But what if we want to check the functionality of a method where we haven't yet set a breakpoint? This is what the Step Into action is for.

When execution is currently paused on a statement that when executed will result in a method or procedure invocation, the Step Into action transfers control into that method (or procedure) and pauses execution again at its first executable statement. If we want to know what goes on in the gotoItemNum method of myPointsList, we can Step Into this method, as follows:

1. Make sure the current line highlight indicates that `iBLine` is paused at the `[myPointsList gotoItemNum:indexPath.row]` statement.

2. Click the Step Into action icon at the bottom of the main Editor area.

Control transfer to the `BetterList gotoItemNum` method, where you can examine variables and again step, continue, or otherwise maneuver in the paused application.

Using the Step Out Of Action

When you have finished exploring in the `gotoItemNum` method, returning to the `FlipsideViewController` method that called `gotoItemNum` is easy. Just click the Step Out Of button, and any remaining instructions in `gotoItemNum` are executed, control return to the `FlipsideViewController`, and execution pauses again, on the line immediately following the call to `gotoItemNum`.

One Dog, Many Tricks

You should already see that the capabilities of the debugger are a good replacement for the variable-checking uses for which we've previously abused `NSLog()`. However, the debugger is not limited just to stopping at every breakpoint it encounters and reporting variable values. In addition to this already-quite-useful functionality, the debugger can make "intelligent" choices about pausing at breakpoints, perform automated actions when it encounters specific conditions at a breakpoint, and it can also edit live variables in a running application. Put together, these move the debugger far beyond a tool for simply reporting or exploring the state of an application and convert it into a tool that, in collaboration with unit tests, can be used proactively to watch for and report errors.

Conditional breakpoints, or watchpoints, are breakpoints that have been configured to only pause program execution when certain conditions are met. Causing `iBLine` to fault, due to trying to add a new item after a `nil` `BetterList` tail node is reasonably easy because we just have to add a point and then delete it and try to add another one. But what if the error only happens if we have a dozen (or a hundred) points allocated? Hitting the breakpoint in `remove` and continuing every time just to get to see what happens when the list is on its last item seems painful. It would be much easier if the breakpoint for `remove` activates only if the current node is the only node.

Conditional breakpoints can do that. To configure the breakpoint for `remove` so that it only activates when it is about to delete the only node in a list, follow these steps:

1. Navigate to the breakpoint for remove and right-click it. You can do this using the Breakpoint Navigator in the Navigator area.

2. From the pop-up menu, choose Edit Breakpoint.

   A pop-up dialog appears where you can set a condition for the breakpoint, configure how many times to ignore it, add an action that should be carried out when the breakpoint is encountered, and configure the breakpoint to automatically continue after the action if that serves your purposes.

3. In the Condition field, enter the text **head == tail**. If the head and the tail are the same item when you are entering this method, there must be only one node in the list. Your configuration should look like Figure 19.11. Click Done.

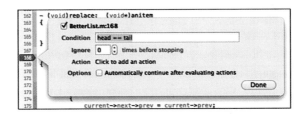

FIGURE 19.11
Setting a conditional breakpoint for when the head and the tail are identical.

4. Go ahead and run iBLine, add three or four points, and then start deleting them.

5. When the debugger pauses at the breakpoint in the FlipsideViewController, disable that breakpoint by left-clicking it once. It turns a dim bluish-gray to indicate that that it is currently disabled. Click Continue Program Execution to get things moving again.

6. Continue to delete points until you get to the last item in the list. Xcode should let you delete all of them except that last one without pausing in the debugger any more.

7. Try to delete the last point. The iOS simulator pauses, and Xcode comes to the front, paused at the BetterList remove method. If you examine the variables in the Variables View, you'll see that head and tail do indeed point to the same location (and not coincidentally, current does, as well).

Instead of configuring a condition based on program variables, you could have configured the conditional breakpoint to become active only after the code had passed through the routine some number of times, or configured automatically executed actions to be conducted when the breakpoint was reached. Consult your debugger reference to learn about some of the actions that you can connect to a breakpoint, but be aware that you can also attach execution of shell scripts, AppleScripts, and other actions of essentially arbitrary complexity. A sufficiently demented application of this capability could have a running program conditionally detecting an adverse condition at a breakpoint and using an action to externally reconfigure program parameter files in an attempt to alleviate the problem. With a sufficient dose of determination, there are very few questions regarding program state that you can't answer with breakpoints and actions.

The other jaw-droppingly useful capability of good debuggers is the ability to modify program memory contents (its variables) on-the-fly while it is running. As a dramatic example of the power of this, let's try an experimental fix for our problem with the `BetterList` remove method.

Thinking through the problem, it is clear that the `remove` method itself doesn't fail. It successfully removes the final item from the list. The thing that fails is the attempt to add a new thing to a now-empty list. We might be able to fix this by adding a new method to `BetterList` to repopulate a list that has lost its last item, but maybe a better solution is just to pitch lists that have become empty into the trash and instantiate new ones when necessary.

Looking at the `plotPoint` code in the `FlipsideViewController`, you'll find that it issues the append (where we've been having trouble) if the `pointsList` is non-nil, but in cases where it is `nil`, it invokes the `DataPhile setupPointsList` method to create a new list. This sounds promising.

To test whether it is worth the effort of adding code to `BetterList` so that it zaps itself more completely out of existence when the list becomes empty, we can use the debugger to simulate this condition. Follow these steps:

1. Make sure your breakpoint for `remove` is still in place and still configured as a conditional breakpoint that will pause only when the head and tail are identical.

2. Run `iBLine` and add a few points to verify that everything is working properly.

3. Delete the points. The breakpoint at remove should not activate until you delete the last point in `iBLine`.

4. Use the Step Out action. This should bring you to the code for the `FlipsideViewController` on the line immediately following the message `[myPointsList remove]`.

5. In the Variables View, reveal the variables under the self compound variable group.

6. Find the entry for myPointsList. It contains a BetterList pointer and a valid memory value, as shown in Figure 19.12. This is our culprit. If the BetterList remove method were set up to annihilate the BetterList instance when the list became empty, this variable would be nil, and there's a good bet that a subsequent add would properly reinitialize a new BetterList instance and everything would continue to work.

FIGURE 19.12
Our problem is that myPointsList has a BetterList pointer and a valid memory value. The BetterList remove method should annihilate the BetterList instance when the list is empty.

7. Variable editing to the rescue! To find out what happens if BetterList zeros this pointer, double-click the value shown beside myPointsList, and enter **0x0** as a new value, as shown in Figure 19.13 and then press Return.

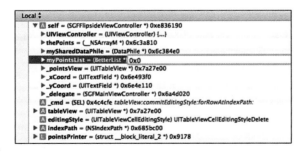

FIGURE 19.13
Editing the pointer's value to 0x0 (hexadecimal zero, nil) to see what happens if BetterList zeros the pointer.

And Another Bug Bites the Programmer

In all likelihood, when you press Return to submit your edited value for the myPointsList pointer, several variables previously accessible in the Variables View vanish. This shouldn't happen, but at the moment, the only way to get them back appears to be quitting Xcode and restarting it.

If you find yourself in this situation, you can still access and edit the contents of variables by right-clicking them to bring up their datatip and then editing the value presented in the datatip line.

8. Click Continue Program Execution and try adding a new point to iBLine. Voilà. No more error, the point adds, and iBLine runs along quite happily, as though nothing is wrong.

With that little bit of experimentation, and no code written at all, you have just verified that you can you can fix BetterList and repair the crash by making sure that the entire list instance is torn down when the last list item is deleted and making sure that the DataPhile keeps itself updated with respect to the actual state of the underlying BetterList instance.

Summary

In this hour, you learned about using a debugger under Xcode. Because the functionality currently available for lldb and gdb are identical in Xcode (minus the unintentional differences due to bugs), what you have learned applies to either Apple's preferred lldb for OS X targets or the legacy gdb for iOS targets. It might still take you a few days practice of setting a breakpoint and using the Variables View to completely replace NSLog() output in your programming habits, but after you have made that transition you'll find that the debugger becomes an incredibly powerful tool for both verifying your program's functionality as you are building it and for identifying problems when something goes wrong.

Q&A

Q. *Is there a way to cause the debugger to output specific variables when it hits a breakpoint, rather than all of them in the scope?*

A. You can limit what's shown in the Variables View, using its search field, but this capability is not very flexible. If you require more flexibility, you can configure an action for a breakpoint and set the action type to Debugger Command. Using the p command (or one of several other output-control variants, see your debugger reference), you can tell the debugger to print the value for a specific variable or variables. The output from these commands appear in the console output area.

Q. *Can the debugger be used to debug unit tests as well as the main program?*

A. Yes. The behavior is a little bit flaky at the moment, especially if you're trying to do this with gdb. When you are using gdb, Xcode doesn't know quite as much about what the debugger is doing internally and seems to sometimes get a bit confused about exactly where it's pausing and how it got there. This will almost certainly improve when Apple finishes the transition to lldb.

Q. *Sometimes when I step through program execution, I can step over a perfectly explicit statement like x=x+5, and watching the Variables View, nothing happens to the value of x. What's up?*

A. You mostly likely have optimization enabled, in addition to the debugger. The optimizer rewrites portions of your code so that it runs more efficiently, and there is not always a line-per-line match between the code you wrote and what the optimizer produces. As a result, when you are debugging an application that's used the optimizer, the "current line" in your code doesn't necessarily correspond to exactly what the program is doing at any given point.

Q. *What does that big Breakpoints button up on the toolbar do?*

A. It enables or disables all breakpoints in the code (without changing their individually enabled or disabled status).

Q. *What happens if you step into a system framework method?*

A. That depends on whether the source for the method is available, but in general, the debugger does exactly what you asked. If the source isn't available, you end up in an assembly language listing derived from the library object file, but you are paused at the first executable statement of the framework method.

Workshop

Quiz

1. How can you make the debugger skip over a breakpoint when it's hit for boring setup purposes in your application and only begin pausing once the breakpoint is being encountered for interesting user interaction?

2. What happens if you try to "Continue to Here" but the program runs across code containing another breakpoint along the route to "here"?

3. Can you Continue Program Execution after stopping for an EXC_BAD_ACCESS fault?

Answers

1. Edit the breakpoint to make it conditional. If you're always doing the same setup, you will probably hit the breakpoint a fixed number of times before interesting things start to happen. In this case, you can simply set the breakpoint to ignore that number of passes before beginning to activate.

2. Execution stops at the intervening breakpoint anyway.

3. That's a trick question. Most literally, yes, although your program will still be suffering from the same memory fault and will immediately fall on its face again. If you're clever and can alleviate the fault by editing a variable value, however, it is possible to rescue a program from this condition.

Activities

1. Set a breakpoint in one of the anonymous blocks used by iBLine to pass functionality to BetterList's walklist method. Trace execution through the walklist method as the block is called.

2. Replace the annoying NSLog() statements in iBLine that are just producing status messages to confirm that execution has reached specific routines with breakpoints that have logging actions attached and Automatically Continue selected. Observe that you can silence all that annoying logging by using the global button on the toolbar to turn off all the breakpoints.

HOUR 20

Keeping Things Organized: Shared Workspaces

What You'll Learn in This Hour:

▶ How to use workspaces to manage projects with shared components
▶ How to create workspaces
▶ How to add projects to workspaces
▶ How to adapt projects built outside workspaces into workspace members

Workspaces are Apple's new way of trying to reduce the clutter and difficult-to-maintain, manually specified path information that inevitably gets hard-coded into large projects composed of many independent parts. An Xcode workspace is a collection of projects and other documents that are developed together.

In several previous hours, you set up projects where a primary application project contained a subproject for a library or framework. If you're like most programmers, you quickly recognized that the machinations that were necessary to configure header search paths or locations for loading libraries were a recipe for disaster if files or projects were moved. The Xcode 4 workspace concept simplifies such co-development designs by recognizing implicit dependencies between the projects and doing much of the work of configuring the build process so that the compiler can find the necessary files without having to build explicit paths into the projects.

This makes the build process much more resilient to rearrangement of code content and files, while simultaneously reducing the amount of configuration work you need to do. It's a clear win, all around, or at least it would be if it actually worked properly. Unfortunately, Apple still has some work to do in this area, and the process is not as smooth as it should be. Still, it is a good-sized step in the right direction, and it seems reasonable to assume that Apple will polish up the rough edges as time goes by. In the meantime, it is still worth enjoying the benefits of the parts that do work.

Did You Know?

Don't confuse Xcode 4 workspaces with the identically named workspaces concept from earlier versions of Xcode. Before Xcode 4 and its single-window design, Apple used the term *workspace* to mean the collection of windows and tools that were used together in developing a project under Xcode. There's even an official Apple Xcode Workspace Guide that you'll encounter in many places around the Web. Don't read it; it is no longer relevant to Xcode 4.

Watch Out!

Slow Down, Construction Ahead

Xcode's workspace functionality is still a work in progress, and many minor details are all in flux (such as the exact naming of choices in dialogs, the existence of some dialog confirmation buttons, and the placement of some details). If you encounter a step where what you're looking at on your screen does not match what is written here, it is almost certainly because Apple changed something to make your life easier. The functionality is still there, and if you look in the most natural place for it, you should find it easily.

Using Workspaces

Taking advantage of the workspace concept in Xcode is simple. You just create a new workspace, add projects to it, and build them. This is quite similar to what you've already done several times before. Where things differ is in the amount of information that you have to give Xcode about where you have put things. Specifically, for workspaces, you mostly have to explicitly *not* tell Xcode where you put things, so that it can find them itself. With workspaces, the more information you give Xcode, the more narrow its search strategy for finding interdependent parts. Therefore, in general, the less specifics you provide, the better the automatic dependency finding performs.

To see how this works in real life, let's deconstruct our BeeLine OS X and iBLine iOS projects, which previously both contained references to the `BetterList` framework and static library. Let's build a workspace that contains the BetterList project, the BeeLine project, and the iBLine project, all as peer projects within the workspace.

To get started, copy the BetterList2, BeeLine2, and iBLine2 project folders from the Hour 20 folder in the code archive from http://teachyourselfxcode.com, and then follow these steps:

1. First, remove the implicit BetterList subprojects from BeeLine and iBLine. Launch Xcode and open the BeeLine.xcodeproj file in the BeeLine2 directory.

2. Open the Project Navigator and select the BetterList project in it.

3. Right-click the BetterList project in the Project Navigator, and from the pop-up menu that appears, choose Delete, as shown in Figure 20.1.

FIGURE 20.1
Deleting the
BetterList
project.

4. If Xcode can find both the BeeLine project and the BetterList project, a dialog appears asking if you want to actually delete the file or just the reference. If this dialog appears, click the Remove Reference Only button, as shown in Figure 20.2. Otherwise, if Xcode cannot find both projects simultaneously, it just asks if you want to delete BetterList, without giving you the option of deleting the reference. In this case, it is safe to tell it to go ahead with the delete.

FIGURE 20.2
Clicking the
Remove
Reference Only
button.

It is almost always safer to delete the reference in Xcode, even if you really want to also remove the files from disk. This way you can go to the directory in the Finder and delete the files that you want to delete and be sure that you're removing the ones that you intend. If you ask Xcode to delete the files for you, it might delete something that you had not intended (which occurs about half the time, in my experience).

5. Select the BeeLine project in the Navigator, and the BeeLine target in the side-bar of the Editor area.

6. Open the Build Settings tab.

7. Enter **BetterList** in to the Search box, to find places where we have previously hard-coded paths to the framework.

8. The list of options should reduce down to a single line showing Framework Search Paths. Double-click the path that is displayed.

9. In the dialog that appears, select the path line that starts with $(SRCROOT), and click the – button at the bottom of the dialog to remove that path, as shown in Figure 20.3, and then click Done or close the window using the standard title bar controls.

FIGURE 20.3
Removing the
path that
starts with
$(SRCROOT).

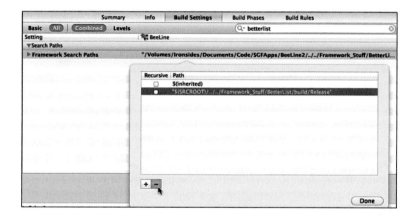

10. Display the Build Phases tab and open the Target Dependencies, Compile Sources, and Link Binary with Libraries groups. Verify that BetterList does not appear in any of them, as shown in Figure 20.4.

11. Choose File, Project Settings from the menu. The dialog for configuring the Derived Data Location will appear, as shown in Figure 20.5. In all likelihood, it will show a path that is not actually the correct derived data location. Click the Advanced button.

12. In the Advanced Build Locations dialog that appears, you need to configure the build location to work with the derived data location. Depending on the version of Xcode that you have, you might see a dialog like that shown in Figure 20.6, or like that shown in Figure 20.12. If you have the Figure 20.6

version, select the option for a shared folder of Xcode's derived data location, and leave the optional field value at its default. If you have the Figure 20.12 version, select the Derived Data Location option.

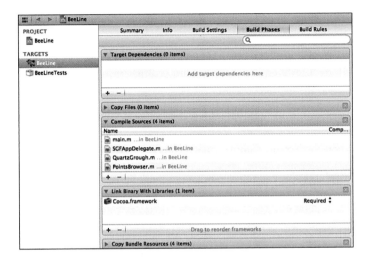

FIGURE 20.4
Verifying that BetterList does not appear in Target Dependencies, Compile Sources, and Link Binary with Libraries groups of the build phases.

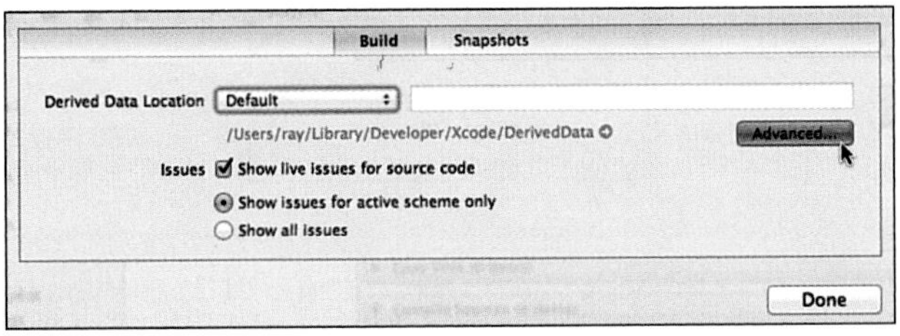

FIGURE 20.5
Clicking the Advanced button to configure the derived data location.

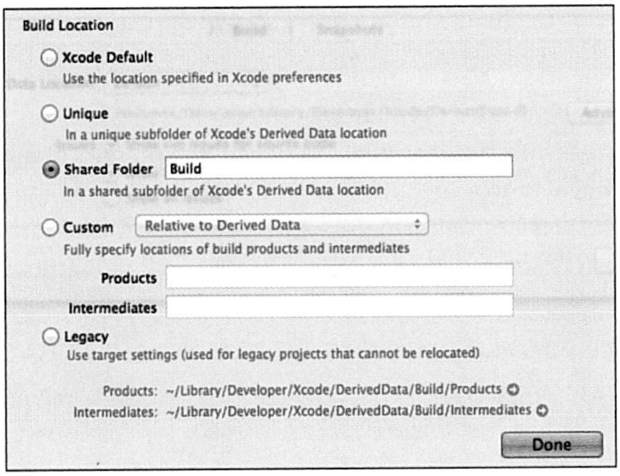

FIGURE 20.6
Selecting Derived Data Location as the build location.

Did You Know?

Yes, when working on libraries and frameworks and building your first OS X and iOS applications in Hours 14 through 16, you learned that using the Locations Specified by Targets option is the way to keep a sane build hierarchy. This is true if you're going to manage the build hierarchy yourself. However, Xcode workspaces perform this task for you automagically. For the magic to work, though, you have to give up control of the build hierarchy.

13. Click Done, and then click Done again to finish removing all traces of BetterList from the BeeLine project.

14. Just to confirm that BetterList is really gone, and that BeeLine no longer builds, try building the project from the Product menu or by clicking the Run button on the Xcode toolbar. You should be greeted with a collection of errors similar to that shown in Figure 20.7. Clearly, BeeLine is no longer a complete and functional project.

FIGURE 20.7
BeeLine has errors now.

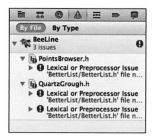

Now it is time to perform the same cleanup on iBLine. To do this you need to open the iBLine.xcodeproj file in the iBline2 directory and retrace the same steps that you took for BeeLine. After you delete (remember to just remove the reference) the BetterList subproject, the iBLine build phases should appear as shown in Figure 20.8.

Remember to delete the header search path for BetterList, as shown in Figure 20.9. If you had to add an explicit library search path for your static library subproject (we did not for libBetterList in the example, but depending on several factors, you might in your code), remember to search for it and delete it, too. If you use a search that will catch both the header and the library in the Build Settings Search box, you can see from the search results whether you have any other build settings to edit.

FIGURE 20.8
Showing how
the iBLine build
phases look
after removing
the reference to
the BetterList
subproject.

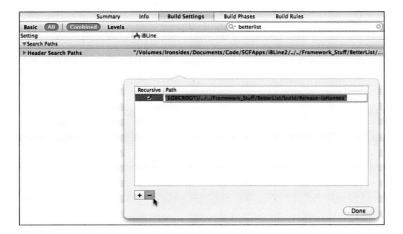

FIGURE 20.9
Deleting the
header file
search path for
BetterList.

Creating a Workspace

After you have finished cleaning iBLine, it is time to build and populate a workspace. To do so, follow these steps:

1. Close any open Xcode projects.

2. Choose File, New, Workspace from the Xcode menu bar.

3. In the dialog that appears, pick a name for your new workspace and a place
   to store it. As shown in Figure 20.10, we use **BsNees** in this example. I recommend keeping your workspaces all collected in one directory for neatness.
   Click Save when you're satisfied with the name and location.

FIGURE 20.10
Giving the new
workspace a
name.

The main Xcode window opens. All three of the main Xcode content areas are empty, as shown in Figure 20.11, because the workspace is just a container and you haven't added any content yet.

FIGURE 20.11
Now we have a
completely
empty
workspace.

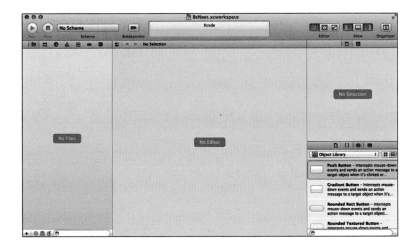

4. Just to make sure that the workspace will operate consistently, choose File, Workspace Settings from the Xcode menu to bring up the dialog for the derived data location for the workspace. Click the Advanced button, and make sure

that the build location is set to the derived data location and that the default subfolder is selected, as shown in Figure 20.12. Alternatively, your version of Xcode might show a dialog like that shown in Figure 20.6. In this case, the correct option is again the Shared Folder of the derived data location.

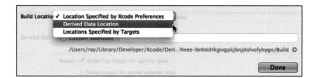

FIGURE 20.12
Verifying that the build location is set to the Derived Data Location.

5. Click Done, and then click Done again to finish setting up the workspace.

At this point, you have a workspace built and appropriate defaults configured so that you can start adding projects and have them behave properly in cooperation with each other. In the next section, you fill that workspace with some active projects and configure them to use the workspace features.

Adding Projects to the Workspace

Having created a workspace, you can now add files. If you have new project content, you can do that by choosing File, New, Project from the Xcode menu and developing your new project just as you have in previous hours. If you're moving old projects into a coordinated workspace, however, you need to complete a few more-involved steps.

We walk through those for the BetterList, BeeLine, and iBLine projects now. First, we add the BetterList project in steps 1–3, which builds both a framework and a static Cocoa Touch library. We repeat these three steps for BeeLine and IBLine before moving on to step 4:

1. Choose File, Add Files to BsNees from the Xcode menu bar, as shown in Figure 20.13.

2. Navigate to the BetterList2 directory, open it, and select the BetterList.xcodeproj file in it.

3. Check the Copy Items into Destination check box, and then click Add, as shown in Figure 20.14.

FIGURE 20.13
Starting to add files to the new workspace.

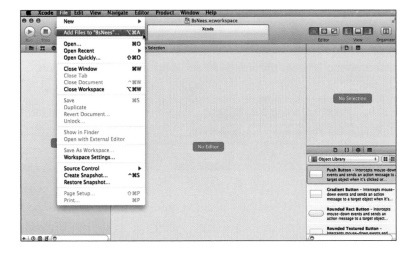

FIGURE 20.14
Adding the BetterList.xcode proj to the workspace, with the Copy Items into Destination check box checked.

Repeat steps 1–3 for the BeeLine.xcodeproj file in the BeeLine2 directory and for the iBLine.xcodeproj in the iBLine2 directory. After doing so, if you reveal the contents of each project in the workspace Project Navigator and reveal the contents of each project's Products group, your Xcode window and workspace should look something like what is shown in Figure 20.15. If your projects are not all peers (at the same level of the hierarchy in the Project Navigator), delete any that are subprojects and re-add them to the workspace. Note that all the products are red, indicating that none of them are current.

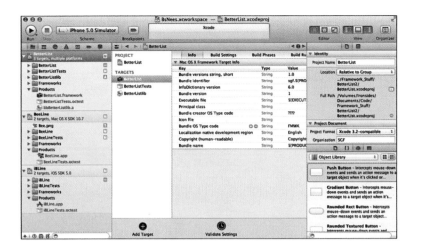

FIGURE 20.15
After adding
more projects,
we see that all
of them are red,
indicating that
none of them
are current.

4. Choose Product, Manage Schemes from the Xcode menu bar, clean up any extraneous schemes you have laying around, and set all of the main project schemes to Shared. When you have finished, the Scheme Manager dialog should look similar to what is shown in Figure 20.16.

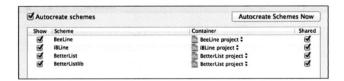

FIGURE 20.16
Setting all the
main project
schemes to
Shared.

Configuring the OS X Project to Work in the Workspace

In an ideal world, Xcode's automatic detection of dependencies would recognize when linking to the library and framework is necessary (for example, if BeeLine and iBline include the header from BetterList and call methods from the BetterList class). Unfortunately, this is not currently possible, but it is probably not Xcode's fault. The Betterlist.framework and the libBetterListlib.a static library both define the same library routines, so it is not really possible for Xcode to choose between them for you. Instead, you still have a little bit of work to do:

1. Select the BeeLine project in the Project Navigator and the BeeLine target in the Editor area.

2. Display the Build Phases tab for the BeeLine target, and open the Link Binary With Libraries group, as shown in Figure 20.17.

FIGURE 20.17
Opening the
Link Binary with
Libraries group
of the Build
Phases section
for the BeeLine
target.

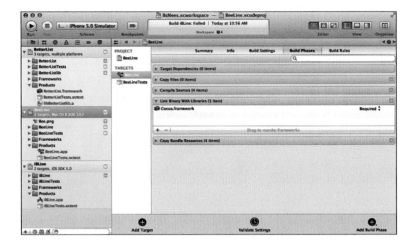

3. Click the + button at the bottom of the Link Binaries with Libraries group.

4. From the dialog that appears, select BetterList.framework, as shown in Figure 20.18. Then click Add.

FIGURE 20.18
Adding
BetterList.
framework.

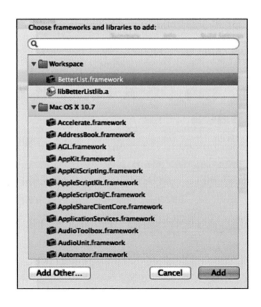

5. In the Scheme drop-down on the Xcode toolbar, select the BeeLine scheme and your appropriate build architecture, as shown in Figure 20.19.

FIGURE 20.19
Selecting the BeeLine scheme and build architecture.

6. Choose Product, Build from the Xcode menu bar. If all goes well, you receive a Build Succeeded notification. Note, as well, that the BetterList.framework product in BetterList and the BeeLine.app product in BeeLine have turned from red to black, as shown in Figure 20.20, indicating that the build has gone according to plan.

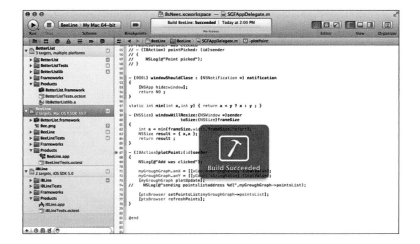

FIGURE 20.20
After these changes, the build is successful.

If all does not go according to plan, you may be greeted by anything from a BeeLine program that runs, but an Xcode notification that it failed, to strange errors in the Xcode interface, to an Xcode indication that everything went fine, but a BeeLine application that crashes. The most likely source of this difficulty is an inconsistency where Xcode thinks it is supposed to find the framework for which you added a dependency in step 3.

To determine whether this is the problem, follow these steps:

1. Reveal the Utilities area.

2. Select the BetterList.framework product from the BetterList project in the Project Navigator.

3. Observe the location and full path that is shown for the BetterList.framework in the Identity area of the Utilities, as shown in Figure 20.21.

FIGURE 20.21
Noting the location and full path settings.

4. Select the BeeLine project in the Project Navigator and the BetterList.framework framework that is linked within it. Again observe the location and full path that is shown for the framework in the Identity area of the Utilities area. If a framework location mismatch is the problem, you will see something different for the linked framework than what you observed for the actual framework in BetterList, as shown in Figure 20.22.

FIGURE 20.22
You could experience a framework mismatch.

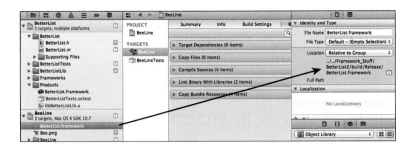

5. To correct this, display the Build Phases tab for BeeLine and open the Link Binary with Libraries group within the build phases. Select the BetterList. framework in the Link Binary with Libraries group and click the – button to remove it. Then click the BetterList.framework in the Products group of BetterList and drag it into the Link Binary with Libraries group for BeeLine, as shown in Figure 20.23.

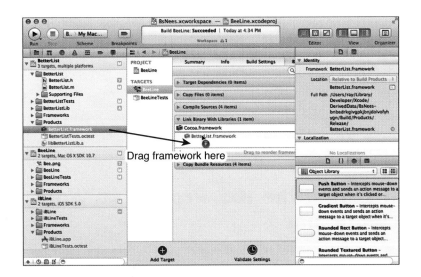

FIGURE 20.23
Fixing a frame-
work mismatch.

One Click Is Good, Two Is Not Better

Do not single-click and release on the BetterList.framework product before you start your click and drag; otherwise, the Editor area will switch to the appropriate view for the framework rather than the build settings for the BeeLine target. You need to do the click and drag in a single smooth action after removing the offending framework version. (We would recommend this process for all the steps that require adding a library or framework if we were better at remembering this and weren't constantly having to open the build settings twice.)

Watch Out!

You'll have better luck clicking and dragging it if you click the name of the framework rather than on the icon for it.

By the Way

6. Try building again. This time you should be rewarded with a successful build and a runnable BeeLine application.

7. Even though BeeLine runs in Xcode, you have one more step to do before you can run BeeLine in the Finder. As before, when you were building your first OS X application in Hour 15, you need to add a Copy Files phase to the Build phases for BeeLine, and add the BetterList framework to the list of files to copy. For reference, this should look exactly as shown in Figures 15.42 and 15.43.

You now have rebuilt your BeeLine project, using BetterList as a peer project in the workspace rather than as a subproject within BeeLine. For a single project and single library/framework, this has little advantage. However, as you accumulate more projects that use the same underlying frameworks and libraries, and that share other resources and code, the advantages begin to pile up quickly. One of the most significant is that with BetterList as a peer in the workspace you can have multiple projects that use it open at the same time, and not have one of them constantly complaining about the BetterList resources already being in use.

In the next section, you add a second project to the workspace to demonstrate this convenient feature, and you learn about configuring different peer projects to make use of different components out of the framework/library project.

Configuring the iOS Project to Work in the Workspace

Configuring the iBLine iOS project to work with the automatically discovered dependencies in the workspace is quite similar to the process for the OS X BeeLine project. However, the fact that the iOS project uses a static library rather than a framework makes things work just slightly differently. Unfortunately, some of these differences seem to be Xcode bugs.

To start, you follow the same procedure that you did to connect BeeLine to the BetterList framework, only this time you select the libBetterListlib.a static library, as follows:

1. Select the iBLine project in the Project Navigator and the iBLine target in the Editor area.

2. Display the Build Phases tab in the Editor area for iBLine and open the Link Binary with Libraries group, as shown in Figure 20.24.

FIGURE 20.24
Opening the Link Binary with Libraries group for target iBLine.

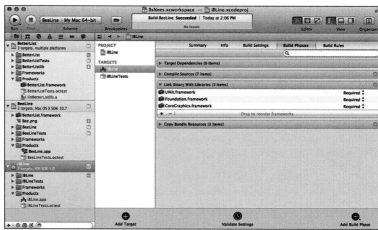

3. Click the + button at the bottom of the Link Binary with Libraries group.

4. In the dialog that appears, select libBetterListlib.a from the BetterList project, as shown in Figure 20.25, and then click Add.

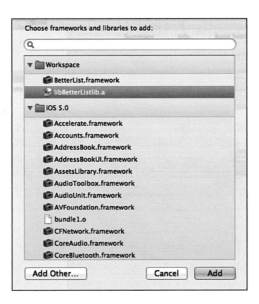

FIGURE 20.25
Adding the libBetterListlib.a from the BetterList project to the iBLine target.

> Yes, we are aware that we just told you that dragging the product from the BetterList project could avoid problems with Xcode confusing itself about locations. Unfortunately, that works only for the framework. Because of what appears to be a bug in Xcode, BetterList will never believe that the static library is actually built (it will always remain red), and dragging the unbuilt red static library produces random crashes as of this writing.

Did You Know?

5. In the Scheme drop-down on the Xcode toolbar, select iBLine and the iPhone simulator, as shown in Figure 20.26. Build iBLine by choosing Build from the Product menu. It won't work.

6. Examine the errors that appear in the Issue Inspector. You should see several complaints about not being able to find BetterList.h, as shown in Figure 20.27. (Actually, you shouldn't see them, but Xcode's ability to find the implicit dependencies falls down on the job here.)

FIGURE 20.26
Selecting iBLine
and the iPhone
simulator.

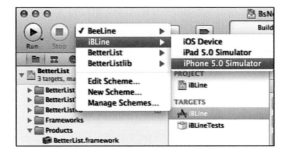

FIGURE 20.27
A number of
errors involving
not being able
to find
BetterList.h
appear after
the build.

To correct Xcode's difficulty in finding the headers, and the resultant failure to find the libBetterListlib.a static library itself, we need to add a few settings in the build settings for iBLine. To do so, follow these steps:

1. Select the iBLine project from the Project Navigator and the iBLine target in the Editor area.

2. Open the Build Settings tab for the iBLine target.

3. Enter **header search** into the Search box for the build settings. This should limit the displayed settings to just a few, including header search paths.

4. Double-click in the value area for the header search paths.

5. In the pop-up dialog that appears, click the + button to add another search path, and then enter the value **$(BUILT_PRODUCTS_DIR)** and select the Recursive option (which might not actually have a column header for Recursive but only an unlabeled column of check boxes, depending on your Xcode version—probably another bug), as shown in Figure 20.28. Then click Done.

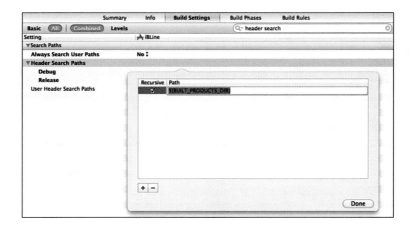

FIGURE 20.28
Adding a recursive header search path.

6. Change your search to **library search** in the Search box. The list of displayed settings should change to a list including library search paths.

7. Double-click in the value area for the library search paths.

8. In the pop-up dialog that appears, click the + button to add another search path, and then enter the value **$(BUILT_PRODUCTS_DIR)** and select the Recursive option, as shown in Figure 20.29. Then click Done, or dismiss the dialog by clicking outside it.

FIGURE 20.29
Adding $(BUILT_PRODUCTS_DIR) to the library search path.

9. Again, select the iBLine scheme and iPhone simulator from the Scheme pop-up on the Xcode toolbar, and then choose Build from the Product menu. You should be rewarded with a report that the build succeeded, as shown in Figure 20.30.

FIGURE 20.30
This time
the build
succeeded.

Bizarrely, even though that build will succeed, if you examine the interface, there's a good chance you'll see that Xcode is simultaneously reporting no issues and complaining that it still cannot find BetterList.h. Chalk up another bug. If you try to use code completion for methods and variables that are within BetterList, you're likely to find that they do not work properly either. Make that two bugs.

If you're happy enough that the build is succeeding and do not need code completion, and aren't bothered by spurious complaints about not being able to find things that are clearly being found, you can stop here. If you want to make code completion work, and silence the erroneous errors, however, you can do something rather hackish instead. This makes your project and workspace a bit less elegant, and requires you to remember to do more maintenance if you change files or file contents around in the future, so there is a tradeoff. If that sounds like an acceptable tradeoff to you, here's a simple trick that will work until Apple fixes the bugs:

1. Add a new group to the iBLine project, by right-clicking the iBLine project and selecting New Group from the pop-up menu that appears, as shown in Figure 20.31.

2. Double-click your new group in the Project Navigator under iBLine and change the name. This example uses the name **BustedCruft**.

FIGURE 20.31
Right-clicking the iBLine project to get the menu with the New Group option.

> **By the Way**
>
> In what I'll call yet another bug, causing the group name to become editable by double-clicking it isn't as easy as double-clicking the name of a file in the Finder (or other slow-double-click processes you're probably already familiar with). I know it sounds silly, but try "scrubbing" your mouse back and forth while double-clicking the name. For reasons probably not even known to Apple, this seems to produce the desired results much more reliably than a standard double-click.

3. Reveal the contents of the BetterList project and the BetterList group within it.

4. Click the BetterList.h file in the BetterList group, drag it to your new BustedCruft group in iBLine, and drop it there, as shown in Figure 20.32.

5. In the dialog that appears, deselect all targets in the Add to Targets list, and then click Finish, as shown in Figure 20.33.

> **Did You Know?**
>
> Since you've gone down this rabbit hole, if you have to change the name of BetterList.h, or add other headers to BetterList and rearrange method definitions, or otherwise modify things so that BetterList.h no longer completely defines the interface for code in the libBetterListlib.a static library, you'll need to revisit the headers you've referenced here.

iBLine will build now, code completion will work properly, and it will not complain about missing headers that it can really find.

FIGURE 20.32
Adding
BetterList.h to
the new group,
BustedCruft.

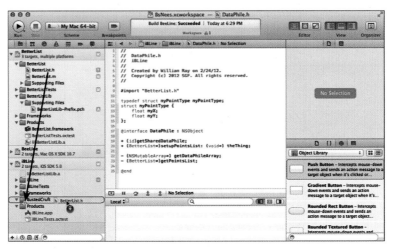

Drag BetterList.h from the BetterList project
and drop it in the new group in iBLine

FIGURE 20.33
Deselecting all
targets and
clicking Finish in
the dialog.

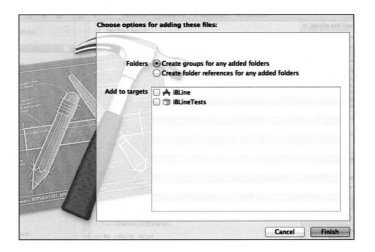

Summary

In this hour, you learned a better way of managing projects that share components. Managing each component as an independent project is sometimes your only choice if you want to share development with others but keep some code private. However, if you are not obliged to partition your projects by such external concerns, the ability of workspaces to automatically deal with dependencies can save you a lot of headaches.

Q&A

Q. *Can projects that are members of workspaces also be opened as stand-alone projects outside the workspace?*

A. Yes, though you're running a risk if you try to open a project in a workspace and also open it separately. In addition, if you open a project independently outside of its workspace, it won't receive all the benefits of the workspace's automatic dependency resolution. This might require you to do some additional manual configuration for some tasks.

Q. *Can projects in workspaces contain subprojects?*

A. Yes. Subprojects within other projects in workspaces are especially useful in keeping your workspace organized. You could, for example, have a Frameworks project in which you keep all the frameworks that you develop and use. And, with more and more varied projects around, BeeLine and iBLine probably start looking more like they should be two subproject peers in a parent project that contains them.

Workshop

Quiz

1. What incantation enables you to replace explicit search paths to other in-workspace projects' products?

2. If code completion is not working for members of a framework or library that is in your workspace, how can you fix it?

3. If you add a shared framework to a sister project in a workspace and it continues to act like the framework is missing, what is the likely problem?

Answers

1. $(BUILT_PRODUCTS_DIR)

2. Create a new group in the project that's having difficulty resolving the symbols, and make reference copies of the headers for the problematic library or framework. Hopefully, this won't be necessary for very long.

3. Xcode probably added the wrong path to the framework. Try deleting it from the Link Binary with Libraries group and then dragging it back in directly from the framework project.

Activities

1. Download Apple's GLEssentials project from https://developer.apple.com/library/ios/samplecode/GLEssentials/GLEssentials.zip. This project contains a pair of Xcode projects, one for OS X and one for iOS, that implement the same program and that share a lot of code through the somewhat dangerous mechanism of both living among the shared files on disk. (Consider what happens if you delete a file from one without realizing that it is used by the other.) Convert these two independent projects into a pair of sister projects under a workspace, and using shared code resources from the workspace instead of each compiling and linking the shared files independently.

2. Try splitting the libBetterListLib product out of the BetterList2 project in the BsNees workspace and make it another peer in the workspace. Single projects that can build multiple targets for different purposes, such as the original BettterList/BetterList2 project that built both a framework and a library, are a great way to keep your functionality together and organize features when you're stuck working with a bunch of independent projects. Under the workspace model, however, they actually place unnecessary restrictions on the way you work. Breaking out the static libBetterListLib library and dynamic BetterList framework into their own sibling projects, both using the same code resources, is a much more flexible solution when using workspaces. If you think about it a bit, you might be able to figure out how to make one of them function as a wrapper project that simply includes the product of the other to build its target.

HOUR 21

Advanced: Analyzing Code with Instruments

What You'll Learn in This Hour:

▶ How to use the Instruments feature to trace the operations of your program

▶ How to repeatedly automate user interface actions with instruments

The Instruments application is Apple's Xcode-like interface to a collection of tools that enable you to observe the status of a process, or of numerous processes on a running system. They also provide reports about things such as open files, memory usage, network usage, or user interface events.

Instruments operate primarily by observing method invocations and messages within the system at a very deep level, mostly via a command-line tool (although this is hidden when using the Instruments interface) called dtrace. dtrace itself can report on essentially every byte allocated or deallocated, every memory location changed, every process register, every command that runs through the CPU, the status of all the files on the disk, the status of all the network connections, and numerous other pieces of information. dtrace's output, however, is voluminous and not particularly easy to read. Instruments take this output, parse portions of it that are useful to you, and display them in easy-to-read graphs and detailed summaries.

Whereas some of the features of the Instruments application are easy enough to use productively right away, others require a deep understanding of the underpinnings of the OS X kernel, interprocess communications, network technologies, and so on. The examples in this hour barely scratch the surface of what is possible. In fact, an entire book this size would probably barely make a dent in the available options.

By the Way

> Don't be shy about using the tremendously valuable features, such as leak detection, that can be used without much study, but be prepared to get your hands dirty and to spend a lot of time deep in the man pages if you want to make full use of the profiling power that the Instruments application provides.

The Instruments Interface

The Instruments interface is designed much like the Xcode interface, layering all features into a single window. Shown in Figure 21.1, the Instruments window contains several areas. Like most Mac OS applications, it has a toolbar and a main window area. The main window is broken up into an Instruments pane, a Track pane, a Detail pane, and an Extended Detail pane, with functions as detailed here.

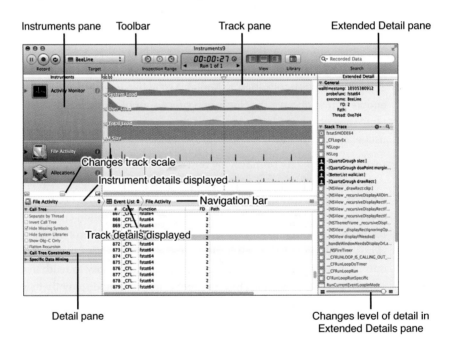

FIGURE 21.1
The Instruments window has an Instruments pane, a Track pane, a Detail pane, and an Extended Detail pane.

▶ **Instruments pane:** The Instruments pane contains a list of the currently active instruments, enabling the control of the features that each instrument captures, and some parameters that affect how results display.

▶ **Track pane:** For each instrument in the Instruments pane, the Track pane displays a tickertape-like or chart-recorder-like graph of the events that the instrument captured while an application or applications were running. Multiple runs of the application can be carried out, creating multiple parallel tracks for an instrument.

▶ **Detail pane:** The Detail pane displays details about the currently selected instrument in the currently selected run and, when possible, about the currently selected portion of the currently selected track. The details are generally contextually appropriate for the track selected, and you can configure the variety of details shown by selecting different options for the details from a navigation bar (which falls between the Detail pane at the bottom of the window and the Instruments pane and Track pane above it). At the left of the Detail pane, you can configure some additional features and capture options for the selected instrument.

▶ **Navigation bar:** The Navigation bar extends horizontally across the top of the Detail pane and controls the type of details shown for the selected track. The detail options range from different presentation styles for the details to overall details for the application run, such as its console output. The leftmost field in the Navigation bar, falling directly under the Instruments pane, enables the selection of the different instruments in the Instrument pane (and has the same effect as clicking on the instrument in the Instruments pane). The next field to the right enables selection of the types of details to be displayed in the Detail pane. Additional navigation selections are contextually available depending on the selected instrument and details displayed.

▶ **Extended Detail pane:** The Extended Detail pane shows fine-grained detail about one detail line selected from the Detail pane. It may show this as a single collection of information or in a number of group summary areas like the inspectors in the Utility area in Xcode.

At the right side of each instrument in the Instruments pane is a small round *i* button (of the style typically used for information dialogs) that opens a pop-up configuration dialog where you can configure data-capture features of the instrument and data-display features of the track.

Within the toolbar itself, you can select the target to which you want to apply the instruments, run the Instruments (by clicking the Record button), and customize the layout and features of the Instruments application itself, by adjusting the inspection time range, the panes within the application that should be shown or hidden, and the run to examine. There is also a button that displays the library of available instruments, and a Search field from which you can search for features of interest within your recorded data.

At the top of the track pane is a timeline. By clicking in the timeline, you can drag an indicator called a thumb to select the precise point in the timeline that you want to examine. As you scrub the thumb back and forth across the timeline, the details in the Detail pane will update to reflect those appropriate for the point in time that you're indicating, and small detail notification flags will appear in the track graphs, indicating the nearest, or most salient, events in that track to the time point you have selected, as shown in Figure 21.2.

FIGURE 21.2
Small detail notification flags appear when you select a point in the timeline to examine.

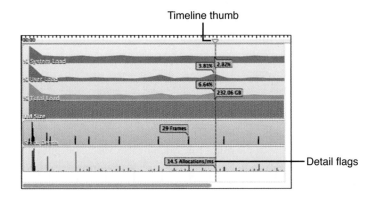

Timeline thumb

Detail flags

Using Instruments

Using instruments on applications you are developing in Xcode is quite simple. You access this functionality by clicking and holding the Run button on the Xcode toolbar until the Profile option appears. Then you select it. When you do so, a dialog opens in which you can choose the type of instrument to use for profiling your application. To get some practice using instruments, let's returned to the BeeLine application and find out if I've left any memory leaks.

Checking for Memory Leaks

Memory leaks occur when all the pointers that point to a block of memory that is allocated during execution (for example, in response to a `malloc()` call) lose track of the address of that block of memory. For example, if `foo` is the only pointer to a block of `malloc()`ed memory, and you assign `foo=0`, there is no longer any way to access the `malloc()`ed block of memory because nothing knows where it is. Because you cannot access it, you cannot `free()` it, and it will hang around, still taking up space until your program ends. This is no big deal if it is one leaked block of memory, but if that kind of leak happens in a loop or in response to user interaction with the program, the amount of memory your application will require will continually grow as long as it is running. This is not a recipe for happy users or a stable system.

To check BeeLine for memory leaks, follow these steps:

1. Locate the BsNees workspace you created in Hour 20, "Keeping Things Organized : Shared Workspaces," or retrieve a new version from the Hour 21 folder of the source downloadable from http://teachyourselfxcode.com/.

2. Open the BsNees workspace in Xcode. Select the BeeLine project in the Project Navigator and the BeeLine target in the sidebar of the Editor area.

3. In the scheme drop-down in the Xcode toolbar, select the BeeLine scheme and the appropriate architecture.

4. Click and hold the Run button at the upper left of the Xcode toolbar until the available Run options appear, and then drag down to the Profile option and release. The button should change from Run to Profile so that you only have to click it the next time.

5. In the dialog that appears, choose the Leaks instrument, as shown in Figure 21.3, and click Profile.

6. BeeLine launches, as does the Instruments interface. It is collecting information as soon as it launches. Add some points to BeeLine.

7. Continue adding points for 40 seconds or so.

8. Then click the Stop button on the Instruments toolbar, or quit BeeLine by choosing Quit from BeeLine's File menu.

FIGURE 21.3
Choosing
the Leaks
instrument.

After you quit BeeLine, you should be greeted with an Instruments window that looks much like Figure 21.4. It should come preconfigured with an Allocations instrument and a Leaks instrument. The Allocations instrument shows you all the memory that has been allocated by the process and when the allocations occurred. The Leaks instrument shows you times when, as far as the instrument can tell, memory that was allocated by BeeLine became unreferenced. When you click the Allocations instrument, details for it are shown in the Detail pane. When you click the Leaks instrument, likewise, its details appear.

FIGURE 21.4
The Allocations
instrument
shows all the
memory allo-
cated by a
process and
when the alloca-
tions occurred.
The Leaks
instrument
shows when
memory alloca-
tions became
unreferenced.

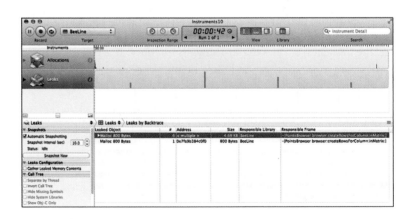

If you want to adjust the granularity of the information display (for example, if all your data is bunched up at the left side of the track pane, or if the track pane is showing only a few milliseconds in the middle of your 40-second run), you can try to do this using a small horizontal scrollbar that appears directly under the Instruments pane. Dragging this to the left zooms out, making more time fit within the Track pane. Dragging it to the right zooms in, expanding the tracks within the pane so that you can see finer detail than if all the events were compressed into your available window or screen space.

If you want to make the entire duration of your run fit exactly within the Track pane, you can do this by selecting Snap Track to Fit from the View menu in Instruments.

Watch Out!

Gentle Touch Required

The Track Scale slider is incredibly sensitive (almost uselessly so). The difference between 20 seconds and 20 milliseconds on the slider is a matter of only a few pixels on the screen. When you try to use it, pay attention to the current value that it is displaying and make very small moves with your mouse. Otherwise, you will find the track display zipping back and forth from too compressed to be useful to too wide to be useful at an uncontrollable rate. We hope this is a bug.

Within the Detail pane for the Leaks instrument, you can see that there have been multiple leaks of 800 bytes from memory allocated by `malloc`. In the rightmost column of the Detail pane, you will see a list of the methods where the memory was leaked from these `malloc`s.

Did You Know?

You probably should be able to double-click the method indicated in the responsible frame column and have Instruments take you straight to the guilty bit of code. Unfortunately, this doesn't currently work. Peculiarly, while double-clicking the method currently does nothing, double-clicking the allocation size attempts to take you to the code. However, it fails to do so correctly, and induces erratic behavior in the Instruments application.

Getting Additional Information About Leaks

To find out where in the method calling stack the offending method was called, and to gain the ability to jump to that code, reveal the Extended Detail pane by clicking its icon in the View options on the toolbar.

In the Extended Detail pane, you will see a bottom-up trace of the call stack, ending at the top in the allocation that eventually was leaked. Immediately below the allocation is the method that invoked the allocation, as shown in Figure 21.5. If you double-click the calling method in the Extended Detail pane, Instruments will successfully find the source and display the offending line in the Detail pane, as shown in figure 21.6.

FIGURE 21.5
In the Extended Detail pane, we can see which method leaked the allocation.

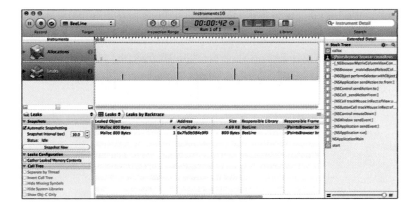

FIGURE 21.6
Double-clicking the calling method takes us to the offending line of code in the Detail pane.

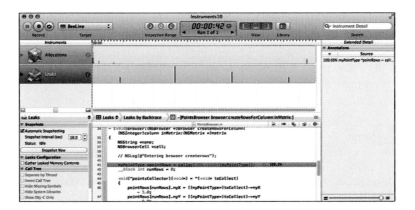

Watch Out!

Don't Squash the Bug

Although the error I've left here is fairly obvious, don't fix it just yet. You need it for the rest of this hour.

Additional Runs

Instruments can also collect multiple runs from the same application so that you can compare those runs and determine whether there are commonalities or differences in the behavior of your program. To add additional runs of your program to the Instruments display so that you can compare them to the first run, just click the Record button and interact with BeeLine again. Try to keep your run about the same duration as your first run, and then click the Stop button again. Do this two or three times. Try to have add lot of points in one run, and only add a few in another run with some long pauses between points. When you have finished, click the disclosure triangle on the Leaks instrument in the Instruments pane. Instruments should show you an Instruments pane and a Track pane that look much like those shown in Figure 21.7.

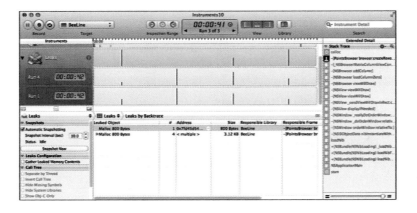

FIGURE 21.7
Collecting multiple runs to compare.

As you can see, although there are some distinct similarities in the leaked memory pattern, some differences also exist. The similarities are primarily due to the granularity of sampling in how Instruments look for leaked memory. The differences are because of the differences in timing of how I interacted with BeeLine when I was adding points.

You can adjust the granularity of sampling by changing the snapshot interval for the Leaks instrument. Select the Leaks instrument from the leftmost field in the navigation bar, and a parameter group for Snapshots will appear beneath it. The snapshot interval controls how often the Instruments application collects data from the running process being profiled and provides it to the Leaks instrument for analysis. So, setting this field to smaller values causes the Leaks instrument to check for leaks more frequently. Different instruments have different ways of configuring their snapshot interval or sampling rate.

Memory leaks like this, which depend on what you do and when you do it, can be particularly hard to diagnose. This is especially true if it requires a lot of time interacting with the user interface before the error occurs. Thankfully, the Instruments feature has a powerful tool for replicating interactions with the user interface: the Interface Recorder. In essence, it can record a series of interactions with the interface of a program, including where the mouse moved, what text was entered, and what buttons were clicked and when. It can then play those events back to a freshly started copy of the program as though you were pressing the buttons and entering the text yourself. Using this tool lets you consistently replicate user interactions so that you can consistently replicate problems for debugging.

To use the Interface Recorder instrument, follow these steps:

1. Quit Instruments and return to Xcode.

2. Click the Profile button on the Xcode toolbar. In the dialog that appears, find the UI recorder trace template, and click Profile.

3. The Instruments application will launch and again begin recording a trace of BeeLine. This time it is recording actions that you take in the user interface. Begin entering point values. Again enter four or five values for different points, clicking Add after each one.

4. When you have finished, wait a few seconds, and then choose Quit from BeeLine's File menu.

The BeeLine interface will disappear, and the Instruments interface will display a track similar to that shown in Figure 21.8. In the Track pane, a series of overlapping thumbnails showing the various actions is presented. Each thumbnail is a mini screenshot of the region of the interface where the action occurred. The Detail pane will display, line by line, each of the thumbnails and also what type of event was recorded for the thumbnail and any value parameters that were entered. The Record button on the Instruments toolbar changes from Record to Drive & Record. This indicates that it is ready to play back the collection of events that it just recorded and record new data.

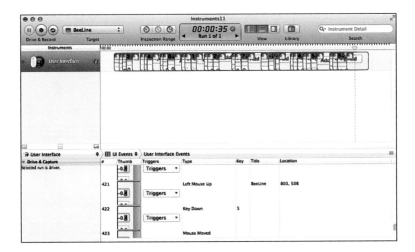

FIGURE 21.8
The Interface Recorder instrument recorded actions taken in the user interface and is displaying thumbnails of the actions in the Track pane. In addition, the Record button has changed to Drive & Record.

Collecting Data from Additional Instruments Simultaneously

You can add additional instruments to the Instruments pane. All of them will record data simultaneously. To use our recorded user interface interaction to look for leaks, we can add a Leaks instrument to the Instruments pane and let the User Interface instrument drive BeeLine for us, while the Leaks instrument records data and reports leaks. To do this, follow these steps:

1. Click the Library button on the Instruments toolbar to reveal the Library browser.

2. Find the Leaks instrument in the Library browser. You can do this by scrolling through the list or by using the Search field at the bottom of the Library browser to filter the instruments shown.

3. Click the Leaks instrument in the Library browser and drag it to the Instruments pane. Release it where you want it in the list of instruments, as shown in Figure 21.9. Alternatively, if you're happy with it at the bottom of the list, just double-click it.

4. Now click the Drive & Record button on the Instruments toolbar. The BeeLine interface will appear, and the User Interface instrument will proceed to drive your cursor and attempt to carry out the exact same user interface actions that you took when you recorded the session.

FIGURE 21.9
Adding the Leaks instrument to the Instruments pane.

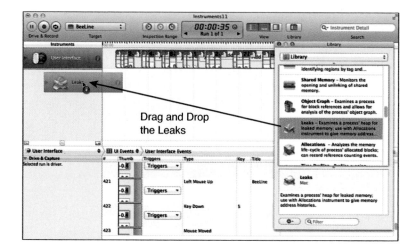

Drag and Drop the Leaks

Don't Touch Anything

Don't move your window, or the Instruments window, or move other windows on the screen between recording the user interface session and using it to drive the interface in Drive & Record mode. The Instruments application tries to reproduce your actions literally, but its idea of *literal* involves "the same place" rather than "the same thing." If you've rearranged windows, Instruments will happily click on, and interact with, whatever is in the same place on the screen as your target program was previously.

5. If you need additional duplicate runs, you can continue to click Drive & Record as many times as you need. Additional tracks of data from the Leaks instrument and from the User Interface instrument will be collected for each run.

By the Way

At this point, we cannot recommend using the loop option for the Drive & Record action. The loop option, enabled by a button found next to the Drive & Record button, is supposed to run your user interface action track over and over and over. Unfortunately, there seem to be a number of bugs in this function at the moment. Not only is it almost impossible to make it stop properly, it also has a bad habit of losing its focus on the application it is supposed to be interacting with, and spamming your user interface events into other applications that you have running. The outcome is rarely healthy for your blood pressure or your computer.

As of Xcode 4.2 and 4.3, the User Interface instrument is unlikely to function as described here. This is the way it is supposed to work. However, as shown in Figure 21.10, it does not produce perfect replicates of the user interface actions that were originally carried out. It does not even produce identical erroneous runs.

This is not simply a matter of user interface timing, as examination of the console output from BeeLine (viewable by selecting a track in the Track pane, and the Console output details from the navigation bar) demonstrates that BeeLine is in fact receiving different values. It appears as though a significant portion of this problem is due to the user interface actions not being properly indexed spatially to the program interface, even if nothing is moved. This is a critical failure on the part of the Instruments application and one that we expect Apple will address soon. Perhaps (we at least hope) it will be working properly by the time you read this.

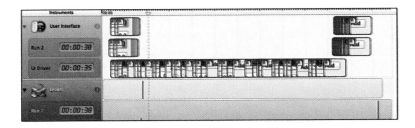

FIGURE 21.10
Unfortunately, the User Interface instrument does not produce perfect replicates of the actions that were originally carried out.

Summary

In this hour, you got a brief introduction to the Instruments application and learned how to use two of the most immediately powerful instruments together, to augment your ability to debug your code. The instruments within this feature are so much more than we have space to cover here. They can inform you of just about every change that takes place in your machine, almost on an instruction-by-instruction basis.

By using the full panoply of instruments that are available, as well as leveraging the ability to easily create custom instruments by wrapping Apple's provided interface around custom dtrace scripts, you can take your programs and programming to a whole new level. Start slowly, use the tools that are easy to use, and one day when you think "I wonder if there's some way that I could find out what the system does when…," turn to the Instruments feature. They'll do that for you.

Q&A

Q. *Can you save the traces from instruments for additional analysis later?*

A. Yes. You can also pare down what is saved by picking unneeded traces in the Trace pane and selecting Delete Run from the Instruments menu. Saved user interface tracks can be reloaded for later playback. However, remember that they are quite literal about the location of features on the screen, so you need to position your application exactly identically if you want user interface playback to work from a saved run.

Q. *Is the Instruments application limited to working with Xcode projects?*

A. No. The Instruments application is actually a completely separate tool kit from Xcode. Xcode and Instruments simply interoperate fairly easily, making it a useful tool to use along Xcode for diagnosing problems with your projects. Instruments can actually profile the operation of any program (that your userid has permission to peek into) on the system, including the kernel. In addition, it can profile multiple programs simultaneously, enabling the debugging of situations where multiple intercommunicating programs are involved. You can access this additional functionality through the Attach to Process selection in the Target drop-down menu on the Instruments toolbar.

Workshop

Quiz

1. How can you get a better idea of the connection between user interface actions and memory leaks?

2. Where do the additional runs appear when you make several recordings in the same Instruments session?

Answers

1. Create an Instruments setup with a UI recorder instrument. Stop the run and delete it to get back to the initial Record mode. Then add a Leaks instrument. Set the Leaks snapshot interval to a small value, 1 second or less. Record a session, and use the timeline thumb to identify the UI recorder thumbnail frames that correspond to the reported leaks.

2. They are initially hidden, but can be revealed by clicking the disclosure triangle on the instruments in the Instruments pane.

Activities

1. Correct the memory leak in BeeLine. Profile it again to make certain that the leak is really gone.

2. Profile iBLine and determine whether it has any leaks. If it does, see if you can fix them. Remember that there is still a bug in the BetterList code, if you haven't fixed it already, that causes a crash if you delete every point in the list and then try to add another.

HOUR 22

Managing and Provisioning iOS Devices

What You'll Learn in This Hour:

▶ How to prepare iOS applications for distribution
▶ How to create a distribution certificate
▶ How to create an App ID
▶ How to create and install a distribution provisioning profile

Once your application works as you want it to, you have to start thinking about the big picture: getting it out of Xcode and onto the devices (whether iOS or OS X) where it will be used.

If you're developing just for yourself, you really have no reason to go beyond the rapid development provisioning for iOS devices that you were introduced to in the first hour (or beyond just building your application for use on your own Mac). However, if you want to distribute your application, you need to complete a few additional steps.

These steps fall broadly into two separate categories: housekeeping steps to ensure that your application is distributable, and steps that Apple requires if you want to make the application available via the App Store.

In this hour, you learn how to prepare your iOS devices to receive your software and how to inform Apple about resources that must be allocated (such as a namespace for your iCloud data storage) to enable other devices to receive your app. In the next hour, we look at the App Store itself and Apple's requirements for distributing for iOS and OS X.

> Unlike most other hours in this book, you cannot follow the instructions here entirely literally. We create several configuration documents for application distribution that are required, by virtue of how Apple manages the App Store, to be completely unique among all apps. To avoid conflicts with other readers of the book, and confusion when the App Store complains that an identifier is already taken, make sure to use your own email addresses and company and bundle identifiers when following the steps in this hour.

Creating an iOS Distribution Certificate

The first thing that is necessary for distributing, as opposed to developing, iOS applications is a distribution certificate. Distribution certificates consist of unique public and private key pairs, used by the distribution process and the users who will receive your application to verify that it really came from you. They're necessary to prevent some malicious third party from sneaking out an update version of your software that might contain damaging code and fooling your users into thinking that it is an official release from you.

> You need to fully understand two key terms used repeatedly through this and the following hours:
>
> ▶ *Certificates* are a mechanism to ensure that you are who you say you are (or rather, that anyone who says they're you, really is you). Certificates are used to sign applications to provide a guarantee that the application is authentic and belongs to a specific developer or development team.
>
> ▶ *Provisioning profiles* are used to associate specific certificates with specific hardware devices and specific applications. They effectively specify combinations of who, where, and what may be run, enabling you to control how your team uses your development resources and enabling Apple to limit the damage that an unfinished application can do "in the wild," by restricting its distribution to only those devices where you have explicitly enabled that application.

As of Xcode 4.3, you can create a distribution certificate in several ways. The way that Apple hopes that you use is automatic provisioning, letting Xcode manage the creation of the necessary certificates for you. Unfortunately, this process doesn't always work.

To determine whether you are already set up, open the Organizer from the Xcode toolbar and pick devices in the Organizer and profiles in the Organizer sidebar. If you see an iOS device distribution profile there, along with an IOS device development profile, and you can select it and it doesn't tell you that it is an invalid profile,

Xcode's automatic creation of the certificates for you has worked. If you don't see the distribution profile, or it tells you that it is not a valid distribution profile, something went wrong in the process, probably in the insertion of the certificate parts into your keychain. In this case, you must clean up Xcode's mess and create the certificates and profile manually.

If you're one of the lucky ones for whom everything worked, you can skip ahead to "Creating an App ID." If all that appears in the Organizer is your development profile, and not a broken distribution profile, you can skip ahead to "Creating a New Distribution Certificate and Provisioning Profile by Hand."

Fixing Broken Distribution Certificates and Profiles

If Xcode starts the automatic process but leaves you with a broken distribution profile, follow these steps to get back to a clean slate so that you can build a working profile by hand:

1. Open the Organizer from the Xcode toolbar and pick Provisioning Profiles under Library in the sidebar.

2. Select the distribution profile that was partially created. It may have a status line showing "Valid signing identity not found," or it might only show a warning when you select it.

3. Delete the problematic profile and close the Organizer.

4. Launch the Keychain Access program from the Utilities folder of your Applications directory.

5. Pick the Login keychain, and the Certificates category, from the Keychain Access sidebar.

6. Use the Search field on the Keychain Access toolbar to search for "iPhone."

7. Select any certificates with names that start with "iPhone developer" and delete them.

8. Cancel the search for "iPhone" and delete the Apple Worldwide Developer Relations Certificate Authority certificate.

> **By the Way**
>
> It seems likely that in the future Apple will start using certificates named iOS Developer rather than iPhone Developer. You might want to keep an eye out for these, as well.

Now Xcode's Organizer and your keychain should be clean and ready to accept a new certificate that you create and install by hand.

Creating Distribution Certificates and Provisioning Profiles Manually

To create a new distribution certificate and provisioning profile manually, you work through the Keychain Access program and Apple's Online Provisioning Portal in addition to Xcode. The process has several parts. You must first use Keychain Access to create a request for a certificate, and then use the Provisioning Portal to actually obtain the certificate. After you've obtained the certificate, you can install it in your keychain again, and then you use a combination of Xcode and the Provisioning Portal to create provisioning profiles for distributing your application. Let's start with creating a request for a certificate.

Creating Certificate Requests with Keychain Access

Keychain Access enables you to configure a request for a certificate that you can send to a certificate authority. To use Keychain Access to configure the request, follow these steps:

1. Launch Keychain Access from the Utilities subfolder of your Applications directory on your Mac.

2. Open the Keychain Access preferences and click the Certificates tab.

3. Configure the preferences as shown in Figure 22.1, with both the Protocol and the Revocation List set to Off. Close the preferences.

FIGURE 22.1
Setting the Protocol and Revocation options in the Certificates section of the Keychain Access preferences to Off.

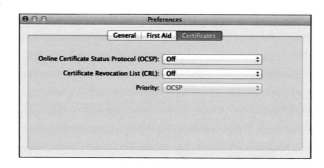

4. From the Keychain Access menu, choose Certificate Assistant, Request a Certificate from a Certificate Authority.

5. Provide the team agent email address as it appears in your iPhone Developer Program registration.

> The team agent is the sole individual allowed to actually submit files to the App Store. If you have already registered the team agent under a different user ID or on a different computer, you must duplicate their already-created distribution certificates and public and private keys into your keychain. Apple provides a tutorial on how to do this in Tech Note TN2250 available at http://developer.apple.com/library/ios/#technotes/tn2250/.

6. Provide the common name that should be associated with your certificate. This can be your company name or your personal name. If you've requested other certificates for other purposes, be consistent with this value.

7. Select the Save to Disk option, and check the Let Me Specify Key Pair Information check box.

8. You should not have to specify a certificate authority email address because you are going to save the request to disk rather than have Keychain Access submit it automatically. However, Keychain Access sometimes insists that you put something in this field before it will let you click Continue. Because it will not be used, it is safe to just use your own email address here if Keychain Access wants a value before proceeding.

9. When you have everything filled in, your request should look something like what is shown in Figure 22.2. Click Continue, and then choose a place to save the certificate request. The default filename and your desktop are good choices. Click Save.

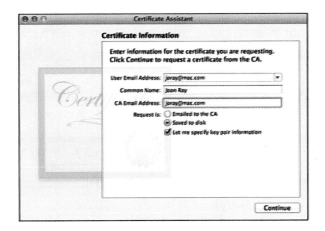

FIGURE 22.2
Here is the completed certificate request before clicking Continue.

10. In the dialog that appears, specify a key size of 2048 bits and the RSA algorithm. Click Continue.

11. A dialog appears indicating that your certificate request has been saved. Click Done.

Requesting the Certificate Through the Provisioning Portal

Now that you've created the certificate request, you can send it to the Provisioning Portal, which requests the actual certificate for you. To use the Provisioning Portal to request your certificate, follow these steps:

1. Navigate to the Provisioning Portal (http://developer.apple.com/ios/manage/overview/index.action) in a web browser and sign in using your developer ID.

2. Click the Certificates category in the navigation list on the left. Then click the Distribution tab along the top of the work area.

> ### Don't Let the Tabs Fool You
>
> The contents of the Distribution tab and the Development tab look an awful lot alike, and every time you make an action in the portal, the portal defaults back to the Development tab. Sometimes it even seems to default back to the Development tab when you look away from your screen for a few moments.
>
> You don't want to know how many times I've gone through all the steps of setting up certificates or creating profiles only to discover that I've accidentally missed a switch to the Development tab somewhere in the middle of the process and have to delete everything and start all over again. Pay really close attention to those tabs, and hopefully you'll pull out less of your hair than I have.

If you've just deleted a broken distribution certificate and profile from your keychain and organizer, you will probably see a current distribution certificate listed.

3.   **a.** If, and only if you just deleted the broken certificate from your Keychain Access application, make sure you're really on the Distribution tab, and then revoke it, and continue with step 4.

　　　b. If there was no distribution certificate in your Keychain Access application, but a distribution certificate already appears here, ready for download, the certificate may have been created properly and just not downloaded. Skip ahead to step 9.

4. Beside the line that says "You currently don't have a valid distribution certificate," click the Request Certificate button.

A page opens with instructions for this certificate-creation process that you're currently in the middle of, and a note that Xcode's automated process is really the preferred way of requesting these certificates. If Xcode had done it right, you wouldn't be here now, so forge ahead.

5. Near the bottom of the page, you'll see Choose File. Click it.

6. Navigate to the certificate request that you saved to your desktop in step 9 in the preceding section, select it, and click Continue. Back on the Distribution tab (you're still on the Distribution tab, right?), click Submit.

The page for the Distribution tab on the Provisioning Portal then reloads and shows your new distribution certificate, probably with a status of Pending.

7. Wait a minute or two, and then reload the page for the Distribution tab. The status should now be Issued, and there should be a button in the Actions column to download your distribution certificate. If the status is still Pending, wait a bit longer and try this step again.

8. When the Download button appears, click it. The distribution profile then downloads to your computer.

9. Click the link to download the Worldwide Developer Relations (WWDR) intermediate certificate. The link should be located immediately beneath the list of distribution certificates in the Provisioning Portal.

10. Back in the Finder on your Mac, navigate to where you saved the WWDR intermediate certificate and your distribution certificate.

11. Double-click each of the certificate files (the WWDR and distribution certificates) that you just downloaded. Keychain Access should launch (if it is not already open), and the certificates should be installed in the Certificates list for your Login keychain. The private keys for each should be installed in your Keys list for your Login keychain.

12. Select the iPhone Distribution certificate in your keychain and click its disclosure triangle. You should see an associated private key, as shown in Figure 22.3.

FIGURE 22.3
Showing the iPhone distribution certificate in Keychain Access and its associated private key.

If you do not see the key here, try looking directly in the keys under your Login keychain, opening each likely one to see whether there is one associated with the iPhone distribution certificate. If the private key is present, you're ready to create a distribution profile. If the private key is missing, something went wrong, and you must start from the "cleaning up" step again and repeat the process.

This entire process seems rather unstable at the moment, and many people seem to end up having to repeat it several times before everything works properly. According to reports on the Web, some developers even have to quit and restart the Keychain Access program or Xcode between each step to make it through the entire process successfully. Because Apple is moving toward Xcode performing all the steps automatically for you, this process should be easier soon (we hope).

By the Way

Thankfully, because a certificate's purpose is to identify you or your team, you generally will need just one distribution certificate for all of your development work. So, once you get this certificate downloaded and installed properly, you should not have to repeat this process.

Creating an App ID

The next thing you need so that you can make use of your distribution certificate is a registered identifier for your application. App IDs are identifiers that are used to distinguish your application from all others in the App Store and to make certain that Apple's iCloud and push notification services are connecting the right iCloud data, and right push notifications, to your application. You create these unique identifiers through the iOS Provisioning Portal, as well.

App IDs Are like Tattoos

After you've created an App ID, you're stuck with it, and the closest you can do to removing it is to hide it. Make sure you really want a particular App ID before you create it. Apple doesn't currently even give you a way to hide App IDs, although if you create more than a few, some of them will inevitably be hidden off the bottom of your screen (probably not the ones you want though). A kind third-party developer has created Safari and Chrome extensions that parse Apple's iOS Provisioning Portal pages and let you hide selected App IDs. You can find it at https://github.com/simonwhitaker/app-id-sanity/downloads.

To create an App ID in the Provisioning Portal for your application, follow these steps:

1. Navigate to the Provisioning Portal (http://developer.apple.com/ios/manage/overview/index.action) in a web browser and sign in using your developer ID.

2. Click the App IDs category in the navigation list on the left, and then click the Manage tab.

3. Click the New App ID button in the upper right of the Manage tab. A new page loads under the Manage tab, where you set up the appropriate details for your application.

4. Fill in the description with a short descriptive string or name for your App ID. Remember that these IDs are forever, so do not create them unnecessarily, and don't give them descriptions that you might regret later.

5. Enter the bundle identifier for your application. If you don't know the bundle identifier, or you want to use something other than the identifier that Xcode created automatically from your initial project setup parameters, follow these steps:

   a. Open your iOS project in Xcode.

   b. Select the iOS project in the Navigator area, and the iOS application target in the sidebar of the Editor area.

   c. Display the Info tab in the Editor area and find and disclose the Custom iOS Target Properties.

   d. Find the bundle identifier line. If it contains something like `COM.SGF.${PRODUCT_NAME:rfc1034identifier}`, and your target is named iBLine, the bundle ID that is being written into the application is `COM.SGF.iBLine`.

Watch Out!

Case Matters (Kind Of)

There is currently some confusion about case sensitivity of bundle IDs. Although they apparently are not supposed to be case sensitive, it appears that some parts of Xcode and the Provisioning Portal assume that they are lowercase, and some parts do not automatically downcase uppercase characters in the specified string.

The result is that you can get a mixed-case string stuck in the Provisioning Portal, which won't let you delete it, and which won't let you actually use it to provision devices because on their end they downcase the strings and then discover a mismatch with the profile.

So, it is currently safest to explicitly downcase your bundle ID manually if you have previously specified a bundle prefix or application ID that would cause a mixed-case bundle identifier to be created.

By the Way

You can set up a wildcard App ID for all the applications developed with a particular bundle identifier prefix if you use a wildcard in place of the product name in the App ID Request page.

It is probably not a great idea to use something like just your company prefix and a wildcard for the App ID, even though that would let you use the same App ID for any application you wanted to provision. A better use is creating wildcarded App IDs for collections of cooperating products that all need access to the same iCloud data storage and so forth.

If I were planning to develop a whole host of bee-related products for SGF, I might use com.sgf.beez.* for my bundle identifier in the Provisioning Portal and com.sgf.beez.ibline for the iBLine bundle identifier in Xcode.

> **e.** If you need to convert your bundle ID manually to lowercase, double-click the Value for the bundle identifier under the Info tab and specify a lowercase and properly formatted string. In Figure 22.4, I set the iBLine target we've been working on to use com.sgf.ibline as the bundle identifier.

FIGURE 22.4
Setting the bundle identifier to use a name with all lower-case letters.

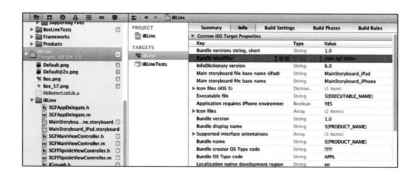

6. Back in the Provisioning Portal, make sure that the bundle seed ID is set to use your team profile. Depending on your configuration, the Provisioning Portal may require that you explicitly set this value, or it may have it automatically configured with no options for you to select.

7. After you have the Create App ID page in the Provisioning Portal configured approximately as shown in Figure 22.5, click the Submit button.

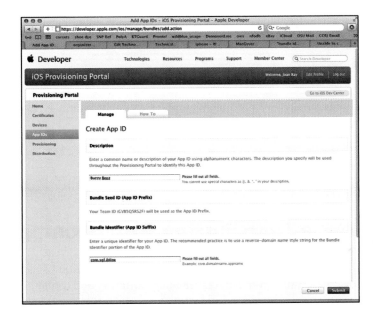

FIGURE 22.5
Creating an App ID with a description of the App ID and a bundle identifier.

8. The App IDs page should reload, and your newly created App ID should show up in the list, similar to what is shown in Figure 22.6. If you need to modify its configuration (for example, to enable access to iCloud data containers, or to configure for access to Apple's push notification service), you can set up those features by clicking the Configure button at the right of the App ID details.

FIGURE 22.6
The App ID has
been success-
fully set up. If
you need to
make any
adjustments to
the configura-
tion, click the
Configure option
at the right end
of the line.

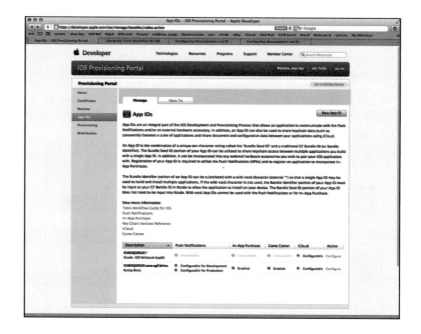

Creating a Distribution Provisioning Profile

After you have successfully installed a distribution certificate and configured an App ID for your product, you can put these together to create distribution profiles for your application. Your distribution profiles can either associate specific iOS devices with the App ID and your identifying certificate or they can be App Store distribution certificates that enable distribution of your application through the App Store for anyone to download or purchase. To create a provisioning profile for your application using your distribution certificate, follow these steps:

1. Navigate to the Provisioning Portal (http://developer.apple.com/ios/manage/overview/index.action) in a web browser and sign in using your developer ID.

2. Click the Provisioning category in the navigation list on the left. Then click the Distribution tab along the top of the work area. Remember that the pages for the Distribution and Development tabs look quite similar and have an insidious and annoying tendency to try to trade places when you're not looking.

3. Click the New Profile button near the top of the page that's displayed for the Distribution tab.

4. Enter a profile name. This should be adequately informative that you can tell what the profile is for from the name. For iBLine, I'm naming my profile App Store Distribution for iBLine.

5. From the pop-up menu for the App ID, pick the App ID you just created for your application.

6. Decide whether you want to distribute your application via the App Store or via Ad Hoc distribution and select the appropriate option. If you decide to use Ad Hoc distribution, you must also pick the devices where the profile will enable the application to be installed.

Usually, you would use the App Store for your final production builds and Ad Hoc distribution for your development team for testing. If you use Ad Hoc distribution, you must send your built products to your team members yourself, instead of using the App Store to distribute your product. In the next hour, we cover Ad Hoc distribution, including the Enterprise type of distribution whereby your users can download and install your app directly on their iOS device.

Developer Apps Are Not for Sharing

Do not use the Ad Hoc distribution mechanism to distribute software to people who are not members of your development team. Unless you have an Enterprise developer account, which enables distribution to arbitrary devices in an enterprise, Apple reserves the right to revoke developer credentials without warning and without recourse if you distribute software to end users, rather than developers, outside the App Store mechanism.

7. After filling out the Distribution Provisioning Profile page approximately as shown in Figure 22.7, click the Submit button.

   A new page loads under the Distribution tab for provisioning in the Provisioning Portal. It should contain a new line listing your just created profile, probably with a status of Pending.

8. Wait a minute or two, and then reload the page in your browser. When your newly created distribution profile status changes to Active and a Download button appears in the available actions for it, click Download.

9. Navigate to the downloaded file (it should have the extension .mobileprovision) in the Finder and double-click it. Xcode launches if it is not already running, and the Organizer opens.

10. Select the Devices tab on the toolbar of the Organizer and the Provisioning Profiles item in the Library group of the Organizer sidebar.

11. Look for a new profile line that matches the Distribution Provisioning Profile you just created. If everything worked, and you've been following along with similar configurations for your iOS application build, the Organizer should show you something like what is shown in Figure 22.8, where the most important detail to check is that the Status line for my App Store distribution for iBLine profile says "Valid Profile."

Congratulations, you've made it through the certificate installation and provisioning profile creation process successfully. Now you can move on to the final step of making Apple's required tweaks in your application for submitting to the App Store and finalizing the submission process.

Begin Soapbox Mode

A lot of people are annoyed that Apple requires all this certificate and provisioning business for distributing iOS applications and wonder why they cannot just build apps and distribute them like they can OS X applications. The answer is that iPhones are phones, and first and foremost as phones, they must function as phones.

That means that if someone picks one up and dials for emergency help, it had better function as a phone and dial properly. If just anyone could write apps and distribute them without restriction, there's a very real chance that a broken application or a malicious application could interfere with the basic phone functionality. This might not bother you on your phone-turned-development platform, but for many people, their iPhone is just a phone (and might be their only phone).

Be careful what you wish for, too. For instance, unless you think your grandmother (standing in for all our grandmothers) is sufficiently savvy enough to keep malicious applications off of her phone, and unless you are comfortable with the fact that her phone could potentially crash during an emergency, don't wish too hard for easy, open development and distribution mechanisms for iOS apps.

Summary

This hour walked you through the process Apple requires to get your application set up to begin the App Store submission process or to prepare the app for Ad Hoc distribution. These steps are the practical requirements that you must complete to create a certificate that guarantees your identity and the app's authenticity; to create a unique identifier so that the app can find its data in the cloud and receive notifications if needed; and to create a provisioning profile that associates the App ID, your identifying distribution certificate, and the hardware on which the app is allowed to run.

There are a few steps where optional configuration is possible, such as configuring the App ID (using the Configure button on the App IDs page in the Provisioning Portal) to enable iCloud support or modifying the Distribution Provisioning Profile (using the Modify button on the Distribution tab of the Provisioning page) to change the profile name. To a large extent, however, the steps in this hour are almost identical for every iOS application that you decide to provision and distribute.

Q&A

Q. *Is there a way to move my distribution certificate from the machine I created it on to another machine?*

A. Yes. To do this, you need to export both the private and public keys for your distribution certificate and copy them to the new machine. It is recommended that you copy them and store them somewhere secure on a CD or other durable media for safekeeping anyway, because if you lose the private key, all your provisioning profiles will become invalid and you'll have to delete them all and start again. Apple details the process for copying the keys at http://developer.apple.com/library/ios/#technotes/tn2250/.

Q. *I'm getting a weird error when I try to install an iOS App Store provisioning profile that says something about there being no devices configured for development under my profile. But I have one (or more) iOS devices set up for development and can see them in the Provisioning Portal. What's up?*

A. Developer, meet another Xcode bug. The problem is really that you don't have an OS X device registered with the development portal. I know you're working on an iOS project. Xcode should, too, but well, it is Xcode. Sometimes you have to remember that it is still growing and treat it like it is a bit daft. To correct the problem, select your OS X machine from the sidebar of the Devices tab in the Organizer. On the page that appears, click the Enable Developer Mode button, wait until Xcode comes back from thinking to itself, and then click the Add to Portal (+) button at the bottom of the Organizer. Now go back and try to install your provisioning profile. Bug, meet developer. Squash.

Q. *This hour talked a bunch about setting up provisioning for iOS devices. Do I have to go through all of this rigmarole for provisioning OS X machines, as well?*

A. Not all of it, at least at the moment. When you build an OS X application, you produce a standalone OS X application that you can double-click and run in the Finder and that you can copy to other machines and run the same way. You do have to do some of this if you want to distribute through the App Store for OS X applications, however.

Workshop

Quiz

1. Why might the Organizer tell you that your distribution provisioning profile is invalid?

2. Can you delete that App ID you created as a joke, with that uncomplimentary reference to your boss's receding hairline?

3. Should you just use the wildcard team App ID for all of your apps and avoid the risk of creating something you'll wish you hadn't later?

Answers

1. There are several possible causes. The most likely is that you do not have a private key installed for the distribution certificate in your keychain. If you have, or can obtain a copy of it from somewhere, finding the file, quitting Xcode, and double-clicking it to install it into your keychain should cause Xcode to improve its behavior on the next launch. If you do not have access to the private key, you must start at the beginning of this hour, delete the broken certificate from your keychain, and create a new one. If you already have the private key and it is already installed, you've hit an Xcode bug. You can do one of two things: Quit and restart Xcode, export the certificate and private key from your keychain, delete them from the keychain, and reinstall them from the exported files, reboot, or various combinations of these things. Alternatively, you can just delete the key and certificate and start over from the top. The "delete and do it again" option is often a faster route to getting Xcode to recognize the key properly than any amount of trying to convince it to pay attention to the already properly configured certificate that's right under its nose.

2. No. App IDs, like diamonds, are forever. This is frustrating, but it actually makes sense. App IDs uniquely associate applications and their iCloud data, notifications, and other resources that really should be unique to the application. If you could delete an App ID, someone else on your team could possibly create another app with the same ID and completely confuse things by having a different app that appears to want access to the same iCloud storage and push notification services. Think twice before creating App IDs that might haunt you later.

3. That depends. If you want to let all your applications have access to the same collection of iCloud data and notifications, using the team wildcard solves your App ID dilemma and keeps your collection of App IDs from growing out of bounds. If you need to partition your iCloud data so that only some is shared between only some apps, you need to create additional, only partially wildcarded App IDs for each application group.

Activities

1. Recruit a friend for your development team and add his iPhone to your list of development devices. Then create a new Ad Hoc distribution profile that includes both your iOS device and his iOS device and install it in Xcode.

2. Sneak a peek in the Build settings for your project, looking for the Code Signing group. Configure one of the Debug or Release build configurations to use your new Ad Hoc distribution profile, and experiment with Archiving and Sharing your application with your new development team member. If you get stuck, don't worry. We cover this in more detail in the next hour.

3. Reenable one of the crash-producing bugs that we previously fixed in iBLine. A good choice would be the bug that bit us when the last point was deleted from the list and then another point was added. Install this buggy version of iBLine on your iOS device, and then crash the app. Now connect your iOS device to your computer, launch Xcode, and open the Organizer. Select the Devices tab, and look under the Device Logs in the group for your iOS device. Pretty cool, huh? This is also the mechanism you use to connect crash reports that your users might generate back to your code. If you receive crash reports, you can drag them into the log area to add them to the list and connect them to Xcode.

HOUR 23

Distributing Your Applications

What You'll Learn in This Hour:

▶ How to prepare your new application for distribution
▶ How to archive your newly built app
▶ How to distribute your app
▶ How to set up iTunes Connect to facilitate your app submission to the App Store

Well, you've done it: You have your application developed and debugged. You have created your developer ID (Xcode created it automatically for you when you created your first provisioning profile) for OS X applications and distribution provisioning profiles for your iOS applications. Now the App Store awaits.

In this hour, you learn about the final changes to your application code, project configuration, and build settings that enable you to distribute your iOS apps through the App Store and through Ad Hoc distribution. For your OS X applications, you learn about the process for distributing through the App Store and via direct distribution yourself. You also learn about signing applications with your developer ID so that they can be validated with Apple's upcoming Gatekeeper software authentication system, and how to avoid signing if you prefer not to use Gatekeeper at this time.

Just When You're Getting the Hang of Things   Watch
                                                                   Out!

As of this writing, Apple's developer ID and Gatekeeper (the default mechanisms for application distribution) are still under development and so subject to change. Therefore, the exact steps you follow to use them might differ somewhat from what is shown in this book. But, from what you learn here, you'll be able to improvise and achieve distribution. After all, Apple only makes the process easier with each change, right? You've made it this far in this book, so now you'll be able to figure all this stuff out.

Your developer ID should have been created automatically when you first set up a provisioning profile, way back in Hour 1, "Xcode 4." However, sometimes this slips through the cracks. To check whether the automatic process worked for you, open the Organizer, display the Devices tab, and then click your ID under the Teams group in the sidebar.

If you see a listing for you, with the name Developer ID Application, you're good to go. If you do not see that item listed, you can try to convince Xcode to request a developer ID again by selecting Profiles under the Library group in the Organizer sidebar and then clicking the Refresh button in the lower right of the Organizer window. Xcode should automatically request missing IDs for you.

Finalizing Your Distribution Build

You need to make a few final tweaks to your app before it is ready for distribution. These involve adding features that are required by the App Store and configuring code signing for your apps and a few "common courtesy" fixes that you should do just to keep your users happy. The required modifications differ slightly for OS X and iOS applications.

OS X Applications

For an OS X application, you must decide whether to sign your application with your developer ID, add icons (as appropriate), and you must ensure the archive settings for your scheme are configured properly. You also want to remove any unnecessary `NSLog()` statements that you have left hanging around in your code.

To sign your app with your developer ID, follow these steps:

1. Open your project in Xcode, select the project in the Navigator area, and again select the project in the sidebar of the Editor area.

2. Click the Build Settings tab.

3. On the Build Settings tab, enter **Code Signing** in the Search field.

4. Find the Code Signing Identity line and click where it says Don't Code Sign.

5. In the pop-up that appears, select your developer ID signing certificate. Several options appear in the dialog, as shown in Figure 23.1. Apple's developer ID documentation indicates that the correct value is your Developer ID Application certificate. We expect that in the future the value that Xcode recommends will default to this certificate, but at the moment the recommended default does not appear to work.

If you do not want to sign your app with your developer ID, you can just leave the Code Signing setting alone.

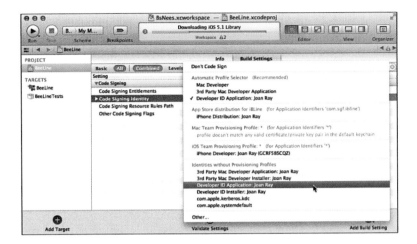

FIGURE 23.1
Selecting the Developer ID Application identity to sign the app.

Confirming Archive Settings in Your Scheme

Because you haven't been archiving your apps for distribution so far (if you have been archiving them at all), you need to check the settings for the Archive build in your scheme. If you're like me, you can and probably have gotten away with some settings for your own archive purposes that are not acceptable for distribution archives. To make sure that your scheme is configured properly, follow these steps:

1. Open your project in Xcode, select the project in the Navigator area, and again select the project in the sidebar of the Editor area.

2. Choose Edit Scheme from the Product menu.

3. Open the Build pseudo-action, and make sure that the target you're planning to distribute is the only thing selected for the Archive action, as shown for the BeeLine app in Figure 23.2.

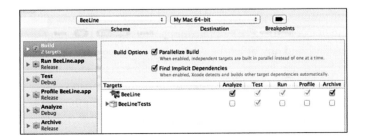

FIGURE 23.2
Making sure that the target we plan to distribute is the only item selected for the Archive action.

Open the Archive action and make sure that Build Configuration is set to Release and that an appropriate archive name is specified. Make sure that the Reveal Archive in Organizer check box is checked, and then click Done, as shown in Figure 23.3.

FIGURE 23.3
In the Archive action, we set Build Configuration to Release, make sure that the archive name is appropriate, and check the Reveal Archive in Organizer box.

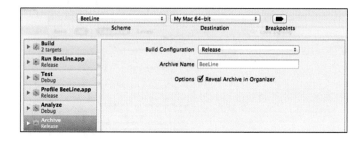

Final Code Cleanup

It's that time: Those last lingering NSLog() statements that are still hanging around like a security blanket have got to go. Your users do not want their system logs filled with notes about traversals of your data structures and congratulatory exclamations that your application successfully launched. Either delete them completely, comment them out, or wrap them in conditionals dependent on a variable that you can globally configure in your header to turn them all on or off simultaneously. You can use the Find, Find in Workspace item under the Edit menu to locate all the NSLog() instances across your entire project. If you want to comment them out, you can do that using a Find and Replace, replacing **NSLog(** with **//NSLog(** across the entire workspace.

Also, remember to go back and either connect or remove any interface components that do not currently have attached functionality (for example, menu items that were created in the default menu in the NIB that are not relevant to your application).

Attending to Additional Details

The last thing you need to do is add those little touches that make your application fit in with the flock of other OS X applications. These include adding application icons, screenshots, and any other metadata that is required for distribution and installation of your application. Mac users expect a certain look, feel, and style to your application icons and onscreen presentation; and although you can get away without providing these polishing touches for simple distribution to a local circle of friends, if you want your application to shine in the App Store, providing high-quality graphics is a near necessity. Providing minimally acceptable graphics is an absolute requirement; after all, Apple won't accept an App Store submission without them.

Did You Know?

Despite Xcode apparently wanting, and accepting, a PNG file dropped into the App Icon space on the Summary tab for OS X application targets, what it really needs you to put there is a ICNS file built from your PNG files. To construct the ICNS file, launch the Icon Composer by picking Open Developer Tool, Icon Composer from the Xcode menu. Then, drag appropriately sized copies of your icon image into the provided slots in Icon Composer. Next, from the File menu, choose Save As and save the collection to an ICNS file. You can then drag this file into the App Icon space on the Summary tab for your application, to properly configure its App Icon resources.

You can find the full details about what Apple requires for submission in the iTunes Connect documentation available from https://itunesconnect.apple.com/docs/iTunesConnect_DeveloperGuide.pdf.

Building Your App Archive

After you have collected these final bits for your application, it is time to build an archive for your application so that you can submit it to the App Store (or distribute it outside of the App Store to your users). Building an archive is no different from invoking the build actions that you have done many times already while working through each hour's projects in this book, with the sole difference being that the Archive build action does not appear as an option under the Run button on the Xcode toolbar. Instead of the Run button, to invoke an Archive build action, pick the appropriate scheme and architecture from the Xcode toolbar, and then choose the Archive item from the Product menu. Xcode builds an archive, and if you elected to code-sign your application, prompts you for access to a keychain key with which to sign the archive. Allow it access to the keychain key, and you should (after Xcode finishes building, linking, and archiving) be greeted with a new archive for your application in the Organizer.

If You Don't Get a Clean Archive Build

Your OS X application might not build cleanly when you try to archive it. For some reason, despite using the Release build configuration for archiving and a having a Release build configuration that's perfectly functional when you Build for Running, the Build for Archiving action sometimes gets confused and loses track of the autodiscovered framework dependencies.

By far the easiest way to solve this problem is as follows:

1. Select the scheme for your embedded framework on the toolbar, and make sure that it is set to use the Release configuration for building.

> **2.** From the Product menu, choose Build For, Running.
>
> **3.** Select the scheme for your application on the Toolbar, and again choose Build For, Running from the Product menu.
>
> **4.** From the Product menu, choose Archive.
>
> The archive should build cleanly now.
>
> This issue seems to have something to do with the same framework location issue mentioned in Hour 20, "Keeping Things Organized: Shared Workspaces," where the location of the BetterList.framework in the Linked Frameworks and Libraries group of the Summary Tab for the BeeLine target changed depending on how the framework was added to the list. You might want to experiment with removing your framework from the list and adding it back using different methods, such as directly from the + button in the Linked Frameworks and Libraries group, or dragging it, or in the Link Binary with Libraries group in the Build phases. If you experiment with this, remember that you must add the new framework back to the Copy Files build phase so that it will be embedded in the final application.

At this point, from the Archives tab of the Organizer you are ready to select the application archive and distribute it, depending on your preference, via the App Store, as a code-signed (or unsigned) directly distributable application, or as an Xcode archive for other people to use in Xcode.

iOS Applications

As with OS X applications, you must change a few of your iOS application's build settings and configuration details to ready it for distribution. For instance, remove any unnecessary NSLog() invocations and confirm that your the Archive build action in your scheme is configured properly. Unlike with OS X applications, you have no choice about code signing. You also need to attend to a couple of details that are not necessary for OS X distribution archives.

To configure code signing for your iOS application, follow these steps:

1. Open your project in Xcode, select the iOS project in the Navigator area, and again select the project in the sidebar of the Editor area.

2. Click Build Settings for the iOS project. Enter **Code Signing** into the Search field for the build settings.

3. Locate the Code Signing Identity group and expand it.

4. For the Release identity, click the value setting to the right and configure it for the recommended Automatic Profile Selector iPhone Distribution, as shown in Figure 23.4.

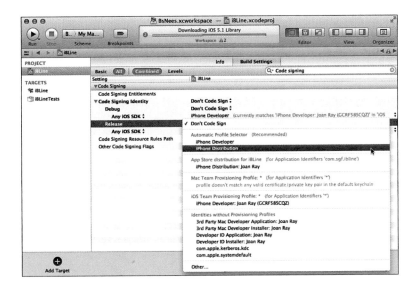

FIGURE 23.4
Selecting
iPhone
Distribution for
the Release
identity.

5. For the Any iOS SDK code-signing identity, click the Value setting and configure it for the same iPhone Distribution certificate.

To configure your scheme settings for proper archiving, follow these steps:

1. From the Product menu, choose Edit Scheme.

2. From the Scheme selector at the top of the Scheme Editor dialog that appears,
   select the scheme for your iOS target.

3. Select iOS Device for the destination at the top of the Scheme Editor dialog.

> If you see your iPhone or other hardware iOS device listed in the pop-up list of
> destinations, rather than the generic destination iOS Device, unplug your iOS
> device. For some reason, the generic iOS Device destination sometimes disap-
> pears when a hardware iOS device is available.

By the Way

4. Select the Build pseudo-action and verify that your iOS app target is the only
   target selected for the Archive action.

5. Select the Run build action and configure it to use the Debug build configuration.

6. Select the Archive build action and configure it to use the Release build configuration, make sure that it has an acceptable archive name specified, and then
   select the option to Reveal Archive in Organizer. Click Done to close the
   Scheme Editor dialog.

If for some reason you really need your Run build action to use the Release configuration, and you want it to use your development provisioning profile instead of
your distribution provisioning profile, you can configure the Run build action as you
want and create another build configuration with which to apply the distribution
provisioning profile. To do this, create a new build configuration (on the Info tab for
the project, under Configurations) for your iOS application and set up code signing
with your distribution provisioning profile with it. Then add a new scheme dedicated to archiving that uses your new build configuration in its Archive build
action.

You can also use this trick to set up an iOS target so that it can be built for either
Ad Hoc distribution or App Store distribution simply by changing schemes. In this
case, you add two new build configurations for the project (on the Info tab for the
project, under Configurations), one for Ad Hoc distribution and one for App store
distribution, and then assign the appropriate distribution provisioning profiles to
each configuration (on the Build Settings tab for the target, under Code Signing).
Then, two new schemes are required, with each selecting the appropriate build
configuration for its Archive build action.

Final Code Cleanup

If you did not get rid of any remaining NSLog() invocations in your iOS app when
you globally cleaned your OS X application, do so now.

Also, remember to check your interface layout on all the devices that your app supports, and for all the device rotations that are enabled.

Attending to Additional Details

As with your OS X application, your iOS application needs icons and screenshots. It
also needs one or more launch images. Unlike OS X applications, instead of specifying these images by providing a collected group of them in an ICNS file, for iOS
applications Xcode requires you to add the plethora of images required directly to
the target's Summary tab into many scattered image-drop spaces. Hover over each
of the image-drop spaces to bring up its tooltip hint, to find out what the resolution
requirements are for each image.

You can find the full details about what Apple requires to submit iOS apps in the
iTunes Connect documentation available at https://itunesconnect.apple.com/docs/
iTunesConnect_DeveloperGuide.pdf.

Also unlike OS X apps, which really can contain just about anything in their internal directory structure, iOS apps for distribution are more rigorously constrained in
what they can contain. Therefore, it is possible to have an iOS app that builds and
runs fine, both in the simulator and on development hardware, but that cannot
build an archive that is acceptable for either Ad Hoc or App Store distribution.

Building Your App Archive

After you have collected the final bits for your application, it is time to build an archive so that you can submit it to the App Store (or outside of the App Store via Ad Hoc distribution). The process is identical to building an archive for an OS X application:

1. Set the scheme as appropriate for your iOS application and set the architecture to iOS Device on the Xcode toolbar.

2. From the Product menu, choose Archive.

   If your changes to the code or other configuration details require that the app be rebuilt, Xcode builds it, and then it constructs the archive and puts it in the Organizer. If Xcode asks for permission to access a key from your keychain during the build, click Allow so that it can properly sign the app archive. After Xcode is finished building, signing, and archiving your app, the Organizer opens, and you should be greeted with a new archive of your iOS app.

Derived Data Interference

If, when you try to build your app for archiving, you get a silly error about not being able to find files in directories that look suspiciously like the name of an iPhone, or you get complaints that build directories that should be standard (such as build/Release-iphoneos/) are missing, it is because you have, or recently had, an iOS device plugged in.

For reasons known only to Apple, some parts of the automagically constructed derived data path take cues from the name of the device that's plugged in, while other parts of the automatic dependency discovery and linking mechanism ignore the device information. As a result, certain orderings of build steps and device connections and disconnections can leave Xcode with a completely confused notion of the derived data directory structure.

If this happens to you, plug in your device, select the appropriate scheme, and from the Product menu choose Clean. Unplug your device and repeat the cleaning step. Then, make sure the architecture is listed as just a generic iOS device on the Xcode toolbar and retry the Archive build action. If you have multiple iOS hardware devices, you might need to repeat the connect-and-clean step for each device.

If the archive of your iOS app looks like a spiral-bound notebook in the Organizer's list of archives, as shown for iBLine in Figure 23.5, rather than like a typical rounded-square iOS app icon, the format of the archive is not correct. To diagnose the problem, follow these steps:

1. Click the Distribute button on the Organizer.

2. Use the Save Built Products option to save the archive to your desktop.

3. Open the archive and find out what it contains other than your intended iOS app. From this information, you should be able to figure out what portion of the build process is including the unneeded information.

   If you try this with the iBLine iOS app from the BsNees workspace from Hour 20, you'll find that what gets saved to your desktop contains a directory hierarchy and a copy of the BetterList.h header. Embedded headers are meaningless to iOS applications, and it turns out that there is an erroneous Copy Headers build phase set up for the `BetterListLib` target in the BetterList project in BsNees. Removing the Copy Headers phase for that target and rebuilding the archive will fix the archive structure and cause iBLine to appear properly in the Organizer.

FIGURE 23.5
A successful archive of an iOS app that can't be successfully distributed, looks like a spiral-bound notebook.

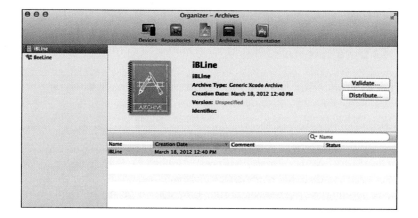

Configuring an iTunes Connect Application Record

You need to set up iTunes Connect records only if you plan to distribute your OS X or iOS applications via the App Store. iTunes Connect is a moving target, and full documentation fills several volumes of Apple's Developer Documentation, making it impossible to do more than touch on the highlights here. Apple's current introduction to the documentation is stored in a PDF file that you can download from http://itunesconnect.apple.com/docs/iTunesConnect_DeveloperGuide.pdf.

To get started with iTunes Connect and create your first application record, follow these steps:

1. Open https://itunesconnect.apple.com in your web browser. Enter your Apple developer user ID and password. Click Sign In.

2. If you need to set up a contract so that you can receive payments for your app through the App Store, click the Contracts, Tax, and Banking link in the main body of the page.

   At the top of the page that opens, you can request new contracts for regional or worldwide distribution. The iTunes Connect Developer Guide contains information on how to properly configure requests for contracts.

   If you plan to distribute your app for free, you can use the free distribution contract that was autocreated for you when you joined the Developer Program, so you do not need to request a new contract.

3. Click the Manage Your Applications link in the main body of the iTunes Connect page. A new page opens listing your current apps and most recent activity with your submitted applications.

4. Click the Add New App button in the upper left of the Manage Your Apps page. If you have not previously added an app to iTunes Connect, a page opens requesting that you specify a company name.

Did You Know?

Think carefully about what you enter for the company name. Like App IDs, company names are forever. The one you configure this first time will apply to all applications that you submit to the App Store in the future.

They're also much more public. The company name you enter is exactly the company name that will be shown for your app in the App Store. This is also the value that the App Store uses to collect all the apps that you submit so that users can find other software that you have written, so it is both an important field for organizing your submissions and highly visible public information.

---

5. After you have configured your company name (or immediately after clicking the Add New App button, if you configured your company name previously), you are launched into the App Information Entry process.

   This process is documented in detail in the iTunes Connect Developer Guide. As part of this process, you specify many details about your application, such as the range of devices on which it can be installed, the pricing information, variable rights for different territories, educational discounts, version information, screenshots to be included in the App Store listings for the app, and numerous other pieces of information.

As the App Store evolves and new iOS devices with new capabilities and new OS X technologies become available, the information that Apple requires changes. Download and read the iTunes Connect Developer Guide sections that apply to your application carefully. You should download and peruse this document before each app submission, just to be sure that you are working with the most current version of the document and understand Apple's requirements at the time of submission.

While you're configuring your app record in iTunes Connect, you need to provide your app name. Things will go more smoothly if you can use the app name exactly as you have named the target in Xcode. If that app name is already taken, you should probably edit your Xcode project to use a different name, instead of playing games with renaming the application binary after Xcode builds the archive. You also need to configure your bundle identifier exactly as it is set for your app in Xcode and upload all your image assets for the app when requested.

After all your app details are filled in, you reach a page that shows an overview of your app information and which shows a status of Waiting for Upload. When you get here, you're ready to distribute your archived application via the App Store distribution method.

It's All in the Details

Make sure that you are very familiar with the current requirements when you're submitting your apps. Many seemingly minor details in the submission configuration and requirements can come back to haunt you if you aren't thoroughly familiar with them. For example, the Developer Guide contains a note pointing out that after you have created a new app submission record, future versions can expand the list of supported devices but can never revoke existing device support. As a result, if you accidentally create an app record that specifies that it supports a device that you do not actually intend to support, you will end up being forced to add support for that device to your program. Apple won't add apps to the App Store that do not support all the devices that their submission record lists, and there is no way to get rid of the erroneous specification (both now and forever in the future).

Distributing Your Archived Application

Now that you have your OS X or iOS application archived, it is time to take that last big step and distribute it. For direct distribution with OS X applications, this is really no step at all; you just need to give your application to someone, and you have just distributed it. For Ad Hoc distribution of iOS applications, you give out copies of an *application*.ipa file, and your users install it through iTunes, which is hardly any more difficult. For Enterprise distribution of iOS applications, you need to add a few steps to the Ad Hoc distribution, but if you can edit a web page, enterprise distribution is easy enough. Finally, for App Store distribution, the steps get quite lengthy, for both OS X and iOS applications. Regardless of which type of application or what distribution process you choose, distribution starts in the Organizer. To distribute your apps, follow these steps:

1. Open the Organizer and go to the Archives tab.

2. Select the app that you want to distribute from the sidebar on the left, and select the appropriate build of the app from the list that loads in the Organizer window.

3. Click the Distribute button beside the description of the app and build you just selected.

4. In the dialog that appears, choose the type of distribution that you want for your app. As outlined in the following subsections, several different distribution types are available, depending on the type of app you have selected for distribution.

Distributing Unsigned OS X Applications

To directly distribute unsigned OS X applications, follow these steps:

1. Choose the Export As, Xcode Archive option and click Next.

2. Save the archive to your desktop, and then locate it on the desktop in the Finder and right-click it to Show Package Contents.

3. Open the Products directory, and then open the Applications directory.

4. Drag your application from there out to your desktop.

Now you have a file you can distribute any way that you see fit. You can zip it up and put it on a web page, create an installer package, or put it on a CD or thumb drive and physically hand it to your users.

Watch
Out!

Exports Damaged in Transit

Yes, you should be able to simply export an unsigned application using the Export As option for either the Application type or the Installer Package type, resulting in an easier process for getting to your app for distribution. Unfortunately, this currently does not work. Apple's evolving developer ID system seems to have gotten its fingers in here where they don't really belong, and the Organizer attempts to validate the code signature on unsigned archives and, of course, fails to do so, making these options currently useless.

Distributing Signed OS X Applications

To distribute signed OS X applications, follow these steps:

1. Choose the Export Developer ID-Signed Application option and click Next.

2. In the next dialog, confirm that the same developer ID is configured in this dialog as was configured to code-sign the application in the build settings, and then click Next.

3. Xcode asks you for permission to access your keychain (perhaps once, perhaps a dozen times). Click the Allow button, and keep clicking it until Xcode stops presenting that dialog and brings up a Save As dialog instead.

4. Give your application a name and save it where you can find it.

> Yes, for some reason even though you have code signing turned on in the project, you have to do it here again. If you did not code-sign during the build, it is not clear what will happen if try to code sign now (and it is even less clear that what does happen is the intended behavior). If you code-sign with a different developer ID here than you did within the project itself, we have no idea what Gatekeeper is going to think.

Using Ad Hoc Distribution for iOS Applications

To distribute your iOS applications via Ad Hoc distribution, follow these steps:

1. Choose Save for Enterprise or Ad-Hoc Deployment, and then click Next.

2. In the dialog that follows, select the appropriate code-signing identity. This should match the code-signing identity that was used when creating your Ad Hoc distribution provisioning profile (and should match the owner of your distribution certificate).

3. Click Next, provide a filename, and then click Save.

A file with the extension .ipa is created. You can distribute this file however you want to distribute it, via the web, CDs, or even email. When your users click it, your iOS app loads into their iTunes library for installation on their device.

> An Ad Hoc distribution can be installed only on the iOS devices that were selected for it when the Ad Hoc distribution provisioning profile was created. Users with other devices can install it in the iTunes library, but they cannot install it on their devices.

Using Enterprise Distribution for iOS Applications

Enterprise distributions are loaded directly to iOS devices through links on web pages. So to use this option, you must first save your iOS app archive, and then upload it and some associated resources to a web server. Then, you must construct a web page with a link that your users can click to download your app.

To save the app for Enterprise distribution and upload it and some associated resources to a web server, follow these steps:

1. Choose Save for Enterprise or Ad-Hoc Deployment, and then click Next.

2. In the dialog that follows, select the appropriate code-signing identity. This should match the code-signing identity that was used when you created your Ad Hoc distribution provisioning profile.

3. Click Next, provide a filename, and then click Save.

4. At the bottom of the dialog, check the Save for Enterprise Distribution check box, and fill in the various fields that appear. Provide the URL where you are going to store your iOS app for your users to download. You also need to make a large and small application image available on a web server and provide URLs for those in this dialog, too. Then, add a title and a subtitle if appropriate, and if you want Xcode to automatically add the canonical iOS icon "shine" to your images, check the box for that option. Then click Save.

Two files are created: one named *appname*.ipa, the other named *appname*.plist.

Figure 23.6 shows the Save for Enterprise Distribution dialog filled out for iBLine, to be distributed from the iOSapps directory on my server at someguys-farm.com.

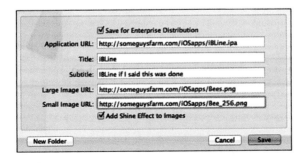

FIGURE 23.6
Filling out the details in the Save for Enterprise Distribution dialog.

By the Way

If at some point later time you need to change the URLs that you used here, you can edit the plist file and change them there, instead of re-exporting the archive from the Organizer.

5. Upload both the application (.ipa) file and the plist file so that they are available at the URL you specified in the Save for Enterprise Distribution dialog.

   If you specified that your application URL was http://mycompany.com/dir1/myApp.ipa, you need to download the file from that URL, and you need to download the associated plist file from http://mycompany.com/dir1/myApp.plist.

   You also need to upload a 512 x 512 PNG app image URL to be available from the URL specified for the Large Image URL, and a 72x72 PNG app image to be available from the URL specified for the Small Image URL.

Now you must construct a web page with a link that your users can click to download your app, as follows:

1. Construct a link with the following syntax:

```
<a href="itms-services://?action=download-manifest&url=itms-services:
//?action=download-manifest&url=<URL for your plist>" id="text">Download
➡My App</a>
```

2. Embed it in a simple HTML page, such as the following:

```
<HTML>
<H1>BZZZZZZ! Get your Bs in Line!</H1>
<a href="itms-services://?action=download-manifest&url=itms-services://
?action=download-manifest&url=http://someguysfarm.com/iOSapps/iBLine.plist"
➡id="text">Tap
Here to install iBLine</a>
<hr>
Now Buzz on!
</HTML>
```

3. Upload the HTML page to your web server and share the URL for that page with your users so that they can install your iOS app.

When users visit that page on their iOS device, they can click the link to download and install the application on their device.

Remember that unless you have an Enterprise Developer account, users can install your Enterprise distribution app only on devices that were specifically included in the Ad Hoc distribution provisioning profile when you configured it in the Provisioning Portal.

Distributing Applications via the App Store (OS X or iOS)

You cannot proceed with the App Store submission process unless you have already configured an application record in the iTunes Connect system. If you have an application record configured in iTunes Connect, follow these simple steps:

1. Select Submit to the (Mac or iOS) App Store and click Next.
2. On the next dialog that opens, provide your iOS developer username and password.

Your app then begins its journey into the App Store validation process, and you interact with iTunes Connect from here on out, to configure additional information about your app, such as the purchasing options and so on.

Summary

Congratulations. You have finished your journey through Xcode's twists and turns, and have developed both an OS X application and an iOS app from start to finish in Xcode. You now have a lot of details to remember, and several of Apple's developer guides will be your constant companions in the future. But, you're ready to submit your apps to the App Store, or distribute them through other means, and enter the wide world of professional developers building high-quality applications for Macs, iPhones, and iPads. There's a world of opportunity out there. Make a BeeLine for it!

Q&A

Q. *What's this gatekeeper thing mentioned in conjunction with the developer ID?*

A. Gatekeeper is a new technology that Apple is currently testing that provides users a way to validate the origin of OS X applications that they receive. As currently envisioned, when enabled for a user account, the user of that account will only be able to install apps that are signed with a valid developer ID. The exact details of Gatekeeper seem likely to change as it nears final release, but the mechanism of developer IDs to use with Gatekeeper appears to be relatively stable, even if it is hit or miss that Xcode creates your developer ID automatically when it should.

Q. *Is there any way to add more iOS devices where an already provisioned Ad Hoc distribution can be installed?*

A. Not without resorting to some undocumented tricks that may not work in the future. The approved route is to create a new Ad Hoc distribution provisioning profile in the Provisioning Portal and create a new, signed build of your app.

Workshop

Quiz

1. How can you obtain a runnable, distributable copy of your unsigned OS X application?

2. Why doesn't the PNG app icon that you added to your OS X app show up when you look at the app in the Finder?

3. Why do some devices refuse to install the Enterprise distribution (download) of your iOS app?

Answers

1. Unfortunately, the obvious answers like exporting an unsigned application or installer are broken at the moment because Xcode tries to sign them even if you ask it not to. As of Xcode 4.3.1, you need to save an Xcode archive of your unsigned app and dig the actual application out of the archive bundle that Xcode creates. Hopefully, the unsigned-export options will begin working again in the future.

2. The PNG app icon that you added to your OS X app does not show up when you look at the app in the Finder because Xcode accepts a PNG for the app icon in the interface but cannot actually use one to build an icon for the application. You need to use Icon Composer to build an ICNS format collection of PNG files and add them to the app icon slot instead.

3. This can be for a number of reasons. The most likely is that those devices were not included in the Ad Hoc distribution provisioning profile. However, they also might not be compatible with, or have installed, the versions of iOS that you have required for your app, or perhaps they are not listed in your app's list of compatible devices.

Activities

1. Set up schemes to create both App Store and Ad Hoc distributions for your iOS app.

2. Create an Ad Hoc distribution archive, and then set it up for distribution via the Enterprise distribution (download) from a web server. Install it on your team's iOS devices wirelessly.

3. Create your company ID and an app record in iTunes Connect, and then submit your built application archive to the App Store for validation and distribution.

HOUR 24

Xcode CLI Utilities

What You'll Learn in this Hour:

▶ How to use tools from Xcode from the command line

▶ How to get more information about command-line tools

▶ How to automate the Xcode build process using command-line tools

Xcode is rapidly evolving into a first-class integrated development environment (IDE) for OS X and iOS applications. For many users, it serves its purpose perfectly in that capacity, providing an environment where users can go to develop and test applications. However, some users, and some uses, need to develop and build projects without wrapping the process in the development environment. Some of these uses are purely preferential because some programmers prefer to maintain code using command-line tools such as emacs. Other such uses are entirely practical, such as the collaborative development of cross-platform projects where some developers are not even using Xcode.

Conveniently for either use, Xcode exposes almost all of its GUI IDE functionality to the command line, enabling you to perform the same actions that you can using clicks in the interface by using commands in the Terminal instead. The primary tools you work with to use Xcode functions from the command line are xcode-select, xcodebuild, and xcrun. Several others are also available, including commands for code signing and product signing.

<table>
<tr><td>To use command-line tools, you can launch Terminal.app (located in /Applications/Utilities) on your workstation, or if you're not at your workstation you can connect to it using an ssh (Secure Shell) program, enabling you to work with your Xcode projects from almost anywhere that you can find a network.</td><td>**Did You Know?**</td></tr>
</table>

With a little creativity, you can set up a system so that a development team working on a heterogeneous collection of hardware can all submit code changes to a central Xcode build server, which can continuously compile their work, construct Enterprise distribution ad hoc builds of an iOS app based on it, and email out app-download links for your development team, all automatically and without you needing to interact with the Xcode IDE other than for initial configuration.

Using xcode-select

To use the Xcode command-line tools, the first thing you have to do is tell the command-line tools where the Xcode folder is. You configure the location of the Xcode folder using the xcode-select tool with a command such as this:

```
xcode-select -switch /Applications/Xcode.app
```

Depending on your user and machine configuration, you might need to run xcode-select with administrative privileges. Use sudo `xcode-select ...` if the command complains that you do not have permission to use it.

If you move your Xcode installation, rerun this command to reflect the new path. If you have multiple versions of Xcode, you can also use xcode-select to switch between them.

To verify that xcode-select is set to the Xcode that you are expecting, run the following:

```
xcode-select -print-path
/Applications/Developer/Xcode.app/Contents/Developer
```

Note that the path that this command returns is an expansion of what was actually set. From this, we can also see that I have moved my Xcode installation from the default location.

If you set your Xcode path as shown here, but when you run the check you do not see the expansion, your system might have the wrong version of xcode-select. So far, this most commonly occurs if a system has OS X 10.7.3 and then Xcode 4.2 is installed. OS X 10.7.3 comes with xcode-select by default, but installing Xcode 4.2 overwrites the system xcode-select. You can fix this by installing the 10.7.3 combo update.

By the Way

You do not really need to install the command-line tools package to use the Xcode command-line tools discussed in this hour. However, if you want to make common UNIX developer tools like the gnu compiler suite readily available systemwide, install the command-line tools package either via the Downloads in the Preferences or via Xcode, Open Developer Tool, More Developer Tools.

The man page for xcode-select is included in Table 24.1.

By the Way

For those developers who might be a bit old fashioned and who really appreciate having decent printed documentation that they can read, mark up in the margins, and on which they can highlight examples of successful uses to reference, here you go. This hour reproduces a few relevant man pages so that you don't have to print them out later and stuff them in here as your own personal (and binder-breaking) addenda.

TABLE 24.1 xcode-select Man Page

xcode-select   Manages the path to the Xcode folder for the Xcode BSD tools.

Synopsis

`xcode-select [-help]`

`xcode-select [-switch xcode_path]`

`xcode-select [-print-path]`

`xcode-select [-version]`

Description

Specifies which Xcode folder is used by these Xcode BSD tools: agvtool, ibtool, open-diff, xcodebuild, xcrun, instruments. It can be used to switch between Xcode versions or to update the path to the current Xcode folder if it is moved after installation.

Options

`-help`	Prints the usage message. Also prints the usage message when invoked with no options.
`-switch xcode_path`	Sets the path of Xcode to *xcode_path*. Must be run as the superuser. To set this without superuser permissions or only for the current shell session, use the `DEVELOPER_DIR` environment variable.
`-print-path`	Prints the path of the current Xcode folder.
`-version`	Prints xcode-select version information.

Environment Variables

`DEVELOPER_DIR`	Specifies the search path for locating the current developer tools and overrides the xcode-select default.

Using xcodebuild

xcodebuild is the command-line tool that builds targets from Xcode projects and workspaces. It has access to the schemes and build configurations of the project or workspace and to some of the build actions (Build [the default], Clean, Archive, and Test).

xcodebuild for Projects

To build a project, use Terminal.app to run xcodebuild in the directory with your *project*.xcodeproj file, and if you have multiple projects in the directory, specify which project to build with the -project option:

```
xcodebuild -project some-project -target target -scheme schemename
➡[build action]
```

For example, to build and archive our original BeeLine application target from within its directory, I can issue the following commands:

```
cd /Volumes/Lump/SGFApps
cd BeeLine
xcodebuild -target BeeLine -scheme BeeLine archive
```

Xcode takes some time and prints a considerable amount of detail to the terminal. All of this same action is taking place behind the scenes when Xcode is running a build in response to a click in the IDE interface. When it is finished, it prints ** Archive Succeeded ** to the terminal and returns you to the command prompt.

Did You Know?

If you do not specify the build action, xcodebuild compiles the target as per the Build for Archive settings, but does not actually construct the archive.

By the Way

The target and the scheme do not need to be the same; they just happen to be in this instance, and many others, because schemes are often autocreated with a name shared with their target.

If I have multiple .xcodeproj files in the same directory, I can identify the one that I want xcodebuild to use by adding the -project option to the xcodebuild invocation:

```
xcodebuild -project BeeLine.xcodeproj -target BeeLine -scheme BeeLine archive
```

Both of these commands compile any source required to build the BeeLine target, using the BeeLine scheme, and submit the compiled BeeLine.app product into the Archives section of the Organizer.

If I want to build the project only to check for compile errors, and not build an archive, I can simply omit the archive build action keyword. In that case, BeeLine.app is built but not copied into the Organizer as an archive.

Did You Know?

The documentation says that you can omit the -scheme parameter for project builds and just use the -target parameter, but builds do not seem to work properly in some situations when the scheme is omitted. It is possible that there are other situations where it breaks if it is included. If your builds produce errors rather than successful archives, try removing or adding the parameter for the appropriate scheme.

xcodebuild for Workspaces

To build a workspace, you must first change directories to the directory containing the .xcworkspace file. Then you invoke xcodebuild adding a -workspace option to the xcodebuild invocation and dropping the -project option.

```
xcodebuild -workspace some-workspace -scheme schemename
➥[-configuration Release|Debug] [-sdk thesdk] [-arch thearch]  [build action]
```

For example:

```
xcodebuild -workspace BsNees.xcworkspace  -scheme iBLine -configuration
➥Release -sdk iphoneos -arch armv7 archive
```

Xcode will build iBLine, and a bit oddly, if you have not yet told it to Always Allow access to the code-signing keys, it opens a dialog box at the end of the build requesting your permission to access the keychain for code signing. If you do not want to have to deal with clicking the button to allow access, you can either grant default access or compile your app without code signing into an archive for the Organizer and then code-sign the result when you actually export it for distribution.

Did You Know?

Don't be alarmed if you see a list of errors pop up first, before seeing a successful build at the end. Xcode's ability to correctly identify implicit dependencies does not seem to work quite properly when using the xcodebuild command, and for the BsNees workspace, it erroneously attempts to build the BetterList framework as a prerequisite for iBLine builds and for the libBetterListLib static library.

Despite these errors on the (irrelevant) target, xcodebuild will eventually get to the correct targets and build them properly. It's likely that you can avoid the creation of these unnecessary errors by explicitly specifying the dependencies for your target, but that defeats the purpose of the workspace implicit dependency mechanism, so it's probably better to just live with them.

xcodebuild for Release Builds

If you need to save the build products directly to the file system rather than into the
Organizer archives, you can also use xcodebuild for that. To use this option, you use
xcodebuild and explicitly specify the build action Build:

```
xcodebuild -workspace BsNees.xcworkspace -scheme iBLine
➥-configuration Release -sdk iphoneos -arch armv7  build
```

> Yes, the Build build action is the default, but for this specific type of invocation,
> you get different behavior if you omit it, even though it is the default. This is prob-
> ably yet another Xcode bug.

When xcodebuild returns control to the command line, look at the last line of output. There will be a path to your derived data location ending in *appName*.app,
which is the on-disk location where the output is stored. Keep track of this path; you
will need to provide it to other tools for automatic packaging or autodistribution of
your product.

Other Uses for xcodebuild

You can also use xcodebuild to display which software development kits (SDKs) are
available in the current version of Xcode that has been set with xcode-select.

For example, in the current version of Xcode, we see that both macosx10.6 and
macosx10.7 SDKs are available:

xcodebuild -showsdks

```
Mac OS X SDKs:
        Mac OS X 10.6                    -sdk macosx10.6
        Mac OS X 10.7                    -sdk macosx10.7

iOS SDKs:
        iOS 5.0                          -sdk iphoneos5.0

iOS Simulator SDKs:
        Simulator - iOS 5.0             -sdk iphonesimulator5.0
```

Upon switching to a different Xcode, we see that macosx10.7 and macosx10.8 SDKs
are available:

xcodebuild -showsdks

```
Mac OS X SDKs:
        Mac OS X 10.7                    -sdk macosx10.7
        Mac OS X 10.8                    -sdk macosx10.8
```

```
iOS SDKs:
        iOS 5.0                             -sdk iphoneos5.0

iOS Simulator SDKs:
        Simulator - iOS 5.0                 -sdk iphonesimulator5.0
```

As of this writing, Xcode changes regularly. If you find that you are forgetting which versions of Xcode you have installed, you can use xcodebuild to find out what version of Xcode is the current version.

It turns out that Xcode 4.2.1 is what gave us the first batch of SDKs shown:

xcodebuild -version

```
Xcode 4.2.1
Build version 4D502
```

Xcode 4.4. gave us the second batch of SDKs:

xcodebuild -version

```
Xcode 4.4
Build version 4F90
```

Table 24.2 provides the man page for xcodebuild.

TABLE 24.2 xcodebuild Man Page

xcodebuild	Builds Xcode projects and workspaces.

Synopsis

```
xcodebuild [-project project-name] [-target target-name . . .]
[-configuration configuration-name] [-sdk sdk-full-path¦sdk-name]
[build-action . . . ]
[setting=value . . .][-user-default=value . . .]


xcodebuild -workspace workspace-name -scheme scheme-name
[-configuration configuration-name] [-sdk [sdk-full-path | sdk-name]
[build-action . . . ]
[setting=value . . .] [-user-default=value . . .]


xcodebuild -version [-sdk [sdk-full-path | sdk-name] [info-item]


xcodebuild -showskds
```

TABLE 24.2   Continued

`xcodebuild -list [-project` *project-name* `|` `-workspace` *workspace-name*`]`

Description

xcodebuild builds one or more targets contained in an Xcode project or builds a scheme contained in an Xcode workspace.

Usage

To build and Xcode project, run xcodebuild in the directory containing your project, which is the directory containing *project-name*.xcodeproj. If you have multiple projects in the directory, use `-project` to specify which project to build. By default, xcode-build builds the first target listed in the project with the default build configuration.

To build an Xcode workspace, pass both the `-workspace` and `-scheme` options to define the build. The parameters of the scheme control which targets are built and how they are built, although you may pass other options to xcodebuild to override some parameters of the scheme.

Options

`-project` *project-name*	Builds *project-name*. Required if there are multiple projects in the same directory.
`-target` *target-name*	Builds *target-name*.
`-alltargets`	Builds all targets in the specified project.
`-workspace` *workspace-name*	Builds *workspace-name*.
`-scheme` *scheme-name*	Builds *scheme-name*. Required if building a workspace.
`-configuration` ↪*configuration-name*	Uses *configuration-name* when building each target.
`-arch` *architecture*	Builds each target for *architecture*.
`-sdk [`*sdk-full-path* `|` ↪*sdk-name*`]`	Builds an Xcode project or workspace against the specified SDK, using build tools appropriate for that SDK. SDK can be specified by an absolute path or canonical name.
`-showsdks`	Lists available SDKs that Xcode knows about.
`-list`	For a project, lists the targets and configurations. For a workspace, lists the schemes.
build-action . . .	Specifies a build action or actions to perform. Available build actions are as follows:
	`build` Builds the target in the build root (SYMROOT). This is the default build action.

TABLE 24.2 Continued

	archive	Archives a scheme from the build root (SYMROOT). Requires specifying a workspace and scheme.
	installsrc	Copies the source of the project to the source root (SRCROOT).
	install	Builds the target and installs it into the target's installation directory in the distribution root (DSTROOT).
	clean	Removes build products and intermediate files from build root (SYMROOT).
-xconfig *filename*		Loads the build settings defined in *filename* when building all targets. These settings override all other settings, including settings passed individually on the command line.
setting=*value*		Sets the build setting to *value*.
-*user-default*=value		Sets the user default *user-default* to *value*.
-version		Displays version information for this install of Xcode.
-usage		Displays usage information for xcodebuild.
Environment Variables		
XCODE_XCONFIG_FILE		If set, provides the path to a file for build settings that should be loaded and used for building all targets. These settings override all other settings, including ones passed at the command line and those in the file passed with the -xconfig option.

Using xcrun

You can use xcrun to run or locate other necessary development tools. One of its most important uses is invoking the PackageApplication tool, to create distributable packages from the output of xcodebuild.

Packaging Applications with xcrun

The basic syntax for xcrun is as follows:

```
xcrun [-sdk thesdk] toolname arguments
```

For example, to package the iBLine.app output created by the `xcodebuild…build` command earlier, I can use xcrun like this:

```
xcrun -sdk iphoneos PackageApplication -v full path to Release-iphoneos dir
➥/iBLine.app -o ~/Desktop/iiBBLine.ipa --sign "iPhone Distribution Cert"
➥--embed full path to mobileprovisioning profile
```

The *full path to Release-iphoneos dir* component is taken from the last line of the xcodebuild invocation that built iBLine.app in build mode.

You can find the *iPhone Distribution Cert* value by using Keychain Access and looking in your Login keychain certificates for a certificate starting with the words *iPhone Distribution*. The search for this key is slightly smart, and it is sufficient to specify only a portion of the name of the certificate, as long as that portion is unique among all of your certificates. For example, if you have only one distribution certificate, it is sufficient to use **Distribution Certificate** for your search. In my case, iPhone Distribution is adequately unique.

The *full path to mobileprovisioning profile* value can be the full path to an Ad Hoc distribution certificate that you downloaded from the Provisioning Portal, if you've saved these somewhere convenient on disk. It cannot currently look these up from Xcode's stored copies of the provisioning profiles.

If you did not save a copy outside of Xcode, you can find Xcode's stored copy as follows:

1. Open the Xcode Organizer and display the Devices tab.

2. Select Provisioning Profiles under the Library group in the sidebar.

3. Right-click the desired Ad Hoc distribution provisioning profile and choose Reveal Profile in Finder.

4. If you drag and drop the revealed .mobileprovision file into a Terminal window, it places a copy of the path to that file in the Terminal.

Fully filled in with the values that my system produces for iBLine, this command looks like this:

```
xcrun -sdk iphoneos PackageApplication -v
➥/Users/ray/Library/Developer/Xcode/DerivedData/BsNees-
➥bnbedrkgivgpkjbnjdolvofyhygn/Build/Products/Release-iphoneos/iBLine.app -o
➥~/Desktop/iiBBLine.ipa --sign "iPhone Distribution" -embed
➥/Users/ray/Library/MobileDevice/Provisioning\
➥Profiles/6BC2A945-5A7D-4336-83AE-2D43A33E50F3.mobileprovision
```

Other Uses for xcrun

You can also use xcrun to locate tools that are stored within Xcode and that you might need to use at the command line. For example, to locate ibtool (the application for validating and compiling Interface Builder documents), you can use xcrun like this:

```
xcrun -find ibtool
```

It responds with the following:

```
/Applications/Xcode.app/Contents/Developer/usr/bin/ibtool
```

Table 24.3 shows the man page for xcrun.

TABLE 24.3   xcrun Man Page

xcrun	Runs or locates development tools.

Synopsis

```
xcrun [-sdk SDK] -find tool_name
xcrun [-sdk SDK] [-log] tool_name [tool_arguments]
tool_name [tool_arguments]
```

Description

xcrun provides a means to locate or invoke coexistence- and platform-aware developer tools from the command line, without requiring users to modify makefiles or do other inconvenient things.

The SDK defaults to the boot system OS SDK, and can be specified by the SKDROOT environment variable or the -sdk option, which takes precedence over SDKROOT.

Usage

The first usage returns the full path to tool_name.

The second usage executes tool_name with tool_arguments.

The third usage is when xcrun is used as a replacement for any of the standard UNIX developer tools (typically in /usr/bin), by duplicating xcrun and renaming the duplicate as a standard UNIX developer tool. When invoked in this fashion, xcrun uses the name of the tool it is replacing, tool_name, to locate the corresponding tool within the evaluated DEVELOPER_DIR and SDK. In this usage, tool_arguments are not parsed by xcrun.

Options

-verbose	Displays information about how the redirected path is constructed.
-no-cache	Does not consult the cache when looking up values.
-kill-cache	Removes the cache and causes all values to be recached.

TABLE 24.3   Continued

`-sdk` *SDK*	Specifies which SDK to use. Overrides `SDKROOT` environment variable.
`-log`	Prints the full command line that is invoked.
`-find`	Prints the full path to the tool.
Environment Variables	
`DEVELOPER_DIR`	Specifies the search path for locating the current developer tools and overrides the xcode-select default.
`SDKROOT`	Specifies the SDK to use. Overriden by the `-sdk` option.
`xcrun_log`	Same as specifying `-log`.
`xcrun_nocache`	Same as specifying `-no-cache`.
`xcrun_verbose`	Same as specifying `-verbose`.

Other Xcode Command-Line Tools

Some other Xcode command-line tools that might prove useful include agvtool, ibtool, opendiff, instruments, codesign, and productsign. We do not discuss these commands in depth, but knowing about them will be helpful, and you can always access their documentation through the built-in man pages:

▶ **agvtool** is the Apple-generic versioning tool. You can use it to manage version numbers, if you have versioning enabled in your project:

To display the current build version, you can use agvtool to query the project version, as follows:

```
agvtool what-version
```

To increment the CFBundleVersion across all your Info.plist files, you can use agvtool like this:

```
agvtool next-version -all
```

Alternatively, if you want to update your CFBundleVersion to a specific value, rather than increment it, you can use agvtool, as follows:

```
agvtool new-version -all 2.0
```

You can also query your marketing version (the CFBundleShortVersionString in your Info.plist file) like this:

```
agvtool what-marketing-version
```

And you can update your marketing version in all of your Info.plist files simultaneously using agvtool like this:

```
agvtool new-marketing-version 4.0
```

Unfortunately, if you need different marketing versions in different Info.plist files, you will need to update these manually.

► **ibtool** compiles, prints, updates and verifies Interface Builder documents. It is commonly used when localizing applications.

► **opendiff** launches FileMerge from the command line to graphically compare or merge files or directories.

► **instruments** reads an Instruments template from the command line.

► **productbuilder** creates a deployable product archive that can be used with the OS X Installer.

► **codesign** and **productsign** are components needed for working with the Developer ID program. Man pages for these tools might still be in flux as Apple refines the Developer ID program.

► **codedesign** creates and manipulates code signatures.

► **productsign** signs an OS X Installer product archive. It can be used in three different modes:

  ► Creating a product archive using a distribution file

  ► Creating a product archive from one or more bundles (or component packages)

  ► Creating a distribution for one or more component packages

► **PackageMaker** is another utility that is needed for the Developer ID program. It is included in the Auxiliary Tools download from the Developer site. You can open it in the Finder or run open *path-to-auxiliary-tools*/PackageMaker.app to launch it from the command line.

Bigger and Better Command-Line Uses

While simply managing and building projects from the command line can give you enhanced development flexibility and convenience, a much more sophisticated use of the tools, and one that can take your development efforts to a whole new level, is using these tools to put your projects under the control of a continuous integration server. Using a continuous integration server (CIS) pushes the job of building your application, and even potentially distributing it to your users, into the hands of a continuously running back-end process that can compile, verify, package, and deliver your application, even if your workstation is turned off.

Under this scenario, your entire development team would submit their changes to the project to a centralized CIS server, which would handle the build process, independent of any of their workstations. Xcode, on each of their workstations, would become a front end to developing the code and project, rather than the mechanism of building it and distributing it.

Although you can build a sort of CIS yourself, using the UNIX cron command to periodically execute shell scripts containing the appropriate xcodebuild and xcrun commands, a plethora of quite sophisticated CIS tools already exists. If you are interested in pursuing this option, we recommend that you look into Jenkins (http://jenkins-ci.org/) and TestFlight (http://testflightapp.com/), although many of their competitors are also worthy of your consideration.

Summary

In this hour, you learned how to use the Xcode suite of command-line tools to build targets without having to launch into the Xcode IDE itself. You also learned how to package those built targets into actually distributable versions of your applications.

These capabilities can be immensely useful for several reasons. At the simplest, these command-line tools enable you to check the validity of code changes in your project, regardless of whether you are at the keyboard of your workstation or connected to it from a remote terminal on the other side of the world. At their most sophisticated, they can be used to completely customize your build environment and process to work the way that you want it to.

Q&A

Q. *Why should I use* `xcrun` *`sometool` rather than just using the tool directly?*

A. Because xcrun knows about your currently selected Xcode version and will always point to the correct tool binary.

Q. *Is there some way to make that (horrible) path to the Release build of an app less of a pain to work with?*

A. It doesn't seem like Xcode provides a neat solution at this point, but you can always use other UNIX tools to make your life easier. For example, you could create a Perl script like this:

```
#!/usr/bin/perl

$apploc = "";
while($inline=)
{
   if($inline =~m/Validation (.+\.app)/) { $apploc = $1; }
}
print $apploc;
```

Put it somewhere that your shell can find it and make it executable, and then run the xcodebuild like this:

```
export apploc='xcodebuild -workspace BsNees.xcworkspace -scheme iBLine
➥-configuration Release -sdk iphoneos -arch armv7 -target iBLine  build |
➥xcodebuildparse.pl'
```

The final directory and *appName*.app result will now be stored in the shell variable $apploc, which you could use in your xcrun command like this:

```
xcrun -sdk iphoneos PackageApplication -v $apploc -o ~/Desktop/iBLine.ipa
➥--sign "iPhone Distribution" --embed /Users/ray/Library/MobileDevice/
➥Provisioning\ Profiles/6BC2A945-5A7D-4336-83AE-2D43A33E50F3.
➥mobileprovision
```

Q. *I set up a cron job to run my xcodebuild commands. It works for some, but not for others. What's the problem?*

A. The builds for which it is breaking are ones that require access to your keychain. When you're working in a terminal, inside a logged-in session directly at your workstation, you have full authentication to your Login keychain. For security reasons, when you log in to the machine remotely, the shell you're working in, at least with OS X 10.7.3, doesn't have access to your Login keychain. If you want to make this work, copy your development/distribution certificates from your Login keychain into one that's available to a remotely connected shell. The process for doing this is the same as Apple documents for moving your identities around between different machines (see TN2250 at http://developer.apple.com/library/ios/#technotes/tn2250/). You have to identify the correct keychain by adding the command security list-keychains to a cron job and capturing the output to see which keychains are available. They probably include one for named /Library/Keychains/System.keychain, where you could store your credentials if you do not mind them being available to the entire system. If you prefer to keep your credentials more private, you can use the `security` command in your script to unlock additional key-chains. See the man page for the `security` command (`man security` in the terminal) for complete details on accessing keychain resources.

Workshop

Quiz

1. How can you find out which of your installed Xcode versions is being used by the command-line tools?

2. xcodebuild for projects uses the `-target` parameter to specify what's going to be built. What controls the build target for xcodebuild for workspaces?

3. How can you learn more about the syntax, typical uses, and other documentation for these (and other) command-line commands?

Answers

1. `xcode-select -print-path`

2. xcodebuild for workspaces uses the targets specified by the scheme for the provided build action.

3. From the man pages: `man commandname` at the command line.

Activities

1. Test build your apps using the command-line tools.

2. Write a shell script that invokes both xcodebuild and xcrun to produce a final packaged app.

3. Write the next killer app for the App Store, change the world, and don't forget to say nice things about us when you're rich and famous!

Index

shared frameworks, adding, 376-382

signed applications, distributing, 580

unsigned applications, distributing, 579

outlets, 195-196

connections, creating, 198-200

creating, 206-208

P

PackageMaker, 599

paid developer programs, 8

joining, 9-11

registration, 9-10

panes, Instruments application, 534

parameters, 27

parents, 26

paused applications

continuing, 499

maneuvering, 498-499

stepping forward, 500-502

Perl, 321-322

placeholder objects, 169-170

pointers, 40

pop, 230

pragma marks, 131

prebuilt actions, 203

predicates, 437

prepareForSegue:sender method, 228-229

preparing iOS device for Xcode development, 17

primitive data types, 39

proactive debugging, 493-496

procedural programming, 24

productbuider, 599

products, 253

productsign, 599

Profile action, 255, 268

program execution

continuing, 499

stepping forward, 500-502

programming

Cocoa, 50

arrays, 52

dates, 53

dictionaries, 53

numbers, 53

strings, 52

URLs, 54

versus Cocoa Touch, 51

imperative development, 24

language, selecting, 312-313

Objective-C, 25-28

ARC, 49

categories, defining, 37

class structure, 36

expressions, 44-45

if-then-else statements, 45

implementation files, 34-36

interface files, 28-33

messaging, 41-43

objects, initializing, 40-41

protocols, creating, 38

releasing objects, 49

switch statements, 45

variables, declaring, 38-40

project files, 88

Project Navigator, 97-98

Build Phases tab, 263

Build Rules tab, 264

Build Settings tab, 263

files, renaming, 106

filters, 98

templates, adding, 99-103

projects

adding to workspaces, 517-519

commits, 298-299

configuration, reviewing, 89

creating, 13, 83

template, configuring, 85-87

template, saving, 87

template, selecting, 84

files

adding, 105-106

locating, 107

removing, 106-107

frameworks

adding, 108-109

headers, 109

removing, 110

groups

adding, 110-111

removing, 111

loading into repositories

Git, 293-294

Subversion, 291-293

S

sample code, 153

saving templates, 87

scenes, 217

adding to storyboard,
218-219

multiscene projects, 216

naming, 219-220

segues

advanced segues,
creating, 230-239

configuring, 225-227

creating, 223-225

dismissing, 227

push segues, creating, 243

creating, 243

sharing information between,
prepareForSegue:sender
method, 228-230

supporting view controller
subclasses, adding,
220-223

schema, 437

Scheme Editor

Analyze action, 268

Archive action, 268

Build action, 266

Profile action, 268

Run action, 267

Test action, 267

schemes, 256

adding, 270-271

SDKs, displaying with xcodebuild
tool, 592-595

Search Navigator, 129-130

searching Xcode Help viewer
library, 157

segmented controls, 198

segues, 217

advanced segues, creating

navigation controllers,
230-234

tab bar controllers,
234-239

configuring, 225-227

creating, 223-225

dismissing, 227

push segues, creating, 243

selecting

programming language,
312-313

static libraries, 331-333

template for projects, 84

selection handles (IB), 178

setting

breakpoints, 497-498

object identities (IB), 191-192

shared frameworks, adding to
OS X applications, 376-382

sharing information between
scenes, 228-230

signed applications (OS X),
distributing, 580

Simulate Document command
(IB), 189-190

simultaneous data collection, performing with Instruments,
543-545

singletons, 26

Size Inspector (IB), 179-182

snapshots, 279

auto snapshots, 282

creating, 280

exporting, 282

managing, 282

restoring, 280-282

viewing, 280-282

snippets

adding, 140-141

editing, 141

viewing, 138

source control

branching, 284, 304-306

changes, 284

commits, 298-299

merging, 284-285, 306-307

pulls, 299-300

pushes, 298-299

repositories, 283

connecting to, 287-290

Git, creating, 286-287

projects, loading into,
291-294

revisions, viewing, 301-304

snapshots, 279

auto snapshots, 282

creating, 280

exporting, 282

managing, 282

restoring, 280-282

viewing, 280-282

status codes, 297

trunks, 284

updates, 299-300

X-Y-Z

Sams **Teach Yourself**

When you only have time
for the answers™

Whatever your need and whatever your time frame, there's a Sams **Teach Yourself** book for you. With a Sams **Teach Yourself** book as your guide, you can quickly get up to speed on just about any new product or technology—in the absolute shortest period of time possible. Guaranteed.

Learning how to do new things with your computer shouldn't be tedious or time-consuming. Sams **Teach Yourself** makes learning anything quick, easy, and even a little bit fun.

iOS 5 Application Development in 24 Hours, Third Edition

John Ray
ISBN-13: 978-0-672-33576-1

Core Data for Mac and iOS in 24 Hours

Jesse Feiler

ISBN-13: 978-0-672-33577-8

Android Application Development in 24 Hours

Lauren Darcey
Shane Conder

ISBN-13: 978-0-672-33569-3

HTML, CSS, and JavaScript All in One

Julie C. Meloni

ISBN-13: 978-0-672-33332-3

Windows Phone 7 Game Programming in 24 Hours

Jonathan Harbour

ISBN-13: 978-0-672-33554-9

Your purchase of **Sams Teach Yourself Xcode 4 in 24 Hours** includes access to a free online edition for 45 days through the **Safari Books Online** subscription service. Nearly every Sams book is available online through **Safari Books Online**, along with thousands of books and videos from publishers such as Addison-Wesley Professional, Cisco Press, Exam Cram, IBM Press, O'Reilly Media, Prentice Hall, Que, and VMware Press.

Safari Books Online is a digital library providing searchable, on-demand access to thousands of technology, digital media, and professional development books and videos from leading publishers. With one monthly or yearly subscription price, you get unlimited access to learning tools and information on topics including mobile app and software development, tips and tricks on using your favorite gadgets, networking, project management, graphic design, and much more.

Activate your FREE Online Edition at
informit.com/safarifree

STEP 1:   Enter the coupon code: UJLPXAA.

STEP 2:   New Safari users, complete the brief registration form.
Safari subscribers, just log in.

If you have difficulty registering on Safari or accessing the online edition,
please e-mail customer-service@safaribooksonline.com